The Unchained Man

The Alpha Male 2.0

by Caleb Jones

Published in 2014 by DCS International
6715 NE 63rd St. #127
Vancouver, WA
USA

ISBN: 978-0-9862220-2-3

Printed in the United States of America

Second Printing January 2016

Table of Contents

Happy-Fun Disclaimers

Disclaimer 1

While this book will be extremely helpful to you in building a new, powerful life of freedom and happiness, there will be statements and concepts within that may make you angry. You may even perceive these statements as a personal assault upon you, your relationships, or your life choices. This will be especially true if this is the first time you've been exposed to these concepts. I'm telling you this in advance. There. Now you can't say you weren't warned. Read on at your own risk.

This book is about facts and systems. Any controversial fact given in this book has its source referenced in the footnotes, so if you don't like the fact, go yell at them; I'm just the messenger.

Nothing I say here is an attack against you, your current relationship, your current business or career, or any decisions you've made up until now. If you view anything in this book as such, that's your own interpretation and not what was intended.

Disclaimer 2

This is a book for men. If you're a woman, you're certainly invited to the party if you're curious, and a few of the chapters can apply to both sexes. Just remember that this a book written specifically for guys. Keep this in mind if anything you read in this book offends you, which it is likely to do, or doesn't make sense to you, because it was written for a man.

Remember that at any time you are more than welcome to put this book down and go read a book, magazine, or web site written for women, of which there are more than enough.

That being said, over the years I have been pleasantly surprised at the number of women who enthusiastically support the concepts and structures this book outlines. You ladies give me hope.

Disclaimer 3

I am not an attorney. I am in no way qualified to render legal advice, and no advice in this book should be considered as such. While I will not be recommending anything illegal, laws do vary greatly from region to region. Please check with a local attorney before attempting any relationship or business structures described in this book if you have any questions or concerns.

All names of non-famous individuals used in this book have been changed to protect anonymity.

Part One

The Alpha Male of the 21st Century: The Alpha 2.0

Chapter 1 –

The Five Traits of the Alpha Male 2.0

The meaning of life is not simply to exist, to survive, but to move ahead, to go up, to achieve, to conquer.

Arnold Schwarzenegger

Winter, 1982.

In a vast and powerful empire known as United States, at the edge of a small and unimportant city, there was a normal family living in a normal home. I was a ten year-old child living there. There was a severe recession, though I knew little of it at the time. My troubles were far more personal and internal.

I was in my bed, unable to sleep, thinking tortured thoughts. Slowly, I crept from my bed and made my way down the dark hallway to my parent's room. Seeing they were still awake, I entered silently, hoping they would be have the answer to the question that made peaceful sleep for me impossible.

My parents were good, honest, normal people. Like most normal people, sometimes they were happy and sometimes they were not. My dad was the typical high-stress guy who worked very hard at a job he hated, and was often either irritable or exhausted unless it was a Saturday. My mom, a former Catholic nun before she married my father, was always in chipper spirits, but raising five rowdy children, a dog, and two cats on one man's barely adequate income during a recession often took a toll on her.

As I entered the room, I was relieved to find them in good spirits, for my questions for them required clear minds. They were already in bed but with the lights still on, reading magazines and talking quietly to each other. They greeted me warmly, but I was in no mood for small talk.

"I have a question for both of you," I said gravely.

They gave me the look that you might expect from two adults watching a ten year-old trying to convey concepts of great depth. I was used to this look. As a child, I received it often.

"Okay," my mom said, trying not to offend. My dad looked up from his magazine, a smile on his face.

"Alright," I said, beginning to pace back and forth like an attorney delivering his final summation, "I think I've figured this out. I'm going to run it past you and I need you to tell me if I'm right or wrong."

"Okay," they said, smiles forming but remaining politely interested.

"Alright," I said again, "I think this is how life works. First, you're born, but for about four or five years you really can't do anything because you're little. Then you have to go to school for 12 or 13 years straight. Then, if you're 'lucky,' you go to more school for another four or six or eight years. After that, you have to go to work…for 40 years! Then, after all of that, if you're 'lucky,' you can retire and stop working. But by then you're old and grey, and so you can't really do much because you might break a hip or something. You get about ten years of that, then you reach age 75 and die."

I stood there waiting for a response. My parents just stared back at me.

"Well?" I said, "Is that how life works?"

The answer they gave me haunted me for decades. So terrifying was their answer that it was the turning point in my life.

They smiled, nodded approvingly, and both said "Why yes, Caleb. That's exactly how it works. Very good!"

The Prison

If you're not paying very close attention to life, or if you allow the animalistic desires of your mind and body to operate on autopilot, you are living within the confines of an invisible prison, a reinforced cell made from bars forged from your own fears and obsolete biology, constructed by old and powerful men long dead, hundreds or even thousands of years ago. Your life doesn't belong to you. It belongs to them and their descendants.

This is "The Prison."

Paradoxically, you were never designed for life within this prison cell. As a man, you are designed for adventure, excitement, achievement, freedom, sex, strength, power, constancy, and happiness. The Prison allows for very little of these things. Your role is not to be happy or fulfilled. Your role is to serve, conform, and stay quiet. You are to serve The Prison, not yourself.

Many have compared this to the society of blissfully unaware captives portrayed in the movie *The Matrix*. This is an inaccurate comparison.

Rather than an ignorant slave, you are a fully willing drone, doing what you're told to serve The Prison, but on some level you're also convinced it's the right thing to do. Your role as a man in The Prison is to go to school, get a job, then as the saying goes, "buy things you don't need, with money you don't have, to impress people you don't like."

You are to carefully date one woman at a time, get married, spend years following your wife's orders, have 2.3 children, get divorced, lose a bunch of money, marry another woman, and then follow a new set of orders.

You're supposed to get angry at distant and unassailable politicians, CEOs, Wall Street bankers, and anyone diametrically opposed to your political opinions.

You're supposed to go into debt, be terrified of terrorists and climate change, go on one decent vacation a year, then grow old and expect your neighbor and your kids to kick in for your retirement, if any.

Questioning any of these things invokes the ire of others. Words like "selfish" or "immature" or "narcissistic" are thrown at you. No one wants to be called selfish. So you learn to step back into line. The Prison endures.

Once when I was 12, my dad was grumbling about waking up early in the morning for work.

"Why do you wake up so early when you hate it?" I asked, "You have your own business. Can't you wake up whenever you want?"

"I have to be at work by 8am," he said resignedly, "That's what the marketplace expects."

The Prison isn't questioned.

When I was 17, I told my mom I was planning to "skip" going to college.

"You have to go to college!" she cried, "You'll be a loser if you don't go! You'll be a bum! If you want to be a bum on the street, then fine!"

The Prison is defended.

When I was 23, I told some of my coworkers about my goal to have a six-figure income before I was thirty, and then only work three or four days a week while traveling often.

"Oh right," they laughed, "We had goals like that too when we were your age. Ha! You'll learn."

The Prison is reinforced.

When I was 37, I was explaining to my friend my system of how I am able to date three or four women at a time, and not be cheating because all the women know I'm dating others and continue to see me anyway.

"Oh, bullshit," he cried, "You can't do that. Women won't let you do that."

The Prison is solidified.

Men must shut up, step back into line, obey, and conform.

The Prison must continue.

The Alpha Male 2.0

There is only one type of person able to break from The Prison and live a life of consistent freedom and happiness. He's called the Alpha Male. Through his strength, rational thinking, confidence, bravery, individuality, and hard work, he can break free of The Prison and live a life exactly of his choosing.

The problem with the term "Alpha Male" is that every man has a different picture of whom or what that is. Cultural differences will also create some surprisingly different ideas as to what exactly the term "Alpha" means. For many years, I have discussed this subject in detail with hundreds of men from all over the world, and there is really no solid consensus. So before we endeavor to travel down the path of the 21st century Alpha Male, the definition must be clarified.

When someone hears the term "Alpha Male" they often envision a big, tough Marine-looking guy with bulging muscles, a scar on his face and a knife in his pocket. The kind of guy that scowls a lot, laughs a lot, gets into fights, and loudly bosses his girlfriend around. That kind of guy certainly has some traits worth emulating in that he is strong, tough, confident, and masculine, but he's not exactly the evolved, twenty-first century version of Alpha that will be discussed here.

Perhaps your vision of an Alpha isn't so negative or stereotypical. Perhaps the word conjures up visions of a 1840s East India trader on the high seas, the ship's wheel in one hand and a percussion cap Derringer in the other. Perhaps it's a guy like Rambo, mowing down enemies somewhere in the jungle with an M2 machine gun. Maybe it's a classy lady's man from the various ages, like Casanova, Humphrey Bogart, Warren Betty, Bill Clinton, and James Bond. Or maybe it's a craggy-faced, steely-eyed badass like Clint Eastwood or John Wayne.

If you live outside of the United States, it may be none of these guys, and you may contend that my Alpha Male examples are too

American-centric. Men in Europe would easily consider guys like Johnny Depp or Russell Brand as Alphas.

Whatever your vision of an Alpha Male is, it's more than likely the standard style of Alpha similar to the above examples, what I call the Alpha Male 1.0. In this book, I will be discussing a new type of Alpha, one who lives life exactly the way he wants, whenever he wants, however he wants, regardless of what The Prison demands of him; a man who is consistently free and happy.

It's the Alpha Male 2.0.

The Three Types of Men

All men in modern, Western society fall into one of three categories. The percentage breakdowns of each are not scientific. Rather, they are close estimates based on my research and experience over the last decade or so.

The Beta Male: Approximately 70% of today's men are beta males. Betas are typical "nice guys." They're hardworking, submissive, needy, fearful, and play it safe. They spend their lives being controlled by girlfriends, wives, bosses, religious dogma, societal pressures, and external circumstances. They range from completely hopeless pussies to decently cool guys who have lots of regular "relationship drama" and unfulfilled dreams.

The operating goal of the beta male is to **not risk**.

"I can't do that; my wife won't let me."

"I can't do that; my girlfriend said she'd break up with me."

"I can't start my own business; I might not be able to pay my bills."

"I can't stand up to my dad; he's my dad."

Betas are true inmates of The Prison.

The Alpha Male 1.0: This is the classic definition of Alpha Male, and what most people think of when they hear the term. They make up about 25% of the modern male population. Alpha 1.0s are tough, masculine, confident, dominant, capable, and successful men. They take charge and get things done. Unlike betas, Alpha 1.0s rule others rather than being ruled themselves.

The problem with Alpha 1.0s is that they are highly sensitive to what others in their lives do or say. If an Alpha 1.0's girlfriend or wife doesn't play ball, he gets upset. He starts commanding, lecturing, and setting rules. The same goes for his family members, friends, and co-workers. When everyone around them does exactly what they're told, Alpha 1.0s are happy guys who are fun to be with. Whenever anyone doesn't act in accordance with their specific parameters (which is often), these guys are nightmares. They often live lives of 70% joy, 30% anger.

The operating goal of the Alpha 1.0 is to **control** and to **be heard**. They love to boss other people around and to issue lectures about proper behavior. They love to get pissed off and to "set people straight." Having other people listen to them and acknowledge them is of extreme importance to these strong men.

The Alpha Male 2.0: The remaining 5% of men out there are Alpha 2.0s. The Alpha 2.0 is exactly the same as the Alpha 1.0 with a few significant differences.

The operating goal of the Alpha 2.0 is **freedom** and **long-term consistent happiness**. This means two things.

First, he has structured his life so that every morning he wakes up and does whatever the hell he wants, the way he wants, any time he wants, without having to check in with anyone. He is free from the agenda of girlfriend, wife, boss, or society. That doesn't mean he is without a special woman in his life; he certainly can have one. It means he can do whatever he likes without having to get permission from her, or anyone else.

Secondly, the Alpha 2.0 is very different from the Alpha 1.0 in that he doesn't care what other people in his life think or do. He has structured his life so as to maintain a high level of happiness and well-being no matter what happens with anyone else. If the woman in his life throws a tantrum, he shrugs and has sex with someone else. If his boss ever treats him poorly, he quits his job without fanfare and quickly gets hired somewhere else. If he has problems with a customer, he calmly terminates the relationship and continues on his merry way. He doesn't argue or lecture; that would damage his happiness. He simply moves on.

Since everyone in his life knows his modus operandi, people quickly learn not to give him all the relationship drama, anger, rules, and problems betas and Alpha 1.0s regularly have to wrestle with.

The Alpha 2.0 is truly free.

What Is Possible For You

The Alpha 2.0 is the only type of person who has the ability to break free of The Prison.

Beta males cannot. They fear The Prison as much as they cling to it. They see no other options than The Prison, though they may wish to and complain about it often. Doing anything that may oppose the will of The Prison fills them with fear, so they remain trapped.

Women, with very rare exceptions, also cannot break free. The vast majority of women enthusiastically agrees with, supports, and reinforces The Prison. Without The Prison, they believe they have no power. They're wrong, but that's what they believe. The Prison ensures this.

Alpha Male 1.0s can break free of The Prison, but only partially. They have the ability to leave The Prison for temporary periods only, but even then there's a steel chain attached to them ensuring they don't wander too far. Soon, their desire for control and overwhelming concern for what others in society think and do force them to return to The Prison over and over again throughout their lives.

That leaves the Alpha Male 2.0. Only he has the ability to break free of The Prison and never return.

The good news is that any beta or Alpha 1.0 can choose to reorient their thinking and their lives and move into Alpha 2.0 status. That's what this book is all about. In the modern era, any man can make whatever money he likes, have sex with as many women as he likes, live and travel wherever he likes, have any type of marriage or relationship he likes, and live an adventurous, exciting life.

It's very doable. I've done it. Since that fateful night with my parents over 30 years ago, I have spent my life proving to myself that I did not have to follow the dreary existence I had described to my parents. Here are a few of the things I've done since then:

- I have started multiple companies, beginning at age 24.
- I have made a six-figure income by age 27, starting from nothing.
- I have slept with more women than the average 10 men in their entire lives combined. These women have ranged from high school cheerleaders to corporate vice presidents, self-made millionaires to bimbo trash queens, accountants to models, to strippers, to attorneys and everything in between.
- I have dated women as much as 24 years younger than me (yes, they were legal) and much older than me as well.

- I have worked with literally hundreds of companies, from among the Fortune 500 to small mom-and-pop operations, churches, and nonprofits.
- I'm rarely dating fewer than three women at a time, all of who know I'm dating other women and continue to date me anyway.
- I have worked with hundreds of interesting and dynamic people, ranging from those relatively unknown to world famous men like Phil Knight, Brian Tracy, and many others.
- I have had every type of romantic or sexual relationship with a woman it's possible to have. I have had serious exclusive girlfriends, played the field, been married with children, been polyamorous, and have had periods where I was totally alone (by choice). I have had relationships ranging from friends-with-benefits to being deeply and mutually in love at a rich and spiritual level.
- I have had wild, exciting experiences, all over the world. I've eaten snails atop the highest skyscraper in downtown Tokyo; sat in the ocean hundreds of feet off the coast of the Yucatan while watching a distant thunderstorm; closed a business deal with a Pakistani steel baron while overlooking his multimillion-dollar estate; made $3000 in 30 minutes playing blackjack in Vegas with one of the inventors of the automobile fuel cell; had a threesome with two women who later were featured on national television; exchanged sunglasses with a billionaire; and debated the nature of the universe with a Buddhist monk in an island monastery off the coast of Hong Kong.

That's only a partial list, and I'm only in my early 40s. I'm just getting started.

I'm trying to show you what's possible for you, but lest you think I'm bragging (which I am), I will also demonstrate that Alpha Males are still human, and are thus imperfect. I've had my share of upsets and defeats on my journey to Alpha 2.0 status…

- I've been poor. I remember what it was like to watch with dread as my $300 limit credit card was swiped by the cashier at the grocery store, hoping beyond hope it would work so I could eat that night.

- I've had my face and body bloodied in martial arts matches.
- I have been handcuffed, fingerprinted, and thrown into a small concrete jail cell with 20 inmates of the huge, smelly, angry, tattooed kind, none too pleased to see me. As I walked in, one of the inmates said "Nice shirt! Let me guess! DUI! Right?" I answered, "No. Contempt of court." He frowned. Apparently that's not a very impressive reason to go to jail.
- Even after some financial success, I've been on the verge of bankruptcy twice. I've spent countless hours with tax collectors, attorneys and bill collectors as a result of my own mismanagement in my earlier years.
- I have been through the pain of divorce. I remember listening to my small daughter cry on the phone while I was unable to do anything to help her.
- I have lost serious money on real estate and business deals gone bad. Once while married, I lost so much money I had to sell the house and the cars (one was repossessed) and move my family of four into a tiny apartment.
- I have been fat. Standing at hair under 5'11", I have weighed over 250 pounds, and it was fat, not muscle.

No journey is perfect. Don't expect it to be. Regardless of the upsets I've had in my past, today I live the Alpha 2.0 lifestyle. I am free to do literally whatever I want, whenever I want, and I take advantage of that daily in wonderful and varied ways. I am one of the most consistently happy men I know, or have ever met, at any age or income level.

Why You Can Do This Right Now

You can live like this too, if you choose. For thousands of years, this kind of lifestyle was impossible. No longer. Just in the last few decades, many men have pioneered new methods, viewpoints, and technologies to improve upon the old Alpha 1.0 model. For the first time in history, it is now possible to live the life of an Alpha 2.0.

With business…

In the 90s, authors like Michael Gerber of *The E-Myth* fame showed us how to run a business outside of The Prison, by structuring a company that didn't require you to be present. Over a decade later, other men like Tim Ferriss and his *4-Hour Workweek* came along and perfected Gerber's concepts with new technological enhancements and realities.

With sex and relationships...

For decades, even after the sexual revolution of the 1960s when women started gaining power in society, men were still imprisoned in the "take a girl out to dinner, hope to get lucky" 1950s model of dating and sex, until a few guys with names like Mystery, Style, DeAngelo, and Jeffries showed them how to attract women without having to do any of that. This was many years ago and other men have further improved upon those concepts and techniques (your not-so-humble writer among them).

With success...

There have been big-muscled men since the dawn of civilization, but the concept of the perfectly formed male body was an impossible one, until a flamboyant Austrian with barely a command of English showed them they were wrong. Just look at Arnold Schwarzenegger's entry in the Guinness Book of World Records. He said he was going to be the best bodybuilder in the world, and did it. He then said he would be a multimillionaire businessman, and did it. Then he said he would marry a Kennedy, and did it. Then he said he would be the highest paid actor in Hollywood. People laughed. Then he did it. Then he said he would be elected governor of the seventh largest economy in the world. People didn't laugh this time, and he did it.

He later had trouble of course, but only because he insisted on adhering to the relationship models of The Prison. More on this later.

Arnie's success is not a unique exception. Steve Jobs said he would revolutionize computing, and did it. Then he said he would revolutionize music. People scoffed. You can only revolutionize one thing in your life, not two. The audacity! Then he did it. He didn't think that was quite enough, so then he decided to revolutionize cell phones too. While he was at that, he also revolutionized animated movies with Pixar. Oh, and he did all of this before he reached his early fifties.

I'm not saying these men are Alpha 2.0. I'm saying these men, and thousands like them, have developed or demonstrated new systems and technologies to allow men like you and me to become Alpha 2.0s if we chose. Most of these systems were not in existence just decade or two ago.

The Five Traits of the Alpha Male 2.0

The Alpha Male 2.0 has five specific traits, the combination of which differentiates him from women, betas, and Alpha 1.0s. These are:

- He is consistently happy.
- He is confident.
- He is masculine.
- He is free.
- He lives an abundant life.

He has all five of these traits at the same time, all the time, simultaneously and consistently. If a man is ever missing any of the above qualities, he is either an Alpha 1.0 or worse; a beta male.

I will describe each trait.

Consistent Happiness

The Alpha 2.0 lives in a constant state of happiness. Experiencing emotions such as anger, fear, loneliness, jealousy, or sadness are extremely rare occurrences in his life. If he ever experiences unhappiness it is only because of some unusual rare event beyond his control, like a parent dying or an entire economy crashing. On the rare occasions he feels sadness, it is an experience of compassion motivating him to help or defend others.

A man who is happy sometimes but upset others is either a beta male living within The Prison or an Alpha 1.0 angrily banging against the bars. A man who is not truly and consistently happy is missing the entire point of masculine existence. Happiness is such an important trait in the Alpha 2.0 that I've devoted the entire next chapter to it.

Confidence

The Alpha Male 2.0 is a confident man, striding boldly though life, with full knowledge of what he's doing and the path he's on. Confident does not mean fearless or soulless. The Alpha 2.0 is still a human being with human emotions, but he is never paralyzed or demoralized by fear, indecision, or timidity.

A man who is not confident will not possess the drive or desire necessary to achieve and maintain Alpha 2.0 status. He cannot attract money or women in abundance whenever he desires. A timid man will not be able to sit in meetings with potential clients or dealmakers and come out a winner, nor can he ask that super-hot woman on a date, nor do the bold things necessary to turn that date into fast sex. He is destined to live a life of mediocrity at best.

We'll be discussing confidence in detail in Chapter 15.

Masculinity

A man who is not masculine may be a perfectly fine person, but he's not an Alpha 2.0. Nothing's wrong with a more feminine man, particularly if he lives in a culture where more effeminate men are accepted and celebrated. I'm also not talking about sexual orientation here; I'm referring to demeanor and outlook. There are certainly many high-functioning men in modern society who range from moderately masculine to not masculine at all.

The problem goes back to the first trait of the Alpha 2.0, which is consistent happiness. An Alpha 2.0 is not a man flying high because he's just snagged a great new girlfriend and who then is crying in his beer a year later because she dumped him.

One of the hallmarks of masculinity is constancy, and one of the core traits of femininity is inconsistency and change. As we'll be discussing in Chapter 13, women (and by extension, more feminine men), value not only positive emotions, but a full range of emotions, both the good and the bad. This requires constant change, not stability. Maintaining only positive emotions for feminine people is not only damn near impossible, but they really don't want it. Being happy all the time is "boring" to them. They desire change.

Therefore, while both a masculine and effeminate man can achieve happiness, only the masculine man will have the ability to maintain it in some consistent fashion. More neutral or feminine men will sometimes be happy, sometimes be unhappy, and sometimes be somewhere in between.

Freedom

A man who is not free cannot live the life of an Alpha 2.0. While all five traits of the Alpha 2.0 are necessary, freedom is perhaps the most important of them all.

A man can be extremely tough, muscular, and masculine, but if he's sitting in a real-life prison cell, he's not capable of living the life he chooses.

A man can be charismatic, good-looking, great with women, and the life of the party, but if he only makes $25,000 a year, he'll never have the resources to live the life he really wants.

A man can be intelligent, educated, wealthy, and successful, but if he's married to a woman who won't let him buy that new truck, or screams at him whenever he's ten minutes late, he is nowhere near Alpha 2.0.

The Alpha 2.0 wakes up every morning of every day and is able to, within legal and realistic financial constraints, do whatever the hell he wants, whenever he wants, without having to check with anyone.

There are four types of freedom that comprise the Alpha 2.0 lifestyle:

1. Freedom of Action
2. Financial Freedom
3. Sexual Freedom
4. Social Freedom

<u>First Freedom: Freedom of Action</u>

Freedom of Action means that the Alpha 2.0 is able to live his life any way he chooses, free from any unreasonable limitations from work, government, family, or lifestyle. This means:

1. He lives in a country that is more or less free, peaceful, and prosperous. If you live in an oppressive dictatorship or communist country, you cannot be free no matter how amazing you are. The same goes if you live in an unsafe area where violence and threats to your physical safety are the norm.
2. He lives in a society that is technologically advanced, since only through technology can he achieve comfort levels high enough to maintain consistent happiness. You cannot be an

Alpha 2.0 if you live in a hut with no electricity or running water. You could visit places like that, and you probably should, but live there? Nope.

3. He can do whatever he likes without having to get approval from anyone. That includes parents, a spouse, or a boss. This also means you cannot depend on your family for your income. Work for your dad if you really want to, but you'll never be Alpha 2.0 that way (since he will be controlling you in ways beyond just your job).

This extends to your wife or girlfriend. "My wife won't let me" is the credo of the beta male. An Alpha 2.0 can be in love with, and share a life with, a special woman whom he cares deeply for, but he is either legally unmarried or has an unconventional marriage (such as an open marriage with an enforceable prenuptial agreement) that we'll be discussing in later chapters. A man with a typical, traditional wife or girlfriend can never be an Alpha 2.0. By adhering to that system you must obey at least some of her rules and put up with at least some of her drama. A traditional relationship or marriage might be fun for a while, and it might impress your friends and family in The Prison, but it's not freedom. We'll discuss all of this in much more detail in upcoming chapters.

This also extends to raising children. Alpha 2.0s can certainly be fathers. I have two kids myself and it's even possible I will have more at some point. However, an Alpha 2.0's life cannot be limited by the fact he has kids. Having children is wonderful, but being responsible for raising small children 24/7 is not freedom. An Alpha 2.0 either:

A. Has no children.

B. Has children, but none that live with him full-time.

C. Has grown children that don't require supervision.

D. Has smaller children who do live with him, but he has an unconventional wife or girlfriend who is at least 90% responsible for the day-to-day child rearing tasks. He serves as a role model to his kids and a support system for their mother, but he is not a mother himself.

Again, just like with the trait of masculinity, I'm not saying having children is undesirable or un-masculine. Be very sure you hear me on this: having children is great. It's such an important topic I've devoted two full chapters to it in this book. I'm saying that having children that require daily care from you personally is not freedom, nor will it make you consistently happy.

4. He does not work too many hours per week, at least not for an indefinite period of time. You cannot be Alpha 2.0 if you're working 70 or 80 hours a week for years and years on end. Doing that will force you to miss out on other key areas of your life you consider important. Eventually, this will damage your happiness...and likely your health as well.

The exception to this rule is if you're starting a new project or business that temporarily requires you to put in some long weeks. That's perfectly fine and often necessary. However, I'm talking about your overall work life. If you're working more than 50 hours a week for more than three years straight, you're more than welcome to do that, but you won't be experiencing the Alpha 2.0 lifestyle.

<u>Second Freedom: Financial Freedom</u>

The second type of freedom critical to the Alpha 2.0 is financial freedom. Financial freedom as it's typically understood means financial independence, i.e. the condition of having so much money in the bank you literally don't need to work anymore. When I talk about financial freedom in this book, I'm not talking about financial independence, though a financially independent man certainly qualifies as financially free. Rather, financial freedom means being free from circumstances and unhappiness created by financial lack.

Let's say there's a car you really want. I don't mean one of those "that'd be cool to have" thoughts. I mean you really want this car. If you can't buy it because you can't afford it, you're not financially free. The fact you want it badly but can't buy it causes you some degree of unhappiness, and thereby violating one of our five key Alpha 2.0 traits.

You can apply this to anything within the financial realm. If you can't dress in the kinds of clothes you really want, travel to the kinds of places you really want to visit, or live in the home you really want, you're not financially free. Again, I'm talking about the strong yearning for these things, not a casual desire. Of course it may be possible that you simply don't want any of these kinds of things in the first place. As long as you're being completely honest with yourself, that's fine.

You are certainly not financially free if you have all kinds of financial problems, like being unable to pay your bills or having significant debt.

The Alpha 2.0 doesn't have to be rich, but he has the ability within his current income to provide the kind of life he really wants. He never thinks, "Damn! I wish I could but I can't afford it!"

We will be discussing money and finances in part five of this book.

Third Freedom: Sexual Freedom

Part Four of this book is devoted to the concept of sexual freedom. Most guys understand the concept of financial freedom, but sexual freedom may be new to you. Men understand why being free is a good thing, or why having money is a good thing, but in regards to sexual freedom, Societal Programming and Obsolete Biological Wiring get in the way (more on those evils is in Chapters 3 and 4).

Men, especially Alpha Males, are highly sexual creatures. We want sex often. We also want variety in our sex. Sex with the same woman over and over again tends to bore us, even if we love her dearly.

This is because love and lust are two completely different things and two completely different needs, even located in different parts of the brain. Your desire for sex resides within your hypothalamus, specifically its preoptic area. This area is twice the size in men as it is in women. It controls our more basic human desires, such as sex, hunger, and sleep. However, the feeling of romantic love occurs in your ventral tegmental area, which is linked to the hypothalamus but is still a very different part of your brain that serves a very different function.

Sex is one thing. Love is another. Often, sex has nothing to do with love or even a romantic connection. Only in The Prison do they try to convince you otherwise.

The Alpha Male 2.0 does not shy away from this reality. He does not try to suppress it for some greater good like beta males do, nor does he try to deny this and lie to himself about it like Alpha 1.0s tend to do. The Alpha 2.0 makes no apologies for who he is and what he is, and he does not allow society to dictate what he should or should not be.

Sexual freedom is the option of having mutually consensual sex whenever you want with whomever you like without having to get permission from anyone. That means that long-term monogamy is not a part of the Alpha 2.0 world. You can have long-term relationships, or even marriage, but you cannot be monogamous beyond short stretches. All of my relationships, even serious ones, are 100% sexually open. Whenever a woman catches my fancy, I have condomed sex with her, even if I'm dating or in love with someone else. There is no cheating. I never promise sexual monogamy, and the women continue to be with me anyway.

Now and throughout history, Alpha Male 1.0s, and even many betas, have destroyed their happiness, finances, families, careers, and even their lives by deluding themselves into thinking that long-term monogamy will work for them. The Alpha Male 2.0 follows a different path.

Fourth Freedom: Social Freedom

The final type of freedom is social freedom, which means the ability to take action without regard to negative reaction from society. As you might be able to see by now, many things the Alpha 2.0 does will not be readily accepted by those within The Prison. As a man breaking free of The Prison, some people are going to be upset at how you live your life. This might include people close to you, such as your friends, family, co-workers, women, people in your neighborhood or city, and people you communicate with regularly online.

If you hesitate to take needed action to improve your life because you fear some of those people are going to give you a hard time (which some will), then you are not socially free. You are still an inmate of The Prison, snapping yourself back into line for fear of disapproval from others.

This all goes to the concept of Outcome Independence, something I'll be describing in Chapter 15. Outcome Independence simply means you don't give a shit. If someone screams at you, or rejects you, or insults you, or tells you you're being a horrible person, or tells you to change, you shrug and move on. You don't get mad. You don't argue with them. You just smile and get on with your life.

This is not to say there are no constraints you must abide by. Obviously you must obey the law. Nowhere in this book will I advise you to do anything illegal. Obeying the law is actually a requirement of the Alpha 2.0, since violating the law means you will eventually get caught. Getting caught means fines and/or imprisonment, which will remove both your happiness and freedom, two of our key traits.

However, if you live in a country with an excessive amount of laws that infringe upon your happiness, it does behoove you to leave that country and find a new one with a minimum number of laws restricting your freedoms. This will be covered in Chapter 22.

It's also critical to not infringe upon the freedom of others. Chapter 8 will be explaining your personal code of conduct, and adhering to this is every bit as important as following the law.

The point here is just because the Alpha 2.0 lives a life of social freedom, it does not mean he's some ravaging barbarian causing chaos and harm to others. He's a good man, and he's good for the world around him.

An Abundant Life

If you're a desirable, single man, have great dating skills, but are not currently having sex with any women, what's the point of all that freedom and ability?

If you have a very outgoing people personality, have strong skills in business, marketing, or finance, but sit on your ass all day and play Xbox, what's the point of having those skills? What value are they actually bringing to your life?

This brings us to the final key trait of the Alpha 2.0: he lives an abundant life. Unlike the four traits above, abundance is a result of traits rather than a trait itself. An Alpha with all four of the key traits and who puts them into action will very quickly begin living an abundant life.

Abundance in this context is highly subjective. Different Alphas will often have different opinions on what things like "lots of money" or "lots of sex" means, based on one's individual personality, culture, upbringing, and desire. I'll define some basic parameters in a minute, but realize the exact ideal amounts of things like money, sex, love, social relationships, and even health are going to be largely up to you. I can't tell you what a "good income" is for you or what an "appropriate" amount of regular sex is, and neither can anyone else.

The point is the Alpha 2.0 does not go without these things.

How Much Is "Abundant"?

This all begs the question, how much money is needed? How much sex? Although these are subjective concepts based on many factors, we have to start somewhere, and this means we must quantify at least a basic starting point.

I will describe some specific baseline minimums an Alpha Male 2.0 must have to live a consistently happy and free life. They may apply to you perfectly, or they may require some modification based on who you are or where you live. Regardless, they should give you a good idea of what to shoot for and maintain.

Money Baseline

There are three financial minimums for the Alpha 2.0 lifestyle:

1. Annual income of at least $75,000 in US dollars or the equivalent.

2. The ability to earn the above income without having to work more than 40 hours a week on average. Fewer than 30 hours a week is ideal.
3. The ability to recover the above income within 6–12 months if you ever lost it for reasons beyond your control.

I had been teaching the $75,000 minimum annual income figure for many years based on some research and some educated guesses on my part. Then I read a study quoted in the book *Abundance* by Diamandis and Kotler, where they surveyed over 450,000 Americans on exactly what made them happy. The study discovered that the more money people made, the happier they became. Interestingly, this dynamic leveled out once people hit an annual income of $75,000. Making income beyond this point didn't seem to make people any happier, at least on average, but $75,000 annually was required to get to that happy state.

This is not a hard and fast number that applies in all circumstances. If you live in downtown New York City and support three children, $75,000 isn't nearly enough. If you live alone in Thailand or rural Wisconsin and have no debt, it might be too much. Feel free to make some adjustments, but if you don't make at least $75,000 per year, it's very likely you are suffering from financial lack, and thus are missing our Alpha 2.0 requirements of consistent happiness and financial freedom.

As we discussed above regarding Freedom of Action, it's also important that your $75,000 per year income doesn't require you to work long hours. The world is full of men who make way more than $75,000 but have to work 60+ hour weeks to maintain it. These men are not free, and thus not living the Alpha Male 2.0 lifestyle. We'll be discussing time management in Chapter 11.

Most people understand the value of a good income and not working too hard, but they tend to forget about the replicability of that income, which is item number three in our above list. Not only must you make at least $75,000 per year on fewer than 40 hours per week, but if you suddenly lost that income due to factors beyond your control, you should have the ability to fully restore that income within a matter of months.

If you instantly destroyed all of my current sources of income and threw me into a distant city, within 6-12 months I would be making my current income once again, or damn near it, even if the economy was poor.

That's true financial freedom. I know way too many men with decent incomes who are fearful that someday they may get laid off from their jobs, or that some change in the economy, law, or their industry will wipe out their business. They live in a constant state of nagging fear because they know in their hearts they could never make the income they now enjoy if that were to happen.

That's not happiness, and that's certainly not Alpha 2.0.

Sexual Baseline

Now we need to cover sex. Regular and abundant sex is critical to a man, and even more so to the Alpha Male. Here are the three sexual baselines for the Alpha 2.0 lifestyle:

1. The ability to have sex with at least two new women within four weeks of losing your current wife, girlfriend, or friend with benefits.
2. Having sex at least twice a week, regardless of whether or not you currently have a wife or serious girlfriend.
3. You consider these women at least "cute." Only having sex with ugly or average-looking women isn't going to satisfy you in the long run.

Once a man has accomplished the three sexual baselines above, he never needs to worry about going without sex or female companionship ever again. Never again will he be clingy with a girlfriend or wife. He knows that his vibrant, passionate and exciting sex life will continue uninterrupted even if he breaks up or gets divorced.

We're going to cover all three of those items in detail in future chapters, but here I'll cover some initial questions you may have.

The reason the Alpha 2.0 needs to have sex with *two* women in four weeks instead of just one is that if you have the ability to have sex with only one new woman, you are much more likely to start thinking that one woman is your only source of validation, sex, love, and/or companionship. You will very likely start getting needy, jealous, clingy, or territorial with her; all of which are beta or Alpha 1.0 traits. I've known and worked with hundreds of men and this kind of thing happens all the time. (Don't believe me? Ask women about it!) You must know that you can always have sex with someone else; moreover, someone else *cute*. This keeps your confidence and Outcome Independence levels high.

The "sex twice a week" minimum is where things may indeed get a little subjective. Every Alpha is different. You may be a horny bastard and need sex four times a day, or you be a more even-keel guy and may need sex just once a week. The point here is to never go long stretches without sex, and to never "get used to" going without sex or reduced sex just because you're married or "too busy." As a masculine Alpha Male, sex is important, and you need to have it often! Don't bullshit yourself about this. Too many betas and Alpha 1.0s do this to their detriment.

The Tires or the Engine

Before we wrap up this chapter and get to the good stuff, I have to pause for a minute here and deal with a problem I already see growing in your mind. Because of Societal Programming (something we'll be discussing in Chapter 3), when I start talking about all this "money and sex" stuff, the brainwashed part of your mind might start saying something like:

"Jeez this guy is shallow! Money and sex? Is that all that's important? Why does he keep harping on those two things? What about things like love, children, commitment, fitness, spirituality, giving back to your community, and making the world a better place? Money and sex isn't all that matters to a man!"

Correct! It isn't all that matters. In Chapter 7, we will be discussing the importance of those other areas, including physical fitness. Yet, those two things are required as a foundation in your life to accomplish all those other things. Visualize this:

Picture the coolest motorcycle you've even seen in your life. Even if you've never ridden one, imagine you're cruising down the freeway on that motorcycle, blasting through the wind, having a great time.

All of a sudden, the cycle starts fishtailing badly. You glance behind you and see that the rear tire is going flat. So you yell a few choice words, and are lucky enough to carefully slow down and pull over without an accident. You hop off and examine the tire.

Sure enough, there's a small screw embedded in the thing. No problem! You're a prepared guy, so you pull out your portable tire patch kit and get to work.

While you're working, a guy walking his dog passes by and stops to observe you. You see him and give him a friendly nod. He glares back at you and shakes his head, disapproval in his eyes.

"My goodness, you really are shallow, aren't you?" he says.

"Excuse me?" you respond, not understanding.

"Here you are," he says, "Doing all this work, spending all this time and effort on your tire. Is that all that's important to your motorcycle? The tires? Is that all that matters? What about the transmission? Or the engine? Do you seriously think the motorcycle's engine is less important than the tires? You are so superficial."

You smile silently to yourself, realizing this poor guy is brainwashed by The Prison, and you answer, "No, I don't think that at all. The engine is indeed more important than the tires. *But without two working tires on a motorcycle, the engine doesn't really accomplish much, does it?*"

The Importance of Money and Sex

A motorcycle's engine is more important than its tires, yes. Regardless, I don't care if you have the most expensive, top of the line motorcycle money can buy with the most advanced engine in the world. If that cycle doesn't have two working tires, it's not going anywhere. It literally can't move. It's no longer a motorcycle at that point; it's just a big hunk of expensive metal. However, if you put some tires on that thing, even if they're used and bald, now it actually moves. Now it's a motorcycle.

As a man, money and sex are the two tires on your motorcycle. Things like love, family, fitness, Mission, spirituality, self-actualization, and just about anything else you can think of are all part of the engine. They might be more important than money or sex in the long run, but as a man you need money and sex as a *fundamental baseline* to accomplish and enjoy all of those other things.

Still don't agree? Consider this.

Let's say you have a fantastic relationship with a woman you deeply love. Let's also say you are physically fit, have great hobbies, lots of friends, and a strong spiritual belief you have committed to that brings you great peace.

Sounds nice, doesn't it? Now let's also say you have zero money in savings, you're deeply in debt, and you've had zero income for two years.

Given the above situation, is your life generally okay?

If you're being honest, the answer is no. You're in a consistent state of stress because you can't pay your bills. Angry letters and phone calls from creditors are assaulting you constantly. You worry about getting kicked out of your home. You rely on others to help you with financial basics, always worrying that they may cut off their assistance at any time. Your self-esteem as a man plummets.

As a result of your lack of money, one of the tires on your motorcycle, your life is in chaos. Even with those other important areas of your life going great, you've got some extremely serious life problems due to your financial situation.

What about sex?

Regular sex is a requirement for you whether you want to admit it or not. The only possible exception to this is if you have an unusually low sex drive or suffer from low testosterone or other similar issues. For the remainder of this book I will presume your sex drive is typical and healthy.

Let's say you have tons of money in savings, have a great income, are physically fit, have lots of friends you enjoy immensely, have one or two fun hobbies you enjoy, and have a great family life. Let's also say you haven't had any sexual contact with a woman whatsoever in two years.

Yikes! You probably had an evil shudder run through your body as soon as you read that last sentence. I certainly did! Do I even need to ask you the "Are you generally okay?" question? Hell no! You're unhappy and you know it, regardless of other positives in your life. You feel weak and un-masculine. Women treat you like a "friend" or a "brother". You masturbate to porn way too much, possibly to the point of addiction. Whenever around women, your confidence suffers. You may even experience feelings of anger and resentment towards women. You have powerful feelings of longing that never go away.

Once you have a decent income *and* are having sex on a regular basis, all the other areas of your life can finally bring you the happiness, fulfillment, and rewards they were meant to give you.

As a man, and particularly as an Alpha Male, money and sex are the two core baselines for all other joys you can and will experience in your life. The Alpha 2.0 recognizes the importance of these two things, and he does not discount them as being frivolous or shallow desires. To denigrate the importance of money or sex to your personal fulfillment as a man will cause you guilt, unhappiness, and misdirection in your life.

Regardless of any other life problem you can think of, be it being overweight, or lonely, or spiritually stifled, or bored, or whatever else, once you have a steady flow of money and sex, you are now in a position to easily resolve any of those problems, and likely with great speed.

Money and sex. You need both. Now let's go get 'em.

Chapter 2 –
How to Accomplish Long-Term Happiness

There is an incessant influx of novelty into the world and yet we tolerate incredible dullness.

Thoreau

The early 1980s.

I was a child and my parents had very little disposable income. My dad worked hard for an average income supporting five kids and a stay-at-home housewife. Regardless, my religious mother demanded that her kids be raised in a Catholic private school.

Private schools were far less expensive in those days than they are now, but it was still a decent chunk of money for my dad to spend. My parents pinched pennies so hard they screamed, and they were able to send their two oldest children, myself and one of my sisters, to a private Catholic school…at least for a while.

Soon my parents ran out of money and could no longer afford it, so after eighth grade I was suddenly transferred to the local public high school.

Therefore, I had the interesting experience of being schooled during my childhood in an oppressive, politically conservative, Catholic school, while being schooled in my adolescence in a free-spirited, politically left-wing public school. Going from one extreme to the other was a shocking experience to say the least.

Which was better?

The truth is that they both sucked, because they suffered from the same problem: they both thought and taught that personal happiness was bad.

During my Catholic school years, I was taught, with great detail and enthusiasm, that living a free life was a terrible idea. Both God and Jesus wanted me to be a good little boy who followed the rules and who grew up into a good adult who also followed the rules. Hell awaited me if I wanted to go off and do my own thing. The Bible's teachings were about sacrifice, not happiness; humility, not laughter; following rules, not freedom; the virtue of being simple, pious, and meek; not wealthy, free, and confident.

My teachers, most of them angry nuns, constantly glowered at me with judgmental, angry eyes. The happier I was, the angrier they got. I was a happy, talkative kid, so I was punished often.

Then I hit the left-liberal high school, and that all changed. Spontaneity, laughter, and even some ostensible freedom was encouraged and celebrated, but there was still something rotten in Denmark.

Intelligent but wimpy beta male teachers told me all about how "women are the boss" and how I would "understand someday" that a "happy wife means a happy life."

Many of the female teachers were even worse. Frustrated feminists with short haircuts would stand in front of the classroom and go on and on about how America, the country we all lived in, was a selfish nation because we had more money than anyone else, and that wasn't fair. We also had more military might than anyone else, and that really wasn't fair. They hated talking about President Reagan and glossed over him whenever they could, focusing a huge amount of social studies class time on guys like Ralph Nader. Over and over again, I heard about how we wiped out the Indians and enslaved the blacks hundreds of years ago, and how bad we should all feel about that.

When I asked why I should personally feel bad about something neither me nor any of my ancestors did hundreds of years ago to people who were now long dead, I was told that I was insensitive for not feeling bad. Feeling bad was a virtue. Kids that felt terrible about things received knowing nods of approval. Kids who were happy received angry looks and eye rolls.

In the end, I couldn't tell who was worse, the conservative nuns or the progressive feminists. Both as distant opposites as possible, yet both teaching me the exact same thing. Feel bad. Feel guilt. Walking around happy all the time? Not cool.

Why the Desire for Happiness Is Not Selfish

Thousands of years ago, a smart guy named Aristotle announced that he found the purpose of life. Not the meaning of life. That's a little more esoteric. Instead it was the purpose of life. It was to be happy. He immediately received criticism for this. Left-liberal-minded folks screamed, "What about other people? What about service to your fellow man? What about poor people? No one will help them if everyone if focused on their own happiness!" Conservative-minded folks cried, "What about bad people? What about standards? You can't just run around doing whatever you want!"

Like I said, Aristotle was a smart guy. His answer to all of this was that only the good can be happy, and only the virtuous can be good. This means you've got to be a nice person or you'll never be truly happy. It's built into the system. This answers all questions about whether or not happiness is "right" or "selfish." How can something be wrong or selfish if it requires one to be a good person? The fact happiness requires you to be a good person makes happiness inherently good, not bad, and certainly not selfish.

The universe is a self-managing, self-correcting system. If you want to be happy, you have to be a reasonably good person. If you're a bad person, even if you get away with doing bad things, you will not be a happy person, at least not in the long run. This is because eventually our cause-and-effect universe will ensure that bad things will happen to you. It will also ensure that, eventually, good things will happen to you if you're a good person.

In both cases, these bad or good things may not happen immediately. It may even take years for them to manifest, but manifest they will. It can't be any other way.

It's an impressive system if you think about it. Do good things, and you will be rewarded with happiness, at least eventually. Do good things, and other people will be rewarded automatically, since the only way to be happy in the long-term is to do good by others. Happiness really does become its own reward.

The longer I live, the more I find this concept to be accurate. The stronger your desire to be happy, the more you will be motivated to do good things for the world, even if your motives appear to be selfish on the surface.

Here's an example. Most months I donate 5% of my gross profit income to charity. One of my biggest financial goals is to someday raise this to 10%, and perhaps beyond. I don't donate to charity for the reasons you might think. It's not because I'm a right-wing conservative, and thus think that God owns my money, and I am but an undeserving steward, and if I don't donate money I've committed some sort of sin I need to feel guilty about.

Nor do I do it because I'm a left-wing liberal/progressive, and thus think that money is bad, that rich people are evil assholes, that I should feel guilty because I have more money than others might, and the only way I received my money is either by deceiving people or ripping them off, and therefore the poor deserve my “excess” money more than I do.

Nope. I thoroughly disagree with both of those positions.

Instead I donate money to charity for the primary reason that *it makes me feel good.* I experience real joy by seeing the good my money does. It helps give deep meaning to my work. If you don’t already regularly donate your time or money to charity, I strongly suggest you do. You won’t believe how good it makes you feel.

Many books and papers have been written on the concept of happiness, rational selfishness, and rational self-interest. I’m not going to rehash all of that here. Let’s just start with these two concepts:

1. Your personal happiness is the most important thing in your life.

2. You can only achieve and maintain that happiness if you’re a generally good person who helps others.

The only reason people in The Prison disagree with item one is because they don’t understand item two. Once you thoroughly understand item two, item one becomes your new standard automatically. It makes happiness “okay.” If you winced a little when I first said that your happiness is the most important thing in your life, it’s because you think the only way for you to be happy often is to do bad things to others, or at a minimum not do good things for others.

It’s a false belief structure and it’s a standard part of The Prison. We’ll talk about why you think this way in Chapter 3, but for now I’ll help dash this false premise from your brainwashed mind.

Joe, Dan, and Larry

Let’s talk about something that ostensibly makes people happy: money. A common belief in The Prison is that if you have a lot of money, the only way you got that money is by being an asshole. If you’re “rich” (and everyone has a different opinion of what that word means), then somehow, somewhere, you ripped someone off, took advantage of someone, or lied. An even worse assumption is that you sat on your lazy ass and inherited all the money from rich relatives, doing zero work to earn it yourself.

In other words, you got that money by being bad. Therefore, if you don’t have money and want to get “rich,” you’ll have to do bad things to get there since there's no other way.

Let’s examine that belief. Take Joe, a normal guy. Joe starts a small construction company out of his home, building starter-family houses for lower-middle class families. So far, I don't think anyone would say he's doing anything bad.

Let's say Joe works very hard for 25 years, busts his ass, grows his business, and now he's a millionaire. Let's assume that he's always been a good, honest person, which, in my extensive experience in working with over 400 business owners for decades in my corporate consulting career, I have found overwhelmingly to be the case.

He now owns a decent-sized construction firm with 130 employees, building two or three-bedroom homes for middle and lower-middle class families. As a result, he now makes a decent six-figure income, lives in a nice house, drives a nice car as does his wife, and his two kids go to high-quality schools.

He regularly gives money to charity, pays a lot of taxes, provides the economy with inexpensive housing, and has created 130 jobs.

Is Joe bad? Did Joe do bad by becoming what many would call "rich?"

The answer is no. It's quite the opposite. By pursing his very selfish desire for money, he's done the world a great service.

Of course it's not always that clear. "Oh come on!" some might say, "Not all rich guys are like Joe!" That's true. Joe is a pretty simple example, though his example is very typical of people at his income level. Regardless, let's get a little more complicated.

Across town from Joe is another construction company owner, Dan. Like Joe, Dan makes a very good income and experiences a lifestyle that most would consider "rich." Unlike Joe, Dan is an evil, manipulative bastard. He screams at his employees and makes them work long hours for little pay. To save money he secretly and illegally violates all kinds of building codes, making his homes unsafe. He pads his invoices to his customers, ripping them off. He cheats on his taxes. He cheats on his wife with his secretary. He never gives any money to charity. He even kicks homeless people as he walks down the street, laughing with an evil glee. He's truly an Evil Rich Guy™, the kind Hollywood loves to portray.

Let me ask you a simple question: Is Dan happy?

Really think about that.

The answer of course, is no. Dan lives a terrible existence. Because he treats others poorly, he has no choice but to be unhappy. That's how the universe works. As I said, it's quite an ingenious system.

Moreover, because of the imperfect though sublime beauty of free market capitalism, if Dan really does all of these things, eventually he'll go out of business. Customers are going to stop giving him jobs. People are going to start quitting and he's going to have a tough time finding decent employees. His wife will eventually catch him cheating and divorce him. Lastly, even if the IRS never audits him, even if he somehow stays in business, he'll eventually get sued into oblivion because of his business shenanigans, and could even wind up in jail.

Would these things make Dan happy? Nope.

"Okay, fine," some in The Prison might say, "But what about the people like that who get away with it?"

Now you're really pushing the envelope of reality, and you should be aware you're doing that in order to make your point. What you're proposing is pretty damn unlikely. Eventually, at some point, guys like Dan will wind up paying the piper, even if takes 25 years. Regardless, let's run with that excuse anyway.

Let's take yet another construction business owner in the same town. His name is Larry. Like Dan, Larry is an Evil Rich Guy™. However unlike Dan, Larry is much craftier about it. Larry actually treats his employees and customers somewhat nicely (or at least pretends to) and is generally considered a nice guy. He pads and steals from his customers, but unlike Dan, he does it inconsistently and very carefully, so that he's never caught. It's the same story when he violates building codes or cheats on his taxes. He's so good at it and subtle, he never gets caught. Soon he amasses a small fortune, and now he's "rich" like Joe is. He buys his wife a nice new car, gives her a sweet kiss and tells her he loves her; then he secretly has sex with her sister. In an amazing feat of improbability, he beats the odds and gets away with it all of it.

I'll ask the question again: Is Larry happy?

"Yes!" the Prison folks answer.

Is he? Really? Do you think when Larry is all alone with himself, he feels good about himself or his life? Fulfilled? Proud? At peace?

I promise you he doesn't. Larry may put on a plastic smile, but inside he feels like crap. There's a gigantic hole inside him that never goes away. He feels empty and unfulfilled, and possibly guilty. If you look at his life more closely, you'll often find he's a closet alcoholic or addicted to painkillers. He has serious marital problems and/or kids who hate him or are on drugs. He's at the doctor all the time with problems like ulcers or headaches, or even cancer.

Because he's a bad person, he's unhappy. It can't be any other way. I have known and worked with a few Dans and Larrys in my life and this is how they work. Business, churches, organizations, and politics are full of Dans and Larrys, both male and female. Sometimes, to the casual observer, they do indeed look happy. You see Larry with a smile on his face wearing a fancy suit and driving his $80,000 car, so you assume he's happy. He looks happy, he acts happy, but behind closed doors his life is dysfunctional and damaged. He's anything but happy.

Moreover, I'm going to again challenge the assumption that Larry gets away with all of this stuff forever. Remember, the universe is a self-correcting system. As happy as you think Larry is now, life is going to catch up to him. At some point in his life, and it could be a decade or more down the road, some very bad things are going to happen to him. His wife will leave him, his kids will hate him, and he'll die a lonely and broken man. Perhaps instead he'll die of an overdose, or be in and out of drug rehab for the rest of his life. Maybe he'll wind up in jail sitting right next to Dan.

Being a bad person makes you unhappy. Eventually. There's no getting around it.

If you still have a hard time accepting this concept, look to the people you know in your own life. Can you find a person who's been consistently bad for at least 10 or 15 years, even in secret, "successful" ways like Larry, who you believe is truly and honestly happy, deep down in his or her heart on a consistent basis, including behind closed doors? I think you won't be able to come up with such a person.

I'm also not presenting this concept as a spiritual one (though if you chose to interpret it that way, that would be fine). I'm not talking about mysticism or karma, I'm talking about real-life statistical probability. If you seriously believe that a person can be bad for years on end and not eventually experience a persistent level of unhappiness, then you have a very skewed view of how probability functions in the real world.

People who are happy, who "selfishly" set their priorities on being very happy, must be good people who help the world. People who selfishly but honestly seek their own long-term happiness as their greatest ideal are the most benevolent people in society. It simply can't be any other way.

If you're sure that getting rich will make you happy, go get rich! As long as you go about it in an ethical manner, by selfishly pursuing your own happiness, you'll serve the world at the same time.

You can replace "get rich" with "having sex with 100 women" or "moving to a different country" or "getting divorced" or "switching careers" or anything else you're sure will make you happy, regardless if society approves of your choice or not. In all five of those examples, you'll benefit society by pursuing your own happiness.

- Getting rich means you've created jobs and provided needed products and services to others.
- Having sex with a lot of women (and remember we said "in an ethical manner") means you've provided great pleasure, and thus happiness, to many women who desired it.
- Moving to a different country enriches your life with new experiences, as well as the lives of those you meet in the new land.
- Getting divorced means that once you overcome the temporary unhappiness of such an event, you'll be free to pursue a new life as you chose. Forever more you'll be a happier man, and everyone around you will benefit from this new happiness.
- Switching careers means you'll be happier doing something you were meant to do, and your new employer (or customers) will be happier by having someone better suited to the work they need done.

So stop worrying about The Prison lecturing you about how happiness is "wrong" because it's "selfish." *Your happiness helps the world.*

Long-Term Happiness vs. Short-Term Happiness

Alright, so happiness is the primary reason for life, and it should be your number one purpose in it. However, there's one wrinkle to this; happiness can actually be dangerous under certain conditions.

There are times during the day where, while I'm working, I get a little lazy and I'm tempted to stop working and watch a movie on my big-screen TV. I'm a very motivated guy, but I'm still human, and sometimes I'll think to myself, "Hm. Taking a little break and watching *Blade 2* sounds like a really good idea right about now."

Why not chuck my work and watch a movie? I love loud, badass action movies. Watching those movies makes me happy, and happiness is my number one goal in life. So why not do it?

If I indeed stopped working on my important projects and had a six-hour Wesley Snipes marathon by watching all three Blade movies in a row, yes, it would make me happy. However, that evening, or the next day, or a few days down the road, I'd be very unhappy. Why?

- I would lose sleep and experience stress by being behind on projects I consider important.
- I could lose money by not getting my projects done.
- I would get behind on my personal financial and business goals, which would really piss me off.
- I may inconvenience or severely disrupt my clients or business partners, and that would cause me all kinds of headaches, hassle, and lost time and money.
- Most importantly, my self-esteem would take a hit. I would start to doubt my abilities to achieve my important goals in life, and that would make me extremely unhappy.

So watching a movie when I should be working would make me short-term happy while I was actually watching the movie, but make me long-term unhappy in the days and weeks that followed. In effect, I would have traded temporary and short-lasting short-term happiness for long-lasting and much more important long-term happiness.

Here's another example many people in our high-carb society can relate to.

I have an endomorphic body. This means my body gains mass quickly (as opposed to an ectomorphic body, which would represent a really skinny guy). The good news is that means I'm a big guy, which I like. As a man, having size is masculine and intimidating, both good. It also means when I lift weights, I get huge beautiful muscles very quickly without having to blow my brains out lifting weights. It's really nice.

The bad news is if I even look at a glazed doughnut, I gain three pounds of fat. I gain muscle fast, but I also gain fat fast. One meal at Taco Bell and I get jiggling man boobs. It sucks. I have to watch what I eat very, very carefully, much more so than a lot of other guys, and have had to wrestle with this challenge my entire life. Several times in my life I've been clearly overweight because of it.

The funny part is that I have very thin, ectomorphic brothers. One of them can eat an entire pizza and not gain a pound. Whenever he does this, I call him an asshole. However, then he goes to the gym to get ripped, after three months of very hard work he looks...exactly the same. I can hit the weights, lightly, and within two or three weeks my shoulders and thighs are noticeably bigger when I flex. That's when he calls *me* an asshole.

Being a trim, good-looking guy makes me long-term happy. If I'm trying to lose weight, which is a frequent occurrence in my life, and I decide to chuck it one day because I want to eat a jalapeno and cheese bagel slathered with cream cheese, it will make me short-term happy for about 15 minutes, but long-term unhappy for about two days (or longer), especially when I step on the scale the next morning.

I could rattle off a thousand more examples of how people, especially Americans, stupidly pursue short-term happiness at the expense of long-term happiness. Short-term happiness is easy, but fleeting. Long-term happiness is harder, sometimes very hard, but it lasts much longer and has a much stronger positive effect on your well-being and your life (not to mention everyone around you).

Therefore, it is not enough to say that "happiness" is our primary goal. It must instead be *long-term* happiness. Your goal should be to be as consistently, long-term happy as possible. Everything you're going to learn in this book revolves around that specific goal. Not inconsistent short-term happiness. Not happiness sometimes and pain and unhappiness others. No. The primary goal of the Alpha Male 2.0 is consistent, long-term happiness.

It is the condition of long-term happiness that defines and differentiates the Alpha 2.0 from everyone else. Generally speaking, women cannot be long-term happy (we'll discuss exactly why in Chapter 13). It's the same with beta males and Alpha 1.0s. They either lack the ability to achieve and maintain long-term happiness or refuse to pursue it.

The Barriers to Happiness

If happiness is the goal, why don't people just be happy? Why don't people simply do the things necessary to make themselves happy?

We've already discussed two reasons. The first is that they mistakenly believe being happy is somehow a bad or selfish thing that harms other people rather than helping them. The second is that they pursue short-term happiness which always results in eventual long-term unhappiness.

However, even those two aren't the biggest impediments to happiness. I know that even if I convince someone that happiness should be their number one priority in life, that it's a good thing to do, and that long-term happiness is better for them than short term happiness, they likely are still not going to take action on many of the principles and techniques described in this book.

Why?

It's because happiness actually isn't their highest objective, despite what they say or think. Something else is.

"Wait a minute. Why would someone NOT want to be happy?" you ask. Good question.

In the modern era, we human beings have two powerful enemies that confound our desire and accomplishment for long-term happiness. The first is Societal Programming. The second is Obsolete Biological Wiring. Before you take the path of the Alpha, you have to deal with these two bastards first. We'll discuss them in detail the next few chapters, but for now let's continue with some other reasons.

Justifying Negative

Another common reason for unhappiness is that many people in The Prison are under the mistaken impression that feeling negative feelings is somehow good. Here are some examples of the justifications they make.

"Problems make you stronger. They build character."

Generally speaking, that can be accurate. The issue is that I've seen the above statement used to justify all kinds of horrible, needless problems that need never have happened; problems caused by people being stupid, reckless, immature, irrational, or impatient, on purpose. I've seen it justify the behaviors of people with a long string of self-created life challenges.

If you're using that statement to justify a single problem you had years ago that you took care of quickly and never repeated, then fine. It did make you stronger. However, if you're using that statement to justify a long negative pattern of behavior, a series of never-ending problems lasting years and years, then you're just making excuses. Problems are not good in this case, and they are not "making you a stronger person" or "building your character." They are in fact making you a weaker and more miserable person.

Always be very, very careful when trying to justify consistent problems or negative feelings in your life. That's victim-talk.

"Walking around happy all the time means you're not considering all the pain and suffering in the world."

Does this mean that walking around angry all the time will help feed starving children in Africa or help end the wars in the Middle East? It won't. You can be as sad or as angry as you want; your negative feelings won't feed any starving children or liberate any oppressed people.

The argument could be made that if one is angry enough, one will take action to help the world be a better place. In the real world, I don't see this happen very often and neither do you. Take an honest assessment of most angry or sad people you know. Are these successful, passionate activists who really change things, get things done, and donate lots of time and money to charity?

If you're being honest, the answer is no. The vast majority of unhappy people make the world a worse place, not a better place. Those very few who channel righteous anger into positive action are the very rare exception to the rule. Frankly, even with those folks, once they start acting to improve the world, there's no reason for them to remain angry. They can certainly be more effective at changing things if they do it with a smile on their face rather than a scowl.

Bertrand Russell said, "The men who thought happiness the end of life tended to be the more benevolent, while those who proposed other ends were often dominated unconsciously by cruelty or love of power."

"You need bad feelings to know what good feelings are. If you never feel bad, you won't appreciate it when you feel good."

Ah, this is the biggest excuse of them all. Many people in The Prison cling to that statement like a child clings to a teddy bear at night.

On the surface, that statement is indeed accurate. If you grew up in Minneapolis and then go to Maui, you will certainly appreciate the beauty of Maui much more than someone who spent their entire life there. If you were married to Janet for 15 years and she routinely hit you with a baseball bat, then divorced her and married Suzi who never did that, you would certainly appreciate Suzi much more than I would if I had married her, simply because I've never had a wife who beat me with a baseball bat.

Now here's the question: In order to continue to appreciate your new, nonviolent wife, would you need Suzi to occasionally beat you with a baseball bat so that you could remember what it was like?

The answer is HELL NO. I think after 15 years of getting your ass kicked with a Louisville Slugger you would remember it quite vividly for the rest of your life. You would not need a refresher course. You would continue to appreciate your new circumstances without having to re-experience the negative feelings that caused your enhanced appreciation of the new condition.

If you told your new wife to occasionally hit you with a baseball bat so you could "feel bad in order to appreciate feeling good," she'd think you were insane (and she'd be right). Forget the damn baseball bat and enjoy your new wife.

So yes, one appreciates the good when one has experienced the bad. However, I would submit that for most of us, by the time we reach age 25 or so, we have experienced plenty of horrible, negative experiences and thoughts. We don't need to keep repeating these things forever in order to somehow further appreciate the good stuff. I suppose it's statistically possible that there may be some people that go from infancy to age 25 with every aspect of their lives being perfect the entire time, but again, those are the very rare exceptions to the rule.

Think about it. By the time you were in your mid-twenties or so, you likely experienced suffering, anger, fear, sadness, physical pain, emotional pain, financial lack, emotional upset, rejection, and all kinds of unfulfilled needs and desires. Do you really need to keep repeating that stuff in order to feel good?

You don't.

Unless you're well under the age of 25 and have never had anything bad happen to you, you no longer need to feel negative emotions ever again. I'm serious about this. Of course it's impossible to live the rest of your life with only positive emotions; some negative is going to happen to you occasionally no matter how good you are. I'm saying that you don't *need* any negative. With only two notable exceptions we'll cover in a minute, you should consider negative emotions as completely useless from this day forward. You cannot achieve the Alpha 2.0 lifestyle if you if you believe negative emotions should be repeated from time to time.

The Facilitation of Happiness

How does one achieve long-term, consistent happiness? There are really only two ways:

1. Organize your life so that happiness-creating events occur more often and unhappiness-creating events occur as infrequently as possible.
2. Organize your mind so as to reduce the number of things that make you unhappy.

Let's examine both items.

Structuring Your Life for Minimum Unhappiness

Item one is simple to understand but not easy to put into practice, which is why most people disregard it.

If you hate doing paperwork, you should never become an attorney, regardless of the other compelling reasons you may want to become one. If you dislike small children and love an orderly, clean lifestyle, you should never have kids, regardless of how hard your wife, girlfriend, or mother is pressuring you to have some. If you love having lots of sex with a variety of different women, you should never promise monogamy to any one woman, even if everyone in The Prison tells you it's the only "appropriate" way to love someone. There are so many examples of how people purposely violate, and even destroy, their long-term happiness by purposely structuring their lives in a way where unhappiness is a common occurrence.

- People who go into jobs that include tasks they strongly dislike or are unsuited for.
- People who go into debt, only to have painful financial problems down the road.
- People who get college degrees (and worse, go into debt for them) that they will never use.
- People who get into long-term relationships with partners who they know have extremely irritating behaviors.
- Women who hate being mothers and don't have the personality for it who have kids anyway.
- Men with extremely high sex drives and are who are accustomed to sexual variety who promise forever monogamy to one woman.
- People who strongly dislike the country, city or neighborhood in which they live, but never move.
- People who regularly vote for politicians who do things they hate.
- People who cling to religions or other spiritual beliefs that "force" them to behave in ways completely opposed to their personality and what makes them truly happy.

The list is endless. Doing anything similar to any of these things would create a life where unhappiness-creating events would be happening to you all the time. You might have spurts of short-term happiness occasionally, perhaps even often, but consistent long-term happiness would be impossible.

Any time you make any non-minor decision in your life, you must come to a complete stop and evaluate whether or not this decision will make you happy or unhappy in the long-term. Ask yourself, "I understand this will make me happy now, but will this keep me happy five years from now? How about ten years from now?" Be very honest about the answer. Way too often we agree to all kinds of life commitments that temporarily make us happy, or temporarily take the heat off, only to be stuck with a situation that makes us unhappy down the road.

Whenever I make a non-minor decision in my life, I pull up a blank document or spreadsheet and I write out exactly how this decision will affect my consistent, long-term happiness. If I determine the decision will make me happy now *and* will not decrease my future happiness in any way, then I go with it. If I determine that it will or might decrease my happiness later in life, then I chuck it. I do this even if it means I will make other people very upset with me. Invariably, these people are inmates of The Prison (women, beta males, and Alpha 1.0s), so I don't expect them to understand anyway. I may even do this if it might require more work or sacrifice in the short-term. My long-term happiness is well worth it. We'll cover this in more detail in a minute.

Structuring Your Mind for Minimum Unhappiness

Your life is external, but you must also cover your mind, that which covers your thought processes and emotions. Socrates said, "He is richest who is content with least, for contentment is the wealth of nature."

Let's take the classic example of the old man yelling "Get off my lawn!" at the neighbors' kids, and apply it to my real-life situation.

My house is sandwiched between two homes containing big families with lots of small children. In the summer time, these kids are always playing outside and having a good time. Because of this, sometimes when I come home from work or a date, or when I leave the house in the morning, there will be toys, trash, or even a bicycle or two in my driveway or my front lawn. Sometimes this happens many days in a row, every day bringing me a new surprise.

It's not fun to see trash in your front lawn. It's not fun to be unable to pull into your driveway because a big toy is in the way. This would really upset most men. 15 or 20 years ago, it would certainly have enraged me. I would have gone all Alpha Male 1.0, picked up that toy, walked over to both of my next door neighbors' homes, and bang on their doors. When they answered, I would have shoved the toy into their hands and lectured them like a grouchy old man about how they need to keep their damn kids off my yard, and how they need to parent their kids better so as to respect other people's property.

Being typical suburban Americans, they would have nodded and placated me (or worse, screamed right back at me) and promised to do so. Then a few days later there would be another toy, bike, or piece of trash in my lawn. That's how kids work.

Oh damn, then I would really lose it. This would go on and on and on, until I finally moved away.

I'm not like that anymore. Today, when I see a stuffed animal or an empty soda can on my lawn, I just chuckle and ignore it. If it's still there after a day or two, then whenever I feel like it I'll just pick it up and throw it in the trash, or perhaps toss it over to one of my neighbor's yards, then laugh and get back to work without a second thought. Whenever I see the kids playing in my lawn, I just wave at them and tell them to have fun. I'm completely Outcome Independent about it. (We'll discuss the concept of Outcome Independence in Chapter 15.)

Why the change? Because years ago I realized that being an anal retentive guy was a direct violation of structuring my mind for maximum happiness. It was clearly damaging my long-term happiness. I knew then, as I know now, that most people in the world are chaotic and incompetent. As a younger man, this used to really make me angry. Now I just accept it. Moreover, I usually find it humorous and laugh at it, which increases my happiness rather than reducing it.

A wise man once told me, "You can tell the size of the man by the size of the things that make him mad." Exactly. The longer the list is of things that upset you, the harder it will be to achieve or maintain consistent, long-term happiness. Therefore, it is in your best interest to keep that list as short as possible.

Learn to not give a shit. Learn to laugh things off. Learn to refocus your mind on positive, constructive things whenever you feel yourself getting frustrated at other people's behaviors. Remember that most people in The Prison are flawed, limited, irrational creatures, and they're going to stay that way no matter how mad you get or how many lectures or threats you issue. Do whatever is necessary, including counseling if you feel you need it, to reduce the number of things that make you unhappy to their absolute minimums. It's well worth the endeavor.

Is Unhappiness Ever Necessary?

Are there any times where temporary unhappiness is necessary to achieve long-term happiness? Yes. There are only two times where negative emotions, or unhappiness, is indeed necessary for improvement. The first of these is when you experience temporary unhappiness as a motivation to improve your condition.

I used to be poor. There were days I was worried I wasn't going to be able to buy groceries to eat dinner, or pay my electric bill, or put enough gas in my car to get to work. I hated that existence with a white-hot passion. This discomfort compelled me to do what was necessary to start making a good income. I started to work hard, and very soon I was no longer poor and no longer unhappy. As we've already discussed, I've never felt a need to occasionally go back to being poor so I could more appreciate being prosperous. Once was enough, thank you very much.

If I had never felt unhappy at my financial situation, it's unlikely I would have ever put in the action necessary to improve my life. Therefore, you could make the argument that the unhappiness I felt was a good thing.

However, notice that I eliminated the unhappiness. I made the unhappiness *temporary*. Many people unhappy with a condition in their lives simply keep these conditions (often defending them or making excuses for them), and thus maintain their unhappiness for a very long time. I'm talking about years or even decades. This is not what I would call "temporary."

Another common occurrence is that people will remove their unhappiness only to have it come back to them, over and over again. These are people who make good money, and then lose it all, and repeat that throughout their lives. Another example is people who have been married three, four, or more times.

So while discomfort with your current condition can be a powerful catalyst for positive change, that argument is only valid if:

1. You eventually eliminate the unhappy condition.
2. Don't repeat the unhappy condition.

Then, and only then, were the initial negative emotions of value to you.

The Happiness Change Curve

The second instance when negative emotions are necessary is when we make a significant change to improve our condition. Why don't people stick with new habits or actions they know they need to in order to be happy? *Occam's Razor* suggests the answer is because new habits are uncomfortable (i.e. unhappiness-causing), so we stop doing them.

This brings me to something I call the Happiness Change Curve. It's a chart that I always keep in mind whenever I pursue some new activity or project in order to improve my condition to ensure my long-term happiness. It's as simple as it is accurate. It looks like this:

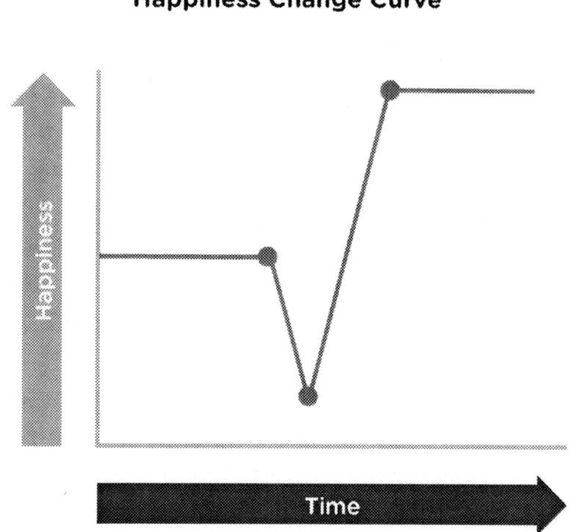

The Happiness Change Curve shows that you start at a state of discomfort, enough to want to change. Then you make a change to better your condition. Examples of this change could be a divorce, starting a new business, starting to exercise to lose weight, going back to school, or practicing a new skill you're unfamiliar with.

When you first start into the change and new behavior, it soon gets painful. Your happiness drops. However, if you stick with it, you start to see results, your life starts to improve, and you get happier. Soon, when the habit or system becomes second nature and the new results become part of who you are, you are now at a new level of happiness, higher than when you started.

Let's say you look in the mirror and see a beer gut where your flat stomach used to be. You are dissatisfied. Your happiness level is about a three on a scale from one to ten. For the first time in your life, you decide to start running three miles every morning to lose weight. Over the next week, you're running through your neighborhood, your fat bouncing up and down, panting like a dog. Are you happy? Hell no. You're sweaty, you're cramping and in pain, you feel like your heart is going to explode, you look silly, and you feel embarrassed. You're actually less happy than before you started exercising. Your happiness level was at a three, but now you're at about a one and a half. It sucks.

It's possible you might quit because of this unhappiness. Then you'll snap right back to a three and stay there. Forever.

However, if you push through the low point of the running (and the dieting), soon a few things will happen:

1. You'll start losing weight and your stomach will start getting smaller.
2. You'll start hating running less.
3. Making the effort to run daily will seem like less "work."

Over time, your new habit, and the results it creates for you, will boost your happiness to seven or eight, where it will stay forever (as long as you keep exercising and watching what you eat). I'm using exercising and losing weight as an example, but again, this can apply to just about any new habit or project you're going to undertake in order to better yourself.

When I was a young man, I worked in the corporate world with a normal eight-to-five job. I hated it. I wanted my own business. So I took action and made it happen. As I discuss in detail in Chapter 19, when I first quit my job and started my business full time at age 24, the subsequent two years were a very stressful time. I had little money, very little business, and there were many months I could not pay my bills. At one point I almost lost my house and was pennies away from bankruptcy. I was worse off and less happy than when I had my corporate job.

I stuck with it, and soon my income began to rise. Eventually I was making more money and working fewer hours than when I was working at my old job. Then I doubled the income I was making at my old job. Then I tripled it. I had achieved a new high level of happiness and have maintained it since. However, I had to persevere through that sharp but temporary dip in happiness that comes at the low point of the Happiness Change Curve. The temporary unhappiness was well worth the long-term happiness I now experience every day.

One of the few core differences between a successful person and an unsuccessful one is that unsuccessful people either fear the dip, or leap back to the status quo when the dip starts becoming uncomfortable. These people are stuck forever at their current (low) level of happiness.

Any time I start a new endeavor to achieve a new goal or make some positive change in my life, I always remember the Happiness Change Curve. I know that once I start with the change my happiness will actually decrease. I know I will have to suffer through this *temporary* unhappiness for a while until I can get to the point where my happiness will be higher than when I first started. I do two things:

1. I make sure that the low point of the Happiness Change Curve will be as brief as possible, and I try to get it over with as fast as I can.

2. I make sure not to quit when the unhappiness is at its worst, and stick with it. I remind myself the unhappiness is temporary, and the good stuff is coming right around the corner.

Remember the Curve as you move forward in this book. Once you start making big changes in your life, you're likely going to need it.

More importantly, remember that the only two times unhappiness is acceptable is when the unhappiness is temporary, as per the above two examples.

<u>Part Two</u>

Your Enemies

Chapter 3 –

How Society Programs You, and How to Overcome It

Men are not born stupid. They are born ignorant. They are made stupid by education.

Bertrand Russell,
paraphrasing Claude Adrien Helvétius

Summer, 1985.

I stood in line at the pizza joint in Queens, New York. At age 13, it was the first time I had been to a city far away from my home near Portland, Oregon. My best friend, whom I was visiting, stood next to me, as did his mother and older sister. New York was a very interesting place during the 1980s. Crime and grime were commonplace, and a strong pungent odor seemed to never leave my nose while I was there. How different it was from the woodlands of the Pacific Northwest were I was born and raised!

Finally it was our turn to order. My friend's mom placed the order for the pizzas, and then asked us all what we wanted to drink. My friend and his sister ordered soda. I ordered a small milk. Throughout my childhood I drank nothing but milk with all of my meals. It was a common thing to do in my hometown.

As soon as the word "milk" left my lips, three things happened at the same time. First, my friend's mom, who was a New York native, looked at me with a shocked, almost disgusted look on her face. Second, two burly guys sitting at a nearby table looked at me and made loud, half-laughing, half-snorting sounds. Third, the young woman behind the counter sneered and said, "We don't have milk here."

I was very confused. I looked at the woman and thought, "No milk? Why would a pizza restaurant not serve milk? What an odd thing." Then I noticed the nearby guys making fun of me and my friend's mom's expression.

When the two guys started snorting louder, the mom's look went from disgust to embarrassment. She turned to the two guys and said, "He's from out of town," shaking her head as she said it. The two guys laughed, throwing a few muttered insults about me and milk. The woman behind the counter kept looking at me like I was an alien from Mars.

I was amazed. It's not just that the restaurant didn't serve milk, but it actually *bothered* these people that I wanted to drink some.

As we walked to our table with our pizza, my friend's mom explained to me, "Look, in New York, we don't order milk with food. Ordering milk to drink is like ordering a bagel with no cream cheese. So you don't want to do that again. You should order Coke or Pepsi next time."

Societal Programming

All societies in the world, now and throughout all of human history, have been controlled by a small few. The elites. The primary objective of the elites is to achieve and maintain control over the masses. Sometimes they do this in a nice way, other times not so nice. There is usually nothing inherently evil about this control. It's simply part of human nature. Under any political system, be it free market capitalism, corporatism, quasi-socialism, real socialism, communism, oligarchy, monarchy, or a dictatorship, you'll always have a small group of elites ruling over everyone else in some form or fashion. It's human nature and unavoidable.

In order to maintain the power they have over the masses, the elites do their best to manipulate the thought processes of the people in a way most conducive to keeping the people organized, obedient, and docile. The more people in a society like that, the easier it is for the elites to maintain their power.

If it served the elites' power structure for the masses to believe that eating large amounts of doughnuts was good for you, then even if you lived in a "free" country, you would eventually start hearing about how eating doughnuts was good for you.

1. You would see good-looking famous people in movies and on television eating lots of doughnuts while looking and feeling great.

2. You would hear big corporations pushing doughnuts as a healthy food.

3. You would hear religions talking about how eating doughnuts was moral and right and how not eating them is sinful and selfish.
4. "Eat doughnuts to be healthy" would be taught in schools in programs pushed hard by teachers and politicians.
5. Parents would constantly scold their children, whether young or fully grown, that they should be eating more doughnuts.
6. Your friends and peers would eventually start making fun of you (or at least start looking at you strangely) if you didn't eat doughnuts regularly.

At some point, and it may take many years for this to happen, you would start to think, even a little, that eating doughnuts often was the best way to go. Likely, you would think this to some degree no matter how smart or independently-minded you think you are. Eating doughnuts is not good for you of course, but that's irrelevant. It would have been said so many times, so many ways, from so many sources, all your life, it would now be implanted in your subconscious mind, and you would believe it, or at a bare minimum you would assign credence to it to some degree.

Multiply that by a thousand different opinions in all the different topic areas you've learned throughout your life. All your life, you have been programmed by society to think a myriad of incorrect things by many different trusted sources. Since the day you were born, the following sources have been hammering away at you with untruths, 24 hours a day, seven days a week:

- Schools
- Corporations
- Governments
- Religions
- Advertisements
- Authors
- Politicians
- Television
- Movies

- Music
- The news
- The internet
- Your friends
- Your parents
- Your extended family
- Your lovers

Many of them actually have good intentions by doing this, and many do not, but all of them are reinforcing falsehoods in your brain. What they're really doing, whether they realize it or not, is bolstering the elites' ability to maintain their control over The Prison.

It works very well. The elites couldn't be happier.

This is sometimes called societal conditioning. I use a more accurate and memorable term: Societal Programming, or SP.

As a result of this constant programming, your brain has literally hundreds of "facts" and opinions that sound right but are completely false. You have been inaccurately programmed by society.

A very small amount of this programming is accurate to reality, such as "Don't kill people." The problem is for every one of those, you've got twenty incorrect ones like "They hate us for our freedom," or "Schools need more money," or "Get a good job and everything will be okay," or "Open marriages don't work."

SP includes all kinds of things…

In politics:

"Republicans make government smaller."

"Democrats don't go to war."

In history:

"The North invaded the South in order to free the slaves."

"FDR was completely shocked when the Japanese attacked since he had no idea that would ever happen."

In relationships:

"Women are attracted to men who buy them things."

"Once you find that one special person, you won't ever want to have sex with anyone else."

In economics:

"The crash of 2008 was caused by too much capitalism."

"Real estate always goes up in value."

In fitness:

"Weight loss is mostly about exercise."

"Eating fat makes you fat."

In business:

"Entrepreneurs who own successful businesses have more time and freedom."

"The most important thing is to cut costs."

All of the above statements are false. I'm not going to spend time going into detail regarding the above topics, since most are well outside the scope of this book. Don't believe a word I say; feel free to do your own objective research if you strongly agree with any of the above items, and you'll discover that they all sound right, but are actually false.

There are many common statements you and I could make that would sound perfectly accurate and logical to you but are completely wrong, because of your own ingrained SP. Based on the culture you live in, your upbringing, and your political views (all of which are various forms of SP) you might agree with some of them and not others, yet all of them would be false. This is because these lies have been repeated to you, since childhood, over and over again, so you believe them. The fact they're untrue doesn't factor in at all.

The Purpose of SP

So what's the problem with this? So what if people think doing crunches will spot-remove fat from your abdomen? What's the harm?

The problem is the goal of SP is not to make you happy. Therefore SP is not compatible with our primary life goal, which is, as we discussed last chapter, to be consistently long-term happy. SP isn't necessarily designed to make you unhappy either. In many cases, unhappiness tends to be an unintentional byproduct of SP. As I said above, the goal of SP is to maintain the power structure for the elites. This includes people like upper level politicians, Wall Street bankers,

Fortune 500 CEOs, celebrities, and their ilk. You can call them the ruling class, the political class, or whatever you like. These are people with far more power over society than you or I will ever attain. They're the people in charge, and naturally they want to stay in charge.

On a certain level, I don't begrudge the elites for wanting this. If you were one of them, you'd probably want to stay in power too. Although often the elites do things I consider quite evil and terrible, it's a natural part of the human condition to have a small group of bosses and a large group of followers.

Here's where things get problematic for those seeking the path of the Alpha 2.0. The elites need you to do things like obey, conform, consume, vote, and fear. Your personal happiness is nowhere in there. They'd actually prefer you'd be docile or angry (at the right people) than happy. This means the elites' goal of continued power and your goal of long-term happiness are mutually exclusive. You cannot be long-term happy if you follow the elites' program. Either you follow the agenda of the elites and be happy sometimes or never, or you reject their agenda and achieve long-term happiness. There is no third option.

To achieve long-term happiness as an Alpha, you must actively reject Societal Programming.

I'll be honest with you...this is difficult. You face a tough battle on two fronts. First, you must question and attack all the false SP that has built up in your mind over the course of your life. I've been doing this for many years, and to this day I still catch myself falling prey to a little SP on occasion.

The second problem is even tougher. On a day-to-day basis you'll have to deal not only with your SP, but the SP within everyone around you. If you overcome your own SP and start pursuing long-term happiness, you're going to be doing all kinds of things that look very odd, perhaps even offensive, to all the other SP-filled people around you. The Prison inmates are going to be very uncomfortable watching you break out of The Prison and engage in freedom-based, happiness-maintaining, non-Prison behaviors. You're definitely going to get some feedback about that.

There are many examples of this, but I'll give you a really easy one to chew on. If you're a 45 year-old man and you start casually dating a 19 year-old woman, some people are going to get very angry and consider you a disgusting person. In the Western world, particularly in the United States, we have been filled with strong SP for about 100 years that older men should not date younger women that age.

On a purely rational and technical level, is there anything wrong, evil, or destructive about a 19 year-old woman choosing to have a consensual, casual relationship with a 45 year-old man of her own free will? If you take your emotional reactions out of the equation, the answer is no. As a matter of fact, I have argued that a 19 year-old woman is usually going to be better off and safer dating the typical 45 year-old man than the typical 19 year-old man. Think about it. Picture the typical 19 year-old guy. Now picture the typical 45 year-old guy. Which guy is more responsible? More trustworthy? More conscientious? More safe? Which one is smarter? More educated? Has more financial resources? Again, if you're thinking rationally and not emotionally (i.e. not under the influence of your SP) you'll have to answer that the typical 45 year-old man has the typical 19 year-old man beat soundly in all of those areas.

However those are facts, and SP isn't about facts. If a 45 year-old man walks into an office party with an 19 year-old woman on his arm, he's going to have to deal with some viscerally negative reactions from other people his age, all due to false SP. Dealing with this kind of bigoted SP from other people is not fun. Just ask any men who are black or openly gay, and they'll tell you all about it.

Dealing with negative SP from others requires some strength and courage. Is it worth it? Absolutely. By avoiding SP, the reward is vast amounts of happiness. When that 45 year-old guy goes home with his 19 year-old he'll be far more happy than his buddy at the party who has to go home with his bitchy, jaded, non-sexual, overweight 45 year-old wife. Trust me on that one. I've been circumstances similar to both of these scenarios, and many other men who have been in both situations will say the same thing.

Obviously I'm using an extreme example to illustrate the point. Often the situation is much more subtle and insidious. If you're from an Asian family and decide to not go to college, you're in for some serious negative SP from your parents. The same goes for you if you're a black guy and marry a white woman, or if you quit your job as a doctor to become an artist, or if you walk around with a purple Mohawk. There are thousands of possible things you can do that that will generate ire from the normal, SP-brainwashed Prison inmates. This is something you'll have to learn to accept, expect, and overcome.

Sources of SP

SP comes from various powerful and influential sources in your life. Here are the big ones, listed in the usual order of when you encounter them.

Your Enemies

1. Your Upbringing

Your parents are the very first people to start filling you with false SP. Men are often raised by single mothers and taught to "respect women," which in reality often means to be submissive to women's demands. You could also have been raised by an abusive or Alpha 1.0 father who taught you all kinds of falsehoods not only about women, but about other races or cultures.

Your political beliefs were likely implanted by your parents as well. Most conservatives were born into conservative households, just like most left-liberals were born into left-liberal households. Most didn't come to these political bents because of rational, objective analysis. They simply adopted the beliefs their parents told them to believe. Others angrily reacted to their parents' beliefs and thus adopted opposite beliefs in rebellion. Neither of these are rational responses; they're both classic SP.

2. Your Education

Is it any wonder that left-liberal colleges tend to crank out left-liberal progressive students more than they do conservative Republican students? Or that private Catholic schools crank out more Catholic students?

How you were educated, from the time you were a small child until the time you got your high school diploma or college degree, is a powerful contributor of false SP in your brain.

3. Your Country and Culture

If I were to pick one source of SP as the most powerful, it would likely be cultural SP. Sometimes people can break free of some of the SP their parents or teachers programmed into them, but cultural programming is extremely difficult for most people to expel from their minds.

For example, if you were raised in Asia, you likely have an extremely strong desire to please and obey your parents, especially your father, even if you're well past the age of 25. Because of powerful cultural SP, you're going to find it extremely difficult to pursue your own happiness, since often that requires you doing things your parents will not approve of. Contrast this to folks raised in the United States, where by the age of 20 or so, we often consider our parents old fuddy-duddies who are completely full of crap, even if we love them.

When talking to large numbers of men online, I often run into an interesting and predicable problem when talking to men raised in the United States versus men raised in Europe. When I start talking about long-term monogamy being a pipe dream and not working, some guys will get very upset. Invariably, almost all of these guys are men in my own country, the United States. As Americans, with a strong conservative, religious past, men in my country have been brainwashed with powerful SP that says long-term monogamy is wonderful, moral, and easy to accomplish as long as you pick the right girl. Thus, many American men can't stand it when I talk about long-term monogamy not working and being a waste of your time. While I'm arguing with these guys, the European guys remain very quiet. As Europeans, they know that long-term, absolute, sexual monogamy doesn't work at all, which is one of the reasons cheating is a common and accepted practice in most European cultures.

Here's where things get really interesting. When I switch topics and start talking about how great business is and capitalism is, and how important making money is, and how men should make as much money as possible, the entire situation reverses. The American guys are very supportive and ask lots of great questions, but some of the European men get furious with me to the point of accusing me of all kinds of terrible things. SP in European cultures is somewhat anti-capitalist and anti-money. Financial success in America is often celebrated, but financial success in Europe is viewed with strong suspicion.

In both cases, men are reacting to these topics purely based on cultural SP, not on logic or reality. Such is the power of Societal Programming.

4. Religion

Though religion as a force for SP is far less powerful in the Western world than it was in years past, it is still a strong factor. If you were born in the United States, you're likely a Christian or an agnostic. If you were born in Saudi Arabia, you're likely a Muslim. If you were born in India, you're likely a Hindu. If you were born in China, you're likely not religious at all, but hold some very superstitious beliefs. In all these cases, the only reason for your beliefs was the country you happen to have been born into, not any objective analysis on your part.

The key problem for religious SP for the Alpha 2.0 is the sexual restrictions it places on you as a man. If you belong to a religious faith, it is very likely you have some false SP in your brain that's telling you sex is bad, or at least is only acceptable under certain, specific conditions. Religion is probably the biggest source of anti-sex SP there is. This is such an important topic to your long-term happiness, I have devoted an entire chapter to overcoming your false sexual SP (Chapter 12).

5. Hollywood and the News Media

Even if you live outside of the United States, films, television shows, and commercials from Hollywood and the news media are a tremendous source of SP. Hollywood fills people's heads with all kinds of false SP such as:

- Businessmen are evil.
- Wives and girlfriends are tough, strong, and independent; husbands and boyfriends are incompetent and stupid.
- Finding someone special is very hard, but once you find them, the relationship is very easy.
- Women deserve everything.
- Women should not be feminine.
- Seeing sexual imagery is good, but actually having sex is bad.
- Single mothers are heroes.
- Crime is rampant.
- The government is here to help.
- Rich people are evil; poor people are hardworking and honest.
- Government knows best.

Not only is the much of SP coming from Hollywood and the news media completely inaccurate, but very few of the above messages are conducive to a free, happy, Alpha 2.0 lifestyle.

I don't really watch TV shows, but I'm a huge movie nut and watch them often. However, I have to be extremely careful every time I watch a movie, especially one I really like, to be aware of the often subtle SP Hollywood is trying to shove into my brain that will damage my long-term happiness as a man and an Alpha. You should also.

6. Politics

The single, most irrational area of modern day life is politics. The SP that comes from political groups and political leaders on all sides of all political spectrums is staggering. The sheer amount of completely false SP flowing from the mouths and keyboards of otherwise very intelligent people on all sides of the political debate is stunning in its intensity and vastness. It's really gotten bad out here, and it will likely get worse. It's actually reached a point where if you are completely nonpolitical, you are likely better off in terms of SP and rationality than someone who is very politically informed and opinionated.

For the purposes of full disclosure, I'll state up front that my political views are mostly libertarian. However this is not the time and place to discuss my political opinions. All I'll discuss here is your political views as a support or deterrent to the Alpha 2.0 lifestyle.

Speaking very generally, and there will be many exceptions, achieving and maintaining the lifestyle of an Alpha 2.0 is easiest for men who are either nonpolitical or libertarian in their political leanings (since personal freedom is such a strong and critical component of the Alpha 2.0 life). Next best would be men who are left-liberals or very mild conservatives. The worst would likely be men who are strongly socially conservative. That's simply because as a strong conservative, you likely are still clinging to some false SP regarding things like sex, marriage, children, and the lack of rights for women, and relationships. This is equally true of left-liberals/progressives in the areas of business, money, income, finance, and investing, since as a lefty you're going to have some false SP about how evil or "bad" some of these things are.

If you are strongly political, even if you're a libertarian, constantly be aware of the shortcomings of your political beliefs in terms of your journey towards a happy Alpha 2.0 life. Just like with religion, any strong beliefs in the political area can often be a source of problems for you.

7. Your Social Circle and Work Circle

Birds of a feather flock together. The people you regularly hang out with are a compelling source of SP, and you need to be aware of this.

As I mentioned back in Chapter 1, my mother was Catholic nun prior to marrying my dad and having me. As you might imagine, throughout most of my childhood she was a devoutly religious, God-fearing, conservative Republican. When I was a kid, I remember her seeing Democrats on television and telling me how "slimy" they looked.

She never said this about Republicans. Therefore the SP she was attempting to program me (whether consciously or not) with was "Democrats bad, Republicans good."

Then something strange happened. When my siblings and I grew older, she didn't need to be around the house nearly as often, so she got a job as a teacher. At first she taught middle school and later, college. She enjoyed teaching immensely and continued doing so until retiring at the age of 70.

Are teachers and school staff usually conservative or left-liberal? They're overwhelmingly left-wingers, of course. The more my mom hung out with teachers, worked with teachers, befriended teachers, and became involved with teachers unions, the more I started hearing more left-wing stuff come out of her mouth.

Today, after decades of being in that environment, my mom is now one of the most left-wing people I know, with a love for men like Teddy Kennedy and Barack Obama that borders on worship, as well as strong hatred of anything Republican. Wow! What a change from when I was a kid!

That's the power of SP from your social and work circles.

How to Overcome SP

Overcoming this river of false information that has been flowing into your mind on a daily basis is not easy, and that's the first thing to be aware of. You will never overcome all of your SP. It's impossible. You can do a thorough cleaning of your brain and get rid of a good 80%, or even 90% of it, but pieces will remain despite your best efforts. That's okay. You don't need to be perfect to be an Alpha, you just need minimal influence from SP.

There are three specific ways to combat SP's influence over your life.

Method 1: Qualified vs. Standard Information Sources

In any area of your life you deem critical, you need to educate yourself by looking beyond the standard, universally-accepted information sources.

Here's the simplest example. If you think you know a lot about business because you went to college and got a business degree, I guarantee you've all kinds of false SP in your brain about building a successful business. In order to remove this SP, you would research and find the best business books written by self-made business owners who had been successful in the real world. You would avoid business books written by college professors, researchers, corporate managers, or any business owners who inherited their businesses from their parents. You would pay attention to the *qualified* business owners' advice over the *standard* advice you learned in college.

In other words, you would listen to people who have actually done what you want to learn about, rather than those who study or teach the topic without actually having done it. Moreover, you would only listen to people who achieved their circumstances starting from circumstances similar to yours.

The above example goes for any area of life. If you think you know accurate American history because you learned it in high school, or if you think you know how to make marriage work because of lectures you received as a child from your parents, or if you think you know how to lose weight or gain muscle mass from your two weight-lifting buddies who were born with mesomorphic body types and fast metabolisms, in all cases you're getting advice from standard sources, rather than qualified sources.

Whenever analyzing information, you must determine where that information came from, then determine if the source was a standard source (like your parents, your school, Hollywood, your buddies, etc.) or a qualified source. A qualified source is someone who has accomplished what you want to accomplish, having started in a very similar situation as you, who has also worked with many other people and seen similar results in them. As you can see, this disqualifies all the usual sources of SP, from Hollywood to your high school history teacher.

Method 2: Rational Answers to Challenges

I once had a very interesting conversation with a woman I was dating. She was in her late 30's, highly intelligent, and college educated. She had a healthy sex drive but came from a strong religious Christian background. Our relationship was sexual, but not serious, and we had this conversation right after having sex.

"Premarital sex is bad," she said, "People shouldn't do it."

"You do it," I responded, "Hell, you just did it."

"I know I do it. I do it a lot. But I shouldn't."

"Why not?"

"Because. I just shouldn't."

"Why not? You're not hurting anyone by doing it."

"Well…I just shouldn't do it."

"Why not?"

"Well, what if everyone was doing it? What kind of world would that be?"

"Everyone does do it."

"Well, yeah, but they shouldn't."

"Why not? You're not answering my question. You just keep repeating yourself."

"It's about respect. It's disrespectful."

"To whom?"

"To everyone. To everyone doing it."

"How are two adults who are unmarried, having consensual sex while using a condom, disrespectful to either one of them?"

"It just is! It's disrespectful!" she screamed.

The conversation continued like this for another minute or two until she became visibly upset with me. The problem here is I was using logic to communicate with a woman I was in a sexual relationship with about a sexual topic, which is almost always a mistake, but we'll talk more about that in Chapter 13.

Notice that although she had a very strong conviction regarding a topic, she had no logical or rational explanation for the source or reason for her opinion. This is the ultimate tell-tale sign of SP. Any time someone is challenged on something they say or believe, and they can't give a clear, rational, logical reason why it is they believe it, you've just uncovered some clear SP in that person's mind.

Though she probably wasn't aware of it, the reason she thought premarital sex was disrespectful was because of decades of false religious SP. Sadly, now as an intelligent adult woman, she was carrying around all kinds of guilt because of her love of sex while her false SP that kept telling her premarital sex was wrong.

If I am strongly challenged on any of my strong life opinions (of which I have many!), I can instantly lay out a very clear, rational, logical, fact-based set of reasons as to why I feel the way I do. I have found that most people with strong opinions cannot do the same. Like my friend above, they have strong opinions, believe certain things very passionately, but they cannot tell you why they believe them. All they have is SP backed by emotion, which is a strong combination, but a false one.

On the other hand, if I realize I have an opinion that upsets me when challenged, but where I can't back it up with logic, reality, and/or facts, I come to a complete stop and do a gut-check. I'm likely suffering from some false SP, and need to re-orient fast.

As an exercise, write down a list of all the things you believe strongly. Make that list as complete as possible. Then go back to the top of the list, and for each belief, write out a clear, rational, fact-based reason why you believe that item. This should be something another person can Google online and fact-check relatively quickly. If you can't do this, you've likely uncovered some SP in your mind that needs weeding out. I did this exercise myself years ago, and believe me, it was a mind-blowing experience. You'd be surprised at what kind of garbage you'll find lurking in your own mind.

Always make sure that anything you believe strongly has a basis of something rational and clear. Ensure your beliefs are based in reality rather than SP. Does this mean you'll always be right? Of course not! Even very intelligent, rational, well informed people can be wrong. It happens to the best of us. Regardless, the odds of you being right are far beyond those who base their lives on SP, since those folks are virtually guaranteed to be wrong.

J. Paul Getty, one of the wealthiest self-made men in American history, once said, "If you want to be successful, look at what everyone else is doing, and do something different." He was well aware of the pervasive, damaging power of SP.

Realize that I am talking about irrational, SP-based reasons for strongly held opinions and convictions. I am not talking about feelings. For example, if you're deeply in love with someone, but you cannot logically explain why, that's perfectly fine. I love lemonade and don't like limeade, and I can't logically or rationally explain why. Things like love and taste are not opinions, they're feelings. Feelings are good. What's destructive are strongly held opinions, convictions, or beliefs backed by nothing but feelings with zero rationality.

Method 3: Be Aware of Hidden Programming

Some SP is overt and clear. When one of your buddies says "Classy women make you wait for sex," that's overt SP that's very easy to identify. However, most SP is subtle and hidden, and is fed to you in sneaky ways. You need to constantly be aware of all hidden Societal Programming whenever you consume any external input from your fellow human beings.

Motivational speaker Randy Gage once noticed that the movies *Spider-Man* and *Spider-Man 2* were filled to the gills with anti-wealth, anti-money SP. To quote from his article "The Danger of Lack Programming" from 2003:

The big hit last year was "Spiderman." It was such a success in big part, because it was filled with insidious lack and limitation messages. If this didn't jump out at you from the screen while you watched it, you've got a ways to go in your consciousness in this area.

Here are just some of the subliminal messages this movie foists on you:

Poverty is noble. We have the poor relatives who bring up Peter, the poor orphan. (By the way, have you ever noticed how many orphans there are in popular literature? Not just Spiderman, but Batman is an orphan, Superman is, Harry Potter is, and plenty more. This is to evoke emotional support from you.) There even is a part in the movie, where Peter's uncle speaks the most lack-centered words that have ever been spoken.

"We may be poor, but at least we are honest!"

Translation to your subconscious mind: Rich people are crooks.

Which is subliminal message number two. The evil villain in the movie, is of course, the billionaire industrialist. He is wealth and ambition personified; the devil incarnate!

These messages were repeated over and over...

Remember the scene where Peter finally gets up the nerve to talk to the neighbor girl. She seems like she cares for him, then the rich kid shows up with his new car (that daddy bought him for his birthday). She drops Peter like a piece of radioactive camel dung and jumps in the new car and speeds off.

Is it any wonder that you grow up hating rich people and subconsciously not wanting to be like them?

Every time you talk to someone, see a movie or TV show, read a book, article, or blog post, watch a lecture, or receive any other input from society, your SP-detector needs to be on full blast. Before I walk into any movie theater, I remind myself that because the movie was made by Hollywood (one of our primary SP sources) I need to be aware of the hidden SP the movie may try to sneak into my mind when I'm not paying attention. I do the same right before I read a book or click on my internet browser.

Be aware that the mounds of SP that lie within you are damaging you and keeping your life down. It is your job to:

1. Clean out as much SP from your mind as you can.
2. Be ever watchful for new incoming SP, and keep it out.

I'll say it again. You cannot be a consistently happy person, much less an Alpha 2.0, if you allow SP to guide any important area of your life.

Chapter 4 –
How Your Obsolete Biology Limits You, and How to Overcome It

The easiest thing is to react. The second easiest thing is to respond. The hardest thing is to initiate.

Seth Godin

Summer, 2007.

I was sitting across from a gorgeous blonde in a bookstore coffee shop. She was in her mid-thirties, talking to me about all the trouble she was having with her 12 year-old son. He was a special needs child, having been born with some serious deficiencies. I was still perfecting the fine art of dating at that point, but I had at least learned by now that the more a woman talks on a first date, the higher your odds are of closing the deal.

So I kept asking questions about her son and kept her talking, which was easy. My eyes roved over her perfect face, perfect long golden hair, and perfect body as she went on and on about all the problems she was having with her son at home, at school, and with her extended family.

This was followed by a long oration about how she had never wanted kids in the first place. When she was young she wanted to focus on her career, and never intended on having any children, ever. Her son was the result of an accident during a dalliance in her twenties with a guy who was just above the status of a one night stand. Though talkative, her thoughts were very clear and her dialog was crisp and thoughtful. She was clearly an intelligent and capable woman.

After all of this, I asked her "When you found out you were pregnant, why didn't you just get an abortion?" I was well aware by this point she was nonreligious and quite left-liberal in her worldview, so I was confident she would not be against the concept of abortion. If I had thought she was, I would have never asked the question.

As soon as I asked the question, she made an odd movement with her eyes, like a neuron in her brain misfired. She hesitated and sputtered out an incoherent, hesitant answer. Instantly gone was her clear cut, eloquent way of speaking. She had gone from a class act to sputtering idiot in the span of fewer than five seconds.

Finally she blathered some incoherent answer about how she "could technically afford a kid" (which was false) and how it "made sense" to have an abortion if she was some bum on the street with no money, but because she "had a job" it "didn't make sense" to do that, even though she "never wanted kids."

The sudden transformation in her was fascinating to watch. Since then I have spoken to several women like this. Women who never wanted kids, who got pregnant by accident, decided to have the kid anyway, and now live lives of hell as the single mothers they never wanted to be. If you watch them long enough, once their child finally grows up and leaves the house, these women go back to being happy again.

What's going on here?

Let's switch this around and use a male-centered example. You're relaxing with your girlfriend. She's cool. You really like her. She's pretty, fun, smart, honest, and loyal. You're both in a good mood and enjoying each other's company.

Suddenly, her phone jingles. She's got a text. It's over on the table and she asks you to hand it to her. You do, but as you do your eyes catch the text on the phone. It reads: "Hey sexy! How's it going?"

It's from a guy named Dave.

Immediately, your blood boils. You crush the phone in your hand like a tin can. You whirl upon her, death in your eyes, and start screaming, "Who the hell is Dave?!? Who is this guy?"

"What are you talking about?" she answers, genuinely amazed at your sudden change.

You hurl the phone at her like it's a missile. "I don't want any of these guys texting you!" you scream, "That's bullshit!"

Then you both proceed to have a huge argument that lasts an hour and ruins the entire evening. The anger and hurt spill over into the next day in the form of angry rants from the both of you to your own sets of friends, as well as some choice Facebook and Twitter status updates.

I'm exaggerating this situation for illustration of course, but you know exactly what I'm talking about.

Here's the interesting part. Your girlfriend has never lied to you nor given you any indication of being unfaithful. Yet for some reason, none of that mattered. You saw that text, and BAM! You suddenly wanted to kill someone. You're a smart, reasonably put-together guy, but none of that mattered at that moment.

Again, what's going on here?

Obsolete Biological Wiring

It both situations above, people became victims of the second of our two great enemies: Obsolete Biological Wiring, or OBW. If you thought Societal Programming was bad, and it is, get ready. In many ways OBW is even worse.

Our physiologies as human beings have changed very little over the past 50,000 years. While our lifestyle and culture has changed radically, we are still walking around in the same bodies and thinking with the same brains as the cavemen of thousands of years ago. This is one of the reasons people in the Western world are so damn fat. Our caveman bodies are designed to store fat whenever we have excess calories so we will survive the winter living in the cave when food is scarce. Our bodies haven't adjusted to the fact that people living in the Western world, even if very poor by Western standards, have access to more free or inexpensive high-calorie food than we could ever want or need. As Ray Kurzweil stated in his book *Transcend*, "Our Stone Age genes ensure that we will still jump at the chance to eat sugary foods whenever we can." So our stupid, outdated bodies get fat for no good reason.

For the same reasons, we start showing signs of aging beginning at age 25. Our outdated caveman bodies are biologically wired to die at around age 25 once we've created a few babies. Nature wanted us to reproduce, but it didn't want a bunch of old people hanging around eating all of the tribe's scarce food. That's why during adolescence, you're horny as can be, and starting at age 25 your body slowly starts to die, a process we call "aging."

Sadly, this obsolescence not only applies to our bodies, but our minds as well. 50,000 years ago, when you were a strapping young caveman, you lived in a tribe of perhaps 30 people. Like all the other young cavemen boys, you wanted to have sex. Badly. Nature designed you to crave sex in order to continue the propagation of the species. So far, so good.

The problem was that only about half of the tribe was female. So now we're down to 15 people. Worse, many of these women were too old or too young for you to get sexually turned on. So now we're down to perhaps five girls of desirable, child-bearing age. Even worse than that, some of those shagable girls weren't attracted to you, and were perhaps more attracted to the more Alpha men of the tribe, so that drops the number even further. In some tribes, some of the remaining women were controlled or protected by other males.

All this attrition left you with one, two, or zero women for you to have sex with.

Yikes! That's pretty horrible. Things were like that for men for many thousands of years. As a result, today your ridiculously outdated psychology is hard-wired to think that women are a scarce commodity, a commodity to be possessed and jealously horded. 50,000 years ago, your biology was absolutely right. If you wanted to have sex with a woman, that was the only way to mentally process it. Today in the 21st century, your biology couldn't be more wrong.

In the modern era, women actually outnumber men. On top of that, thanks to the sexual revolution of the 1960s and first-wave feminism of the 1970s, you don't need to marry any of these women if you want to have sex with them. Your logical left brain is well aware that you can put this book down right now and go down to your local mall and it will be chock-full of hundreds of pretty women, many of whom will happily have sex with you without you needing to promise them money, gifts, children, marriage, or anything else. There are likely more eligible women in a ten-mile radius from your home than you could ever hope to sleep with in an entire lifetime.

Every year there literally millions of new women who become legal sexual age (or whatever age you consider to be your minimum), so there is literally no end to this abundant flow of new women.

Women, and sex from women, have gone from being a scarce commodity to an over-abundant, excessive, ever-renewing resource. The problem is your outdated psychology doesn't know that, or more accurately, doesn't *feel* that. Your biological wiring, even if it might feel right, has become woefully wrong. It's now obsolete.

When you feel neediness, jealousy, territoriality, or possessiveness with a woman, rarely is it based in any reality or facts. More than likely it's just your OBW flaring up. It has nothing to do with reality or even valid emotions. It's just your stupid, out-of-date, caveman biology acting as if you're living in a cave with nothing but a loincloth and a pointy stick.

I'm using jealousy as just one example. OBW can cause all kinds of negative actions and emotions, up to and including actual violence.

Many modern-day military conflicts between nations are, in many ways, the direct result of the OBW of political leaders. In the 21st century, do we really need extra land for prosperity the same way we did back in the 15th century? No. Yet the wars over land continue anyway, as if nothing has changed. OBW is a serious problem, not just for you, but for the world.

The one bit of good news is that we men have less OBW than women. Women have all kinds of powerful and ridiculous OBW that compels them to get into serious relationships with men they shouldn't, have babies when they shouldn't, get married when they shouldn't, terminate relationships when they shouldn't, and all kinds of other destructive things. An Alpha can use women's OBW to his advantage if he understands it while simultaneously controlling his own. We'll discuss this in more detail in later chapters.

Regardless, as a man, OBW is still a powerful negative force in your life you need to be aware of, manage, and control. Several areas where OBW asserts control over you are:

1. Fear (of just about anything).
2. Sexual jealousy.
3. Racism.
4. The desire to cum inside women during sex when you know you shouldn't.
5. Tendencies to get into fights, either physical or verbal, with other men.
6. Feeling threatened, particularly physically threatened, when you aren't.
7. Reacting with anger in situations that don't warrant it.
8. Territoriality. Regarding women like your property.

Your body and brain have all kinds of "hard coded" wiring that made sense in the world of 50,000 years ago, a world filled with danger, death, starvation, and scarcity. You still have this wiring in the 21st century Western world of abundance and safety, and it will compel you to do all kinds of stupid things like get jealous if your girlfriend/wife talks to another guy, get women pregnant when you shouldn't, treat other men as if they're physical threats to your safety when they aren't, and all kinds of other destructive silliness.

I'm not taking about *all* biological wiring, but *obsolete* biological wiring. The biological wiring you have compelling you to have sex with that attractive woman is just fine. The obsolete biological wiring compelling you to cum inside that woman without wearing a condom is not fine, nor is the wiring compelling you to become enraged whenever she talks to one of her guy-friends once you start dating her.

Biological impulses caused by OBW are as powerful as they are useless. If you're not carefully aware of them, and most people aren't, they will cause you fear, anger, chaos, and extreme, needless financial expense.

Combining OBW with SP spells complete disaster, which is exactly how most people in The Prison live. OBW compels you to cum inside that 21 year-old woman, but when she gets pregnant, SP compels you to marry her because of it, even knowing the odds of the marriage lasting are minuscule, making a terrible situation even worse.

Territoriality

There are many forms of OBW you're going to have to manage as you start down the path of Alpha 2.0, but one of the greatest you'll experience is something called territoriality. Sexual jealousy is a subset of territoriality, just as in the above example of you getting angry when another guy texts your girlfriend.

The reason you feel jealous in a sexual, emotional, or romantic context is because you view the woman as your property or "territory." If another man "invades" your territory, powerful OBW will rise within you causing you to lash out at either your property (her) or the trespasser (him).

I'm not saying you think these things in a literal sense. I doubt very much you view your girlfriend, wife, or love interest as your property the way a slave owner from the 19th century would. Rather, this thought process is occurring emotionally, irrationally, and subconsciously. To your logical left brain, yes, that woman is her own person and no one owns her, certainly not you. To your irrational right brain, that woman belongs to you just as much as your laptop computer. If a man comes along and starts touching her in a sexual manner, even with her full consent, you're going to be just as angry and threatened as if a strange man broke into your house and sat on your couch while watching your TV and eating your Cheetos.

A philosophy I follow is a concept called Natural Law. I do not believe it literally, but I follow it as a personal code of conduct for maximum long-term happiness. Much has been written on Natural Law, and I strongly suggest you do your own research on the subject if you have further interest. For our purposes here, the most applicable concept of Natural Law is the concept that you own you. You own your body and mind, completely, 100%. No one else owns you besides you.

That's all well and good when we think of ourselves. The problem is Natural Law also applies to everyone else. You own 100% of you, so you can go have sex with anyone you like as long as it's consensual. However, your girlfriend owns 100% of herself too, so she can go talk to, flirt with, make out with, or even have sex with any other man she likes, whether you approve of this or not.

"Whoa, wait a minute," you say, "We're in an exclusive monogamous relationship. She promised me she wouldn't do that. If she does that anyway, she's violated the contract she made with me."

That's very true, but that's the logical objection, and one we'll deal with in later chapters. Right now we're talking about the irrational, OBW aspect of the problem. When a man gets angry at his girlfriend when some other guy texts her, or when she posts a picture on her Facebook with her and another guy, she hasn't violated any promise to anyone, but he's upset regardless. The same jealousy, or territoriality, a man feels in those situations is the exact same emotion he would feel she actually cheated on him. The only difference is in degree.

Like all OBW, territoriality did indeed serve a valid purpose in ancient history.

- Back when you were a caveman, sexable women were frighteningly scarce. In many cases, when one man took one of these women, that was one fewer woman for you. Today, there are thousands of women all over the place, perfectly available for you sexually, regardless of the amount of men or married women also present.
- Back when you were an agrarian farmer, the only way you could get cheap labor for your farm, and ensure your retirement, was to have children. Children were valuable commodities. They were property. As property, you had to ensure these children were your children and not your neighbor's children. Therefore you had to make damn sure your wife did not have sex with your neighbor, thereby creating more valuable commodities for him instead of you. Today, your children have zero obligations to pay for your retirement or work in your business unless they really want

to (governmental social programs notwithstanding). Moreover, today you can buy a paternity test kit at local pharmacy for $20 and find out in a flash if a baby is your child or not.

- In post-agrarian historical times, women really were treated by society like property. Women were bought and sold to men like livestock via marriage, dowries, slavery, and other SP systems. So if a man had sex with one of "your" women, he really was violating your personal property, at least in a cultural, and sometimes legal sense. Today of course, women are not property, nor should they be in any enlightened society that obeys Natural Law (or at least tries to).

All the logical, societal, real reasons for you to feel sexually jealous are now gone! When you feel territorial regarding the woman (or women!) in your life, it's simply some remnant OBW that was valid when you were Grog the caveman. Because happiness is our highest objective, it's critical to understand that sexual jealousy in today's modern era has no purpose and no meaning. We'll address exactly how to deal with sexual jealousy in Chapter 12.

I'm talking about *sexual* jealousy here. It's perfectly normal to feel jealous if, for example, a woman ends a relationship with you and falls in love with someone else. That's emotional jealousy, not sexual jealousy, and emotional jealousy, while negative, is indeed based in real-world human limitations, since most people don't have the ability to romantically love more than one person at a time (though there are those that do; people who practice true polyamory). Jealousy is also acceptable, perhaps even desirable, when your next door neighbor drives up in that new sports car you've always wanted. You get jealous of his car, and that spurs you on to make more money so you too can drive a cool car like that too. This assumes your desire for that car is real and internal, and not based in SP or a desire to make others like you more.

There are those who believe that sexual jealousy is actually not from OBW at all, but purely from SP. They contend that ancient man wasn't monogamous at all, and everyone happily had sex with everyone else without any problems until the advent of agriculture. Therefore, they contend, sexual jealousy is purely a false creation of SP, and has nothing to do with biology at all.

This historical nature vs. nurture debate regarding sexual jealousy has been hotly debated by researchers since the creation of evolutionary psychology back in 1975. Because there is no consensus on this, we really don't know for sure.

I'm not a historian, anthropologist, or evolutionary psychologist. I have no interest in getting into that particular debate. My layman's view based on my own research and experience is that while SP probably is a factor in regards to sexual jealousy, the majority of it is indeed caused by OBW, even if you only factor in the last 10,000 years when monogamy was practiced or enforced, at least to some degree, in human society.

OBW or SP, the key point is, as I described above, territoriality is no longer needed at all. It has no purpose in your 21st century life, unless you enjoy being jealous or angry.

Is All Biology Bad?

You may get the feeling from reading this that I am anti-biology. Wrong! Much of your biological wiring is good, and should be embraced to the fullest. You have strong biological urges to do things like survive, have sex with beautiful women, and protect your children. These are all wonderful urges, and there is nothing obsolete about them. As long as you protect yourself from their possible downsides (like STDs) you should pursue them. They will make you happy.

There is good biology and obsolete biology, and you need to be aware of the difference. Embrace and manage the good biology and ward off and remove OBW as best you can. Let's talk about how.

How to Deal With OBW

Just like with SP, your awareness and management of OBW is critical if you want to live a life of freedom and long-term, consistent happiness. Also like SP, you will never completely rid yourself of OBW completely. That's impossible. However with a little effort, practice, and awareness, you can dramatically reduce OBW's power over your behaviors.

Method 1: Notice It and Identify It When It Happens

Any time I'm in the grocery store and the aroma of fresh bread hits my nose, I have a very powerful, biological urge to immediately steer my shopping cart in the direction of the scent and shove two or three jalapeño and cheese bagels down my gullet. Instead of acting on autopilot and doing it, and instead of acting on willpower alone while saying "I must not eat bagels, I must not eat bagels," instead, I've trained my brain to say, "Oh, there's Grog the caveman again. He's so cute. Now shut up Grog."

I immediately identify that craving as OBW. Because I do this, the craving instantly loses much of its power. Not all of it, but some. It's exactly the same when I'm out with a woman I care about, and I see another guy starting to flirt with her. Deep down inside, sometimes I have this teeny tiny urge to grab a blunt object, smash the guy over the head, pick up my gal, drive her home, and lock her in a closet. Instead of getting upset or jealous or losing my cool, I immediately know it's just Grog again, with more of his silly, stupid, useless OBW. So I tell him to shut up, and carry on with my happiness.

You must establish the same habit. Every time you feel sexually jealous, or hungry for some pizza, or scared that someone is threatening you (when they aren't), or any similar OBW situation, you need to train yourself to identify those urges as OBW, and therefore a false reaction to a false situation.

Method 2: Visualization - Defeat Grog

Identifying the OBW for what it truly is may not be enough. When it's not, you need to come to a complete stop, pause, and take at least three deep breaths. Ten breaths is better. As you're breathing, visualize Grog in your mind. He's a big, dumb, stupid caveman who's feeling the jealousy, hunger, fear, or anger that you're currently feeling. Look at him and notice how damn stupid and pathetic he looks reacting that way, clutching his stupid little spear and making ape-like grunts. Laugh at him, even out loud. Pity him. Feel sorry for him. Shake your head at him as you would a small child doing something silly.

Then tell him to shut up. If that's not good enough, picture a giant hand, your hand, slapping him so that he flies far, far away, back into the cave he came from. Then visualize yourself walking into the frame. See yourself as cool, relaxed, and confident. Notice you're wearing the coolest outfit you've ever seen yourself wear. Watch that smile on your face as you smirk at how silly Grog is and how evolved you are.

When you get that picture of your confident, relaxed self in perfect clarity, snap out of it and return back to normal. You will find that some of your negative OBW feelings have vanished.

This technique takes practice, so don't expect it to do wonders the first time you try it. As with everything else, the more you do it the easier it gets and the more effective it becomes.

You don't need Grog. You're better than him.

Method 3: Have a Mission

OBW will have a far less effect on you if you have a strong Mission in life that excites you and gets you out of bed in the morning. Your mission is a large part of being an Alpha 2.0, and we'll be discussing it in detail in later chapters, starting with Chapter 9. The point here is having a strong mission in life is a powerful antidote to much of your OBW.

Method 4: Use NLP

If none of the above methods seem to be helping you, you may have to spend some time getting much deeper into your brain. This means learning some basic NLP, or neuro linguistic programming. This is a system by which you link pain to your destructive OBW urges instead of the (false) pleasure your brain now associates with it.

NLP is an entirely different topic and I am no expert in this area. If you wish to pursue this further, you should read the book *Unlimited Power* by Tony Robbins, or any NLP book written by Richard Bandler, one of the founders of NLP.

Chapter 5 -

The Six Societal Values

The conception of one human family, one catholic religion, one universal culture, and one worldwide state, has haunted men's thoughts ever since it's approximate realization by Rome.

Bertrand Russell

Christmas, 2010.

I sat where I always sit when I attend family reunions, at the head of the table. My dad sat at the opposite head as always. Along the sides of the long dining room table were all of my grown brothers and sisters, their spouses and significant others, and many of their children.

My family is a boisterous, talkative, emotional, Italian family. As always, there was discussion and laughing. Soon, the folks meandered to the topic of marriage and relationships, as so often happens with families. During this conversation, one of my sisters was debating with one of my brothers.

"Well, I'm the only one who's made marriage work in this family," she declared.

My brother, my fifth sibling who did not grow up with the rest of us, snorted and gave her a scowl but didn't respond. At the time, he was divorced and unmarried like me. My two other brothers had never been married nor had children despite being well into their thirties. Only my two sisters were currently married, one of them only recently so. The sister who had spoken had been married for almost 20 years, having been married at age 17.

Her statement was true, but only if you use SP definitions for words like "work." In the eyes of society, she alone of all my siblings had "made it work." She married at a very young age, had four children, and almost 20 years later was still married to the same man.

Just one slight problem: my sister was the most consistently unhappy person of all of us. Being married and a mom to four kids had taken its toll on her happiness. Stress, anger, and crying were a regular, almost daily feature of her life. This was a stark contrast to her four unmarried brothers, at least three of which were almost always happy, smiling, and jovial.

Measured against societal standards, my sister beat all of us. Measured against a happy life, my sister had failed, utterly so.

Did she view herself as a failure? Quite the opposite. She was proud of her married status, to the point of bragging rights. Most people in The Prison would probably agree with her. The fact she was consistently unhappy was irrelevant. The external, societal standard had become more important to her than her own happiness.

That's why most people are unhappy.

The Six Societal Values

We've established that primary goal of life is long-term happiness. We've also established the two primary enemies to this goal: SP and OBW. The primary method these two enemies utilize in creating unhappiness in people is that they insidiously insert other goals in front of, and on top of, the goal of long-term happiness. A person living in The Prison, fully infected with SP and OBW, views happiness as nice, but not the most important thing. Rather, happiness becomes number four or five on the list of life priorities. Moreover, the belief that happiness is "selfish" becomes prevalent, making personal happiness even more distant and difficult to obtain.

What exactly, then, do people in The Prison value over happiness? There are six specific items. I call these Six Societal Values, or 6SV. These six things are considered so important to people in The Prison that they will actually forgo their own happiness and the happiness of all those around them in order to possess them.

Here they are, listed in no particular order:

1. Conformity
2. Security (perceived or real)
3. Control Over Others
4. Emotional Validation (or "Drama")
5. Social Validation
6. Not Being Alone

All 6SV pull you towards SP and OBW and away from long-term happiness. More importantly for us, long-term happiness is gained when one consciously resists the 6SV. The lower priority you put on the 6SV, the easier it is to live a life of freedom, fulfillment, and long-term happiness. Therefore it is your goal to beware of and stand firm against the mighty pull of the 6SV.

Let's tackle each one.

1. Conformity

Human beings are highly communal, social creatures. We aren't hermits living far from each other in isolated castles or huts. We tend to clump together in groups. These can be small groups like a family or a neighborhood, or titanic mobs like New York City or Tokyo.

Because of this communal tendency, we have a strong need to look and act like other people in the groups of which we are a part. The more we conform to society at large, the more comfortable or safe we tend to feel.

The need for conformity is so strong that we will actually avoid doing things that make us very happy if they are outside societal norms. For most of human history, gays and lesbians were forced by their need of conformity to hide their sexual natures. Even today, with the Western world's strong acceptance of these lifestyles, many gay and lesbian people still choose to remain "in the closet" due to a strong desire for conformity. Being gay is just one of a hundred different examples. Being repressed like this causes massive unhappiness, stress, and stress-induced medical problems, yet many people continue to do this.

Sometimes in my life I do things outside of societal norms that generate a lot of odd looks or strange questions from other people in The Prison. There are times when I walk down the street while being affectionate with a woman 22 years my junior. There are other times when someone asks me if I have a wife or girlfriend, and when I respond that I have several girlfriends, I get some very uncomfortable sputters as a response. Sometimes these Prison inmates will actually feel sorry for me because I'm not pursing conformity like they are. The irony is that I'm almost always happier in life than these conformers.

Like all the 6SV, conformity does not make you happy. It simply satisfies some of the communal OBW you have within you. Very often, your happiness will come from doing things that do not conform with societal norms at all. Dating younger women and open relationships are just two examples; there are many others. I know people who live on a boat instead of in a house. Not a houseboat, but an actual boat. I also know some folks who live in an honest to goodness commune out in the middle of nowhere with no running water and very little electricity. I also know of a couple who are 32 years apart, and the man is the younger of the two.

These people are not conforming, but I can tell you for a fact they're quite happy. Most of them are more consistently happy than the typical person who conforms. As an Alpha 2.0, you're definitely going to be doing a few things that don't conform to the standard societal model.

I'm not saying you should go outside social norms just because the norms are there. Many teenagers will dress in outlandish ways simply because they're angry or because they want a negative reaction from people, namely their parents and other superiors. We've also had celebrities like Marilyn Manson, Dennis Rodman, and Lady Gaga who purposely behave in outlandish ways for branding reasons or because they want fame or attention. I'm not talking about any of that. Rather, if there is something you know will make you happy but is well outside of established norms, you need to go for it. The only three parameters you should follow are:

- It should be legal where you live.
- It should not hurt anyone.
- It should not involve lying to anyone.

Barring those, pursuing something you know will make you happy will indeed make you happy, at least in the long term, even if it's against societal norms.

2. Security (Perceived or Real)

Human beings, men in general but women in particular, have an overwhelming desire for security. I'm not talking about physical security, since in the Western world we really don't need to worry about that. I'm talking more about financial and emotional security. The desire for this often compels people to create unhappy situations in their lives. Worse, people seek security even if they are aware on some level the security is false. Bad on top of bad.

Women especially have powerful OBW and SP that causes them to seek financial security from a man. Just ask your serious girlfriend or fiancé if she would like to sign a prenuptial agreement before you marry her, and watch the reaction. Ask any woman over the age of about 26 if she would consider marrying a nice, kind, loyal, responsible, good guy who makes less money than she does, and again, watch the reaction. Likely in both cases, her desire for security will quickly overwhelm her logic, preferences, and sense of personal responsibility.

Countries all over the Western world are experiencing massive financial upheavals due to men and women's desire for financial security from their respective governments. Cash-strapped governments are unable to fulfill promises they (stupidly) made to their citizens to provide financial security, and now there are riots, protests, and political unrest all over the world, including in the once cash-rich United States. Such is the power of the desire for security, perhaps the most anger-inducing value of the 6SV.

As stated above, this desire for security stays strong even if the source of said security is clearly false. Women will marry men even if they clearly know they will likely get divorced down the road. Men will cling to shaky government retirement programs or corporate pensions even if they clearly know the very high odds of those programs being long gone by the time they reach old age when they'll need them the most. Since the desire for security is born of OBW and SP and is thus irrational, it matters not if the security desired is or real or false. This is yet another reason why governments continue to get away with promising false security to their citizens, why people continue to rope members of the opposite sex into bad relationships or marriages, and why shifty employers are able to con people into working for them.

Is security so bad? Not at all. Some level of security is critical to your long-term happiness. You should have not only a savings account for a rainy day, but also a retirement fund you regularly contribute to. That's security, and it's good.

There are two kinds of security: internal and external. Internal security is good, external security is not. Internal security is a set of systems you create and maintain yourself. Examples would range from an alarm system in your house; to an insurance policy you pay for; to a very conservative retirement portfolio you contribute to regularly. Internal security is crucial for long-term happiness.

External security is any type of security promised by someone else outside of you. Examples include a woman you marry who promises to never divorce you, a financially indebted government promising to take care of you in your old age, a corporate employer promising to provide fantastic returns if you invest solely in their stock, and a deal you do with a business partner on a handshake rather than from a written contract. External security is extraordinarily harmful to you, your emotional frame, and your entire outlook on life. It's false security.

Relying on external forces for security often results in shattered lives, lost time, or dashed hopes. Perhaps not immediately, but eventually.

Even worse, relying on external security sources trains your mind to the false premise that you are not in control of your life. You will start to view your life as something controlled by external forces rather than yourself. This is a direct assault on your freedom, one of the five required Alpha Male 2.0 traits.

3. Control over Others

Human beings have a strong need to get into other people's business and tell other people what to do. Governments, schools, corporations, religions, families, and both leftist and conservative and schools of thought embrace the system of getting into other people's lives and telling them what to do and not do.

This desire leads to the creation of things called *rules*. Often these rules are stated plainly, like the Ten Commandments or the employee manual at your job. More often these rules are implied rather than clearly stated. You might have noticed that as soon as you enter into a relationship with a new woman, she immediately starts to place rules on your behavior. You also do the same to her. These can range from "answer the phone whenever I call" to "stop going out at night with your buddies" to a thousand other things.

Just like with security, there are times when rules are appropriate, but these are the exceptions to the rule (pun intended). If you raise small children, of course these children need rules like "don't play in the street," just like a country needs some general rules about not killing other people or stealing other people's possessions.

However, the 6SV desire of control over others doesn't stop there. It keeps going, and going, and going. The process of enforcing all these rules makes people very unhappy. One day I was waiting out in the hallway of an office building, sitting on one of the chairs. My phone rang; I answered it, and started talking. As I always do, I did my best to keep my voice low so as to not disturb anyone in the offices.

After about two minutes, a woman, a professional artist I did not know, exited her office from far down the hallway, took a few steps towards me and made some gestures, indicating that she wanted me to talk softer. This was difficult, since I was talking quite soft already, but I nodded at her and did my best.

Several months later, I was coincidently in the exact same hallway waiting for a different reason, sitting in a similar location. This time I was with someone else, and we were talking about an upcoming meeting. Both of us were speaking in a normal tone of voice. Soon a woman exited her office and confronted us. She calmly but angrily suggested to us that we not talk at all, and that we really should go down to the first floor of the building and do our waiting there. I made a smartass crack about the fact that there were, for some odd reason, chairs in the hallway, presumably there for the purpose of people waiting.

After a few seconds it dawned on me that this was the exact same woman who had scolded me several months earlier. Amazing. This woman had a rule in her life: "No one can make any sounds of any kind whatsoever anywhere near my office." As such, she regularly scolded people in the hallway outside her office, almost on a daily basis.

Here's the question: Do you think she was a generally happy person?

What do you think?

That leads to the key point about rules, which is this: *The more rules you are forced to obey and the more rules you have for others, the less happy you will be.*

It's that simple. In all areas of life including business, career, family, politics, sexual relationships, and romantic relationships, you want a minimum number of rules you need to follow, as well as a minimum number of rules you place on others. Why? Because people won't always follow your rules, and you won't always follow the rules of others. We're humans, not robots. What happens when rules aren't followed? Conflict. This means rules always lead to angst, drama, conflict, and unhappiness. The more rules you have for others, and the more rules you must follow, the more difficult it is to live a life of freedom or consistent happiness.

I learned relatively early in life to always avoid getting into situations where I was required to follow a lot of rules. I also learned a little later in life to avoid situations where I had to place rules on others. This was one of the primary reasons I made the voluntary shift from owning a company of employees to a company of just one employee: me. It's also why I made the shift from traditional monogamous relationships, in which many rules are inherent in the system, to open/poly relationships with very little rules on either side. When I made these changes, my happiness skyrocketed, my freedom increased by huge leaps, and my life became better in just about every way.

Realize that SP (and a little OBW) wants you to control others. Men who are Alpha Male 1.0 are particularly susceptible to the desire to control. One of the key traits of the Alpha 1.0 is his strong desire to control "his" woman. Alpha 1.0s love to "lay down the law." The typical Alpha 1.0 has all kinds of rules and regulations for his spouse or girlfriend that are a mile long. If she breaks those rules, which she eventually will, there's hell to pay. This is almost always a catalyst for high-drama relationships. This negative dynamic also extends out into his interpersonal relationships with his friends, family, children and co-workers.

This is all manifests into something called guy-drama. Per the glossary at my dating and relationships blog for men[1], the definition for guy-drama is:

Guy-Drama: A particular form of drama directed from a man to a woman. Unlike drama, which is feminine and takes many forms, guy-drama takes the form of a lecture issued in order to correct behavior. "Setting her straight," "straightening her out," "putting your foot down," "laying down the law," commands to "respect" him, or issuing "rules" are all forms of guy-drama.

Guy-drama is extremely ineffective at managing a relationship and only creates more drama, or at best simply delays (instead of preventing) future drama. You can scream at her to "never be late again!" and you may even get her to agree to this new rule. The problem is, not only is she a human being, she's also a girl. At some point soon, she'll be late again, and you'll feel angry, threatened, and disrespected. Enter more drama!

Conversely, the Alpha 2.0 consciously avoids rules, both agreeing to obey them and setting them for others. He can do whatever he likes, and the people in his life can do more or less whatever they like as long as they don't directly infringe upon his happiness (keeping in mind that he ensures there are few things that make him unhappy, as we discussed in Chapter 2). This virtually eliminates guy-drama and much female drama.

Hey, speaking of drama, that brings us to…

4. Emotional Validation (or "Drama")

This is probably the granddaddy of the Six Societal Values. Emotional validation, or its casual term, "drama," is a source for much, if not most, of people's chronic, day-to-day unhappiness. Drama is the greatest threat of all the 6SV and the biggest source of problems for you as an Alpha 2.0.

---

[1] http://www.blackdragonblog.com/glossary

I define relationship drama as the following:

Drama: Any harsh negative actions directed from a woman to a man where the man is the target of said negativity. Screaming, nagging, complaining, arguing, demands, crying, threats, ultimatums, the "silent treatment," refusing sex because of non-medical reasons, all of these things are drama, and there are many others. Drama is not "anything negative." Specifically, it must be harsh (sweetly lying would not be considered drama) and focused at the man (angrily complaining about her boss at work would not be considered drama).

Drama sucks. You already know this. Everyone says they hate it and want nothing to do with it yet just about everyone experiences it regularly.

Why is this? Because drama is one of the Six Societal Values, placed at great priority by people in The Prison. The majority of women and a sizable percentage of modern-day men actually desire regular drama in their lives. They have powerful needs, born from both SP and OBW, to validate their negative emotions by dumping those emotions upon other people, even if those other people don't deserve it or have nothing to do with the cause. The *target* of the drama is irrelevant, only the *expression* of drama is important.

The need for emotional validation is so powerful, people will throw drama around even when they know for a fact that very bad things will happen to them if they do it. I've always called this Yell at a Cop theory.

Yell at a Cop Theory

Just like everyone else who drives, I've been pulled over by the police several times in my day. Many times I don't get a ticket, instead getting off with a warning. This is because whenever I get pulled over by a cop, for the next few minutes I am the nicest, sweetest, most compliant beta male in the universe. I do this because I don't want a speeding ticket. Tickets are expensive, are a huge hassle, and raise your car insurance premiums. Being nice to the cop for a few minutes, even if I'm furious he pulled me over, even if I think he's completely in the wrong, is well worth the significant financial benefit of not getting a speeding ticket.

I think just about everyone with an I.Q. over 80 knows that if you're nice to the cop, you might get off without a ticket, but if you get upset at the cop, you're virtually guaranteed to get one.

Why is it then, that so many people scream and bitch at police officers when they get pulled over? It's because of their 6SV need for emotional validation. Their desire for emotional validation is so overwhelming that they want to yell at that cop even if they know the price for yelling for two minutes will cost them literally hundreds of dollars and possibly hours of wasted time. They're so pissed off for being pulled over, they can't control themselves. So they yell at the cop, who just rolls his eyes and hands them a $450 ticket.

This is but one example. You can extend this to a the woman yelling at her abusive husband knowing she's going to get punched if she yells at him (and yells at him anyway) to the boyfriend who knows his girlfriend is going to dump him if he yells at her (and yells at her anyway) to the investor knowing he'll lose a profitable real estate deal if he gets angry with the buyer's attorney on some minor point (and yells at him anyway), to thousands of other circumstances you can think of.

One of the primary reasons women desire to cohabitate with a husband (or boyfriend, or female roommates) is simply to have a regular "sounding board" available to them when they need one. They need someone convenient to yell at when they have a bad day at work or with the kids, and poor schmuck husband makes a very convenient target. This also helps explain why very few women live alone. Most unmarried women that aren't living with their parents will typically have roommates. This way they can still maintain convenient targets upon which to unload their negative emotions. Even better, they may even get their emotions further validated when one of them says, "Wow. You're right. She was being a bitch to you."

This is best summed up by the following exchange between Gloria and Jay, played by Sofia Vergara and Ed O'Neil, on the TV show *Modern Family:*

Gloria: I'm not mad at you because you said I snore. I'm mad at you because you didn't say anything!

Jay: Because I didn't want to get yelled at.

Gloria: Well too bad! When you're married to me, you're going to get yelled at many times! You're tough enough to take it! That's what I love about our marriage. We can say whatever we want, but the next day we're still there.

Those last three lines of dialog sum up almost everything about Prison inmates' need for emotional validation and drama, as well as traditional marriage.

Amazingly, people seeking drama will actually start getting uncomfortable if they are in situations or relationships where they don't have it. They'll be in a very happy job, situation, or relationship, and everything will be great. Over time, they will start to get uncomfortable because they haven't had to bitch, complain, or yell at anyone. Then they will actually create situations they know will result in drama. Then, while angrily arguing with their lover, spouse, family member, or co-worker, they can feel "normal" and "human" again. They won't feel happy, but happiness is not their goal. Drama is.

Therein lies the problem: one cannot feel drama and happiness at the same time, regardless of the excuses people try to make to the contrary. Therefore, if your goal is a happy life, you need to avoid drama. Just as importantly, you must avoid situations conducive for drama. We'll discuss this in great detail in later chapters.

5. Social Validation

In a way, social validation is the opposite of the desire for conformity. Conformity compels us to behave like others so we can avoid disapproval. Social validation induces us to do things so we receive accolades from others.

We have a powerful need to receive recognition and approval from our family, parents, friends, peers, and even a wider audience of strangers. We want people to see what we're doing and say "well done!" or "good job!" Every time someone tells you they like what you're doing, you get a little endorphin rush.

There's nothing wrong with that. We like endorphins because endorphins make us happy. If you're doing something you love, and someone gives you a pat on the back for it, that's fantastic. You'll be further motivated to do a good job in the areas you love.

Social validation becomes a problem when we start doing things we don't like in order to receive approval from others. I have many buddies who went into professional fields they hated because they wanted to please their fathers. I have seen women marry men they really didn't like in order to receive approval from their church. I have seen people stay in careers they despise because of all the social validation they get from their spouses. Most obvious of all, we're all well aware of the stupid and destructive things teenagers do because of peer pressure.

These people received accolades and approval from their social circles, but then went on to live lives of resentment, boredom, dysfunction, and quiet anger. Doing things you don't like to get approval from others must be something you never, ever do. If you desire approval and accolades, that's fine, but seek it only in the context of doing what you love and truly believe in.

Of course the best path is to simply not seek accolades at all, and instead receive your validation internally from your own happiness, desires, fulfillment, and accomplishments. I do what I do because I love what I do. I would continue to do it and love it even if no one paid any attention to what I was doing (assuming my monetary results were the same).

6. Not Being Alone

This one is probably the saddest and most depressing of the 6SV. A strong majority of human begins simply do not have the ability to be alone for long stretches. As with security and drama, this mostly applies to women, but it applies to a fair number of men as well.

There are several degrees and variations to this. Many people can't stand the thought of going home to a place with no one there. Others are more extreme and can't stand not being in a "relationship" with someone at all times. Others are even more extreme, and have severe trouble not talking to someone in person for more than a few hours. I'm sure you've met all these types. These people are always with other people, always in a relationship with someone, always interacting with people, at all waking hours, and seven days a week. They can't be alone. They don't know how.

The problem is these people desire this nonstop interaction even if the interaction is negative. They'd rather be in bad relationships than no relationship at all. They'd rather be having a negative conversation than not speaking. Needless to say, drama, chaos and unhappiness are common occurrences in these peoples' lives.

A lot of this is personality driven. Extroverts will usually be more likely to be in a relationship or living with other people, introverts less so. I'm an introvert myself, and I enjoy being alone immensely. However I also enjoy being with other people immensely, especially my children, men of high intellect, and the women I date.

The happiest people on the planet are those who are balanced in this area. They are extroverts who know how to be alone and are perfectly fine with it, and introverts who are very socially calibrated and can enjoy being with people. Unhappiness lies with the hyper, high-drama extroverts who can't be alone just as much as with the reclusive, loner introverts who are always hiding away in their bedrooms on their computers.

As a free, happy, Alpha 2.0, you must have the ability to be alone. This means you are perfectly and honestly fulfilled even if you're not in a serious relationship, and are able to do this without being a reclusive loner who "hates people."

6SV vs. Happiness

The 6SV is the reason why most people in The Prison live lives of moderate unhappiness and numerous restrictions, most of which are completely self-imposed. Instead of placing long-term happiness as their highest priority, they place some or all of the Six Societal Values as higher priorities. Sure, happiness is one of the priorities, but it's not at the top. It might be number three, four, or five on the list, with several of the 6SV superseding it.

There are many common examples of this.

- The person who longs to start his own business but instead stays at his boring, soul-killing corporate job is placing security over happiness.
- The person who goes back to a high-drama, problematic lover is choosing emotional validation over happiness.
- The business owner who could make more money and work fewer hours with fewer employees but chooses to keep those employees anyway is choosing social validation and control over others above happiness.
- The person who admits being married will make them less happy but who gets married anyway is placing conformity, perceived security, and not being alone above happiness.
- The person who reluctantly acquiesces to demands from his lover is choosing perceived security and drama over happiness.

Much unhappiness in The Prison is a result of people choosing to place one or more of the 6SV above their own long-term happiness. Backed by the twin engines of OBW and SP, the 6SV are powerful forces for negativity.

This means the only real way to get to long-term happiness is *to place your personal long-term happiness above the Six Societal Values.*

You can probably already see the problem in doing this. By placing happiness as your highest priority, doing the things necessary to achieve it, and thereby achieving it, you're going to look a little strange to other people in The Prison. Friends and family members aren't going to fully understand what you're doing, or why. Some people may even attack you on your choices.

It won't matter. You'll be happier than all of those people, by far.

Sometimes I will attend large family reunions, or large personal gatherings of business colleagues, or similar. Just about every man at these events show up with a wife or girlfriend. Every man, except me.

Sometimes I show up completely alone, in which case I get a barrage of "Why don't you find a nice girl?" questions. Other times, I show up with a woman who is extremely attractive. So attractive, she looks a little out of place. Sometimes this woman is much younger than me. People are very polite and nice, but I get a lot of odd glances and see whispered conversations. Other times, I get assaulted with "That's great! So when are you marrying this gal?" This is followed by lectures about how important it is (to them) that I settle down and get married as soon as possible.

The interesting part is I am usually one of the happiest adults in the room. I'm not exaggerating. I'm sitting there with a big fat smile on my face, enjoying my life, even if I'm there without a woman. Most other people are complaining about their jobs, finances, or spouses. When not doing that, they're screaming at, correcting, or arguing with their small children. All the while, they're lecturing me about how I should settle down and get married to a "good woman" so I can "live the good life" like they are.

It's amazing that these folks don't see the irony staring them in the face. I marvel at people less happy than me telling me to do what they've done!

Because I lack the Six Societal Values, I look odd to them, but I'm happier. They have the 6SV in spades, but they aren't happy, at least not as a continuous condition.

I'm not saying everyone who follows the 6SV is miserable all the time. Not at all. People who follow the 6SV can be happy and sometimes are, but the happiness is only temporary. Examples would be newlyweds; those people still in the bliss of the honeymoon phase of their new marriages or relationships, or perhaps guys who recently got a new job or closed a new business deal. Nothing wrong with being happy about those things, but the happiness-high from those events is a temporary condition. As we discussed back in Chapter 2, occasional happiness is not the goal. Long-term, consistent happiness is.

Weeding Out the 6SV

You must evaluate the list of Six Societal Values and ask yourself "If I could be truly happy, continuously, for the rest of my life, could I release the need I have for these six things? Or at least reduce the need greatly?" If the answer is no, then be like everyone else, embrace the

6SV, and tolerate a life full of conflict, mediocrity, boredom, and regret. Removing the 6SV from your life is the price for your long-term happiness. *You cannot have the 6SV and be long-term happy at the same time. It isn't possible.*

You *can* have little bits of those six things along the way. For example,

1. You can have plenty of conformity when you walk down a busy city street, since you look pretty much like everyone else. However, you don't go out of your way to do this.
2. You occasionally get social validation from others when you make a big business accomplishment, and that's nice. However, that's not why you do what you do.
3. You can spend time with other people all you want. You can work with people, spend time with family, and date many women. However, if you don't have a serious girlfriend or wife, or live alone for a few years, that doesn't bother you at all.
4. You can work to create your own security. However, you ensure it is all internal security, not external.

So even the Alpha Male 2.0 can get little chunks of the 6SV occasionally, but they are not a priority in his life, nor are they something significant or ever-present like to those in The Prison.

Is your long-term, consistent happiness worth giving up the 6SV? For me, that decision was a no-brainer. Of the Six Societal Values, I despise four of them (conformity, control over others, drama, and not being alone). To me, conformity for its own sake is a form of mental weakness. Control over others is too much work and I have better things to do. Drama I hate with a passion and I want nothing to do with it. Being alone does not frighten me; often it's preferable and enjoyable.

That leaves security and social validation. As stated above, security is fantastic as long as its internal security. I would far rather depend on security I create for myself rather than some other person or organization who may not do what I want, or may not be around several years down the road. I have worked very hard over the years to improve my financial security (by earning money and saving it) and my emotional and sexual security (by mastering the art of meeting, sleeping with, and having long relationships with multiple women whenever I chose). I purposely avoid all forms of external security whenever I can.

Social validation is nice, but I get more than enough of that from my family and career pursuits, and I never plan on completely retiring from the world of work; I love my work.

For you, dumping the 6SV may be easy or very difficult. Regardless, now you know what you're "giving up" by embracing a lifestyle outside The Prison: The 6SV system that was created for the good of society, not you.

What I've just described is the core of everything else we're going to talk about in this book. I'm warning you now, if you choose any of the Six Social Values over your own long-term personal happiness, many of the concepts and techniques in this book will not resonate with you. The single greatest thing you can do for your life is to choose happiness first, and get little bits and pieces of the Six Social Values if you need to, when you can.

I can tell you for a fact, happiness is far better than anything the 6SV can offer.

Chapter 6 –

A Masculine Man in a Feminine World

Were George III to return to life, he would roar with laughter at what a flock of sheep the descendants of the American rebels have become.

Pat Buchanan

September, 1994.

A young guy in my early twenties, I sat on the couch of the much older woman I was sleeping with at the time, flipping through the channels on her TV while she was talking on the phone in her kitchen. Finally I stopped on a show that I had heard much about but hadn't seen.

"Silk Stalkings?" I had asked my buddy a few days earlier.

"Oh yeah," he said, "It's cool. You should check it out."

"Dude," I said, "It's called 'Silk Stalkings.' Why the hell would I want to watch a show called 'Silk Stalkings?'"

"Yeah, yeah," he said, "I know. But the show is still cool. It's about cops. And there are hot chicks too."

I was skeptical. Yet here it was a few days later, right on my friend with benefits' TV set. So okay. I had nothing else better to do, so I watched.

The scene depicted a supposedly hard-boiled cop with his female partner in the police station talking to their captain. Immediately I realized something was wrong. All the walls and furniture in the police station were bright pastel colors; bright oranges, reds, pinks, purples, and yellows.

Um, I had been to a few police stations to pay speeding tickets in my day and I didn't ever remember seeing pastel walls or furniture. Hm.

The next thing that struck me was the pastel colors were also all over the characters, including the male characters. The supposedly hard boiled male cop had a bright pink shirt with a big purple pastel tie. So did the supposedly cranky, crusty police captain. The entire thing was just...off. It looked like I was watching a cartoon.

Against my better judgment, I continued to watch. This pastel thing extended to all the other scenes. Just about all walls in all locations were pastel. Just about all clothing on all characters, including and especially the male ones, were pastel in colors. Even the cars looked pastel and...girly. Moreover, it was a show about cops called "Silk Stalkings."

It was sending a confusing message to my brain. This was supposedly a badass show about tough cops and murders and stuff like that, yet it looked like I was watching some Martha Stewart shit.

Little did I know I was witnessing the beginning of a titanic shift in tone in American pop culture. One moving from tough guys and masculine badassery to nice pretty colors, badass female heroes, and wimpy male characters. Nowadays, this colorful weirdness is normal fare on television. Go watch an episode of CSI (any of them) and look at the police station they all work in. Then go to YouTube and watch a scene from 1980s *Hill Street Blues* and take a look at that police station. See a difference?

Pop Culture's Progression Away from Male Strength
Part One: Television

I was born in the 70s but grew up in the 80s. When you watched TV back then, you were bombarded with mounds of masculine, tough, badass, Alpha Male heroes. Men like Starbuck, Captain Kirk, and Buck Rodgers kicked ass in space. Men like Crockett and Tubs, the A-Team, Hardcastle and McCormick, and Bo and Luke Duke kicked ass here on Earth. Hordes of player-guys like Jack Tripper, Dan Fielding, Arnie Becker and Sam Malone had sex with a new woman every week, and there was nothing strange, insulting, or misogynistic about it. The recurrent theme of "lone man above the law" was epitomized by guys like *Stingray, Spencer for Hire, MacGyver, The Equalizer, Airwolf, Wiseguy, Knight Rider, Street Hawk, Magnum P.I., The Fall Guy, Remington Steele,* and, do I even need to go on?

At the dawn of the 90s, this started to change radically. The tough, masculine, good-looking, suave men of the 70s and 80s were replaced by stupid, pussy, often overweight beta males who cowered in front of strong, attractive, confident wives. These were the men portrayed in shows like *Wife and Kids, Everyone Loves Raymond, King of Queens, According To Jim, Home Improvement* and *Mad About You*. Some shows featured whiney intellectual betas like *Seinfeld* and *Frasier*, constantly confounded by tougher females. Even the cartoons weren't immune. Strong, masculine cartoon heroes like He-Man, Optimus Prime and G.I. Joe were replaced by stupid, fat morons like Homer Simpson and Peter Griffin.

Does that mean that in the 90s there were no tough characters on TV? Of course not. There were plenty tough characters; female ones. TV was invaded by badass babes like *Buffy The Vampire Slayer, Xena Warrior Princess,* Captain Janeway on *Star Trek Voyager, La Femme Nikita, Dr. Quinn Medicine Woman* and the *Powerpuff Girls. The Nanny* screamed her head off, and Greg got his ass kicked by Dharma. Towards the end of the 90s the feminine dominance of the airwaves was complete with the dawn of *Sex and the City*.

I'm not saying there were no masculine shows. Occasionally a *Walker Texas Ranger* would sneak though the estrogen, but shows and male characters like that became the unusual exception rather than the more-than-common norm they had been for decades. Other than sports programming which always remained popular, masculinity had become the exception on television rather than the rule.

Pop Culture's Progression Away from Male Strength
Part Two: Movies

Though I was acutely aware of this change when it started in the 90s, it didn't really bother me, namely because I was never a big TV watcher. Now movies, that's another story! I've been a huge movie freak since I was a small child. Like most men of my generation, I grew up watching Alpha Male characters in movies from James Bond to Indiana Jones to Rambo to Dirty Harry, who was a crusty old guy by the time I got to him in the late 80s, but still masculine and tough.

Movies have gone through a very interesting progression in the last several decades. In eras gone by you had masculine men like Humphrey Bogart. Over time this morphed into even more masculine guys like John Wayne. Can't get more masculine than John Wayne!

Or can you? Yes, you can. At the dawn of the 70s, male heroes became bigger, stronger, taller, and tougher. The Duke was replaced by even more badass guys like Steve McQueen, Clint Eastwood and Charles Bronson. American culture loved it, and begged for more. You can't get more masculine than those guys!

Or can you? Yes, you can. The rough and tumble guys of the 70s were replaced by even bigger and stronger guys in the 80s. Ultra-muscled, Hercules-like monsters like Arnold Schwarzenegger and Sylvester Stallone single-handedly took on entire armies in their movies, and won! Other guys like Bruce Willis, Jean Claude Van Damme,

Steven Segal, Dolph Lundgren, Kurt Russell, Mel Gibson, Harrison Ford, Chuck Norris, and hordes of others flooded onto the movie screens, killing bad guys by the bloody truckload. It was beautiful.

As the 80s ended I couldn't wait for more testosterone-soaked badassery. Little did I know the world had changed! Just like with TV, Hollywood and the culture at large had decided that being masculine wasn't cool any more. In the 90s, action movies went from being a regular occurrence to almost never. When an action movie did appear, the hero was usually a smartass, skinny wimp. Schwarzenegger and Stallone had become men like Keanu Reeves and Nicolas Cage.

This confused me back then. I spent a large part of the 90s screaming "What the fuck?" at both the TV and the movie screens. The slight good news is that many years later in the 2010s there was/is a minor resurgence in Alpha Male movie characters, personified by actors such as Dwayne Johnson, Vin Diesel, and Hugh Jackman, so there is some light on the horizon.

Why Did This Happen?

There was a specific reason this all started in the early 1990s. That's when the more left-wing baby boomer generation started to take societal power from their more traditional, conservative parents, the World War Two generation (otherwise known as the "Greatest Generation"). Arnold Schwarzenegger talks about[2] how during the 1990s, after Bill Clinton had been elected to the presidency (the United States' first baby boomer president), he and other Hollywood heavyweights could see this cultural shift. They wanted to be a part of this new politically correct, mom-friendly (i.e. female-friendly) trend. So, for example, he forbade action toys based on his likeness to include guns or knives, to be replaced with punches and funny catch phrases instead.

So even Alpha Male 1.0s were in on this shift. That's how big it was.

An era had indeed ended. It did not bode well for the future.

Society's Shift from Masculine to Feminine

Today the feminine conquest is complete, and continues.

- Childless women in their twenties make more money than men in their twenties[3].

[2] *Total Recall*, Arnold Schwarzenegger's biography

[3] http://www.forbes.com/sites/realspin/2014/02/24/childless-women-in-their-twenties-out-earn-men-so/

- Women graduate college in higher numbers.
- Single motherhood has gone from being a destructive and horrible idea to something praiseworthy and celebrated.
- Small boys in schools are punished for pointing their fingers and making shooting sounds.
- Men who kill their wives are punished to the full extent of the law, but women who kill their husbands are given a slap on the wrist and are often defended in the media.
- Commercials regularly portray husbands and boyfriends as stupid and weak, but are very careful to never portray girlfriends and wives as such.
- Having a movie called *My Idiot Brother* is a cute and fun idea, but a movie called *My Stupid Sister* would never be made.
- Jeans and leather jackets have become colorful and frilly metrosexual styles.
- Tom Clancy, Robert Ludlum, and Clive Cussler have been replaced by *Twilight*, *50 Shades of Grey*, and *The Hunger Games*.
- In many American states (including Idaho, Georgia, California and others) when consensual sex between two people under the age of consent occurs, the law specifically punishes the man harsher than the woman, even if the woman is older.
- Male fertility has dropped all over the Western world. Sperm counts have fallen by half between the 1930s and 1990s and an additional third since 1990[4].

On and on it goes.

There are many ways in which society is moving away from the masculine and towards the feminine, and how men are becoming more girly, submissive, emotional, and pussified while women are become more masculine, dominant, and bitchy. It's all around you. In The Prison, hyper-masculine behaviors and attitudes are generally no longer considered cool or appropriate unless a woman is doing them (with exceptions like in the sports world and the occasional action movie).

---

[4] http://online.wsj.com/news/articles/SB10001424127887323394504578607641775723354

Traits like independence, adventure, risk, and masculinity are not something The Prison likes any more. Rather, the focus has become interdependence, security, and femininity. As you move down the path of the Alpha 2.0, society and the culture at large are not going to be your friend. Many people, perhaps most people, are going to be disturbed and upset at your masculine, independent ways.

- Making lots of money? You're selfish.
- Having sex with multiple women? You don't respect women and clearly have commitment issues.
- Have sex with women much younger than you? You're shallow and can't handle (read: obey) a strong, intelligent women your age like a gentleman (read: beta) does.
- Love to lift weights to get big muscles? You're a narcissistic douche.
- Like to drive cool, fast cars? You clearly are trying to make up for the fact you have a small penis.
- Smiling, laughing, and making smartass cracks all the time? Wow, don't you realize all the problems the world has?

You're going to face a wall of opposition from The Prison at almost every turn on the road to Alpha Male 2.0. Expect it and plan on it. Remember these people are stuck in The Prison and you are not, therefore your presence is going to make them uncomfortable.

That's okay. It's your life, not theirs. Let them glare at you from behind their Prison bars. You're the one walking into the sunlight. Pity them, smile, and keep moving forward.

The Golden Lining

The good news, and it's very good news, is that there's a flip side to all of this. Even better than a silver lining, it's a golden lining, and this lining is so damn good, in some ways it's actually worth all of society's current anti-masculine tendencies.

It is this simple fact:

While society has become more strongly anti-male, because of technology, globalization, and more liberal cultural attitudes, an Alpha Male free of Societal Programming can live more financially and sexually free now than in any other time in human history.

One of the strangest of modern-day paradoxes is that in one of the most anti-male periods of history, men can live the greatest, freest existence. This is something too many men forget, particularly those in the men's rights movement. Yes, society is against men and it's a problem, but you can simply choose to not participate. Remember, The Prison can only harm you if you choose to not break free of it. Men, or at least the few who choose to, can live more like true men now than at any other time in history if they have the willingness to shed SP and OBW.

You might think men could be more Alpha Male in the Middle Ages where we could just slaughter our enemies with a sword, or during ancient Babylon where men could have huge harems of young wives. Untrue. The historical reality is that true Alpha status was a very rare thing in those ancient times, only achievable by the nobility or the very wealthy. If you were born a peasant, you could not be an Alpha 2.0 no matter how strong, smart, tough, or confident you were. Today, any man can chose Alpha status if he wants it bad enough. Moreover, the quality of life experienced by even a low or middle class modern-day Alpha 2.0 is orders of magnitude superior to even ultra-wealthy Alpha 1.0s of bygone eras.

No, today is the day. Though it may not look like it from a distance, our time is now!

Here are the three factors that make this true despite the current anti-masculine viewpoints of The Prison.

Factor One: Technology

People have looked up to leaders such as Lee Iacocca, Phil Knight, or Steve Jobs. These men are impressive, no doubt. Yet the businessmen I tend to stand in awe before are those rags-to-riches guys who made it decades ago before computers, the internet, virtual assistants, or even calculators. Guys like J. Paul Getty and Andrew Carnegie. Those guys astound me.

I think of my grandfather who started a small insurance company all by himself in the early 1950s. He had no computers or calculators, so he had to do all of his financials by hand. Not only did he have no email, he also had no fax machines and no FedEx, so whenever he wanted to send a piece of communication to someone, he had to wait a week. Imagine that! Waiting a week to send a one-page document to someone! There were no temp agencies back then, and no Elance, Odesk, or Freelancer.com, so if he needed any help whatsoever, he had to somehow come up with the money to hire full-on employees. There was no web marketing, no SEO, no pay per click, no Groupon, no social media, no Ebay, no smartphones. Television was around, but it was brand new and there was usually no way to advertise locally. That meant he had to physically go knock on doors, make phone calls, and if he could find the money, take out expensive newspaper ads.

As a business owner myself, I simply can't imagine what a nightmare starting a small business would have been in the 1950s.

Today, because of the inexpensive, almost Star Trek-like technology at our fingertips, starting a business that actually makes money, and makes money fast, is extremely simple. Chris Guillebeau of *The $100 Startup* fame has profiled thousands of people who started a small business for just a few hundred bucks and who quickly got to the $50,000 per year income brackets or more. Tim Ferriss has profiled many other people making very large incomes on very low hours worked per week.

Prior to the internet age, this kind of thing was impossible. The time, effort, and infrastructure required to start even a small business was gargantuan. Breaking free of the 9-5 corporate grind and starting even a very small business was far beyond the logistical abilities of the vast majority of the population. Even if you could get one started, you had to really bust your ass, for years if not decades, before you personally started to see any extra money in your pocket. My dad stated his own business in the late 70s and worked very hard at it, even though he hated it, for well over a decade before he starting seeing any real money for himself and my mom. That's how things were "back in the day."

Today, it's easy. Throw up a free web site, set up a free PayPal account, and start talking to people in your target market using blogs, forums, email, YouTube, etc., all of which is free or close to it, and you're on your way.

By the way, I've only talked about financial applications here. There are sexual applications as well. As recent as the 90s, if an Alpha wanted to go get find a woman to have sex with, he had to take a shower, get dressed, throw on some cologne, drive down to a bar, and then spend hours upon hours hitting on girls and taking women out on dates.

Today, because of technology, I can press a few buttons on my internet browser or smartphone while sitting at home in my underwear, and I'm having sex with new women, often within just a few hours of actual work. I have a repeatable and reliable system for getting to sex fast using online dating sites (which I describe in detail at onlinedatingsuccessnow.com).

Factor Two: Globalization

When my grandfather needed any help with anything in his business life that cost money, he had one option: hire an employee. Then do all the paperwork, suffer through all the management overhead, set that employee up with an office and a desk and office supplies, listen to that employee bitch and complain, and stress out every two weeks to meet payroll.

Today, the profitable Alpha Male 2.0 doesn't need to worry about any of that. One of my favorite web sites is Elance.com, though there are many others just like it. All I need to do is describe what I need done in a few sentences, click a button, and people from all over the planet bid as low as possible to do my job for me. I simply pick the lowest bidder who has the highest satisfaction rating, wait a day or two, then pay the guy in amounts as low as $20 for a high-quality, professional job.

Geoarbitrage, the art of taking advantage of different price points for different products and services across national borders, has allowed those in the Western world to get a huge amount of fast, high-quality service for literally pennies on the dollar.

Just two weeks prior to me typing these words, one of my business clients required a high-tech database programming job done at one of their offices. They asked their usual local provider how much it would cost and how long it would take. The provider came back with a quote for $2500 and a time frame of three weeks.

"Hold off on that," I told the president one Friday morning, "Let me see if I can do better."

He agreed to let me try. That evening I posted their job on Elance and put in a maximum budget of $500. By Saturday morning my request was full of bids. By the afternoon I selected a database programmer in Pakistan who said he could do it for $100. I immediately paid $100 into an escrow account (only be released to him if I was satisfied with his work) and told him to proceed.

24 hours later, on Sunday afternoon, he was done. On Monday morning I called some of the employees of the client company and had them test everything to make sure it worked. They did, and everything worked fine. I released escrow and paid the programmer.

What a typical Western company said would cost $2500 and take three weeks, some dude in Pakistan did in fewer than 24 hours for $100, with the equivalent level of quality. Even better, later that Monday I told the president of my client company the project was already done and that I was sending him a bill for $500. He was happy as can be, since over the weekend a project was completed he was thinking would take three weeks, and he only needed to pay $500 instead of $2500. I was happy because I made $400 ($500 minus the $100 I paid the programmer) for about one hour of work. The programmer in Pakistan was happy for getting $100 in US dollars, which is a lot of money where he lives, and for the fact I gave him a perfect five-star review on Elance, something that will help him get future work. It was a win-win-win situation.

This kind of story happens in my business life all the time. The business Alpha of the Western world has huge money-making and time-saving leverage men of the past could only dream of.

Factor Three: Increasing Liberal Attitudes

When I went to high school in the late 80s, which was not that long ago, my school had about 1500 students. A grand total of three girls got pregnant during my four years of high school. Do the math on that. That's three girls out of around 750. In all three cases, these three girls where suddenly pulled out of school and whisked away to…somewhere. I don't know where, because I never ever saw any of these girls again.

Why? Because back then, the culture did not approve of single mothers, especially teenage single mothers. Having a baby when you were a teenage girl back in 1987 was considered very, very bad by all involved.

Fast forward 25 years later. I was on a first date with a 19 year-old woman who had just graduated high school. We were talking about teenage girls having kids. She didn't have any kids, but she remarked that out of her core group of seven girlfriends she went to high school with, five of them already had babies already. All of them were age 19 or younger.

I was shocked. This woman was from a typical, suburban, mostly white high school, and five of her seven friends already had babies. Many high schools today, including and especially more upper class suburban ones, have attached daycare centers to watch the babies of the teenage students. Today, according to society, having a baby when you're a teenage girl is a perfectly fine thing. Teenage girls are taking advantage of this in droves: 34% of American teenage girls will have at least one pregnancy by age 20[5].

What a change! In just two decades, American culture has done a complete 180 on the concept of teenage girls having babies. Just a short

[5] http://cdclv.unlv.edu/healthnv/teensex.html

time ago, single motherhood was the mark of a tramp, loser, or a slut. Today, single mothers are applauded on TV, movies, in politics, and in schools. Single mothers are now considered to be "strong, independent" women who are "taking charge" of their lives.

Quite a difference. Every year, Western culture becomes a little more socially liberal, accepting things that just a few years earlier would have been shocking and vehemently opposed. Here are a few examples:

- Teen motherhood
- Single motherhood
- Interracial dating
- Older men dating much younger women
- Older women dating much younger men ("cougars")
- Open relationships
- Open marriages
- Nudity on television
- Non-married live-in couples
- Common law marriages
- Cheating
- One night stands
- Non-lesbian women having sex with other women
- Online dating
- Casual sex
- Porn
- Prostitution (legal or otherwise)
- Sugar daddies
- Friends with benefits
- Sex on the first date
- Divorce
- Multiple marriages over a lifetime

Every year society becomes more tolerant and accepting of these things than it was the year before. Many of these things are now an accepted norm, or even celebrated. The ones that aren't completely yet accepted soon will be. Just watch.

Some of these trends are destructive for society, such as teen motherhood and divorce. Other trends are fantastic, like sex on the first date or open relationships and marriages.

Social conservatives will fight in vain to stem the tide of these things, but they will continue to fail no matter how hard they try. Conservative commentator Joseph Farah once noted that social conservatism simply cannot win in the long-term no matter what happens, since it's a system based in failure. In any given year, even if the social conservatives work extremely hard, score some major victories, and hold back 80% of the left-liberal agenda, that's a great year for conservatives, yet the liberals still won. Liberals still got 20% of their stuff, while the conservatives got 0%. The progression towards social liberalism is inevitable.

While some of this might be terrible news for society, this is fantastic news for the Alpha 2.0. These days I am able to openly date multiple women while having all the women know I'm doing that, and still they date me anyway. I can talk about things like never getting legally married or using prenuptial agreements, and most people, including and especially women, nod their heads in agreement instead of getting offended and angry like they would have just 20 years ago. As a man in my forties, I can date women as young as 18 and 19 years old just as easily as I can date women my age (I date women of all ages), and it's no problem.

If I had been a man in his forties in the 1980s or 1950s, all of these things would have been almost impossible.

Want an open marriage? Want to date women 30 years younger than you (as long as they're legal)? Or 30 years older than you? You can do that now, and as time goes on, society will start accepting even more crazy scenarios.

Again, I'm not saying that everything society now accepts is good for society. On many things social conservatives actually do have a point. There are indeed some conditions that are harmful for society, particularly future society. However, that's not what this book is about. Here, we're talking about what's good for the individual 21st century Alpha Male. Taking advantage of the new technology, globalization, and liberal attitudes to be a happy Alpha 2.0 is a far better option than being an angry, frustrated, hand-wringing social conservative.

Part Three

Your Life

Chapter 7 –

The Seven Key Areas of Your Life

I once watched an older fellow on TV who was lamenting about how he had just been laid off from his job. "I've done this for 25 years!" he said, "I don't know how to do anything else!" What had this man been doing with his life? In 25 years a person could learn to do HEART SURGERY in his spare time!

Earl Nightingale

Summer, 2007.

I had found the "seduction community." If you don't know what that is, it's a collection of men and businesses from around the world who gather online and in local groups called "lairs." Their focus: to discuss and disseminate the best ways to meet and have sex with women quickly.

A year later I went from a lurker and reader to an active participant in the community, asking for advice and receiving it. Some of the advice was terrible and didn't work at all when I tried it. Other advice was fantastic and really helped me improve. In time, I got really good at this stuff, and I was able to render my own advice and help guys who needed it in the areas I had expertise in, namely online dating, older men dating younger women, and open relationships. A few years after that, in the summer of 2010, I started selling ebooks and coaching services focused on those three areas as a part-time side business, and the rest is history.

During all of this, I observed two things I found extremely fascinating.

The first was that I would receive a harsh negative reaction whenever I presented any of the information I had gleaned from the seduction community to "normal" guys outside of the community. These were usually men who were very successful in other areas of their lives, such as financially or in physical fitness.

They told me that these "pickup artist guys" were "sick" or "immature" or "sleazebags" or "hated women." I was often advised to "stop fucking around" with these guys, find a "good girl," get married, and "grow up." The fascinating part was that the men saying these things were invariably very bad with women. Either they were single guys who couldn't get a date, or worse, they were beta males married to bitchy wives who bossed them around constantly, living in terror that these shrews might divorce them and take their children and half their retirement savings with them.

Although these men were very successful in one or two areas, in the women-area of their lives, they were so ineffective that they were harshly angry towards anyone they saw who was experiencing success with women.

The second thing I observed was the exact opposite. This time it was within the seduction community itself. The community was filled with guys who were very successful with women, sometimes amazingly so. At the same time, most of these guys had completely screwed up financial lives. I found men who were unemployed or on government assistance were common, even well before the financial downturn in 2008. Men who lived on friends' couches and went month to month with regular financial problems were not unusual, and those were just the younger men. Many of the older men in the seduction community I noticed were often plagued with failed businesses, projects that never get off the ground, bankruptcies, and lawsuits.

Almost as soon as I started reading stuff from the seduction community, I noticed a strong animosity from these guys towards anyone in the community who were financially successful selling pickup-related products or services. Big name guys who (seemingly) struck it rich selling these kinds of things were reviled in ways that were surprising to a business-experienced guy like me. If anyone tried to start a for-profit business helping men get better with women, often they were instantly attacked, even by men who formerly thought well of them.

This happened to me in 2010. Some of the seduction community men who supported me and thought I was a great guy suddenly did a 180 and hated me as soon as I started selling things (even though I continued to regularly give free advice over forums and blogs). When it appeared I was selling stuff consistently and doing well, this hatred increased. It was only from a tiny percentage of guys, but the intensity of the vitriol was still fascinating.

So just like the financially successful beta males hating woman-advice, the financially poor pickup artists hated any hint of financial success. In many areas of the seduction community, this hatred is part of the culture, just like it's a part of the culture among well-off beta males to hate "players." There were (and still are) lots of guys in the seduction community who decided that being successful with women was the only thing necessary for a happy life.

Comprehensive Success

I was very lucky to have figured out early in life that being successful in one area but being terrible in another was not a path to long-term happiness. As a young man I resolved to "get good" at all the areas of life important to success as a man, not just the one or two that I liked or that came naturally to me.

Even today, I am more convinced of the importance of this as I learn and experience more. You simply cannot be long-term happy or free if you are very good at one or two key areas but have huge, routine problems in others.

An Alpha 2.0 doesn't have to be good at everything. Alphas are good at some things and poor at others, just like everyone else. Where Alpha 2.0s differ is that they have all the important, relevant areas of their lives "handled" to a degree where they have become either irrelevant or no longer problematic for them.

The Seven Life Areas

Before we talk about how to do this, we need to define the different areas of life you as a man must have handled at least to some degree. Specifically, there are seven of these areas. The Seven Life Areas, or SLA, encompass all possible actions and thoughts you will encounter in your life as a man.

In no particular order, they are:

1. Your Financial Life

Your financial life represents all the time you spend earning, spending, managing, or saving money, or learning how to do so. Examples would be:

- When you balance your checkbook.
- When you work at your job or business.
- When you go to college or other continued education (since you are there to improve your ability to earn).

- When you pay your electric bill.
- When you purchase stocks or bonds.
- When you sit in traffic on the way to work.
- When you buy a new jacket or car.

2. Your Woman Life

Your woman life represents all the time you spend with women in a sexual or romantic context. Examples include:

- When you have a one night stand with that hot babe you met at the club.
- When you take your wife of 20 years out to a romantic dinner.
- When you go out to meet new women at the mall.
- When you read a book on dating techniques.
- When you flirt with that cute checkout girl at the grocery store.

Your woman life does not mean "all time spent with women." Spending time with your female co-workers at your job would be your financial life, and hanging out with a platonic female friend would be part of your social life. Your woman life only applies to women you are currently having sex with, are romantic with, or with those women you are trying to reach that status with.

3. Your Family Life

Your family life represents all the time you spend with members of your close family, extended family, in-laws, or children. It would include things like:

- Going to the Christmas family reunion.
- Playing catch with your son in your back yard.
- Talking to your mom on the phone from 1000 miles away.
- Listening to your sister bitch about her husband.
- Having "movie night" with your spouse and your kids at home.

4. Your Physical Life

Your physical life represents all the time you spend working on your body, including maintaining it, nourishing it, damaging it, and dealing with any problems with it. It would include things like:

- Eating your lunch during a hectic workday.
- Lifting weights after work.
- Going to the hospital for your next cancer treatment.
- Taking vitamins with your breakfast.
- Smoking cigarettes or meth.
- Going running with your dog.

Your physical life does not mean "doing anything physical." Having rough sex for an hour would be part of your woman life, not your physical life. Going whitewater rafting with your buddies would be part of your recreational life. So other life areas can have direct positive (or negative) effects on your physicality without being a part of your physical life.

5. Your Social Life

Your social life represents any time you spend with platonic friends (male or female) outside of your family or work. This would include things like:

- Going to the game with your buddies.
- Consoling your best friend after his divorce.
- Going to your high school reunion.
- Screaming at your platonic female friend (whom you have no desire to sleep with) about why she went back to the boyfriend who beat her.

6. Your Recreational Life

Your recreational life represents any time you spend doing something completely for fun, just for the sake of fun and/or relaxation, especially if no one else is directly involved. It would include things like:

- Watching TV on the couch after a hard day's work.
- Going on vacation to the Bahamas.
- Painting, crafting, writing fiction, taking photos, or engaging in any other artistic endeavor.
- Reading a novel.
- Jerking off to porn.
- Wasting time on the internet reading enjoyable but irrelevant web sites.

Obviously there can be some overlap between your recreational life and your family and social lives. However, there is a boundary. Taking your family to the beach would likely involve much more family life time than recreational time, which is why your recreational life tends to be those fun or stress-reducing activities you do largely by yourself.

7. Your Spiritual Life

Your spiritual life is any time you spend in contemplation, reflection, meditation, or religious worship. It is not completely made up of religious activities, though if you belong to a religion that would certainly be a component of your spiritual life. Examples would include:

- When you read a holy book.
- When you meditate.
- When you go to church services.
- When you read inspirational or spiritual books.
- When you pray.
- When you do affirmations or visualizations.
- When you write in your journal or reflect upon the past.
- When you walk alone in the forest.

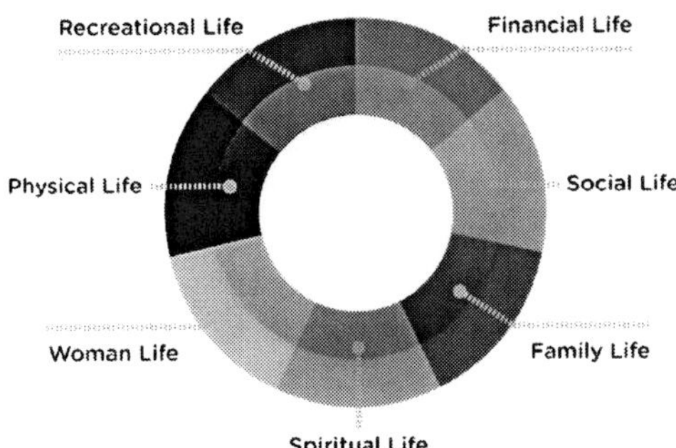

Those are the SLA. Everything you do from the moment you wake up until you go to sleep falls into one of those seven categories. Even when you sleep you're in one (your physical life). I challenge you to find some activity you do that does not fall within one of the SLA. You won't find one.

Relevant Areas

In the above graph, all seven areas are equal in size. Equality in all areas is not only impossible in real life, but it's also rarely desirable. I shall explain why.

In a typical week of your life, you spend a certain amount of time in each area. Take this chart for example:

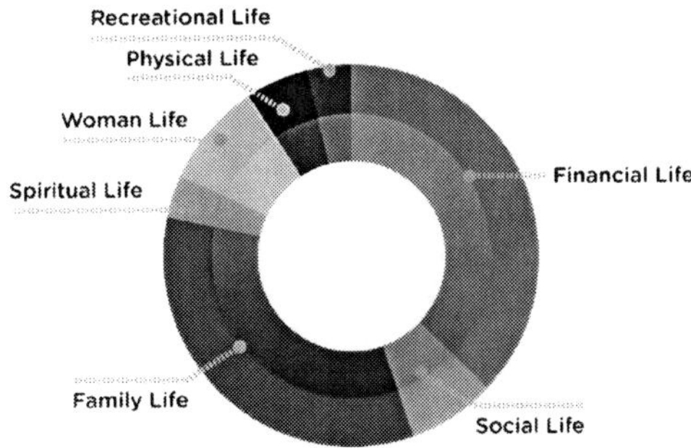

The above would be the typical American man. He's an overweight guy with a typical 8-5 job that consumes about 50 hours a week, has a semi-bitchy wife and two kids at home, never really exercises, and has very little time for things like reflection or spirituality.

He has a wife and kids, which means he has many bills to pay. That means his financial life is pretty damned important, at least in terms of getting those bills paid. That's why his financial life is represented so strongly in the above graph.

On the other hand, he has no religion to speak of and no interest in any spiritual areas. The fact he lacks a spiritual life truly doesn't bother him or make him unhappy. Therefore, his spiritual life is irrelevant. The fact it's so tiny in the graph is okay, at least for him at his current stage in life.

However, we could rightly accuse this guy of having other problems, like the fact that he's overweight. The small slice that represents his physical life should definitely be bigger if he wants to live a full and happy life.

The point here is just because you spend little or no time in a certain area of life does not necessarily mean it's a bad or good thing. Sometimes the absence of one area is indeed a very bad thing, sometimes it's not. The term "life balance" has become popular in the last few years. The implication is that all areas of your life are more or less equally important and you must spend a roughly equal amount of time working in each. This is false. Every man is different, and what may be a very important area to me may be a completely irrelevant area for you, and vice versa.

Take a young man who is unmarried, lives alone, has no children or siblings, and lives 2000 miles away from his parents. Let's assume he has a career he loves, a girlfriend he really likes, hobbies he enjoys, and is relatively fit. If you were to draw a graph showing his SLA, his family life wouldn't even be on there. Is that a problem?

If you're a proponent of "life balance," you might say yes. What then would you recommend for this guy? Should he make sure he calls his mom several times a week? Should he immediately marry and impregnate his girlfriend so he can have kids to be a more "well-rounded" person? Should he regularly buy plane tickets to make sure he spends time with his distant cousins on regular basis?

Of course not. His family life, at this point in his life, is completely irrelevant to him, and that's perfectly acceptable. He's genuinely happy with the way things are. If he ever has children down the road, his amount of family time will obviously change in a radical way, and then he'll have to start spending a great deal of time and energy there. If he never chooses to have children, that's perfectly acceptable too.

Are there exceptions to this? Are there any areas that are considered absolutes to your happiness? As we discussed in detail back in Chapter 1, the answer is yes. *Money* and *sex* are your absolute baselines for happiness as a man in the modern era, so having a near-zero financial life *or* woman life would be a huge mistake regardless of your situation, preferences, or personality. Those are two areas of the SLA that you do indeed need to consider as mandatory priorities.

You might consider physical fitness a priority, and I agree, particularly if you're over the age of 35. If you don't pay attention to your physical life, you're going to have very serious health problems down the road that will damage or even destroy your freedom and/or happiness. If you're a younger guy you have the option of neglecting your body, at least for a while. I'm not saying that's a good idea; I'm saying it's an option. Most men in their late teens or twenties can avoid exercising and eating right and still be completely functional people. However when you hit your mid-thirties or so, this changes, and changes fast.

If the financial, woman, and possibly physical life areas are required baselines for happiness, it's possible that, based on your current life situation and personality, the other areas of your life may not be priorities. In fact, some may not even apply to you at all. When it comes to those remaining four areas, you need to evaluate if you require these areas to be a free, happy, confident, masculine Alpha male. If you don't, ignore them for now. If you do, make them priorities to improve upon in addition to your financial and woman lives (and possibly physical life).

I've done this myself, and I've arranged my life accordingly. Here's a rough estimation of how I spend time and energy currently in my own life:

My SLA

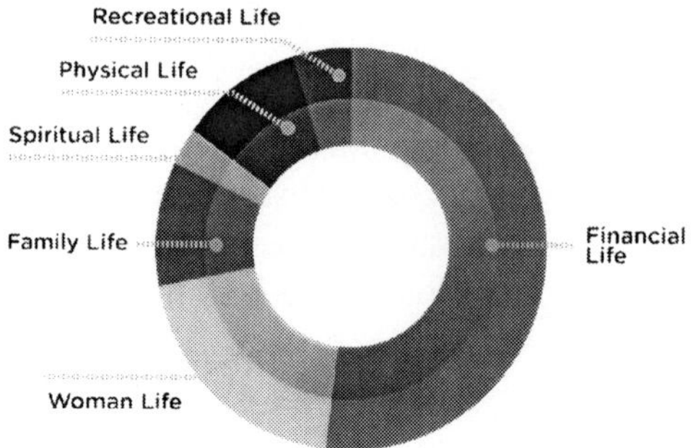

Damn! I really look out of balance, don't I? A way too big financial life...NO social life...a very tiny recreational life...wow! I must be miserable!

Quite the opposite, actually. Living the Alpha 2.0 lifestyle, having designed my life exactly how I like it, I am one of the happiest men I know, and that's no exaggeration. Let's examine why.

- I run three small businesses, I love working, and I am passionate about what I do. Therefore as you can see, my financial life is huge, and that makes me very happy.
- I have sex with multiple women on a regularly basis. Since I'm a high sex drive man, this also makes me very happy, thus the strong showing of my woman life.
- I have two children, but they're older now. My son is an adult and out on his own, and my daughter is a teenager who only lives with me part-time. I'm also not married and do not live with a woman full-time. Therefore my family life is present and important, but somewhat small.
- I exercise daily, take many vitamins and supplements, and do my best to look good, but I'm not a gym rat. Therefore my physical life has a decent but moderate showing.
- I have very few hobbies outside of women and work, so my recreational life is very tiny, but that's fine with me.
- I have a handful of strong spiritual beliefs, but I don't spend a lot time focusing on them. Therefore my spiritual life is also quite small, though I fully plan on expanding this part of my life as I get older.

- My social life is...wait a minute...it's not even on there! I have NO social life! Oh no! I must be a complete loser with no ability to relate to people! Actually, it's exactly the opposite. I realized a long time ago how important it is to interact and relate to people. Therefore my people skills are very strong, and this directly relates to my success with women and in business. I get plenty, and I mean plenty of social interaction from the people I work with every day and all the women I date, not to mention my children. However, I'm also an introvert at heart, so after a day of interacting with people, I love nothing more than to have quiet time by myself. I have no strong need to go spend time with more people for the sake of spending time with people. Therefore, while I have plenty of social interaction, I have zero social life as defined in the SLA descriptions above. That's perfectly fine with me.

Consider the above an example and not what to do. Design your own life "wheel" and makes sure it's customized to your personality rather than my personality or what SP wants you to look like. Be sure to include your financial life and woman life in decent-sized chunks. Add in your physical life if you're over the age of 35 or if you're a younger guy who's into fitness. Then add only the remaining life areas that are relevant to you in their proper amounts. If you're a really social guy, load in some social life. If you're a spiritual man, be sure to add that. If you have no kids and no family, remove your family life, and don't feel bad about it. Also don't feel bad if you're an introvert and don't need a social life (as long as your financial and woman lives are strongly represented). You get the idea.

Once you do this, you'll have a very clear visual representation of the areas you need to focus on, improve, and maintain. It will also show the areas you need to remove from your life, guilt-free.

Natural Strengths, Natural Weaknesses

In going down the list of the Seven Life Areas, you will probably notice that in some of the areas you're already doing very well, while in others you may be lacking. One of the many benefits of identifying the SLA is that it starkly illustrates the areas in which you need improvement.

Everyone is born with different innate talents and weaknesses. There will be slices of the SLA "wheel" you will be naturally good at, and be able to glean results from very easily. There will also be other SLA you will struggle with. This is normal, and you should try to not beat yourself up about SLA in which you have not achieved high results in yet. As a motivated guy, it's probably difficult to "not beat yourself up" about these weaknesses, since as an Alpha (or aspiring Alpha) you'll have a strong desire to be "good at everything."

I'm here to tell you that you'll never be good at everything. Accept it. There will be one or several areas in which you are exceptional, but there will be one or several other areas where the best you can hope for is "decent" or "not bad."

For example, I have always been naturally gifted in my financial life. I have strong skills in that area and a natural, burning desire for financial success that I've had in my gut since I was a small child. In addition, with my more confident and motivated personality, in my 30s I became extremely good at my woman life, achieving some pretty amazing successes (and continuing to do so) without having to spend any money on women. I'm also a very good father, with both of my children being strong, happy, successful, problem-free young adults. This means my family life is also very solid.

Sounds like a charmed life, doesn't it? Well, it is, but it's not all roses and butterflies. Despite my strengths, I have struggled with my physical life pretty much all of my life. I was born with a slow metabolism, an endomorphic body type, and a strong love of abundance and physical pleasure, which includes a passionate devotion to food. Throughout childhood, adolescence, young adulthood, and full adulthood, I have bounced my body between "average," "chubby," and even "fat" on one or two occasions. I love to exercise and have always been a reasonably active person, but my love of food and my slower metabolism gets me almost every time.

These days, I have my body more or less under control, but the reality is no matter how fantastic my financial life, woman life, family life, and other SLA are or become for me, my physical life will always be a little thorn in my side to some degree. I will probably always have a little chub, and I'll probably never have six pack abs, and that's okay. My job is to keep my physical life "decent," and not let it slip back into "bad," while keeping my other SLA at "very awesome" or above.

A helpful exercise would be to write down the SLA relevant to you, leaving out the areas that are not, and rate your current success and happiness in each area on a scale from one to ten. Your goal should be to eventually get all your relevant SLA to at least a seven or higher. The areas in which you're naturally skilled you should get to at least a nine, even if you have to set that as a long-term goal. Your weak areas you should push to at least a seven. This is what I call "decent," which is not great, but certainly not bad.

If you use the excuse of "I'm just not good at that so I'll let it slide" in one of your core SLA, it will permanently limit the amount of long-term happiness you can achieve in your overall life. A fleet of ships must move at the speed of the slowest one, and the SLA is no different. If all of my relevant SLA were tens across the board, but my physical life was a three, I promise you it would severely damage, and limit, my overall happiness. This goes for you if you're physically fit, great with women, but are terrible with money, or have plenty of money but are a timid beta male when it comes to women.

By forcing your weak areas to at least a seven, you can alleviate most of thc limiting influence these areas have on your life as a whole. You don't have to be amazing in your weak areas, but you cannot disregard them either.

Chapter 8 –
Formulating Your Personal Code

Try to develop insights and wisdom rather than mere knowledge, respect someone's character rather than his learning, and nurture men of character rather than mere talents.

Nitobe Inazō

February, 2008.

I lay naked, exhausted on the floor of her apartment. She, a woman I'll call Lisa, was a very corporate lady, one of my favorite kinds. She was a short, beautiful Korean with large breasts. She was naked also, having just finished a few rounds with me, but she was already leaning over to her coffee table and checking her email on her laptop.

"Yeah, you'd better check your email again," I said with a smile, still laying on my back with my eyes closed, "It's been a full 30 minutes since you checked it."

"Exactly," she said, getting my joke but not responding to it, her big, exotic eyes focused on her tiny laptop screen, the only source of light in her living room apartment.

A few minutes later she and I were on her couch talking quietly. Lisa was a friend with benefits; nothing romantic, which was nice, since I could confide in her details about my sex life (namely other women I was sleeping with) in ways I could rarely do with women in romantic contexts, since doing so would cause them to get jealous. Even when women know you're playing around with other women, giving them details about it is rarely a good idea unless they're in the friend with benefits category. Then they don't care. It's nice.

Within ten minutes Lisa and I were deep within a conversation about sex, love, relationships, and even marriage. Not about us, just in general.

"How do you do it?" she asked me, "How do you avoid the mental checklists most people have for what would make a quality mate?"

"It depends on what category a woman is in," I said, "If she's in a friends with benefits category, it doesn't matter if she's mate quality or not. If she's something more serious than that, she might measure up for something more, and if she does that's great. If she doesn't measure up for something long-term, that's okay too."

"Why is that?"

"Because many years ago I made a decision that if I never, for the rest of my life, had a relationship with a woman that lasted longer than three years, that would be perfectly acceptable. I don't plan on *not* ever having a three-year-plus relationship. Don't get me wrong; I'm sure I probably will, especially as I get older. I'd love that. But if it never happens, I'll be just as happy. My life is too good." I smiled broadly.

Lisa sat in silence for a few seconds.

"Yes," I went on, "To most people what I just said is heresy."

"No," she said, "You know me. I get it. But what is it inside you that makes that viewpoint possible?"

I leaned back into her thick, pillowy couch and smiled. I said, "Because my life, and my love it of it, will always be bigger than any one woman."

My life, and my love it of it, will always be bigger than any one woman.

If there was any single mantra for the Alpha 2.0, that would be it.

No matter how much I love a woman, care for a woman, even if she bears my children, no one woman could ever be greater to me than my own life and my own Mission. The love affair I have with my life could never be eclipsed by the love affair I could have with a woman, even if she was the "perfect woman for me."

Yes, there is some very powerful SP that tells you the exact opposite. That you are somehow selfish, immoral, or not a "real man" unless you find a special woman and place her above you. Like most SP, this advice will result in conformity, but not long-term happiness or fulfillment.

I've been in love, very in love. Not very many times, but certainly more than once. Every time was wonderful in ways so intense, I can't even begin describe it to you. Yet even that intense feeling didn't grow beyond the love I have for my life and how I live it. It can't.

A woman whom I passionately love who also demands I make major changes to my first love, my life, will lose every time. It will be a painful loss, to be sure, but there will be no contest. My life, how I live it, and my love of it, will always win over her if there is a conflict between the two. Every single time. The only type of woman who could hope to be with me longer than about three years is a woman who accepts that she will be second, albeit a very close second, to my life and how I live it.

Now that's the woman for me…and should be the woman for you as well.

"Your life and how you live it" is encapsulated in two areas: your Code and your Mission. In this chapter we'll discuss your Code. In the next chapter we'll discuss your Mission.

Your Code

Your Code is both a code of conduct for yourself and a set of standards you will never waver on. You follow these standards 100% of the time, no exceptions, unless specific exceptions are a pre-determined part of your Code. If there are times you don't follow the rules in your Code, then it's probably not part of your Code. Standards in your Code are not guidelines. They are not things that you'd only be able to do when everything is going great. Rather, your Code is a short list of unbreakable, personal laws.

Your Code only applies to you. It does not apply to anyone else. The Alpha Male 2.0 does not spend time concerning himself over what other people choose to do. (That's the path of the Alpha 1.0.) The Alpha 2.0 controls himself, not others. For example, I have never been drunk in my entire life, nor have I ever done drugs (beyond trying marijuana just once and hating it). However I have no problem whatsoever if people in my presence drink, get drunk, or do drugs. I will never do it, but they're free to do whatever they wish.

Because of the absolute nature of your Code, these personal rules and standards are something you need to give a lot of thought to before you put them into practice. Just as an example, I'll give you a few rules from my own personal Code. A man's Code is a very private thing, so I'm not going to give you everything I have; just a few examples to give you an idea of what I'm talking about. I'm not saying you need to have these same rules; you don't and you shouldn't. Your Code will not look exactly like mine or anyone else's. It must be completely customized for you, and you alone.

Here are some examples from mine:

- I will never lie. I am allowed to make mistakes. I am allowed to guess. I can refuse to answer questions. I can joke and be sarcastic; but I will never seriously state things I know to be untrue.

- I will never take overall financial advice from anyone who makes less money than me or has a smaller net worth than me.
- I will never promise a woman complete and total monogamy. I can be serious with a woman. I could live with a woman. I could have more children with a woman. God forbid, I could even get married under an OLTR model (that we'll be discussing in future chapters). Yet I will never promise any woman absolute sexual monogamy.
- I will always own 100% of the stock in any company I consider a primary source of personal income.
- I will never accept any government money for any reason, unless I earn that money by directly rendering a product or service to them (and even that I avoid if at all possible). This relates directly to the concept of internal vs. external security we discussed back in Chapter 5. Government money is *external* security, which is disempowering and risky.
- I will never co-own any debts or assets with a woman I'm in a romantic or sexual relationship with, even if I love her, live with her, or legally marry her.
- I will never do drugs. This includes coffee (which is a horribly addictive drug that just happens to be deemed acceptable by The Prison).
- I will never get drunk. Sipping from a single glass of wine occasionally is okay, but I have never been drunk in my entire life. Getting drunk raises the odds of all kinds of other problems occurring in my life, and I don't like problems. If I really want my body to feel good, I'll go have sex. I have placed a one-time exception to this rule at some point in my future; I wouldn't mind getting drunk once just to see what it's like. However, beyond that, no drunkenness for me.
- I will never get married without a legally enforceable prenuptial agreement. Ideally I'll never be legally married at all, but a legal, prenuped marriage is within the realm of possibly as I get older.

- I will never 100% rely on any one country, city, or region to provide me happiness or regular income (we'll be discussing this in detail in Chapter 20).
- I will remain as physically attractive as is reasonably possible for the rest of my life, regardless of my age or relationship status. This includes things like dressing well, staying in good health, taking care of my body, hair, skin, and teeth, grooming well, and even getting cosmetic surgery if the need arises as I age.
- I will never date a woman past the third date if we don't have sex by then, or at least get very close to it, such as oral sex.

I could go on, but you get the picture. These are all hard standards for me, never to be broken, never to be wavered on. I have others as well, but the above list should be good enough to get some ideas rolling for yourself.

Standards vs. Rules

You may be wondering why I'm advocating a set of personal rules for your own conduct when I just said in the prior chapter, when we were discussing the one of the Six Societal Values of controlling others, that rules were bad, and should be avoided.

True, you should have the least number of rules that you adhere to, and I stand by that. This means we have to clarify the difference between *rules* and *standards*.

In the context of this book, a *rule* is a regulation governing your conduct that is imposed externally from an outside source. A *standard* is a regulation imposed voluntarily by you, upon no one but you. There is a huge difference between these two things.

Rules are bad. Well thought-out personal standards are good.

A law that says you can't drive faster than 55 mph on a desolate rural freeway is a rule. Telling your girlfriend she can't have pictures of her with other men on her favorite social media page is also a rule. Having a personal conviction that you'll never eat red meat is a standard.

Rules damage your long-term happiness, either a lot or a little, but standards will actually increase your long-term happiness, provided they were established without the influences of SP or OBW.

Interestingly, rules are bad and standards are good even if they state the same thing! For example, I have an unbreakable standard that I will never smoke cigarettes, yet I hate living in cities with strong anti-smoking laws. There are few things worse for your health than smoking, so I choose not to smoke. However, if other people want to smoke, let them! I'd prefer the government to not spend my tax dollars monitoring people's smoking habits. It's their bodies, let them do what they will. Freedom is good. It's pretty easy to stay away from people who smoke, and I do so.

As another example, I am against the concept of monogamy and I'm always sleeping with multiple women, but I am thoroughly against the practice of some people in polyamorous relationships who *require* their partners to have sex with other people. I would also be opposed to laws outlawing monogamy. People's lives are their own; let them do whatever they want!

Rules should constantly be avoided, but personal standards are highly advantageous. They serve to guide you and keep you on the path of your own personal fulfillment and long-term happiness. Establishing and following your own personal Code of standards will keep you from faltering when you're not thinking rationally, or when the lure of SP, OBW, the 6SV, or an exciting new woman become enticing.

If your life and happiness is a castle, your Code is the wall and the alligator-filled moat around it. It is your first line of defense against everything that may damage your long-term desires, goals, and happiness.

Developing Your Personal Code

You must develop your own Code, your own list of personal standards that you will hold yourself to at all times. Remember, these are standards, not goals or objectives.

Here are the requirements for the items in your Code:

- Your standards should be very clear and specific. "I will always be happy" is not clear enough, but "I will never take a job that I know will make me unhappy" is fine.

- Your standards should be feasible and realistic. "I will never fall in love" might sound tough and manly, but it's not very feasible. You're a human being so let's be real about this. Notice that even with my anti-monogamy beliefs, I still allow for the possibility of marriage as I get older. So my standard is "I will never promise a woman complete and total monogamy," not "I will never get married." This is much more realistic.

- Your standards should cover all of the Seven Life Areas (SLA) that you deemed relevant to your current life. Also remember that your financial life and woman life, the two wheels on your motorcycle, are required minimums.
- Your standards should not be too long. You don't want a pages-long Code with scores of standards, because it will be too much to remember and adhere to. My personal Code has fewer than 25 short, clear items.
- You don't need to include obvious rules in your Code. You don't need to add an item that says "I will never rob a bank" or "I will never drive my car into an old lady." Normal human standards of decency are already assumed in any Code.
- Your standards should reflect you and only you. Your Code is yours. Not mine, not your dad's, not your wife's, and not your mentor's. You are the only person who is 100% guaranteed to live out the rest of your life with *you*. Putting items in your Code based on anyone else is a severe mistake you'll pay a great price for. Having something like "I will always be in the legal field to impress my father," or "I will never flirt with another woman because I must honor my girlfriend/wife" would be poor Code standards. Be completely selfish when writing your Code.
- Your standards should reflect only items that will help you achieve or maintain long-term happiness. For example, one of the biggest reasons I don't lie is because I know that eventually lairs get caught. This creates drama and drama creates unhappiness. All Code standards must represent a direct link to your long-term, consistent happiness. In the same vein, Code standards that require you to sacrifice and suffer for some greater good are never a good idea. If you are compelled to create such standards, it is very likely you have more work to do in weeding out some more SP from your mind. Speaking of which...
- Most important of all, everything in your Code should be completely free of any OBW or SP. A little of the 6SV is acceptable, but even then you should be very careful. Items in your Code based on the Six Societal Values are only acceptable if you have clearly determined that something in

those categories will make you legitimately long-term happy. However, if that's the case you'd better be damn sure you're not pussing out or rationalizing. Zero 6SV content in your Code is ideal.

Do not expect or attempt to come up with your entire Code in one sitting. Sit down for 20-30 minutes and brainstorm some ideas. Review them a few days later. Over a few weeks you may have to add, delete, or tweak some items on your code, and that's fine.

Once you have a Code, then you can tackle your personal Mission, the core of the Alpha 2.0.

Chapter 9 –

Finding Your Life Mission

Striving implies action; achievement implies inertia, or an end to the action that brought about the achievement. You must have a purpose in life that does not fade away once you achieve a goal or reach a milestone.

Robert Ringer

Winter, 2011.

"I'm attracted to men who have a twinkle in their eye, but I don't want to be that twinkle."

I stared at her blankly, stunned at what she had just said.

"Could you say that again?" I asked.

I sat next to her at a bar on a quick first date. She was a petite and shy 27 year-old. This was the first date she had been on with any man for over two years, having suffered a recent tragedy. I was amazed she had even agreed to meet up with me.

As I always make sure to do on first dates, we were discussing sex and relationships, and something had come out of her mouth that was as profound as it was sublime.

She looked at me oddly, probably not understanding why I was so struck by, what was to her, a very simple and obvious statement. Which it was. She smiled sweetly and said it again.

"I'm attracted to men who have a twinkle in their eye, but I don't want to be that twinkle."

I just sat back and smiled. She had no idea that she had eloquently summarized, in one sentence, the entire reason women are attracted to Alpha Males over betas.

"I'm attracted to men who have that drive in life, a strong drive," she continued, "That's hot! But if his drive in life is me, I just…I don't know…I'm just not turned on."

As she talked, I thought back to a very odd time in my life during my late twenties and early thirties. At about age 28, I had accomplished every major goal I had set for myself. When I was around 18 years old, I set some goals like:

- Have a six-figure income.
- Have my own business.
- Have a good-looking blonde wife.
- Have two kids. One boy, one girl.

By age 28, I had all of those things. I had accomplished all of my goals. My work was "done."

Having all of your big life goals accomplished at such an early age might sound wonderful, and it was...for a while. Very soon I started to stagnate. I had lost that that drive, that fire I had in my early and mid-twenties when I was passionately working towards my goals. I became less motivated and less happy. My masculinity was slowly draining out of me. During the next few years, I experienced a few financial problems, gained weight, and my marriage suffered.

It wasn't until several years later that I re-connected with that inner drive behind those goals that I had set when I was 18. It was something greater than the goals themselves. It was a Mission.

Your Mission

The world is run, changed, and moved forward by men with Missions. A man with a Mission will achieve more in five years than the average ten men will achieve in their entire lives put together, and I mean that in a very literal sense. A man with a Mission will not cry over a girl who dumped him, will not be distracted by petty problems, will not long be delayed by any business or financial setback, will never be bored, and will live longer and have fewer health problems than other men. Women will be wildly attracted to him, and they won't even know why. Other men will naturally trust him and want to be around him.

Most men in society don't have a Mission and never will. About 12% of men in society have clearly defined goals, but only about 3% have Missions.

Your Mission is the rudder of your life. It is the core of your entire Alpha Male 2.0 existence. Everything you do, everything you are, flows from your Mission, your devotion to it, and your love of it. It is what I meant in the last chapter when I said:

My life, and my love it of it, will always be bigger than any one woman.

Your "life", in this context, is powered by one thing: Your Mission.

Your Mission, or Missions (since you can have several), is your overarching, meaningful objective for your entire life. You've heard of companies having mission statements; your personal Mission is similar. Your Mission is why you get up in the morning. It is why you strive, learn, work hard, fail, and get back up. It is the engine of your life.

Your Mission is not a goal, and it's very important you understand the difference between goals and a Mission. A goal is a specific, quantifiable objective that must be achieved by a certain date, and then it's done. A Mission is something that lasts a lifetime or close to it. Rarely do missions have a shorter time horizon than 20 years.

Over time, goals can be, and sometimes must be, heavily modified or discarded. Not a Mission. A Mission can be tweaked a little over time, but that its core it is a steady, unwavering thing. It is something you are committed to for life, or close to it. No other person, including a woman, can or should dissuade you from your Mission. If they do, you never had a real Mission to begin with.

Your Mission is not an obligation to another person. A Mission cannot be something like "Devoting my life to my children" or "Helping my wife survive her cancer." These are all wonderful things, and some of them might make great *goals*, but they aren't Missions. A Mission represents you and your effect on yourself, your life, and possibly the greater world, not one or two other people.

Car vs. Bullet Train

Picture a Japanese bullet train. If you've never been on one, I strongly recommend it. It's a fun experience. Japan's Shinkansen trains fly over the rails at almost 200 miles per hour, but glide as smoothly as any Mercedes. The views from the train ride from Tokyo to Osaka are beautiful, and the experience of being on one is exhilarating.

My life is a bullet train. I have a specific place I'm going, and my purpose is to get there as fast as I can. On the way there, I'm having an exciting, exhilarating time. I see and experience a myriad of fantastic things most people never witness, all while cruising along smoothly at 200 miles per hour.

Let's say I meet a beautiful, intelligent, fun woman, and I fall in love with her. While I'm speeding along in my wonderful Alpha 2.0 life, she comes along with me for the ride, and we're both happy. Let's also say she later decides she doesn't want me to go where I'm going. She tells me to make a hard right and change direction. She also tells me that I shouldn't be going so fast and that I should slow down.

Just one problem; I'm a bullet train. I can't just turn. I'm on a track, going where I want to go, having a fantastic time. She grows upset that I'm not complying with her wishes. I make it clear to her that I'm a bullet train, and that's who I am. I'm not slowing down. I'm not changing direction. Moreover, *the reason she's attracted to me is precisely because I'm a bullet train with these qualities.*

Soon she grows even more upset. No problem. I temporarily slow down and make a stop at one of the train stations along the track, open my doors, and gently escort her off the train. I'm a little sad as she walks away, but then I smile and blast back into the track at breakneck speeds and get back to my exciting life, my long-term happiness, and my Mission. In no time, many other women come along, and I repeat the process, but I never waver on who I am or my destination: my Mission.

The Alpha 2.0 is a bullet train.

Beta males and some Alpha 1.0s are not bullet trains. They're cars. Compared to bullet trains, cars are boring, tiny, weak, slow, fragile, prone to all kinds of problems, and often crash into each other. They only are designed to go short distances, and even when they go long distances, it takes forever.

Cars have no Mission. They drive around, all over the place. When they break down, they're quickly replaced. They're commodities.

That doesn't mean that cars don't have advantages over a bullet train. Women love cars because they're very good at following orders. When you order a car to go left, it goes left. When you tell it to go right, it goes right. It can speed up or slow down whenever you want. It does exactly what you want at all times. Women love that, at least for a while. Cars aren't very exciting compared to bullet trains, but they conform, obey, and fit very nicely into a woman's SP and Six Societal Values (the 6SV).

The vast majority of men are cars, constantly being turned this way and that by their wives, girlfriends, bosses, friends, family, co-workers, governments, cultures, and their own OBW. While the cars run around in circles, never really going anywhere, a few of us are bullet trains, speeding along, having a great time, and achieving our goals and dreams. We're not very flexible as compared to those compliant cars, but we're far happier, more fulfilled, and get far more done with our lives.

The Importance of Your Mission

You must have a mission, or be well on your way to defining one if you desire to live the Alpha 2.0 lifestyle. It's mandatory. An Alpha without a Mission is no Alpha. He's just a cool beta, or at best a conflicted Alpha 1.0.

You might already have a Mission: a burning, passionate life purpose that drives you forward every day like the east wind propelling a sailing ship. If you do, that's great. Well done.

However, more than likely you don't have a Mission yet. You probably have strong desires and convictions. You may have some experiences under your belt that have clarified what you want in life and what you don't. You may already have created most of your Code. You may even have some clarified or written goals. That's a great start, but it's still not a Mission.

Finding Your Mission

A Mission is (usually) not like a goal where you can just think up something you want, put a deadline on it, and write it down. Missions are far deeper and a little more complex. A Mission is the primary purpose of your life. No, it's not the *meaning* of your life. That's something else entirely and is a spiritual/philosophical issue beyond the scope of this book. Rather, your Mission is the *purpose* of your life. Everything you do and accomplish in all of your Seven Life Areas is a direct result of, and effort toward, your Mission. It will drive your big decisions for the next several decades of your life, if not the rest of your life.

If it sounds a little overwhelming, that's because it is. That's why I can't tell you what your Mission should be. It's highly personal to you. The best I can do is give you a few examples of what a Mission is and is not, and do my best to give you some exercises and parameters to assist you in formulating it. The rest is going to have to come from within you.

Because of the sheer size of what your Mission is, it will likely take some real time to completely clarify it. If you have a very active, fragmented personality it may even take several years before you have an absolute, crystal clear understanding of what your Mission is. That's perfectly acceptable as long as you're continuing to improve and clarify it. Just don't let years go by without any Mission because you simply stop thinking about it.

You may have no idea what your Mission is, or perhaps you have a decent notion but need things fleshed out and clarified. If you have no idea where to start, you'll need to uncover possible Mission areas. Then you'll need to clarify your Mission.

Mission Discovery Exercise

This is an exercise that will assist you if you have no clear idea of what your Mission should be. Be sure to do this exercise on a day where you're in a positive, energetic mood. If you're angry, stressed, or tired, delay this exercise until you have a better day.

1. Take at least 45 minutes and withdraw from your life. Get far away from other people and turn off your phone. Go somewhere quiet. Make sure you are not interrupted during this exercise.
2. You may use either a piece of paper, computer, or tablet. Do not use a smartphone (the keyboard is too small to write and edit comfortably and quickly). I'm going to use the term "paper" for the rest of this exercise, but using a computer or tablet is fine.
3. Make four equal-sized quadrants on a blank sheet of paper. Title each quadrant, "Want," "Should," "Good," and "Like."
4. List the numbers one through seven down the inside of each quadrant.
5. On the first quadrant, titled "Want," write down seven things you want to do, either in general or with "your life." Force yourself to come up with seven things. If you come up with more than seven, that's fine too. It's very important to make sure you put things down even if they directly violate OBW or SP. For example, if you honestly want to smoke weed, watch TV, or have sex with hookers for the rest of your life, don't question that right now. Put it down. We'll filter things later. Right now, you need to brainstorm every thought that comes into your head regardless of how crazy it sounds.
6. On the second quadrant, titled "Should," write down at least seven things you feel you "should" do with your life, however you define the word "should." Likely, there are things buried within you that you feel you should do, like give back to the poor, travel, write a book, spend more time with your family, lose weight, or become more spiritual.

Again, don't filter anything based on OBW or SP; put down whatever comes to mind even if you don't logically agree with it. Like with the first quadrant, force yourself to come up with at least seven items. If you're having trouble getting to seven, think back to your childhood or adolescence. Was there anything you felt you "should" do back then?

7. Repeat with the third "Good" quadrant. Write down at least seven things you are naturally good at. This should be pretty easy, since most of us are aware of our natural talents. It's important to write down everything you're good at even if you don't necessarily enjoy the actual activity. For example, you may be naturally good at math, but don't actually like math. Put that down as one of your "Good" items anyway.
8. Repeat with the final "Like" quadrant. Write down at least seven things you honestly enjoy doing, regardless of if you're good at them or if you consider them valid activities. What's the difference between "Want" and "Like"? "Like" are things you have done before. "Want" could be things you've never done, but want to do, or want to do differently. So if you honestly like to water ski, write, have sex with older women, or do legal work, don't question it; put it down.
9. Now you'll have four lists of at least seven items on one page. Go back through the lists and see if you can find any items that link to other items in other lists in any way. Circle these items and draw lines to their linked items in other quadrants. Write a sentence or two (or more) on exactly how these link, and how such a link would benefit you and make you happy or more fulfilled. Keep doing this until you've linked everything on all four lists that have any possible connections.
10. During the linking process, if any new items popped into your mind that you could add to any of the four lists, add them, then see if they link to any other items.

By now you should have a very strong idea of the best directions in which to take your life. Your Mission should be:

- Something you enjoy immensely.
- Something you feel very strongly about, with 100% conviction.

- Something in which you are naturally skilled, and calls upon your natural strengths and talents.
- Something you feel you "should" do. It should have greater meaning beyond just something you like.

If you think you've uncovered your Mission, write it out on a new sheet of paper. See if it excites you. See if it feels right. See if you can see yourself devoting at least the next 20 years of your life to it, regardless of any major life changes you may experience during that time. Remember that if you suddenly derail your Mission just because you get married, or have kids, or move to another city, or change careers, then you never had a Mission to begin with. Missions are stronger than all of these things.

If these things don't quite ring true for you when you re-read what you wrote, then either this is not your Mission, or you need to tweak it some more.

This exercise is just to get you started. From here you may need to do some thinking and soul-searching over the next few days, weeks, or even longer to truly hone in on your Mission. The point here is to get started. Use the following section in this chapter, and the rest of this book, to assist you.

Don't wait. Don't put this off. I'll say it again: Your Mission is the core of your Alpha 2.0 existence. Without it, very little of the Alpha lifestyle will be available to you, or sustainable if you achieve it.

Clarifying Your Mission

Once you have an idea of what your Mission is, you'll need to clarify it. In this section, we're going to discuss the parameters of what an Alpha Mission is and what it is not. Too many men have spent years, if not decades, wasting their lives pursuing the wrong Mission. You don't want to be one of them.

The below parameters will assist you in sharpening your Mission to ensure that it's clear, focused, 100% congruent to who you are, and something that is truly a part of you.

1. **As mentioned above, your Mission cannot rely on one other particular person or small group of particular people**. Therefore things like "I will be the best husband in the world" or "I will be a great father and devote my life to my children" are not Missions, simply because they rely on too small a group of people. Individuals or small groups of people cannot be relied upon long-term to be either present or relevant in your

life. For example, devoting your life to your wife is a nice thought, but what happens if you get divorced? What happens if she dies?

Your Mission must be greater than that. It cannot rely wholly on the cooperation of one or two specific people outside of you. It must be something forged of steel that will stand the test of many decades no matter what happens to your girlfriend, wife, children, family, co-workers, or close friends.

I'm talking here about a small group of people. Missions can rely on a very large group of people, since with large groups the statistics are much more manageable. A Mission such as "To bring food, water, and electricity to the darkest villages in Africa" is a perfectly acceptable Mission, if that's truly what you want and feel. There is clearly a group of people involved, but it's a large, static group that can be relied upon statistically; there is no one or two specific people who can derail or invalidate your Mission.

2. **Your Mission must adhere 100% to your Code.** Your Mission and your Code must be in absolute and complete harmony with each other, since they are tied together closely. At all times during the formulation and clarification of your Mission, you must view it through the eyes of your Code. If your Mission breaks any of the unbreakable personal standards of your code, either it's not a valid Mission, or your Code is not a real reflection of what it should be.

What if your Code and your Mission conflict? The simple, and I hope obvious answer is that your Code comes first. If you're looking at a possible Mission that directly violates something clearly in your code, you either need to choose a different Mission or radically alter your current Mission to fit within your Code. This is because such a Mission will eventually make you unhappy and/or limit your freedom, which we can't have if we're pursuing an Alpha 2.0 life.

The only possible exception to this is if your Code is something you have just formulated and brainstormed, and is perhaps not set in stone yet. If the process of clarifying your Mission causes you to go back and re-evaluate aspects of your Code at this point, that's fine as long as you are very careful. It's possible that if you're rationalizing or second-guessing a problem in your Code it's because there is some OBW, SP, or one of the Six Societal Values creeping into your Mission that you're trying to justify. When tempted to modify your Code for your Mission (or vice versa), always ask yourself:

Will this change make me happy and free now, ten years from now, twenty years from now, and thirty years from now, guaranteed?

If the answer to that question is "maybe" or "no," then you're just rationalizing some residual OBW, SP, or 6SV that's still rolling around in your mind, and you need to rethink that particular change.

3. Your Mission must be something you are truly passionate about. Your Mission must be a labor of love, passionate love, not just something you enjoy casually. Things like hobbies, hanging out with friends, or building a car cannot be Missions. On a scale from one to ten, your passion for your mission must be at least a 9.5, if not a solid ten.

4. Your Mission must challenge you, at least to some degree. At the same time, it must be achievable within reasonable odds of success.

For example, "Maintain a body weight of 160 pounds for the rest of my life" might be an acceptable component of a Mission if you're a naturally short, chubby, stocky guy with horrible genetics, a horrible metabolism, who hates exercising and who's been fighting his weight his whole life, but it's a terrible Mission for a guy who's naturally skinny. At the same time, having a Mission of donating $100 billion dollars to charity probably isn't a great idea either, because the odds of accomplishing such a thing are miniscule no matter how amazing you are.

The best Missions, much like the best long-term goals, are those Missions that push you, challenge you, but are something you can reasonably do.

5. Ideally, your Mission should not have a definite and quantifiable end-point. This is where Missions differ from goals. To "achieve a net worth of one million dollars" is an excellent goal, but it cannot be your Mission. It could certainly be a component of your Mission, but it cannot be your overriding Mission. Why? What happens when you hit that goal of one million dollars? Your Mission is then over. What then?

Just like the "devote your life to your wife" example, if for any reason your Mission suddenly ends, forcing you to stop your life and figure out a completely new Mission, then likely it was never a real Mission to begin with. As they say, "Ask me how I know."

Having multi-part or multi-tiered Missions is perfectly acceptable and we'll discuss that in a minute. Regardless, a Mission is not something that necessarily ends. Your Mission must be your life Mission, something with a minimum time horizon of 20 years, though longer is better. That's how truly BIG your Mission must be! Missions that are not grandiose and exciting will not consistently motivate you or keep you focused.

6. The topic area of your mission can be any of the Seven Life Areas (SLA) you chose. A Mission can include multiple areas. Your Mission can be financial in nature, but it doesn't have to be. It can be philanthropic in nature, but it doesn't have to be. It can be fitness-related, but it doesn't have to be. It can be business-related, or career related, but it doesn't have to be. It can even be spiritual or religious in nature, but it doesn't have to be. It could even be family-related, love-related, or even sex-related! As long as you follow all the other Mission parameters listed here, any of the SLA are acceptable aspects of a Mission. The topic area of your Mission can be anything you want! It's your life! Live it as you choose! The sky's the limit!

Your Mission can even include several different SLA if you wish. My own Mission has elements of my financial, fitness, spiritual, and recreational lives.

Your Mission should be something completely customized to you. If you do include several different SLA within your Mission, make sure your Mission is very clearly defined, even if it takes several sentences to do so.

7. Multi-tiered or multi-part Missions are acceptable. Your Mission can have multiple tiers, phases, and/or sub-Missions, as long as you don't get too complicated. You have the freedom to structure your Mission any way you like. Perhaps your Mission has a "phase one" that will take 15 years, and a "phase two" you'll work on after that. Perhaps you have smaller "sub-Missions" that make up a greater Mission whole.

This is all fine. However, I strongly recommend you don't make it too complicated. Ideally, your entire Mission, including all tiers, phases, and sub-Missions if any, should be completely encapsulated in fewer than one or two short paragraphs. Years ago, my Mission used to be an entire page and a half(!). Today I have it honed down to just a few sentences.

The shorter, more clear, and least complicated your Mission is, the more positive affect it will have on you.

8. Your Mission can be customized to your age. Though your true Mission is a life-long endeavor, you may customize your Mission based on your age and the future phases of your life. If you're 27 years old, it's going to be a little difficult to determine with any precise accuracy what you'll be deeply motivated by when you're 67. So don't try. You could, for example, develop a very clear 20 year mission that you'll focus on until you're in your fifties, at which time you will allow yourself to course-correct into a different, newly-defined phase of your Mission.

That second phase may be something you're only guessing about at this point, and that's okay, just so long as your core Mission for the next 20 years or so is very clear and congruent to who you are as a man.

Examples of Missions

Here are some examples of both good and bad Missions to help you clarify your own. Remember, these are examples only. Copying any of the examples below for yourself is a very bad idea. They are here for you to learn the structure of a Mission and to assist you in formulating your own personally customized Mission.

"I will donate one million dollars to charity."

This is a bad Mission, since it has a quantifiable ending. This is a goal, not a Mission. Once you hit that million dollar goal, then what? Then you'll have to sit down and come up with a new Mission. Not good. A better Mission would be something like:

"I am here to make a positive difference in the lives of children in need. My Mission is to make a noticeable and positive difference in the lives of thousands of children in Africa (or Europe, or Chicago, or wherever). I will do this by setting up multiple organizations that perform X, Y, and Z."

Now that's a Mission, since it lacks a quantifiable end point and comes from a place of real passion.

"I will make my father proud of me, and live up to my family name."

This is another terrible Mission, since it relies on one specific person, your father. It's also dripping with SP, which is never a good idea. Having an objective like that virtually guarantees that you're going to make decisions in your life that, while your father might like them, will make you unhappy. I know many intelligent, capable men who are miserable in careers they hate because they went into them at their father's (or family's) insistence.

The results of your Mission must be something *you* want, not something others what for you. Moreover, it cannot rely on just one person, or even a very small group of people, no matter how important those people are to you.

"I will live a completely location-independent life. I will have the ability to travel anywhere I want, whenever I want, stay there for as long as I want, have no dip in income while I'm there, and be able to financially

support myself easily wherever I am. I'm here to see ALL the world, and all of its people, in all its beauty and glory."

This is a good Mission, and very well-stated. It's relatively simple, congruent to personal freedom, free from SP, doesn't rely on any other person or small group of people, doesn't have a definite end point, and is derived from great passion. It also clearly states there's a financial component that must be addressed, so that specific goals can be derived from this Mission with minimal difficulty.

"I will improve the health and vitality of people all over the world by making great advances in biotechnology. I will help treat and cure disease, lengthen people's lives, and improve their quality of life. I will make my stamp upon human history, and mankind will be made better by my work."

This is a good career-based Mission. It's lofty, but it doesn't attach anything specific enough to make it into a goal. It's just specific enough to be powerfully motivating and to enable specific goals to be pulled from it, which is exactly what Mission should do.

"I will build a series of companies in the energy, hospitality, and construction fields that will be extremely successful. The income from these businesses will provide me and my family a lifestyle of abundance, wealth, and joy. My children will want for nothing, and I will always have enough money to maintain security not only for myself, but for my future descendants for years to come."

This is a wealth-based Mission, and it's a good one. It does mention his children, which technically is a small group of people, but it avoids relying on these people to actually do anything. This Mission is especially powerful because it involves several different SLA (financial, family, and recreational).

"I will be a bodybuilding champion. I will sculpt my body to near-perfection and win multiple bodybuilding titles at the national and semi-national level."

This fitness-based Mission needs a little work. It's motivating and non-specific enough to be a Mission, and that part is good. A Mission such as "I will win Mr. Universe" would be a goal, not a Mission.

The problem is the Mission is very age-dependent, which is fine, but it doesn't accommodate for that. This Mission would be fine for a man's twenties or thirties, but into his forties and fifties, this Mission will be almost impossible as stated. A better Mission would be something like this:

"From now until age 40, I will be a bodybuilding champion. I will sculpt my body to near-perfection and win multiple bodybuilding titles at the national and semi-national level. After age 40, I will be one of the most preeminent fitness gurus on the internet. I will have products and videos that show people how to improve their health and appearance in real and dramatic ways. I will also travel the world giving seminars on effective fitness techniques for all ages. I will make a positive difference in millions of people's lives."

Much better. Instead of its original version that had an implied end point, this is a two-phase Mission with no end point. It also raises the stakes by bringing a greater impact to more people than just himself, which will probably help motivate him, especially if he's a more extroverted guy. However, 100% "selfish" Missions are perfectly okay, like the one above about being location independent. You can better the world, or better yourself, or both. Any of those options are fine. Again, your Mission must be about what you want and what will motivate you, regardless of anyone else.

Just Do It

Does this seem like a daunting task? It is. Relax and man up. Don't worry if you can't figure all of this out right now. As I said above, get started. Take the time to start clarifying a strong Mission you can devote your life to. This is literally one of the most valuable things you can do.

Once you have a clearly defined Code and Mission that drives you forward, all of a sudden just about everything in life becomes easier and more exciting. It becomes easier to earn money, to achieve goals, and to date and be in harmonious relationships with women. You will also find yourself in happier states much more often with less stress, and physical problems diminish or even vanish. It really is amazing.

If you developed a congruent Code and a strong, clarified Mission and devoted your life to it, you could stop reading this book right now and change your life for the positive, forever. That's how powerful this is. For the remainder of this book, everything will be within the context of your Mission. If you still don't have your Mission figured out by the time you finish this book, that's okay. Though I would strongly recommend that you read this book a second time once you do clarify your Mission.

Chapter 10 –

Setting Societally Independent Goals

Stop jumping on the bandwagon and start building your jet.

Alan Weiss

March, 1999.

I sat eagerly, rocking back and forth in my seat, unable to control my energy. I couldn't believe I was actually there.

Sitting across from me, as calm as ever, was a man I had idolized for almost a decade. For years I had read his books, listened to his voice in my car, followed his advice in life and in business. He went from virtually homeless, sleeping on the ground outside his car, to self-made multimillionaire many times over by the time he was 30. He was wealthy, happy, physically fit, wise, intelligent, and a good guy. He was everything I wanted to be.

Brian Tracy sat with his characteristic wry smile, looking at the smartass, badly dressed, overeager 27 year-old before him.

"Well?" he asked, "Go ahead."

I cleared my throat and began. "Okay," I said, "I want to grow my consulting practice and sell it for $2 million…by the time I'm 30! I have some spreadsheets right here you can look at that show the layout of my business and where I'd like to get it to by-"

"Why do you want to sell it?" he interrupted, clearly not interested at looking at any of my stupid spreadsheets.

"Because I want to retire!" I said excitedly, "Retire by 30! I could bust my ass, build it up over the next several years, sell it for $2 million to some big conglomerate, pay whatever taxes I'd have to pay on the sale, then have at least a million left over."

"Why do you want to retire so early?" he asked calmly.

"Because I don't want to work."

"Alright. Then once you're 30 and retired what would you do?"

"Well…I'd travel. And write. And have a lot of sex. You know. Have fun and enjoy myself."

"Okay," Brian said, his smile gone, "That's about year or two, maybe three or four at the most. Now you're 34. You've got another 45 years of life. Now what do you do?"

"Oh, I'd work."

"Caleb, you just said don't want to work."

"Uh, well," I sputtered, "Okay, well, I do like to work. I just don't want to work all the time. You know, I don't want to work 40, 50, 60 hours a week for the rest of my life. I love working but I have other things to do. I'd like to work maybe 20 or 30 hours a week, make a hell of a lot of money on those hours, and spend the rest of the week doing other things in style."

"Then why don't you structure your business so you can do that right now? Why all this silliness about retiring?"

I gave him a confused look.

"Um…you can do that?" I asked.

"Of course you can," he said, "Do you know any successful dentists?"

Dentists? What the hell was he talking about? I was a consultant, not a dentist. I didn't know where he was going but I went along.

"Yeah," I answered.

"Can you set an appointment with your successful dentist on a Friday?" he asked, his slight smile returning.

"Um, no."

"Why not?"

"Because on Mondays and Fridays my dentist goes fishing," I said.

Brian stared at me and blinked.

"Oh," I said, feeling very dense.

Not Just Goals, But Societally Independent Goals

There have been bazillions of books and articles written on the importance of having goals and techniques on how to set proper ones. It makes no sense to repeat all of that here. The one key difference with us is that we are pursuing the Alpha 2.0 lifestyle, where most SP and OBW do not play a role. So while goals are indeed 100% critical for your happiness in life as a man, we must go about the process of goal setting a little differently than the typical guy.

Human beings, and men in particular, are goal-seeking organisms. We're at our best, happiest, and most productive when we are in the process of moving towards a worthy objective. That's what designing your Mission was about. Very little in your life will ever be accomplished unless you determine some very clear goals. This includes short-term goals and longer-term ones.

Moreover, much of chaos and wasted time will occur if you set the wrong goals or if your goals are not congruent with your Mission, like mine were when I had been talking to Brian Tracy. When I was younger, I fell into the SP that said that a "business owner" is a guy with a "big business," a building with his name on it with lots of employees. I also fell into the trap that said a truly successful "young" entrepreneur was one who retired at an early age.

Both of those things sounded great, but were completely incongruent to what I truly wanted in life. As a result, I experienced a lot of misdirection, wasted time, and some problems in my later twenties and early thirties despite my outward successes. How much better my life could have been if I had sat down and determined the goals in life that I wanted, rather than those The Prison told me were ideal or appropriate.

Now that you have a Mission (or are at least on the road to more clearly defining one), you can now set a decent set of goals that are congruent with you and your long-term desires. Because you are aware of the negative influences of OBW, SP and the Six Societal Values (6SV), you've established a Code and a Mission that is created independently of these factors. This creates a blueprint for an Alpha Male 2.0 life for you, as well as a lifestyle geared towards accomplishment and happiness rather than your outdated biology or the elite's agenda for The Prison.

This is why you are now uniquely equipped to create a set of goals that are virtually guaranteed to put you on the correct path in life, and why creating a life blueprint in this sequence puts you light years beyond the typical guy who just sits down and figures out a few goals for himself.

The life blueprint of the Alpha 2.0 looks like this:

Alpha 2.0 Life Blueprint

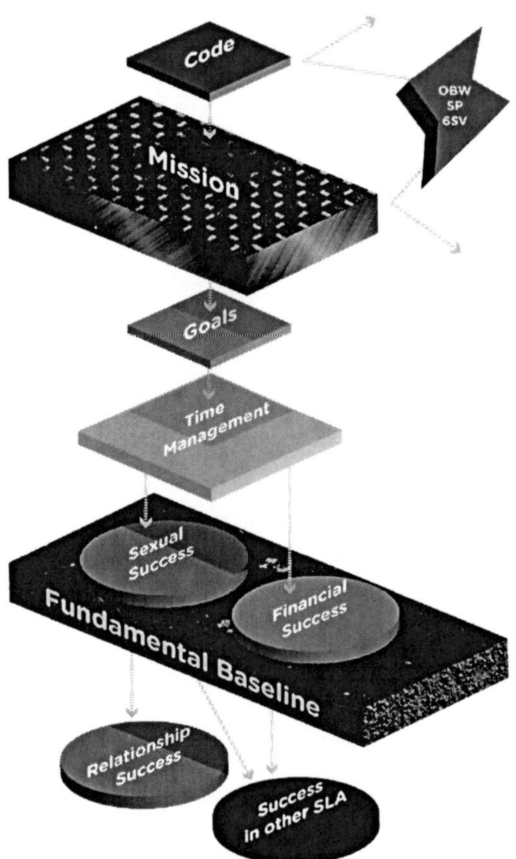

The reason I was on the wrong path so many years ago was because I had established clear goals, but I had done nothing else we've discussed so far.

- I had established no Code of any kind, other than the SP basics of "be a nice person" type things.
- I had only a very hazy and largely incongruent Mission.
- I had allowed OBW and SP to override my desire for happiness, causing me to get legally married and monogamous even when deep down in my heart I had no real desire for either.

- I had allowed the 6SV to influence what I thought I wanted for my business objectives. I didn't want these things. Rather, these were things SP and the 6SV told me were what a "successful businessman" should look like.

As a result, though I achieved a high income in my twenties, I had done just about everything else wrong, and I had achieved my income in ways that were impossible to create long-term happiness and fulfillment *for me*. Short-term, occasional happiness, sure, but not the deep, powerful long-term life happiness and fulfillment inherent to the Alpha 2.0 lifestyle I now live every day. Instead I was a typical, obedient, mildly unhappy, beta male inmate of The Prison, just one at a higher income level.

Retooling Existing Goals

If you're smart enough to be reading a book like this, it's pretty likely you have some written, defined goals ready. That's magnificent if you do, and you should feel good about that, but you're not done. You must now evaluate those goals in terms of the last several chapters you've read. Take those goals out, review them carefully with a critical eye, and ask yourself the following questions:

- Are any of these goals a result of your Obsolete Biological Wiring forcing its will upon you, rather than something you really want?
- Are any of these goals there because you're trying to impress anyone or garner approval from someone?
- Are any of these goals there because you fear being alone?
- Are any of these goals there because have a strong desire to control others?
- Are any of these goals there because you fear criticism or disapproval from your peers?
- Are any of these goals there because you are afraid of going after what you really want?
- Are you avoiding any goals because you fear a negative reaction from others?
- Are any of these goals there just because you're just trying to be a "nice guy" or a "good boyfriend" or a "good

husband" or a "good son" or a "good citizen" or a "good Christian" or a "good progressive" or any other SP-based role or group identification?

- Visualize yourself with all these goals accomplished. Are you now happy? Really happy? Now visualize yourself ten years after these goals are accomplished. Are you *still* happy? Really happy? Be honest! Now visualize yourself twenty years afterwards. Still happy?
- Do any of these goals seek to prevent you from feeling bad rather than making you really happy?
- Are all of these goals actually realistic? For example, does any goal involve you doing something like making a billion dollars, having sex with a particular celebrity, or similar unlikely event?
- Do any of these goals rely on another person external to you to be perfect? As an easy example we'll be discussing later in the book, do any of your goals involve you relying on a woman to never cheat on you, or break up with you, or divorce you for 25 years straight?

When you honestly go through these questions as you review your goals, you might be shocked to find that your current set of goals are riddled with OBW, SP, the 6SV, irrationality, and Disney fairytale expectations. These are bad goals. You need to either delete them completely or seriously retool them so they all become 100% congruent with your Code and your Mission and are free of SP and OBW. Let me tell you from experience, and not just my experience: Having no clearly defined, written goals is very bad, but having *bad* goals can sometimes be worse than having *no* goals.

Setting Goals

In case you have no written goals yet, I'm going to lay out a very simple system for setting goals. There's nothing unique about this and perhaps you've read similar techniques before. There are many good books available on the topic of setting goals and I recommend you read some. The only real difference here is that you have become fully aware of the SP, OBW, and 6SV exerting their insidious influence over you, and you have established a clear Code and Mission before setting any goals.

1. Take at least 45 minutes and withdraw from your life. That means you need to get far away from other people and turn off your phone. Make sure you are not interrupted during this exercise.

2. Using a piece of paper (or a computer or tablet) start brainstorming a list of everything you would like to do, have, or be in the foreseeable future. There are several rules do doing this.

- Don't evaluate what you want. Just put it down no matter how crazy or unrealistic it sounds.
- Let your Mission guide you. Re-read your Mission if you need to.
- Be sure to include all the Seven Life Areas (SLA) relevant to you. Have that list of seven items handy when you list out your goals to help remind you.
- List as many things as you can. The more, the better. You want to completely empty your mind of all the things you would like to do, have, or be.
- Write your goals out as if they have already been achieved. Instead of "I will make $100,000 per year" write, "I make $100,000 per year."
- Write your goals in a positive tense, not a negative tense. For example, instead of "I don't hang out with drug addicts anymore," write "I only hang out with positive, healthy people who are going somewhere in life." Negatively-worded goals that are any variation of "I don't do this" don't work nearly as well on the subconscious as positive ones.
- Your goals must be quantifiable whenever possible. "I make a lot of money" or "I am happy" or "I am ripped" are not goals. Proper goals would be "I make $300,000 a year" or "My net worth is $5 million dollars not including my house" or "On a scale from one to ten, my happiness is at least an eight, at least six days a week, almost every week" or "I bench 350 pounds and have under 7% body fat."

3. When completely done, go back through the list and categorize the items by priority. This is when you start getting critical and realistic. Re-read your list, and put an "A" by the goals you must have, a

"B" by the goals you want to have, and a "C" by the goals it would be nice to have but aren't huge priorities.

4. Gather all of your "A" goals onto one list. Set aside your "B" and "C" goals for the moment.

5. Run down the list of "A" goals and put a number next to each goal that represents the number of years in which you would like this goal. Keep the numbers to one, three, five, ten, and twenty years. Use the number one for any goal that will take less than one year to accomlish. For example, if you want to run the Boston Marathon eight months from now, just write down a "1" by that goal for, denoting one year.

6. Separate all goals that will take five years or longer to accomplish and move them aside for the moment.

7. Prioritize and sort your final list. With the remaining three-year or less "A" goals, ask yourself, "If I could only have one goal on this list, which would it be?" Once you find that goal, place the number one by it. Then temporarily ignoring that one, ask yourself that same question with respect to the remaining goals. Place a two by the next goal. Repeat until you have numbered all the goals on this list. Then sort them by this number.

When done, you now have your core goal list that you need to focus on, and the order in which you need to address them. If you wish, feel free to go back to your longer-term "A" goals and your "B" goals and run then through steps five through seven, though this is not necessary. Your three-years or less "A" goals are what matters.

Using Your Core Goal List

Take your top A1 goal and write at the top of a new sheet of paper (or computer document). Place a specific deadline on it. When exactly do you want this goal accomplished? Use an actual calendar date. Write this deadline right under the goal.

Now make a list of all the actions you will need to complete in order to achieve this goal. Be as complete as possible. Try to list every single thing that must be done. Also list items such as skills you'll need to learn and people from whom you'll need help.

When done, sort the list by priority and sequence. Many tasks will need to get done before other tasks, so sort your tasks in order of procedure, so that the tasks that need to be done are listed first. If the sequence order isn't relevant, sort the items by importance, with the most important items at the top.

There may be some tasks on this list you won't know how to do. No problem! Just put down "Learn how to do X" or "Get so-and-so to do X for me, at a cost of Y."

When done, you will have a real-life battle plan to accomplish your A1 goal. Repeat this process with your A2 goal. Don't worry about your A3, A4, and other lesser goals at the moment. You'll get to those later, for reasons we'll discuss in the next chapter.

At this point, you are now quite literally in the top 3% of all men in the world. You have clarified your Code and your Mission. You have set real goals outside of SP and OBW, with real deadlines, written them down, and developed plans for your accomplishment. 97% of men (and women!) will never take the time to do these things, and they pay the price for this laziness every day. The Prison loves these people.

Your new life has begun!

Chapter 11 –

How to Effectively Manage Your Time

Let me tell you something. Being "in your prime" doesn't last very long. Don't waste time.

Sylvester Stallone

Winter, 1984.

I was sweating and bleeding, though I didn't know it. Blood was pumping through open wounds on my elbows, feet, and knees, staining my karategi. My opponent was James. He was 14 years old, two years older than I, a big curly-haired bastard and a full head taller. This was exactly why my sensei had chosen him.

I was in the middle of my belt test for my Tang So Doo training, a Korean martial art very similar to Taekwondo and Moo Duk Kwan. This particular portion of the test was called Freestyle Defense. It meant I had to stand in the middle of the room, alone, with everyone watching me, and I could not move. James was allowed to approach me from any direction, even behind me, and attack me in some conventional, non-karate way. Examples would be reaching out to choke me, grabbing my shirt, or throwing a punch. I had to defend myself using the techniques I had learned. It was full contact; no protective gloves, pads, or headgear was allowed.

Shit.

My sensei sat before me (though the karate was Korean, the Japanese term sensei was used in the dojo; I never really understood why). He was a stern but bright-eyed Alpha made of iron, and a man I respected immensely. I wanted my belt, and I wanted to make him proud of me.

James had already attacked me twice, and twice I had thrown off his attacks, though badly. He was getting irritated at "losing," and each attack was more intense than the last.

I stood at the ready position, facing my sensei and a few of the other higher-ranking students. I stood as still as I could, feeling the sweat drip off my hair and into my ears. From my peripheral vision I could see James walk around behind me with a sneer on his face.

A rear attack. Great.

Suddenly I felt his hands clamp around my stomach, pinning my arms to my sides. He started crushing me, and I could smell his horrible body odor.

I instantly remembered how to squirm out of such an attack. I was supposed to grab his hands on my stomach, twist my hips to my side, put my right foot behind his left, and then shoot up straight. This would knock him off his balance, pull him off me, and send him flying backwards.

Just one problem. He was aware of this move and was prepared for it. He was also taller and bigger, and that didn't do much to help. I tried twisting behind him. He blocked. I tried again. Again he blocked. I twisted the other way. No go. Time and again I tried, and time and again he stopped me.

"Stop!" my sensei commanded.

James and I instantly parted and assumed ready positions of respect.

My sensei was shaking his head, but he was smiling. This was not good, since it looked like he was actually trying not to laugh.

"Caleb," he said, "When something isn't working, DO SOMETHING ELSE!"

"Yes sir!" I squeaked. He wanted me to do something else? I didn't know anything else. I was screwed.

"Resume your last positions and continue from there," he commanded.

James snapped back behind me and grabbed me around the torso like before. I braced for death.

"Begin!" sensei cried.

The python-like crushing against my stomach resumed. I thought fast. I didn't want to try the twisting thing again. That wouldn't work and make me look stupid to boot. So I improvised.

I grabbed James' arms and locked them in place around my stomach to make sure they wouldn't move. Not that I could have moved them if I wanted to. I tilted my body to the left and lifted my right foot. Then I brought down my heel on his bare toes as hard as I could.

I could hear James scream behind me. His hold on me lessened just a little. It was enough.

Still clamped onto his arms, I crouched downward and then lurched forward. My arms were weak, but my stocky, Sicilian legs have always been strong, even as a child. As my upper body titled forward my legs drove upward, tilting both James and me forward at an angle parallel to the floor.

We both crashed downward. James, being a foot taller than me, met the floor first, which is a nice way of saying his face met the floor at high speed. I could hear a slam followed by him flopping off of me. Dazed, I stood back up, free of him finally, a smile on my face as I could see him rising from the floor while clutching his nose and cheekbone, doing his best not to cry.

"Well done," said my sensei, "Go sit down."

I nodded, bowed, too weak to speak, and trudged back to my spot where merciful rest awaited me. When I sat down, one of my buddies told me to look back at where I had been standing. I did, only to see the bloody red footprints I had made in on dojo floor. Shocked, I grabbed my foot and sure enough, blood was dripping out of it like a leaky faucet.

Hm. Why didn't it hurt?

As soon as I had that thought, it hurt. Like hell.

All this just for a damn green belt? I must be crazy...but the man in me still loved it. I had set a goal to get my green belt before I turned 13, going to karate class three times a week, every week, even if I had to reschedule friends and homework.

After trials were over, my sensei handed me my new green belt. My foot still hurt like hell.

Time Is a Bitch

Time is the only resource you cannot make more of. If you lose money, you can always go make more. Contrary to popular belief, if you lose your spouse or lover you can always go get another one (which is exactly what most people under the age of 60 eventually do anyway). If your house burns down or your car gets totaled, you can buy a new one. If you get fired, you can get a new job. If your business collapses, you can start a new one. Even if your children turn out to be jerks, as a man you can go make more of them whenever you like no matter how old you are.

Human life is one of abundance, full of ever-renewable resources. That's what makes life so wonderful!

The one and only great exception to this is *time*. Once it's gone, it's gone. You can't make more of it, no matter how good you are. Just ask Steve Jobs. Once you end your 25th year, or 37th year, or 53rd year, that year is gone forever. You've lost it and you're never getting it back no matter how smart you are, or how much money you make, or how physically fit you are, or how many people love you.

In the end, time will win. Malcolm McDowell in *Star Trek: Generations* said it like this:

> *Don't you feel time gaining on you? It's like a predator, stalking you. Oh, you can try to outrun it with doctors and medicines and new technologies, but in the end, time is going to hunt you down and make the kill.*

Dramatic, but accurate. Regardless of how old you are, you only have a few years before you die, or at least start getting old, and those years are going to fly by with lighting speed. If you're 25, you're going to blink and be 40. Ask me how I know. If you're 40, you're going to blink and be in your sixties. Don't believe me? Ask a guy in his sixties and he'll tell you all about it.

This is a core problem with most people. People live their lives as if they're immortal, or close to it, like they have hundreds of years of youth of relative health to fart around and waste. They live their lives as if there's plenty of time to put up with all the crap that makes them unhappy. Why worry? They have plenty of time.

You need to live as if you have very little time left, because you really don't have any to spare. Don Draper of *Mad Men* said it like this:

> *I live like there is no tomorrow. Because there isn't a tomorrow.*

It's a cruel irony that the only resource you cannot make more of is the one you automatically lose every day. Time's a bitch.

Fortunately, there are some simple techniques you can use to make the most of your time. I have been teaching time management techniques for many years, and in this chapter I'm going to give you the key portions of my best stuff. These are the same techniques I used to:

- Go from a zero-income, no-experience, no college education 18 year-old to making $45,000 annually ($75,000 in inflation-adjusted dollars) at age twenty.
- Consistently make money in real estate throughout the 90s, often more than at my day job, completely part-time.
- Start a business from scratch and get it to a six-figure income in three and a half years.
- Maintain a six-figure income while working fewer than four days a week.

- Go from a sexless, out-of-practice, divorced beta male to an Alpha getting regular results with attractive women with very little effort in about 18 months.
- Turn around my business during the sudden recession and stock market crash of October 2008, losing over 60% of my income and recovering most of it within six months, more than all of it within 18 months.
- Date as many as six women at the same time while still maintaining a job and regular family life. (Though six women are way too many for a happy life for most men, myself included. I don't want that many women any more. I'm just using this as an example of what's possible. Two or three women is a much more manageable number; we'll discuss this further in Chapter 14)
- Running three small companies in completely different industries while still having plenty of free time to travel and spend with my family and my women.
- Do all of this by age 40.

Mastering time management techniques while being powered by a strong Mission enables you to pull off some truly amazing things. By the end of this chapter, you'll know more proven time management techniques than I knew myself while I was accomplishing most of the items above.

Time Management Customized to Your Personality

There are tons of different time management systems out there. Which ones work?

It's a trick question, because they all do. The problem is different systems work for different types of people. I could give you the theoretically "perfect" time management system, and it might work for you, or it might not. Even if it didn't, it would probably work perfectly for your best friend.

Some people are more visual, others are more auditory. Some people like computers or tablets, others vastly prefer pen and paper. Some people are really disorganized, others are anal-retentive nerds. Therefore, different time management systems will appeal to, and thus work better for, different types of people.

Given this reality, I'm going to give you two completely different time management systems that I have designed, used, and taught: the E3D System and the Check System. You can use one of them, both of them, or combine the two to suit your needs. You may find one system much better than the other. Or you may take pieces of both systems and create your own. Do whatever works, but make sure you have a system that you use regularly in your life to maximize your time.

The system you use for your personal time management must work for you, or you won't do it. Please do customize anything you learn in this chapter as well as any other time management techniques you learn from other resources. Very few systems are going to work 100% "boilerplate" for your unique personality, life, outlook and needs.

This includes whatever type of media you use for you time management. I don't care if you use...

- A day planner booklet you write in
- A binder with papers
- A single piece of paper
- A time management smartphone app
- Time management software on your computer
- A cloud-based time management system
- A spreadsheet or series of spreadsheets
- A word processing document.

All of the above items will work. It doesn't matter which you use; just pick your favorite, the one that will work best for you. Any of those mediums can be used with either system we're about to cover.

The Difference between the Two Systems

The two time management systems we're about to cover appeal to different types of people.

The E3D system will likely appeal to you if any of the following describes your situation:

- You are naturally a little more organized
- You are detail-oriented.

- Your work is extremely varied; you are doing completely different things week-to-week with not much regular "routine."
- You often encounter many small tasks that change often.
- You live a very full life, or relatively complicated life full of different SLA.

The Check System will appeal to you if:

- You are more visual or artistic in nature.
- You're not a naturally organized person.
- You're a more emotional, shoot-from-the-hip type of guy.
- Your regular lifestyle and schedule is not very complicated; you tend to follow a static routine that doesn't change often.

The Check System is more fun and easy. The E3D System is more powerful, though more complicated, and necessary for those with more complex lives or tasks. After reading through both systems, pick the one that makes the most sense to you. Try it out for two weeks and see how it feels. You could always try the other system if you find the first one doesn't work for you. Of course, you may fall in love with both systems, and that's fine too. I use both systems from time to time myself. If my life gets complicated I will use E3D; when things get more focused I will use the Check System. Sometimes I will use variations of both.

Again, use whatever works. The E3D system is more comprehensive, but the Check System is much simpler. We'll tackle E3D first.

The E3D System

Decades ago, people started using daily to-do lists. To-do lists are fantastic. Productivity studies have shown that your output will increase at least 25% the first time you start using a to-do list even if you don't change any other behaviors[6]. Not bad, but there's more to the story.

Around 1990 a smart guy named Steven Covey came along and correctly pointed out that to-do lists only allow you to focus on a time frame of just one day. He argued, again correctly, that doing this kept you focused mostly on fighting fires, maintaining an eternal state of

---

[6] http://www.briantracy.com/blog/time-management/time-management-tools-and-techniques-time-planner-master-list/

crisis management. This is not good for stress, balance, or long-term goal achievement.

His system was to only construct your to-do lists and action plans once a week, or longer! This forced you to take a more nuanced and comprehensive view of your SLA (what he called life "roles").

He was right…when he first wrote those words. When he made that observation it was before full market penetration of mobile phones, email, the internet, texting, social media, globalization, blogging, viable mobile computing, outsourcing, e-commerce, streaming video, Google, smartphones, online dating, and a horde of other life-changing conditions.

The world has become a much faster place since 1990. Back then, once a week was enough.

No longer. If you make some to-do plans on Sunday, by Wednesday the landscape will have changed, perhaps radically.

Yet Covey did have a point when he said focusing on things once a day was not enough. Years ago I experimented with several different systems and time frames to finally develop the E3D System, which stands for Every Three Days.

Once every three days is as close as you can get to perfect. It's looking at a time horizon that is expansive enough to really get some proactive things done in your life, but isn't quite as short a time frame to keep you in firefighting mode. Under the E3D System, you are going to review your goals, plans, and to-do list once every three days. Then you'll go forth and conquer for the next 72 hours. Afterwards you will pause, regroup, and reflect, then attack the next three days, and so on.

E3D is an extremely effective, comprehensive system that puts you in perfect alignment with your Mission and your goals, and allows you to achieve great things in a comparatively short period of time.

Author's Note: This next section describing the specific steps involved in the E3D System gets a little technical. It might be easier to follow along using a separate piece of paper or computer to take notes as you read. If you're unable to do that right now, you're more than welcome to skip E3D and move on to the Check System, then revisit the E3D section when you're able.

Components of E3D

E3D consists of five components you maintain on a regular basis. The components are:

- Your goals list
- Your project list

- Your to-do list
- Your Once-As list
- A calendar system

Your Goals List

This is the list of goals you created last chapter. It is a list of all your current goals, separated into A, B, and C categories. Your two core goals (your A1 and A2 goals) must be on the top of this list in big bold letters. These are the two goals you are going to be focusing on.

Why only two goals? Because as author and blogger Leo Babuta has adroitly pointed out, human beings really can't handle more than two active goals or projects at once. If you try to hit eight different goals at the same time, the odds are huge that you won't hit any of them. If you do hit any, they will likely be the weakest and least important goals you have. However if you attack just two goals at a time, the odds are very high you will hit both of them. Then you simply go back to your goals list, pull out the next two goals, designate them as your new A1 and A2 goals, and proceed to work on them.

A hard and fast rule of time management and goal achievement is to never focus on more than two goals a time. This is probably one of the most difficult pieces of advice I will be giving you in this book. As Alphas, we tend to want to conquer the world and accomplish ten things at once. Very often I will coach or consult with men who tell me things like "Okay, in the next six months I want to get down to 8% body fat, get my black belt in karate, master dating skills, start my own business, and maintain at least a 3.8 GPA in college." Sorry. None of that is going to happen. You must pick two items, and temporarily pause everything else. Once you get one of those two items done, then you can work on the next two items, and so forth.

I know that's tough. I often have trouble with this reality myself. Regardless, I can tell you for a fact it's what works best. You must only have a maximum of two active goals or projects at any point in time. The good news is that if you do everything correctly, you'll be getting things done so fast you will eventually hit all the goals you have listed in your "A" list.

Your Project List

A project is a grouping of individual to-do items that consist of one overall objective or task. Starting an online business would be a project.

Losing 40 pounds would be a project. Achieving a goal of getting five new clients for your business is a project. Setting up your two-week vacation to Spain would be a project. All of these are tasks that require multiple to-do items to complete.

What's the difference between a project and a to-do task? A project is a grouping of many to-do items, like "Create New Lawnmower Sales Web Site." A to-do item is a single task, like "Purchase domain name for new site." Sometimes, really big goals will often include several projects, with each project having many to-do items in each.

Your project list is simply a listing of every project you have that you would like to complete at some point in the near future, with a small sub-list of to-do items under each project.

The lists you brainstormed in the last chapter can serve as a rough draft for the projects you need to get down on this list. In your project list, make a list of every project you need to tackle now and over the next two to five months or so. Give each project a simple title with few words. Under each project title, list every to-do item that must be done in order to complete the project. Then sort every to-do item in order of priority and sequence, placing the first thing that must be done first, followed by the next.

Once you have all your projects listed with a sorted sequence of to-do items for each, assign a single letter code to each project. Use any letters you like. Unlike with our goals, this letter has nothing to do with the priority of the project. It's just a descriptor, so use whatever makes sense to you. Your new web site selling lawnmowers could have a descriptor of "L," and your Spanish vacation could have a descriptor of "S."

Lastly, pick two and only two projects to focus on right now. Use your A1 and A2 goals as your guide. Place these two projects at the top of your project list, and draw a visible line between these two and all the other projects. These two projects are now your "active projects."

Your To-do List

You have a whole pile of things to do in your life that have nothing to do with any particular project. You have to go to the bank, you have to pay your electric bill, you have to call your sister, you need to schedule an appointment with your dentist, you need to fix the fan in your living room, etc.

Your to-do list is simply a big list of all these individual, non-project to-do tasks. Brainstorm and list out everything you possibly need to do and get it on this list. David Allen's now-iconic book, *Getting*

Things Done has some great techniques on how to create a complete to-do list for your life, and I highly recommend it.

Once you have listed everything in your to-do list, run down the list and ask yourself if any of these items could be grouped together as projects. If they can, group them, get them off your to-do list and onto your project list.

Lastly, put an A, B, or C by every to-do task. A items are things that absolutely must get done, and get done soon. B items are things that should be done but are not quite as critical as A items. C items are things that would be nice to do.

Sort your list by A, B, and C items. Then take your A items and number them by priority, placing the number one by the most important item, then a two by the next and so on. Sort your A items so the A1 item is on the top of the list, followed by A2 and so on.

Now you know exactly what tasks need to get done, and the order in which you need to do them.

Your Once-As List

Many tasks in life are recurring. Every month or so you probably need a haircut no matter what else is going on in your life. From running payroll twice a month for your small business to getting a physical once a year from your doctor, these tasks must be done on a recurring basis, more or less forever. I call these types of tasks "Once-As," since they all need to be done "once a" whatever (day, week, month, quarter, year, etc.)

Make a list of all of your Once-As. Be as complete as possible. For example, I have things on my Once-As list like getting my teeth cleaned every six months, charging my electric razor once a week, and getting the oil changed in my car once every five months. I never forget a thing, because everything is in my Once-As list.

I used to have this list in a spreadsheet showing how often they needed to get done, the date they were last done, and a bright colored font that showed if they needed to be addressed soon. Later I changed this to setting up all my Once-As as recurring events on my smartphone's calendar, with reminders that pop up whenever each Once-As task needs to be addressed.

As I said above, the media system you use to manage your Once-As is up to you, just make sure you do it. Too many guys out there forget to pay their electric bills or forget to charge their Bluetooth earbuds.

A Calendar System

Not much to say about this. You need a reliable calendar system to track appointments that must occur at a specific date and time. I don't care what system you use, just use one.

I am continually shocked at the number of people in modern day society who still have not figured out how to use a damn calendar. If you're going to meet up with your friend for lunch at 1:00pm next Thursday two weeks from now, you need to put that down somewhere. Leaving that to your memory is a massively stupid idea. One of the biggest reasons women flake on first dates is that they don't keep a calendar anywhere in their personal lives. Insane! Many men aren't much better.

No goal achievement is possible until and unless you start regularly using a calendar in your life, and not just your business life, but your entire life. If you've already accomplished all of your goals in life, then fine, you can probably forget the calendar; otherwise you'll see how important this is as we move forward.

The E3D Procedure - Prep

Before actually beginning the E3D process, you need to have all the groundwork laid out that we've already discussed. This means you should have:

- A Code
- A defined Mission (or at least a rough idea of one you're clarifying)
- A list of goals sorted by priority
- Your top two core goals (or projects)
- A list of projects with prioritized task items within each
- A prioritized list of to-do tasks
- A complete list of Once-As
- A calendar system you're comfortable with.
- Once you have all the above items in place, you're ready to rock. If you still don't, go back and get those done before attempting the actual E3D procedure.

The E3D Procedure - Execution

Once every three days, you are going to schedule a one-hour appointment with yourself in your calendar. It can be a recurring thing that happens on the same time every third day, or you can schedule it manually. As long as it happens every three days or so, it doesn't matter. Every three days is ideal, but I realize that life is life, and sometimes that won't be possible. If it sometimes ends up being four days or two days, that's okay.

You are now going to keep that appointment with yourself as if it was with your boss or your biggest customer. That's how important it is. That one-hour "meeting with yourself" is your E3D time, and it's going to become the rudder of your life.

When your E3D hour comes, here's exactly what you do.

1. Set a one-hour timer on your stopwatch, smartphone app, or e.ggtimer.com. Do not stop working on your E3D time, don't even take a break, unless you completely finish or until the timer goes off, whichever happens first. If the timer goes off before you're all done, set another timer for 15 minutes, and take a break if you want. (If you feel like continuing to work instead, then do so!) Go outside for a walk or have a quick healthy snack. Then when the 15 minutes is up, set another one-hour timer, and get right back to work.

2. If you're using a computer, unplug or disable your internet connection. That's right. Unplug the damn thing. Email and the web will distract you, so we don't want these things interfering with your E3D work. Another option is to use web browser add-ons such as LeechBlock or WasteNoTime (Google them) to make sure you don't start surfing during your E3D session.

3. Clean your to-do list. Go to your to-do list, and delete any to-do items that you have completed since your last E3D session three days ago. Sometimes, completed items turn into new items, so edit and transform these instead of deleting them. For example, "Call John about New York meeting" could turn into "Call John again" if you called him and left a message and haven't heard back yet.

4. Review your two core goals. Then go to your projects list and if necessary, add any tasks to your projects list that need to be there to ensure your active projects are accurately reflecting your two core goals.

5. Make your project to-dos active. Your two active projects should be on the top of your projects list. Pull the top few to-do items from one or both of your active projects and transfer them over to your to-do list. Place an "A" priority by any to-do item you do this with on your to-do list. Pull as many times you think you can get done over the next three days, but don't go crazy. Make sure to delete these items out of your project list as you pull them over. No to-do item should ever be on your to-do list and your project list at the same time.

6. Schedule in any appointments in your calendar over the next three days (or beyond) that have specific times. Examples would be a doctor's appointment or that hot date on Friday night. Also schedule in any routine time-specific tasks you do, like if you run every morning or pick your daughter up from school every afternoon.

7. Schedule at least two appointments with yourself to work on your to-do list. As always, treat these appointments as if they were a meeting with your boss or your biggest customer. The length of these appointments is up to you, but one to three hours is usually best.

8. Process all of your "inboxes" to empty. An "inbox" would be any place in your life where new task items enter into your zone of control. Examples of common inboxes would be:

    - Your email inbox
    - Your snail mail mailbox
    - Your "in" basket on your desk
    - Your briefcase or work bag
    - Any voice notes you make on a pocket dictator or smartphone app

Go through every one of these items and see if they necessitate any new task items you need to add to your to-do list. When you add an item on your to-do list, "delete" (or archive) that item from its "inbox." Process all of your inboxes until they're all empty. Yes, this means that your inbox folder in your email will be empty by the time you finish your E3D procedure. No more huge, full inboxes!

9. If any new to-do items take fewer than two minutes to do, then stop and do them *right now*. That's right. This is another David Allen

technique. Writing down and/or scheduling a to-do item that takes fewer than two minutes to complete is a waste of time and resources. If you find a new to-do item is “Email Joe to remind him about the appointment next Monday,” don’t bother writing that down. Just fire off a quick, one-sentence email to Joe, delete that to-do task, and get right back to processing your new to-do items.

Be careful about doing this! Don’t get “caught” doing an item for more than two minutes. If you find an item you’re doing will take more than two minutes, STOP IT and make a new to-do item, then continue on with your E3D session.

10. Refer to your Once-As list and see if there will be anything you’ll need to do here in the next three days. If so, make a new task item on your to-do list. It is acceptable to have a to-do task listed on your to-do list and on your Once-As list at the same time. You don't need to delete it from the Once-As list when you copy it to your to-do list, unlike when you move to-do items from the project list.

You don't need to do any of this and can skip step 11 entirely if you're using an automated calendar system with reminders to track your Once-As.

11. Prioritize any new items in your to-do list with an A, B, or C priority. Remember that to-do items moved over from your project list should stay as “A” priority. You could also maintain another column that shows the single letter code of the project you that “owns” the to-do task, so you know when you do that task what project it's assigned to.

12. Quickly review your new to-do list. Make room at the very top for a new, small list. Take your A items, especially any A items you just moved from your project list, and move them up to this list. This will become your “active” to-do list, the things you *must* complete over the next three days before your next E3D session.

A rule of thumb is to not go crazy with assigning yourself too many tasks. Having a small number of items on your active to-do list is far better than having tons of items you probably won't get to. Tim Ferriss is famous for having just a single daily to-do list of whatever can fit on a 8.5x11 piece of paper folded in fourths, handwritten in big letters. You must complete whatever you put on your active to-do list over the next three days, so the smaller the list, the better.

If you don't get all of your tasks done by your next E3D session, or if you get everything done and find you have more time, that's okay. Over time you'll start to get a feel for what you can and cannot do in a typical three-day period in your life.

13. Sort your new, active to-do list by priority. Put the most important "A" item on the top, followed by the next most important task, and so on.

14. If it's not already there, schedule your next E3D session three days out in your calendar.

15. Carry your new active to-do list around with you. Note that this is just your active to-do list, not your entire to-do list.

16. Congratulations! You're all done. Pat yourself on the back and go eat a cookie. You know have the next three days of your life planned out for maximum efficiency and effectiveness. Over the next 72 hours all you need to do is what's on your active to-do list. You'll know exactly what you need to do, when you need to do it, and the order in which it needs to get done. More importantly, you'll be working on key items that move you closer to your goals (what I call "Improvement Work" that we'll discuss in the next section).

Every three days you'll call a time out and do another E3D session to recharge and course-correct if necessary.

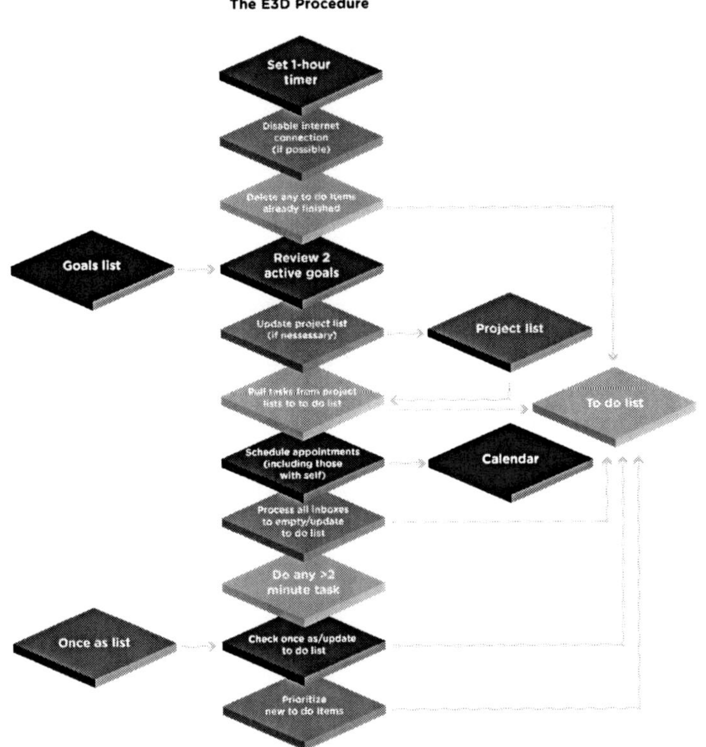

If the above procedure seems like a lot of work, don't worry. I promise that once you do this a few times you'll get this stuff done very fast and it will become second nature. Once you really get humming your E3D session won't take nearly an hour. Mine usually take about 20 minutes, and I live a very full life.

However, if this system really rubs you the wrong way, there's another system you can use that's much simpler...

The Check System

The Check System is far easier and more fun than the E3D System, and that's where its power lies. It's not as comprehensive or specific as the E3D system, but it is still very effective, particularly if you have a hard time staying focused with long-range projects or have difficulty creating new habits. It took me over two years to design this system, and once I did, I wished I had been using it my entire life.

Standard Work vs. Improvement Work

Before you learn the Check System, we need to define the two types of work. Every work task you perform, at least in your financial life, falls into one of three categories:

- Useless Work
- Standard Work
- Improvement Work

Useless Work, otherwise known as "busy work" or "make-work" is work that accomplishes absolutely nothing other than to make you feel busy. It's bureaucratic paper-pushing or time-wasting that serves no purpose other than to help you procrastinate. It's a sad reality that much, or even most work done by employees of large corporations or governments is Useless Work. Useless Work is a waste of time, money, energy, and life. All Useless Work should be identified and removed from your life, permanently.

Standard Work is work that pays the bills. It's important and needs to be done, but that's all it accomplishes. It doesn't make you rich. It doesn't improve your happiness. All it does is maintain your current level of lifestyle, regardless if your annual income is $20,000 or $500,000. It needs to be done, and it keeps you from losing what you have, but it improves nothing.

Improvement Work is work that either definitely or potentially will increase your future income and/or lifestyle. When you do five hours of Improvement Work, it may not pay you any money that day, that week, or even that month. It may be months or even years later before the Improvement Work pays off. The good news is that when it does pay off, it pays off in far more money and profit than your Standard Work. Unlike Standard Work, Improvement Work enables you to improve your income and your lifestyle.

Useless Work wastes. Standard Work maintains. Improvement Work improves.

If you've made the same amount of money for many years, it simply means you've been focusing your financial life exclusively on Useless Work or Standard Work and have done little or no Improvement Work.

Obviously you need to stop doing all Useless Work tasks right now. Once you clarify your Mission and your societally independent goals and projects, it's likely you'll identify a few work tasks that you do at least semi-regularly that you really don't need to do at all. Stop doing these immediately, and use that time instead for Standard Work, Improvement Work, or other areas of your SLA. Just by doing this one step you will have improved your performance and productivity.

Unlike Useless Work, Standard Work isn't bad. You have to do it. If you don't do your Standard Work on a daily basis, you're going to be in big trouble pretty quickly. Soon you won't be able to pay your bills and a lot of people you work with or in your family are going to be very upset with you. The challenge is when you let Standard Work consume your entire work schedule. You need to do Standard Work, yes, but you also need to regularly shove some Improvement Work in there as well, or else you'll literally never improve your life (unless you get lucky).

Improvement Work is extremely important. However, the problem with Improvement Work is that it doesn't pay now. It usually pays later. That's why it's so hard to put Improvement Work into your regular schedule when there's all this Standard Work that needs to get done. Moreover, your Standard Work is guaranteed to pay the rent that's due this week, and Improvement Work won't. Improvement Work just doesn't call to you like Standard Work does. That's why very few people ever do Improvement Work, even if they intend to.

Both Standard Work *and* Improvement Work must be addressed on a regular basis if you want to be a happy, successful, fulfilled man. Not addressing Standard Work means you very quickly won't be able to pay your bills and/or maintain your current lifestyle. Not addressing Improvement Work means you'll always be stuck at your current income forever (and likely will run into huge problems when you try to retire).

The Check System is the solution to this problem.

Non-Financial Work

While Standard Work and Improvement Work apply directly to your financial life, you can apply these two concepts in similar ways to your other Seven Life Areas (SLA). For example, if your diet and weekly exercise routine stays the same forever, you'll likely never lose any fat or gain any muscle. Technically speaking, over time you would slowly gain fat and lose muscle due to aging. So even if you still went to the gym three times a week doing the exact same thing, you would maintain your health at best, but would never improve. Consider that your Standard Work within your physical life. If you wanted to radically improve your body, you'd shift Standard Work into Improvement Work, changing your diet and exercise in order to improve your physique. In all likelihood, physical Improvement Work may take more time and/or effort than Standard Work, but the results would be better.

Standard Work and Improvement Work can be applied to any of your SLA, including ones you wouldn't expect, like your woman life (such as learning and mastering new dating and relationship skills). So while I use financial examples for Standard Work and Improvement Work, remember these two types of work can apply to any area.

Habit Formation

One of the single greatest ways to achieve (and maintain) success in any area is to create new and positive habits in your life. This is a very obvious thing of course, but in our high-speed, information-overload world, this simple truth is often neglected.

The Check System can specifically help you create and install new habits into your daily routine, as well as ensure you put in the proper amount of time into daily Improvement Work.

The Check System Procedure

Here's how to put the Check System into practice.

1. Choose one to four work areas or habits you need to address daily. These should be things you do (or want to do) every day, at least five days a week. They can be in any part of the SLA you wish to maintain or improve

Examples would be:

- Waking up at a certain time in the morning (or going to bed at a certain time)
- Exercise
- Doing one hour of Improvement Work
- Spending one hour of quality time with your kids
- Reading for 30 minutes
- Regular Standard Work tasks that must get done
- Anything else you can think of that should require daily attention

One to four is a somewhat wide range, so base this number on how organized and consistent you are. If thus far in your life you have not been a very organized or focused person, just choose one or two daily items. If you have a much more focused personality you can choose three or even four daily items. The less the better. Rarely do I have more than three daily activities in my Check System; usually I only have two.

As an example, let's say you choose two areas. One is to run for 30 minutes every morning, and the other is to put in at least two hours of Improvement Work daily.

2. Draw or print a chart that represents the next seven days. On the first row, put the calendar date. On the next row, put the day of the week. The new two rows will be a blank square for each daily habit area. So keeping with our example, you would print out a one-week sheet showing the next seven days with two squares on each day. Like this:

The Check System

Date	Jun 6	Jun 7	Jun 8	Jun 9	Jun 10	Jun 11	Jun 12
Day	Fri	Sat	Sun	Mon	Tue	Wed	Thu
30 min run							
2 hours IW							

3. Always have this chart prominent on your desk or kitchen counter with a pen handy, so you're always seeing it.

4. Every time you do one of those things on its corresponding day, put a big fat checkmark into the corresponding box for the current day. So when you're done running on Friday morning, you'd put a checkmark into the "30 Minute Run" box for Friday. Your goal is to get both boxes checked by the end of the day, and have all 14 squares checked by the end of the week.

If you reach the end of the week with all 14 those boxes checked, you had a really fantastic, productive week! Even if you get most of the boxes checked, you still did a great job. Next week you'll have to do a little better. Either way, you've boosted your productivity, enhanced your life, and are well on the way to creating some new, empowering habits.

Make this a game for yourself. The Check System works because it engages the child side of your mind. Do you remember that little jolt of happiness you felt as a small child when your teacher put a shiny star sticker by your name up on the wall when you did something well? Well, I've got news for you: as an adult you work pretty much the same way. Use this to your advantage.

After doing this regularly for about 8-12 weeks, you'll find you have the habit of running every morning and doing daily Improvement Work, *even if you don't bother to check the boxes.* You will have ingrained these two new behaviors as automatic habits. You'll lose weight, feel better, and start making more money, all faster than you ever thought possible.

5. Eventually, one of those items will become such an automatic habit that you won't need to track it on your sheet any more. So delete that item and replace it with a new one. You'll still be doing it, because now it's a habit; you just won't need to track it any more.

Of course if you like tracking it and enjoy giving yourself checkmarks, then by all means continue doing it. Simply add one more item to start working on. The only rule here is that you can't go past four items on your weekly checklist.

This system is much more simple and fun than a to-do list. It's also great since it tells you, literally at a glance, how well you're doing in your current week. It's like having a personal success report card.

You can also get a fancy and customize your chart. For example, on some items I will black out the boxes for Saturdays and Sundays if I want to take a break on those days for those particular items.

If you're the creative type, feel free to get really silly with this. If you want to get big, flashy stickers and use those instead of writing a checkmark, go ahead. I realize that doesn't sound very manly or Alpha, but again, we're engaging the child part of your mind here. Do whatever works. If it makes you feel better, use more manly stickers like footballs, tanks, or TIE Fighters.

Life isn't perfect every day of course, so there will be some days you don't check all of your boxes. Daily recurring perfection is impossible; so if at the end of the week you see some empty boxes staring back at you, don't beat yourself up. You want to make sure that the vast majority of those boxes are checked at the end of the week. Then pat yourself on the back and print out a new fresh sheet for the next week.

If you find you are regularly not checking all the boxes by the end of the week, something is wrong and you need to make some adjustments:

- You probably have too many items. If you have three or four, drop them down to two, or even one. Remember, as we talked about above, you're not discarding those other items, you're just putting them on temporary pause. Once you get your current one or two down as an automatic routine, you can remove them and focus on the next two.

- Giving yourself one or two days off per week for certain items is perfectly acceptable. For example, you may decide that you want to run for 30 minutes a day, but just for five days a week. Pick the two days you want to take off from running, and shade those out with a different pattern or color, indicating that you don't have to place a checkmark in those days. At the end of the week, those days "don't count" for your total check marks.

Focus and regular time management skills are just like any other muscle. Over time, as you use the Check System and get better at it, you can increase its "difficultly level." For example, you can add more items than just two (never go past four however). You can also start tracking time periods longer than one week. Printing out a chart that covers two weeks or even an entire month is fine, just as long as you've been following the Check System with success for several weeks and have the hang of things.

Do not start out at an advanced level. Work up to it. If you've never been a very focused person, you need to take baby steps and start slow or you'll blow yourself out and get frustrated. Start with one-week time frames and one or two items per day, and go from there.

Which System?

As I said earlier, you can use the E3D System and the Check System together, or use just one or the other, or alternate between the two based on your current schedule and goals. Feel free to customize either system to better suit your personality and life situation.

At an absolute minimum, you should pick at least one of the above systems and begin to focus on it regularly. Proper time management is the leverage that makes all your other SLA work. It's just as important as having a strong Mission, for a Mission without a mechanism to get it done is just a pie in the sky dream.

Every remaining technique covered in this book assumes that you have actually done all the exercises starting back in Chapter 7 with your Seven Life Areas, Code, Mission, and goals, and that you are currently using either the E3D System, the Check System or both to manage your time to build (or maintain) your new Alpha 2.0 life.

Now that you've built a solid foundation, we're ready to discuss specific principles, strategies, and techniques for the woman and financial sides of your life.

Let's start with the ladies first...

Part Four

Your Women

Chapter 12 –

Overcoming Your Sexual Programming

Society is organized in such a way that the natural instincts of men are shameful and criminal while the natural instincts of women are mostly legal and acceptable.

Scott Adams

January 2009.

I was sitting across from two of my friends, guys I'll call Beta Bill and Alpha Albert. Beta Bill was the typical beta, several years into his second marriage, getting his ass kicked by his bitchy wife. Alpha Albert was an Alpha 1.0, very successful with women, having slept with more woman than even I had at that point, but often running into all kinds of drama and conflict in his relationships.

We were talking about the concept of women having sex with guys on the first date, and whether or not this was a good idea for women. I thought it was a fantastic idea for women as long as the guy was wearing a condom. Beta Bill and Alpha Albert had different ideas.

"I get hornier for a woman when she makes me wait a few dates," Beta Bill was saying, "So it's probably not a bad thing for women to make guys wait at least a little bit."

"I'm not any more or less horny for a woman on date one or date three or date five," I said, "And that's whether or not sex has happened. But if by date two or three there's no sex or she's still resisting sex, I get the strong feeling I'm wasting my time, and I could probably go have sex with someone else much faster."

"Well," Alpha Albert chimed in, "What if you guys get serious down the road? You don't want your girlfriend to be a slut!"

"How does a woman having sex with me quickly while I'm wearing a condom make her a slut?" I asked, "And since when are sluts a bad thing? Do you really care if a woman has slept with 10 guys or 100 guys? What difference does it make?"

"A lot of difference!" Albert roared.

I was surprised. I expected Bill to say something like that, but not a confident player like Albert.

"What?" I cried, "Albert, you've fucked, what, 180 women or something?"

"133," Alpha Albert said with a smile, "But I'm not counting."

"So you can have a history of fucking gazillions of people, but your future wife or girlfriend can't?" I asked.

"That's right!" Albert said in true Alpha 1.0 fashion, "I'm not going to marry trash!"

"You sleep with over 100 people and you're cool, but if she sleeps with over 100 people, she's trash. That doesn't make any sense. If that number of sexual partners makes her a bad spouse, it also has to make you a bad spouse as well. It's bullshit, Albert."

"No it's not! Would you marry a woman who had been with over 100 guys?!?"

"I don't do monogamy, because it doesn't work, so I wouldn't marry anyone," I said, "Nor would I expect any woman, under the age of about 60, I got into a serious, long-term relationship with me to remain monogamous forever. Eventually she'd either break up with me or cheat on me. In either case she'll end up having sex with some other dude. So this entire thing about how many guys she's been with, and whether or not her number makes for a Disney Fairytale Forever Marriage…it's completely irrelevant to me, and it should be to you too."

"My wife isn't going to fuck anyone else, or I'll throw her out the fuckin' window!" Alpha Albert roared, completely ignoring my point.

"C'mon," I said smiling, "If you got married, you'd cheat. You know you would."

"Well yeah," said Albert, shrugging, "Of course I would."

"So you can, but she can't," I said.

"Yeah," said Albert.

"And you actually think she'll actually put up with that long-term, over years or decades?"

"I'll make it work!" Alpha Albert said, "She'll respect me!"

"You guys are both animals," Beta Bill said, "Is sex all you guys think about? Jeez."

Your Greatest Barrier to a Fantastic Sex Life: YOU

This was one of the first times I realized that men, both betas and Alpha 1.0s, were loaded to the gills with destructive OBW and false SP regarding women and sex. It was a big wakeup call for me. Over the years since then, I have seen these "points," and similar ones, repeated by betas and Alpha 1.0s all over the world. Sadly, these men suffer all the usual consequences once they travel down the standard dating and relationships path of The Prison.

In the next several chapters, we're going to discuss specifically how to attract many women into your woman life (either as casual or serious relationships or both) and how to keep them there, all while maintaining your high levels of happiness and freedom. The biggest challenge to this is we're going to run smack dab into some hardcore OBW and SP you have in your brain regarding how women work, and the roles of women, sex, romance, and love in your life. Much of what you will learn over the next few chapters are going to be diametric opposites to what you've been told your entire life by your fellow inmates in The Prison. Some of your SP is going to be difficult to overcome.

The good news is that once you overcome these things, you will live a lifestyle that you hitherto have only dreamed of in your wildest fantasies.

I know what I'm talking about, since I have proved this in my life, time and again. Over the last several years I have slept with more women than the average 10 or 15 men will ever sleep with in their entire lives combined. These women were all at least an eight on the one-to-ten attractiveness scale (which of course is my opinion, since physical attractiveness is subjective from man to man). A significant percentage of these women were 15 or 20 years younger than me. Many others were around my age, and many were older, all the way to late forties and early fifties.

I've have slept with a diverse group of women, from dumb party "sluts" to lawyers and corporate vice presidents, from models and former models to financial analysts and ivy-league educated businesswomen, from women with five kids to women with no kids. Some women were divorced, some were never married, some had boyfriends, a small handful were married and cheating on their husbands, and several were married but in open marriages.

Life is not all about sex, of course. It's also about relationships. In my life I have been deeply in love, and had deep, serious relationships that lasted many years, including a marriage that lasted nine years. I've also had long-lasting casual friends-with-benefits relationships, and many relationships somewhere in-between these two extremes.

Since I know monogamy is not healthy for high sex drive men, and since I know that an Alpha Male lifestyle is impossible when being monogamous, I have never promised monogamy to anyone. (The one exception was when I was married for a few years as a younger beta male.) I am never dating fewer than three women, and all women I date know I am out having sex with other women, and they happily continue to date me anyway. Some of these relationships have been very serious, some have been casual, some have been somewhere in-between, but all of these relationships have been extremely rewarding, exciting, and happy experiences. The vast majority of these relationships are not short-term things; they last many, many years.

I have been teaching dating and relationship techniques to thousands of men for many years now, many of whom live the lifestyle I now have or a variation of it. This stuff is real, and possible for you if you desire it.

However! In many ways *you* will be your greatest enemy when it comes to meeting women, dating women, having sex with women, and being in sexual or romantic relationships with women. As we discussed back in Chapter 4, you have powerful biological wiring inside your outdated caveman DNA that compels you do to some very stupid things when it comes to women…things that will upset you and make you feel jealous, needy, angry, or lonely. As discussed back in Chapter 3, your mind is also full of completely false SP about how women should behave, how you should behave, and how women are "supposed to be," all of which will make you extremely unhappy in the long-term.

So before we get into exactly how to live the life of the Alpha 2.0, a life full of sexual freedom and fulfillment when it comes to women, we need to do our best to de-program the SP and lessen the OBW within your system.

The Desire for Sex

As we touched on back in the chapter on OBW, not all biological wiring is bad. Some brings us great pleasure as men. Instead of removing or suppressing these biological desires, these particular desires should be embraced. For example, you have strong biological urges to have sex often. Nothing wrong with that at all! Sex is the greatest single source of pleasure you can feel through your physical body alone. In terms of your raw physical existence in this universe, it doesn't get any better than sex. Yes, there are other things in life that are more fulfilling or perhaps even more pleasurable than sex, but all of these things are mental or spiritual, not physical. On the physical hierarchy of pleasures for a man, sex is at the top of the list. Consider these two facts:

- US revenue from porn is more than all the major American networks (ABC, CBS, and NBC) combined. Worldwide porn revenue is more than that of all the top American technology companies combined. That includes Microsoft, Google, Amazon, eBay, Yahoo, Apple, Netflix, and EarthLink[7].

- Besides bonobos and dolphins, no other animal in the entire animal kingdom, besides human beings, has sex completely for the purposes of enjoyment outside of female ovulation[8].

Human beings are more sexual than any other form of life on Earth. Because sex makes us happy, and because consistent happiness is critical for us as free Alphas, sex is good, desirable, and extremely important. You should be having sex regularly and often. I rarely let a week go by without having sex at least several times, even if I'm busy with my other SLA.

Even if sex weren't pleasurable, there would still be many reasons to do it regularly. Sex increases testosterone in men, and the more testosterone you have, the happier you are, the healthier you are, the longer you'll live, and the less health problems you'll have. Overwhelming research has shown that men with lower levels of testosterone are over four times more likely to suffer from clinical depression, fatal heart attacks, and cancer than other men their age with healthy testosterone levels. Men with lower testosterone are more likely to suffer Alzheimer's disease and other forms of dementia. Worst of all, they also have 88% to 200% higher odds of death by any cause at any age[9]. In other words, men with low testosterone are more likely to die in any given year.

Another good form of biological wiring is your desire for *sexual variety*. Back when you were a caveman, there were only several hundred thousand human beings on the entire planet Earth, and it was this way for thousands of years. Nature didn't want you having sex with your mother or your sisters, so it cleverly wired into you a strong desire to have sex with women you don't live with, since it figured that any women you'd be living with would be family members, and thus

---

[7] http://www.familysafemedia.com/pornography_statistics.html

[8] http://www.snopes.com/critters/wild/pleasure.asp

[9] *Sex At Dawn* by Christopher Ryan and Cacilda Jethá

unsuited for bearing your children. Therefore, you are literally wired to get bored having sex with just one woman all the time, especially if you live with her, even if you deeply love her. She's wired to get bored with you too, even more so (we'll be discussing that in the next chapter). You still want to have sex with that one woman, but you want to have sex with other women as well.

I don't even need to explain this to you because likely you've already experienced these desires. If you get a serious, monogamous girlfriend, or get married, and no matter how pretty she is, no matter how wonderful she is, no matter how good she is for you, and no matter how strongly you love her, within a matter of a few months or years, you'll want to start having sex with other women in addition to her.

This is normal and natural. It's the way you are designed from the ground-up as a man. There's nothing wrong, evil, or selfish about it. If you attempt to suppress this desire, you will damage your life, your happiness, and your health.

You need to have a lot of sex, always! The first step to doing this is to clear your false beliefs about sex.

The Four False Sex Beliefs

Because of OBW and the SP of The Prison, often embodied by the 6SV (the Six Societal Values), there are four false beliefs regarding sex likely installed in your head that are causing you all kinds of pain and problems in your life. You may have some or all of them. These are:

1. "Sex is bad / wrong / immature / selfish / inappropriate. It should only be done under certain specific conditions in order to be appropriate and acceptable."
2. "Absolute sexual monogamy at all times is required for serious relationships."
3. "A woman I'm having sex with should never be getting sexual with other men, but it's perfectly fine if I sleep with other women."
4. "A woman who has already had sex with many other men is unsuitable for a serious relationship with me, but it's perfectly fine if I have had sex with a lot of women."

I'm sure that while reading some of those four things, you were nodding your head in agreement with at least one or two of them. This is bad. You read that right. It's bad. Why? Because it is impossible for you to live an Alpha 2.0 life if you strongly adhere to any of those four beliefs. Let me say that again:

It is impossible for you to live the Alpha 2.0 lifestyle if you strongly adhere to any of the Four False Sex Beliefs.

I mean it. If you cling to any of those above four beliefs, the best you can hope to achieve is Alpha 1.0 status, a reasonably good life of being happy sometimes, but while being angry, jealous, hurt, or offended at many other times. You also won't be as free as an Alpha 2.0, since you will (grudgingly) agree to all kinds of rules from the women in your life.

Your desire to cling to one or more of the above beliefs comes directly from OBW or SP. As always, this stuff is completely, 100% false. In no way does it reflect your reality as a powerful, independent man living in the Western world in the 21st century. It is simply outdated "Grog the Caveman" biology and false programming from rich, powerful old men who have been long dead, and frankly wouldn't give a shit about you if they were still alive.

Let's tackle each one of these false beliefs.

Why You Think Sex Is a Little "Bad"

It's quite likely that if you're already reading this book, you probably don't have a huge problem with the first False Sex Belief, that sex is somehow wrong and that it's only appropriate under a few specific conditions. Regardless, this belief is at the root of the other three false beliefs. The more we work to destroy this belief, the easier it will be to deal with the other three.

The SP within you, telling you that sex is perhaps just a little inappropriate, is the result of 10,000 years of false programming from the elites. This first started when cultural monogamy began, way back when humans moved from a foraging existence to an agricultural one. For thousands of years, men were taught that women were property and thus a specific set of rules around the activity of sex were "required."

Over time, this morphed into concept of *guilt* in Western cultures and *shame* in Eastern ones. Guilt and shame are extraordinarily powerful forces the elites have used very effectively to rule over The Prison. People having sex with people they weren't supposed to often meant ostracization, imprisonment, expulsion, torture, amputation, and even death.

This all became even worse about 2000 years ago with the fall of the Roman Empire and the rise of Christianity at the dawn of the Dark Ages. For hundreds of years the Catholic Church ruled the Western world, even requiring sovereign kings to pay it homage. Extremely powerful and intelligent men within the church like St. Augustine spent countless hours writing, lecturing, scolding, and philosophizing about how evil and terrible sex was. Men like him even hated that married people had to have sex, but stated that it was "acceptable" if you had sex with no lust within you as the act was committed. Isn't that nice?

Soon, various powerful religious sects sprang up all over Europe that doubled down on these concepts. They believed, taught, and enforced that sex between two people within a marriage was even worse than infidelity, since marriage involved more sex than cheating did.

They also made it a sin to eat animals; not because eating animals was unkind to animals or because meat was bad for you. No, it was because animals were created from sex, and you didn't want to eat something created by sex, did you? Perish the thought! Humorously, they did offer exceptions for eating fish, since fish reproduce without sex.

Do you see the level of thought and analysis that was put into all of this crap? Not to mention the time, effort, monetary expense, and violence involved in enforcing all these concepts. It's important to reiterate that these were not crazy ideas back then; they were perfectly normal and accepted and as just as real to society as mountains or rivers.

The damage these concepts caused to civilization was extreme and long-lasting. To quote philosopher Bertrand Russell:

It is strange that the last men of intellectual eminence before the Dark Ages were concerned not with saving civilization, or expelling the barbarians, or reforming the abuses of the administration, but with preaching the merit of virginity and the damnation of unbaptized infants. Seeing that these were the preoccupations that the church added on to the converted barbarians, it is no wonder that the succeeding age surpassed almost all other historical periods in cruelty and superstition[10].

As the centuries wore on, these attitudes moved into the more modern ages. In 1850, *The New Orleans Medical and Surgical Journal* declared masturbation was public enemy number one, warning "Neither plague, nor war, nor smallpox, nor crowd of similar evils have resulted more disastrously for humanity than the habit of masturbation. It is the destroying element of civilized society."

Talk about Societal Programming! Just like in the Dark Ages, the men saying these things were some of the most intelligent and knowledgeable men in society. Their words were given great weight and heeded.

---

[10] *The History of Western Philosophy* by Bertrand Russell

Since then, Western society has been blasted with messages like this non-stop for literally hundreds of years. It's even worse in Middle Eastern and East Indian cultures. Only with the sexual revolution of the 1960s and first wave feminism of the 1970s did this barrage of anti-sex SP begin to slow down, but even then the slowdown was minor. That wasn't very long ago, and a few decades of comparatively less anti-sex SP does little to blunt the long centuries of this garbage.

As a result, the damage caused from all of this lingers on in your head right now, whether you know it or not, and whether you believe it or not. If you want to live the Alpha 2.0 lifestyle of freedom and happiness, you can't submit to that false SP anymore.

You need to understand a basic truism of sex, and that is this:

There is nothing wrong, selfish, inappropriate, immoral, hurtful, dirty, or immature about having sex with anyone you want at any time, provided both partners are consenting adults and a condom is used.

If you want to have sex with…

- A woman you're not married to? Fine.
- A woman you're not in a serious relationship with? Fine.
- A woman 25 years younger than you? Fine, as long as she's legal.
- A woman 25 years older than you? Fine.
- A woman you just met and have only known for five minutes? Fine.
- A woman who has promised monogamy to someone else? Fine (if you have trouble with that one, stick with me through the next section on monogamy).
- A woman who's had sex with 200 men? Fine. Be sure to use a good condom!
- The mother, daughter, sister, or best friend of someone you know, or have known, or have dated? Fine.
- A woman who's had six children? Fine.
- A woman who is "low quality?" Fine. Just don't get into a relationship with her; keep it to sex only.

If you had any problems with any of the above examples, let me repeat the only three sexual parameters that do matter:

1. The sex must be 100% consensual for both her and you. That means she can give consent (if she's passed out or on roofies then she can't give consent, so you need to stay away).
2. You must both be legal adults, as defined in your country, state, or province. Remember, as we discussed back in Chapter 1, the Alpha Male 2.0 obeys the law.
3. You're wearing a good condom, unless you're with a very trusted, long-term partner.

I will add a fourth exception that is unusual and situational:

4. If having sex with her will cause serious drama with someone you care about, then stay away.

For example, I would never sleep with the wife of a man I was personal friends with or personally worked with. That's pretty much guaranteed to give me drama and disrupt my life at some point. My happiness will be reduced, and we can't have that. In those rare cases I'll pass, and so should you, no matter how hot she is or how badly she wants you. However, realize I'm not passing because it's somehow wrong, immoral, or bad to have sex. It's because sex in that particular isolated circumstance will reduce my happiness.

Fortunately these situations are rare. If a woman is married to a man I've never met and never will meet and she's gorgeous and dying to have sex with me, I'll go there. If a woman breaks up with a friend or coworker of mine and a year later wants to have sex with me, no problem. In other words, the damage to my happiness is the deciding factor, not the OBW, SP or the 6SV surrounding this thing called "sex."

Condomed sex is strictly a physical act between two consenting adults, just like shaking hands. You're just placing a piece of skin inside a woman's piece of skin. That's all it is. Any other meaning you attach to it beyond a simple handshake-like act is strictly because someone has told you differently (SP) or because the long-obsolete caveman in you thinks it has something to do with being trespassed upon (OBW). We've already established that both of those things are false. *Sex is a strictly physical act where your mind is placing meaning upon something that doesn't exist.*

Am I saying there are no physical, real-world ramifications to sex? Not at all. If you don't use condoms you could get a woman pregnant. If you sleep with the wrong kinds of women while condomless, you could get an STD. Repeatedly orgasming with the same partner releases chemicals such as oxytocin and vasopressin into the brain that helps to solidify a temporary bond. That's nice, but sadly, given several years, those same chemicals will *reduce* sexual passion for that person by interfering with dopamine and norepinephrine pathways in the brain[11]. This is yet another reason why men and women eventually get sexually bored with long-term partners.

I've already covered the issue of pregnancy and STDs by saying that one of the requirements of "valid" sex is condom use. The dopamine problem is alleviated by never getting absolutely monogamous, which we'll discuss in the next section.

Once you take the few physical negatives of sex out of the equation, the remaining ramifications are all positive, such as extreme physical pleasure, happiness, a self-esteem boost (if she's really pretty), exercise, increased testosterone, stress relief, reduced odds of prostate cancer and other ailments, and many others.

Am I saying there is *never* an emotional component to sex? Of course not! There certainly can be a strong romantic, emotional, and/or spiritual connection with a woman during sex if you've been having sex with her for a long time and she means a great deal to you. We'll be discussing love and serious sexual relationships in future chapters. The point here is very often you'll be having sex with women who are quite new to your life, or women to whom you are physically attracted to but not attracted to in any other way. Rarely in these cases will sex be any more than an enjoyable physical act, which is perfectly okay.

Absolute Monogamy Is Never Required, or Even Ideal

Likely you might have already been in agreement with the above "sex is okay" stuff. That's a reasonably easy one to overcome for most people. Yet when we start talking about monogamy, that's where the hard work really begins.

Most people these days, at least those under the age of 50 or so, have no huge problem with people dating, having casual sex, or even having sex with more than one person. The one caveat people add to this is that the sex must be casual in these cases. As long as the sex is casual and doesn't mean anything, then sleep around all you want.

However, if you want a "serious" relationship, or children, or marriage, then you have to "settle down" and "grow up" and be

[11] http://people.howstuffworks.com/love7.htm

absolutely, 100% monogamous in every way for years and years, if not decades.

Just like most other SP, this is completely false. I shall explain why.

I have been teaching open relationship skills to men for many years now. I find that men tend to fall into one of six categories in terms of monogamy belief:

1. Monogamy is the only way to date a woman, period.
2. Monogamy is the only way to date a woman, but occasional threesomes are acceptable.
3. Open relationships are great as long as they're casual. If you really like a woman, then you have to be monogamous.
4. Serious, loving open relationships are great, as long as you don't have kids. If you want to actually have kids with a woman, then you need to be monogamous.
5. Open relationships and open marriages are great, even while having children, as long as one is discreet about it.
6. Monogamy of any kind, at any time, is evil and oppressive.

While I consider category six a little extreme, you should consider mentally achieving category five if Alpha 2.0 status is important to you. Millions of couples, married or otherwise, with kids or otherwise, are carrying on serious open relationships or marriages and having a fantastic time.

A few facts:

- According to a recent article in Newsweek magazine, polyamorous families (where there's three or more people sexually committed to each other) number approximately half a million marriages in the United States[12]. Remember, that's not people, that's marriages!
- That's just *polyamorous* marriages. That half a million figure is dwarfed by the number of marriages where one or both spouses are allowed to go "play around" as long as they keep things discreet.
- In an e-book I wrote called *How to Create or Convert to an Open Marriage*[13], I interviewed over 40 couples who were

[12] http://www.newsweek.com/polyamory-next-sexual-revolution-82053
[13] http://www.open-marriage.com/

married or living together in an open relationship or marriage, and more than 40% of them were raising small children.

- Researchers tell us that couples with open marriages rate satisfaction with marriage and their lives in general higher than people with standard monogamous marriages[14].

You know, those great monogamous marriages where the husband is complaining about all the stuff he's not allowed to do, and where the wife is rolling her eyes about how stupid her husband is? All the drama, rules, fighting, cheating, divorces, custody battles and screwed-up children? Not to mention the lack of sex, since 20% of American couples have sex less than 10 times per year, and 30% to 50% of married women say they have "little or no sex drive."[15]

That's the monogamous world, and it's not a world you can have any part of if you want the life of sexual fulfillment, freedom, and happiness that only an Alpha 2.0 can achieve.

We're going to discuss exactly how to love a woman under a nonmonogamous structure in future chapters. For now, let me state an unyielding truth:

Unless you have a very low sex drive, long-term happiness is impossible for a man if you consider absolute monogamy the only way to love a woman. You must always have the freedom to have sex with whomever you like at all times, whether you are serious or not, in love or not, or a father or not.

I realize that may not be what you wanted to hear, and that your SP may be screaming at you that it's not so, but it's a fundamental reality of the human male, and there is no getting around this. Men are not built for long-term monogamy. We never were.

Betas and Alpha 1.0s spend their entire lives trying their hardest to weasel around this unbreakable law. Beta males constantly struggle sexually with their girlfriends or wives in long-term relationships or marriages, often wanting more sex than their lover provides. Many flee to areas such as internet porn, excessive masturbation, chatting with strange women online, or flirting with other women they know. Others just shut themselves down sexually, damaging their physical and psychological health, resulting in reduced testosterone, weight gain, and other health issues.

---

[14] *Sex At Dawn* by Christopher Ryan and Cacilda Jethá

[15] *Sex At Dawn* by Christopher Ryan and Cacilda Jethá

Alpha Male 1.0s just cheat a lot. Moreover, since men have strong SP to brag about sexual conquests, Alpha 1.0s almost always end up getting caught because they can't keep their big mouths shut. Then massive relationship drama ensues, and often the relationship or marriage ends. Badly.

All of these problems can be avoided by simply refusing to be absolutely monogamous in the first place. We'll discuss exactly how to do this in future chapters.

The True Goal of Monogamy

Monogamy is a direct result of both OBW and SP. Because of this, it's not something that will make you happy long-term. Monogamy serves The Prison. It ensures that you will calm down, shut up, not make too many waves, and behave like a good little inmate. Here's why monogamy is strongly supported by The Prison:

- The government loves monogamy since it makes it easier to tax your income and regulate your personal life (including imposing all kinds of laws on you regarding cohabitation, marriage, child rearing, and divorce).
- Big business loves monogamy because it makes it easier to sell you all kinds of expensive crap you would never consider purchasing if you didn't have a traditional girlfriend or wife. As just one example, back in the 1930s big business used monogamy to successfully trick men into spending thousands of dollars on worthless stones called "diamonds" if they ever wanted to propose to a woman[16]. This false SP persists even to this day.
- Religion loves monogamy since it provides a framework to control you via guilt and fear.
- Women don't really like long-term monogamy (70%-80% of all divorces are initiated by the female[17]) but they love the *illusion* of monogamy because they benefit from it financially, far more than men do.
- Beta males love monogamy because it provides them avenues to have sex with women they wouldn't normally get

[16] http://www.youtube.com/watch?v=N5kWu1ifBGU

[17] National Center for Health Statistics, American Law and Economics Review, Divorce Source Research Center (Atlanta, Georgia), and various other sources

a chance with. By bribing women with free drinks, free dinners, gifts, paying their bills, and paying for the cost of raising their children, beta males are able to get women to have sex with them.

- Alpha Male 1.0s, while they hate monogamy and are rarely *actually* monogamous (no Alpha Male, 1.0 or 2.0, is monogamous for very long; Alpha 1.0s cheat often), they will go along with monogamous structures, even if reluctantly, because they view it as a way to keep other men from having sex with "their" woman. Hypocritically, these men will often have sex with women on the side and eventually get caught and suffer all the usual consequences.

Monogamy's goal is not to make you happy. Its goal is to serve The Prison, primarily the Six Societal Values (6SV), which if you recall are: conformity, security, control over others, drama, social validation, and not being alone. Getting monogamous may give you a temporary high when the relationship is brand new (or when you get married, or first move in together, or have your first baby), and it may satisfy some of your 6SV by making you look like everyone else and making you think your relationship is secure. However, it will eventually make you unhappy, especially if you are a strong, confident, dynamic, sexual man. This also goes for women, who don't like long-term monogamy any more than men do, but do a much better job of pretending they do.

What Is The Real Goal?

Business author Steve Kaplan once posed an interesting question:

"Would you rather own a $1 million business with a $300,000 profit, or a $10 million business with a $100,000 profit?"[18]

This hit home with me when I read it, because as a business consultant with over 20 years of experience, I have indeed worked with business owners in both categories. People with the larger, less profitable businesses often think they're something special, because they can point at a big building and say, "See? I'm successful." They don't realize that the business owner with the small, more profitable business not only makes way more money than they do, but also likely works fewer hours, has less stress, has a more flexible schedule, and is happier.

I know a few people who have marriages that have lasted 30 years or more. While there are some happy, long-term married couples, most

[18] *Bag the Elephant*, by Steve Kaplan

people who have been traditionally married this long are usually stressed out, jaded, snippy, nonsexual, and often deride their spouses (either in public or in private). They're married, but they aren't happy. They can point at their 30-year marriage and say "See? I'm successful." At the same time, the Alpha Male 2.0 likely isn't married at all, but is far happier, less stressed, more excited about life, and still loves and is loved by someone very special.

A commenter on my dating and relationships blog[19] once opined, "Isn't what we want a high number of wedding anniversaries?" Notice where his focus is: on a numerical representation of anniversaries rather than his own happiness.

It's classic happiness vs. the 6SV.

Monogamy Damages Your Health

Human beings were never designed for long-term sexual monogamy. This is why the divorce rate in most American and European cities is well over 60%, and why the infidelity rate in those married couples who never divorce is often as high as 77%[20]. This is also why married men have lower testosterone levels than unmarried men of the same age. Just the act of a man's wife having a baby drops his testosterone levels by as much as 30%[21].

On the other hand, clinical studies have shown us that if a married man does nothing more than a 20 minute chat with a young, beautiful woman, his testosterone instantly shoots up 14%. Older men, including older married men, who have sex with a new young woman experience boosts in their testosterone levels, resulting in increased sexual desire *for their wives*, since more testosterone equals a higher overall sex drive. This is even true if the younger woman is dumber, uglier, and/or worse in bed than his wife![22].

---

[19] http://www.blackdragonblog.com/

[20] http://www.huffingtonpost.com/robert-hughes/is-the-us-divorce-rate-go_b_4908201.html
http://www.dailymail.co.uk/news/article-1377940/Half-parents-split-16-births-outside-marriage-hit-highest-level-200-years.html
http://www.census.gov/hhes/socdemo/marriage/data/acs/index.html
http://www.census.gov/hhes/socdemo/marriage/data/sipp/index.html
http://www.huffingtonpost.com/2013/06/12/gray-divorce_n_3429703.html
http://magazine.foxnews.com/love/cheating-statistics-do-men-cheat-more-women
http://www.washingtonpost.com/opinions/five-myths-about-cheating/2012/02/08/gIQANGdaBR_story.html
http://magazine.foxnews.com/love/are-you-semi-happy-marriage
http://www.care2.com/greenliving/are-only-17-of-marriages-happy.html

[21] *Sex At Dawn* by Christopher Ryan and Cacilda Jethá

[22] *Sex At Dawn* by Christopher Ryan and Cacilda Jethá

Men in the Western world have been fighting monogamy, and losing, for thousands of years. It's time to remove yourself from this battle and join the ranks of the Alpha 2.0s out there who can have sex whenever they choose, and without having to hide it or lie about it.

A Hidden Benefit to Non-monogamy

The obvious benefit to being nonmonogamous is that you can have sex with other women besides your favorite one. No woman will have absolute control over your body and your sexual actions, maintaining Freedom of Action we discussed back in Chapter 1.

However, there is another benefit that is equally beneficial. It is that not being monogamous actually maintains or even increases the attraction the woman in your life has for you, rather than having her attraction decrease over time, which is a standard characteristic of monogamy.

When a man submits to a woman's SP-based relationship rules (monogamy being one of many), saying in effect, "I will do what you want me to do," even if she's outwardly happy, her sexual attraction for him decreases, even if just a little. When a man refuses to submit sexually, even if she appears upset, her attraction increases, or at least stays the same.

When a woman clearly sees that she can't "tame" you, that she can't completely control you, her attraction for you stays strong, even if she is bothered by your actions. This is where the whole "women are attracted to assholes" concept comes from. Of course the goal of the Alpha 2.0 is to handle these relationships in a harmonious way with a woman so as to avoid drama and unhappiness. Being an "asshole" is the realm of some Alpha 1.0s.

It's a difficult concept to describe if you've never been in a nonmonogamous relationship before, but the first time you try it you'll see what I mean (provided you do it correctly).

Open Relationships Must Go Both Ways if Something Long-Term is Desired

The third of the Four False Sex Beliefs likely rolling around in your head is that while it might be okay for you to go have sex with other women, the woman in your life must not be allowed to have sex with other men.

If you're like most men, the thought of the woman in your life getting even a little sexual with another man will send your inner-Grog

OBW into a fierce rage of fiery anger. It will also send your SP into all kinds of righteous indignation about "respect" and "honor" and other false SP concoctions.

The sad reality of this, and I'm no more happy about this than you are, is that long-term nonmonogamous relationships cannot last if only you are allowed to sleep with other people. If you're going to have sex with other women, she must at least have the option of being able to sleep with other men, under whatever rules you both agree to. It simply cannot work any other way, unless all you want in life is a bunch of very short relationships.

Why? Because women in the modern era, even the more submissive ones, are simply not going to stick around long-term not having sex with other guys while you're out playing with other women all the time. It's just not going to happen. Remember I said *long-term*. It is true that in the *short-term* you could bully a submissive or lovestruck woman into agreeing to a relationship like this. Some Alpha 1.0s do pull this off sometimes. That might work for a while, but it never lasts. Eventually the woman either cheats on you behind your back, or leaves.

If you want a *long-term* nonmonogamous relationship, you're going to have to be fair about this. The good news is that often the woman in your life won't be having sex with other men even though you'll be having sex with other women. We'll discuss that in a minute.

Your challenge, then, is your own jealousy. You're going to have to learn to control it. Here's how.

Jealousy Management

Let me start by saying that it's not my contention that I never get jealous when one of my more serious women has sex with some other guy. I'm a confident, outcome independent Alpha Male 2.0 with a strong Mission, so I don't get very jealous, nor do I get jealous often like normal men. I have much more important things in my life to concern myself with than worrying about if the woman in my life is out having sex (usually bad sex) with some beta male who drools all over her like a starving puppy. These men are not my competition anyway.

Regardless, I can feel a little twinge of jealousy sometimes. It's not common but it can happen. I'm human and a little bit of this OBW is unavoidable.

During those rare times when I feel this twinge, I come to a complete stop and remind myself of three facts:

First, I remember that my jealousy is completely obsolete in the modern world, a holdover from my outdated caveman DNA from 100,000 years ago when child-bearing women were scarce commodities and sexual jealousy did actually serve a survival-and-replication-based purpose. As we've discussed, monogamy was further reinforced in society when we became an agrarian people, and needed children to work on our farms. Men needed to make sure that their children were really their children and not their neighbor's children. This monogamy-enforcement was worsened by religion in later years.

The problem is none of these things are factors any more. Nowadays we have DNA paternity testing that specifically identifies if children are yours or not. We also have literally hundreds of millions of single, young, attractive women all over the planet who will happily have sex with you without you having to marry them or promise them anything.

Under these conditions, sexual jealousy no longer serves a rational, functional purpose. It just pisses you off for no reason.

Whenever you're getting sexually jealous, it's just Grog again. He saved your life back when you were living in a cave or on an ancient farm, and that's great. Now, in the 21st century, he's just an obsolete idiot, serving no purpose whatsoever, other than pissing you off for absolutely zero reason and causing you to act like a child.

Second, I remember that plenty of jealousy exists in monogamous relationships too. It's not like being monogamous eliminates jealousy. Are you kidding me? Just watch someone take a good long look at their monogamous partner's phone or Facebook page and you'll see that jealousy is alive and well in monogamous relationships. "Going monogamous" just to avoid jealousy is one of the dumbest things people do.

That brings up another point. If you're a jealous person, you're going to be jealous no matter what relationship type you choose. Monogamous, open, semi-open, swinger, polyamorous, it doesn't matter, if you have a jealous personality, you're going to be jealous. The problem isn't the relationship model you choose, and it's not the partner you pick; no, it's *your* jealousy issues.

I know from experience that the women I've dated who are really jealous in open relationships were just as jealous when they had monogamous boyfriends prior to me (or after me!). I see this happen with men too. A guy is really jealous of his girlfriend; they break up; he gets a new girlfriend, and he's just as jealous again.

Not good.

Third and most importantly, I remember all the huge negatives of monogamy that I never have to worry about. This includes:

1. Drama
2. Rules
3. Boredom
4. Financial expense
5. Financial risk
6. Cheating (both getting cheated on, and getting caught when *you* cheat).
7. Lack of freedom
8. Eventual lack of sex
9. Bad breakups or divorces
10. Restrictions on things like travel, moving, or hanging out with friends

I ask myself this: Would I take the one negative of occasional jealousy (some of which I would feel in a monogamous relationship anyway!) instead of the ten (or more) negatives of monogamy?

Of course I would. I would happily trade in ten negatives for one negative. That's smart. Especially if my goal in life is consistent, long-term happiness, as opposed to intense but temporary happiness followed by unhappiness, which is what monogamy gives people.

This is the thought that usually does it for me. I feel the little pang of jealousy, remind myself it's an emotion with no reason, and it's a very tiny price to pay for the massive amounts of freedom, joy, and happiness I have in my life by not being monogamous. Sleeping with all the women you want with the permission of the women you're already having sex with, without having to hide it, is a really, really good deal.

Having a healthy self-esteem, a full life, exciting goals, and a strong Mission also helps, as we've already discussed in prior chapters.

Anti-Jealousy Visualization Technique

If none of that is doing it for you, you can utilize a visualization technique first taught by Harry Browne back in the 1970s[23], when nonmonogamous relationships started to become more recognized in society.

---

[23] *How I Found Freedom In An Unfree World* by Harry Browne

It's very simple. All you do is calmly visualize the woman in your life having sex with another man. To make this really work, visualize a man who is much better looking than you are. If you are already very good looking, then visualize a man who is older than you or has much more money than you. In other words, visualize the woman in your life having fantastic sex with the most sexually threatening man you can think of.

Just by doing this, you may realize that your jealousy wasn't nearly as bad as you first thought. You may visualize this and get a twinge of jealousy, but then think, "Eh, no big deal. This isn't as bad as I thought."

On the other hand, upon visualizing this for the first time, you may suddenly feel very hurt, violated, or angry. Grog the Caveman will start screaming his head off in your mind, and you may even get visibly upset.

This is fine. The angrier you get visualizing this, the more you need to visualize it. Keep going, keep visualizing. Work through the hurt, fear, and anger you feel. If you're like most men, after a few minutes your anger and hurt will diminish. After a while, it will bother you so little that you may actually be distracted and want to go do something else.

Repeat this technique a few times over the next few days or weeks. Every time you do it, you will probably feel less jealous. Keep reminding yourself of the three anti-jealousy facts above as well.

Jealousy is a solvable problem. Never use it as an excuse to not do what will make you truly happy in the long-term.

Why Letting Her Be Sexually Open Is a Good Deal for YOU

It's more than likely that your SP and OBW are still fighting you on this. So I'm going to deal the final deathblow to your SP and OBW here by describing five reasons why it's a good thing for you to allow your woman to play around with other men if you yourself are playing around with women on the side. (Again, I'm also assuming that you want something long-term and not short-term. If all you want are brief, short-term relationships, than you can forget all of this and do whatever you like.)

1. Number one, top of the list, it frees you from having to babysit her. You have better things to do with your time. At least, you should.

These men who scour their girlfriend's email, phone, Facebook, etc., looking for clues of other men always make me wonder, "Don't you have anything better to do with your time? Do you like babysitting your girlfriend/wife as if she's seven years old? Does that really make you happy? Don't you have any goals, dreams, plans, objectives, and passions that are more important, and that you'd rather be spending your time on? Is this teenage-level jealousy really that important?"

Worrying about whether or not the woman in your life is flirting with or sleeping with other men shows strong outcome dependence on your part. Babysitting her constantly and getting upset when she interacts with other men will never make you happy. It's so much more freeing, both emotionally and logistically, knowing what she does outside of her time with you is mostly unimportant to your life.

2. It makes it much harder for her to get upset with you when you sleep with other women.

Guys often forget about this one. I've already explained how no Western woman will ever go for the you-can-sleep-with-other-women-but-she-can't-sleep-with-other-men thing long-term.

Now let's discuss the reverse. When a woman is allowed to get sexual with men on the side, it makes it very difficult for her to complain that you're doing the same, even if she is currently not sleeping with any men. The point is, she's allowed to, and she knows it.

Some women are not very logical of course, and I'm not guaranteeing you'll never hear about it, but you'll hear far, far less of it if she's at least allowed to play around. This is a huge plus for you as a nonmonogamous man living a life with minimum drama and maximum happiness.

3. The men she has sex with on the side are almost always going to be beta males. This will further demonstrate the contrast between you and typical men in The Prison and will actually serve to heighten her attraction for you. Sounds crazy? I'll prove it.

Here's what often happens. I'll start dating and having sex with a woman. Slowly, we'll start getting more serious, but it takes months for me to do so. Of course I'll keep sleeping with other women on the side. Eventually, she might start having sex with men on the side if she wasn't already (or she might not; we'll discuss that happy situation in a moment).

When she actually has sex with a new guy, he's almost always a beta. We'll call him Poindexter. He'll instantly fall in love with her and start begging her to do things like break up with me, meet his parents, move in with him, marry him, and/or tons of other needy beta male behaviors. Often he'll do these things not after months of dating, but after having sex with her just one or two times.

Men do this all the time. Ever-consumed by SP and OBW, neediness is men's “default setting” when it comes to women. If you don’t believe me, ask a few single women and they’ll tell you all about it.

The contrast between him and me will be stunning. It’s all laid out before her in stark, crystal-clear reality. She now fully understands, likely for the first time in her life, the true difference between an Alpha and a beta.

What do you think happens to her attraction for me? It goes *up*.

There’s an even greater benefit to this, and it’s almost one you have to experience for yourself to believe. She will now fully understand the type of men she’ll have to contend with if she ever leaves me. This really makes women think about the future of their long-term marriages or relationships. “If I break up with him, I’ll probably end up in a relationship with a guy like…Poindexter!” Sometimes this realization alone changes their entire view of men and relationships. I’ve seen this happen with women many times.

Is there a risk that she'll fall in love with all the ass-kissing she receives from Poindexter, and leave you for him? Sure. Just like in normal monogamous relationships, there is a nonzero chance that will happen. However, unlike in monogamous relationships, if a woman does leave you, there's a high probability she'll come back. Ass-kissing from beta males is enjoyable to women for a while, but eventually, women get very, very bored with this. If they instead opt for an Alpha Male 1.0, eventually women will tire of the rules, arguments, and drama from these men. They will once again desire the fun, excitement, great sex, and drama-free aspects of the Alpha Male 2.0.

I've kept careful track of this over the years. In well over 30 nonmonogamous relationships with women, 94% of them who “left” me for a “normal” monogamous boyfriend eventually came back to me and resumed the sexual relationship. I'm not bragging. I'm telling you exactly what you can have if you assume this relationship model. The Alpha 2.0 is more attractive to a woman than a beta (or even an Alpha 1.0) and always will be regardless of her temporary provider-seeking needs generated by her SP and OBW.

4. The fantasy of “I can have sex with other women but she can’t have sex with other men” does not work in the Western world.

I mentioned this above but it’s so important I’m going to hit you with it again. I have found that many men, usually Alpha 1.0s, fantasize about a relationship where they can have sex with hot women on the side while their wife or girlfriend is at home knitting a sweater while 100% faithful, never leaving him and never getting sexual with other men, ever.

That system might work in some areas of the Middle East or Southeast Asia, but every man I have seen attempt a serious relationship like this in the Western world always ends up with a fed-up woman who divorces or breaks up with him, or a resentful woman who eventually has covert sex with other men in an attempt to make things more "fair" in the relationship.

I have never seen this type of one-sided relationship work longer than about a year or so without one of those two things occurring. Plan on that result if you intend on pursuing this fantasy.

5. Much more often than you would think, women won't have sex with other men even if they're aware you're having sex with other women.

This is somewhat the inverse of number four above, yet it's still true.

I have vast experience over many years of having open relationships with many women, including some very serious ones. I also know and have worked with many other men all over the world who possess a similar level of experience in this area. I can tell you for a fact that very often, women won't have sex with other men even if they know you're out playing around. Sometimes they will, but sometimes they won't. A lot of men tend to disbelieve this because they assume women are just like us when it comes to sexual desire. They aren't.

Men are always horny. It doesn't matter if you had a good day or a bad day. It doesn't matter if you're having a horrible month or the greatest month in your life. It doesn't matter if you're 22 years old or 47 years old. It doesn't matter if you have no kids or five kids. You still want to have sex almost all the time. That's how men work.

Women are not like this. Yes, women are horny too, extremely so. I have made the argument that women are more sexual than men are. The difference is that women aren't always in "horny mode." Sometimes they are, but sometimes they're not.

As we'll discuss in more detail in the next chapter, women are highly cyclical people, constantly changing, constantly going from one phase to the next. Here are some phases women go through, just to name a few:

- High sex drive, horny phases
- "Slutty" phases

- "Sex is no big deal" phases
- "I'm liberated and can have sex whenever and with whomever I want!" phases
- "I can't have sex unless he's my boyfriend because I'm a lady" phases
- "I'm too busy for men in my life right now" phases
- "I feel too bloated to have sex" phases
- "I hate men right now" phases
- "I have a new baby so I can't have sex right now" phases
- "I'm a Christian and can't have a lot of sex" phases
- "I just got divorced and I need to focus on my kids" phases
- "I need to focus on my career (or education)" phases

Most women hit most of those phases at some point in their lives. During some of these phases she's going to be very horny and have lots of sex, possibly with more than one man. During other phases she won't have sex with anyone. During yet other phases she'll have a little sex with one man. All of these varied phases are a normal part of being a woman.

Moreover, women have powerful SP and OBW that often prevents them from playing around on the side; internal inhibitors that men lack. For example, scientific studies have often shown that married men who cheat report that they are "very happy" with their marriages and their lives. Only one-third of married women who cheat report the same[24].

Just to be clear: I am not advocating cheating. I am advocating nonmonogamous marriages and relationships, where you are sleeping with other people with full consent of your partner. Cheating is part of the Alpha 1.0 model, not the Alpha 2.0 model. Cheating involves hiding, lying, and drama, none of which has any place within the Alpha Male 2.0 lifestyle.

Bottom line: Sometimes your open-relationship girlfriend or wife will want sex from other men besides you, but very often she'll just want you. Just because you always want to have sex with other people doesn't mean she will always want the same. You're a man, and women are not men!

---

[24] http://ideas.ted.com/2014/01/23/10-facts-about-infidelity-helen-fisher/

Slut Shaming

The final of the Four False Sex Beliefs is another tough nut to crack for many men. It's the false assumption that a woman who has already had sex with many men before meeting you is somehow automatically disqualified from certain types of relationships with you. Men consumed with this false SP belief only want to have serious relationships with women who are sexually inexperienced. Men with extreme versions of this only desire serious relationships (or marriages) with women who have had sex with fewer than three or four other men (ideally zero).

This belief is the result of extremely powerful SP from both men and other women, originating from various historical (and false) religious beliefs we discussed earlier. This viewpoint is especially treasured by Alpha Male 1.0s.

The result of this is slut shaming is where men hold two contradictory views simultaneously: “I want to have sex with lots of women” and “Women shouldn't have sex with lots of men.”

Here are the points which slut shamers typically try to make and their refutations:

Point: “You don't want a girlfriend/wife who was out having all kinds of casual sex before you!”

Answer: But you had casual sex too. By your logic, doesn't this mean that you are now unworthy or unable to have a serious relationship?

There are men who have had sex with over 100 women who are seriously looking around for a woman to marry who's had sex with just two or three men. A man like this forgets that he's 50% of the relationship equation. Even if she's perfect for a long-term relationship, by his own logic he has disqualified himself for being so. Therefore, again by his logic, his marriage is doomed to fail no matter what he does, since he's already had sex with 100 women. He's now a “slut.”

Point: “Studies have shown that women who've had more sexual partners are more likely to divorce you!”

Answer: There have been two of these studies that I know of and I have examined them both. Their focus is not so much the number of sexual partners a woman has had, but the number of live-in cohabitation relationships she's had prior to marriage. Secondly, the studies show that there is very little difference in divorce rates between a woman who's had two or three sexual partners and a woman who's had 15 partners, often with a less than 9% difference. With women who've had an extreme number of partners, like 50 or more, then yes, the numbers do make a larger difference.

But wait a minute. Is a forever-monogamous marriage really your goal as an Alpha Male? Do you seriously want to spend the next 50 years of your life having sex with just one woman? Of course you don't! *Then why is this point even relevant?*

Look, if you want to be a tyrannical, controlling, high-drama Alpha 1.0 with a monogamous marriage where you're not allowed to have sex with other women, married to a woman who's only had sex with two or three other men in her entire life, whom you'll have to watch like a hawk the rest of your life to make sure she obeys your rules, then go right ahead. It's your life, but this is not the path of the Alpha 2.0. Nor will it make you happy in the long-term, especially when you want to have sex with other women, or when you get drama from her (or a divorce) when she finds out you're cheating.

That's the main point that men who make this argument forget or ignore. Even if there were a huge statistical divorce difference between women with lots of prior sexual partners and women with just a few, it would still be completely irrelevant. SP-based, absolute, long-term sexual monogamy cannot be your goal if you want to live the happy and fulfilled life as a man and Alpha 2.0. You can love a woman, be with a woman, marry a woman, and even raise kids with a woman, all without being absolutely monogamous and without planning on a marriage that lasts "forever," something statistically unlikely for you as an Alpha Male anyway.

We'll discuss exactly how to do this in upcoming chapters.

Point: "Promiscuous women get STDs!"

Answer: Remember our three parameters that are required for valid sex. Sex must take place between legal, consenting adults *wearing condoms*. If she was out having tons of *unprotected* sex with various men, then you're absolutely right; she's bad news. Someone at that level of irresponsibility is probably not worthy of a serious relationship.

However, if she was out having lots of casual sex with guys wearing condoms, and you've seen a recent STD test of hers showing she's clean, then there's no problem with her. She's actually demonstrated a great deal of self-control, which is a great trait to have in a woman.

Point: "Women like that will get pregnant out of wedlock!"

Answer: Read what I just said about wearing condoms. If she's having babies with all kinds of strange men, then I agree she's bad news. But what if she hasn't ever gotten pregnant because the men she sleeps with always wear condoms?

Point: "Any woman who hooks up with a guy at a bar she doesn't even know is a slut!"

Answer: Change "slut" to "being very unsafe" and now I agree with you, especially if she's drunk and the guy isn't wearing a condom.

However, what if she's had sex with 20 different men, and she knew all 20 reasonably well, was not drunk when she was having sex, they all wore condoms, and she never got an STD or pregnant? Is she still a "slut?"

If your answer is still "Yes," then you still have some SP to work on.

Point: "I like sexually inexperienced women. They turn me on. I can teach them and mold them."

Answer: That's fine, but what happens when your sexually inexperienced girlfriend or wife is now very experienced because of your teachings? What do you do then? Go through a horrible divorce so you can go find a new inexperienced woman?

By making her this sexually experienced fuck-monster who loves doing all those dirty things with you, you have destroyed that which you were attracted to in the first place. This is why male "virgin-craving" (which is completely based in OBW and SP) is never a need that can be satisfied in the long-term unless you desire to spend the rest of your life having very short-term relationships.

The desire for sexual purity is only within the context of a monogamous paradigm. Once you throw off the bonds of monogamy, it doesn't matter if your serious girlfriend or wife is experienced or not since you can simply go have sex with sexually inexperienced woman on the side whenever you like. One of the fantastic benefits of non-monogamy is that you no longer need this one person in your life to "be everything." If your main woman is sexually experienced, and you desire someone sexually inexperienced, no problem. You can have both. Play with your sexually inexperienced women on the side while you spend your life with your primary girlfriend or wife.

Are you seeing the benefits of cleaning out your false sexual programming yet?

Self-Evaluation

Ask yourself these questions and reflect on the answers:

- Think back to the last time you became angry with a woman you were in a relationship with. Do you remember what the argument was about? Did it stem from one of the Four False Sex Beliefs?
- Have you ever felt jealousy regarding a woman when you had zero real-world evidence or cause to feel that way?
- Have you ever caught yourself feeling that having sex with a particular woman was "bad", even though she was of legal age, you were both physically attracted to each other, it was completely consensual, and doing so would have caused you no drama in your life?
- Mentally run through a list of all the married or formerly married adults under the age of 55 you personally know. Now add up all those who have ever A) gone through a divorce, B) been unfaithful during a marriage, or C) been cheated on while married. Do these three groups add up to more than 50% of the entire group? Does that tell you something?
- Have you ever turned down sex, or the opportunity of sex, from a woman you were physically attracted to? Why did you do that? Don't include any women who may have been married or dating a personal friend. For the rest, why did you turn down that pleasant opportunity? Did it have anything to do with her "quality?" Or slut shaming? Or some other false SP?

The Importance of De-Programming Yourself

Back in Chapter 2 we discussed the importance of putting the minimum number of barriers in front of your own happiness as possible. If you carry around any of the Four False Sex Beliefs, living a life of freedom, choice, happiness, and excitement is going to be that much more difficult.

The Alpha Male 2.0:

- Does not think sex is bad, wrong, immoral, dirty, or selfish. As long as she's consenting and a legal adult, and proper protection is used, sex is perfectly okay at all times.
- Never promises or expects absolute monogamy, especially long-term monogamy. Even if he experiences a period of time where he happens to only be having sex with one woman, it's not because he's promised that to anyone. It's simply because he's too busy with his Mission or other SLA to pursue other women. Regardless, he always has the option and the choice to do so.
- Accepts that in nonmonogamous relationships, his women may sleep with other men too, and that's okay. He may not love it, but he has no huge problem with it. He has bigger and greater things to focus on (like his Mission). He is not threatened by other men.
- Does not consider a woman's past number of sexual partners alone as a factor in determining whether or not to be in a serious relationship with her. He can certainly judge her based on other sexual factors, such as irresponsible sexual behavior, including having sex without condoms or with complete strangers.

The closer you get to the above four conditions, the better. I live by those four conditions above, and I promise you, the life it offers a man is beyond imagining.

Chapter 13 –

The Hidden Ways Women Differ From Men

Men and women age differently. It's unfair, but an immortal fact. A woman sees the lines beginning and the sagging beginning and the skin no longer so fresh and firm but her man's still fine and sought after, and then she sees the young dolly birds and she's petrified she'll lose him to them, and eventually she will.

Ian Dunross
James Clavell's *Noble House*

May, 2007.

She sat on top of me, facing me, as I sat in the front seat of my car. It was night and we were parked in a high-rise parking garage. I pulled her thick blonde hair as we made out. She was a six-figure income corporate vice president at a construction firm in her late thirties, though she looked like an ex-Playboy model.

I pulled down one of the shoulder straps on her dress, moved aside the Victoria Secret bra, and removed one of her fantastic tits. My mouth was on it in a second, still pulling her hair, and she moaned as I growled.

Ever the sexual multitasker, my hands moved to remove her other boob. Instantly she pulled back and slapped my hand away.

"No," she said quietly.

"Uh huh," I grunted, then moved to pull her dress down again.

"No," she said calmly.

"Why?" I growled, the blood still not fully returned to my brain yet.

"Because," she said very matter-of-factly, "This is the second date. So you can suck this boob," she pointed at the prefect breast already hanging out of her dress, "But you can't suck this boob," she pointed to the other breast still hidden under her clothing.

She was not making a joke. She was dead serious. I know, because that's all I got that night.

March, 2012.

I sat in my office working away at a client project while one of my women, a beautiful 22 year-old Asian, sat at the desk across from me at the other computer, messing around with Facebook. Soon she was playing a very sad love song on YouTube and slowly singing along with it.

"Someday," she said with a dreamy look on her face, "When some guy really breaks my heart, this is the song I'm going to listen to." She said it with passion and longing. I looked at her like she was insane. She was a very happy girl, yet here she was looking forward to some future day where she would feel terrible.

August, 1996.

"Maybe I should just date the rest of my life," I said to her, "Being married really looks like a pain in the ass."

The naked and much older cougar-milf whirled to look at me with shock in her eyes as she was pulling her panties back on.

"What?" she cried, "On no! You need to find a good woman and commit to her and marry her. You can't truly be happy unless you're monogamous and committed in a marriage. It's the only way to truly love someone."

I was polite enough not to ask what her husband would think about that, since she had just had sex with me in his house while he was away on a business trip.

Winter, 2008.

I lay in my bed next to one of my friends with benefits, an extremely intelligent and educated woman about my age, her jet-black raven hair spread out over the pillows. I was talking to her about another woman I was dating.

"It was weird," I was saying, "I asked her what she wanted in life, and she sat there and had no idea. She's really smart too."

"Don't ever ask a woman what she wants!" she screamed, "WE DON'T KNOW!"

April, 2009.

I held her close to me in the nighttime darkness on the running track we had been walking on, looking into her deep eyes and caressing her long red hair that cascaded down her back all the way down to her waist. She held my gaze, and I could feel her heart pound hard within her chest. I moved to kiss her and she reluctantly pulled away. She wanted to kiss me, but something inside her held her back.

When I gave her an odd look, she explained.

"Well," she said, "I don't kiss guys on the first date."

"This isn't our first date," I said.

"I know," she said.

"And we did a hell of a lot more than just kiss on our first date," I continued.

"Well, yeah," she stammered, "That's the problem."

"Huh?"

"Well, I don't kiss guys on the first date. I just don't do that. But I kissed *you* on the first date. So now, tonight, on our second date, I can't kiss you at all. We can't do anything like that tonight. That way, the next time we meet, it will be like I didn't kiss you on the first date, then we can, you know, move forward."

Winter, 1999.

The woman who was my wife was in the kitchen screaming at me. It was about the ninth or tenth time she had done so that day, her face red, her eyes harsh, her blond hair dancing like Medusa's snakes.

I interrupted her tirade and asked her in a calm voice, "Hey, why have you been yelling at me all day? You've been doing it since you woke up this morning."

"Because you didn't clean up your mess in the kitchen!" she screamed.

"I cleaned it up eventually," I said in my beta male way, "But you didn't answer my question. I made that mess at noon. You've been yelling at me since 8am this morning. So that's not it. Why are you so pissed?"

"Because you didn't help me with the baby when I asked!" she screamed even louder.

"I did help you out. I just didn't help you out as fast as you wanted because I was on the phone. But again, that happened at about 10am. You were screaming at me hours before then. So try again."

"Because you're an asshole!"

"Why are you not answering my question?"

On and on this went. She got angrier and angrier. I never got an answer. (The answer was That Thing That Cannot Be Spoken™. It starts with the letter "P.")

Summer, 2008.

"I don't mind if you fuck Ashley or Kat, but don't fuck Michelle. Promise me you won't ever fuck Michelle," she said.

To accentuate her point, she forcefully put her balled fists on her 18 year-old hips and glared at me. We had been dating for a few months, and she and I were going over the list of her cute girlfriends I was going to have sex with, with her permission of course.

"Why not Michelle?" I asked. Not that I cared, since the other two friends she had mentioned were both extremely hot.

"Because she's a fuckin' cunt," she said with a sneer.

"So you'd rather me fuck your girlfriends that you like, rather than girls you don't like?"

"Yeah," she answered, "You can fuck the chicks I know and like, but not chicks I don't like, and not any chicks I don't know. And next time we have a threesome, the girl has to be someone I know really well and like a lot, or someone I don't know at all."

I shook my head in confusion at all of the irrational rules she just rattled off and how little sense they made. I decided to refocus on the list of women at hand.

"Okay," I said, "So I can fuck Emma then. Good."

"Oh no! You can't fuck Emma!"

"Why not?"

"Because," she said, "Emma is like my best friend."

Women Are Different than Men

One of the greatest sources of problems for men when they are dating or in relationships with women is that we fail to remember that women don't think like we do and don't view sex and relationships in the same ways. As men, we tend to think that everyone, including other women, view the world and process information exactly the same way we do.

Women don't. Moreover, the differences are extreme; often shockingly so. Most men reading the above stories from my dating life, all of which are completely true (only the names have been changed) would react with shock or laughter at how silly and irrational those women were behaving. However, many women reading those same stories, including very intelligent ones, would probably be nodding their heads in agreement with the above women's behaviors, thinking they would behave similarly in similar circumstances.

That doesn't mean women are dumber than men, nor does it mean women are less capable than men, nor does it mean that women are bad, evil, insane, not to be trusted, or out to get you. In my vast experience with working with and dating women, I have found that 95% of women out there are very nice people with no ill agenda toward anyone.

What it does mean is women see the world, process information, and make decisions using completely different criteria than you do, sometimes in ways that may actually seem irrational or even insane to us men. This is true even if the woman is extraordinarily intelligent, knowledgeable, mature, successful, and/or educated. As a matter of fact, often those very qualities exacerbate a woman's irrational tendencies, not lessen them.

Before we talk about how to best optimize your woman life for long-term Alpha Male happiness, you need to fully understand the differences in the female operating system from your own, so that you won't be taken by surprise by them like most men are.

Difference 1: Men are static, women are dynamic.

Perhaps the greatest relevant difference between men and women you need to understand is that women are dynamic creatures. By "dynamic," I mean the scientific meaning of the word, which would be "characterized by continuous change."

Women are constantly changing. One day she's the "happiest she's ever been." The very next day she's "miserable." One week she'll feel one way about something, the next she'll feel a completely different way. One year she'll want certain things for her life and three years later she'll want a completely different set of things, often the exact opposite of what she just wanted. Women under the age of 50 are constantly changing. They can't help it. It's how they are.

Men are the opposite, at least usually. By and large, men are static creatures ("static" in this context meaning slowly-changing, rarely-changing, or never-changing). They are the way they are, and they rarely go through any radical changes in opinions or desires. A 25 year-old man with a high sex drive, who loves baseball, wants to get married, and have two kids is very likely going to be that same guy with those same core desires when he's 45. While there are always exceptions to every rule, usually very little of those core desires will change over that 20-year time span for him.

However, a 25 year-old, high sex drive woman who loves baseball, wants to get married and have two kids will change all of those opinions drastically, many times, during that 20-year journey to age 45. Sometimes her sex drive will be strong and healthy; sometimes she won't want sex from anyone at all. Sometimes she'll want to be married. Other times she'll hate marriage and think it sucks. Sometimes she'll want two kids. Then she'll want four kids. Then she won't want any kids. Then she'll want one kid. On and on and on this goes, in all of her Seven Life Areas (SLA).

This is how women work, all the way until they reach their fifties when this process of constant change begins to slow once they complete menopause and lose estrogen, thus making them less feminine and more static, like men.

Perhaps one of the greatest mistakes men make when they enter into long-term relationships or marriages with women is that they assume the women will be ever-static like a man. These men are always shocked to find a few months or years later that the woman they're with suddenly wants radically different things than she used to want when they were first dating, or first married, or first moved in together, or had their first child. Static men are constantly frustrated, enraged, confounded, and confused by their dynamic female partners.

Consider the following facts:

- 70-80% of all divorces are initiated by the female[25].
- Approximately three-fourths of all boyfriend/girlfriend relationships are terminated by the female, and men take breakups harder than women do[26].
- Over 20% of the women in the US have children from multiple fathers[27].
- Numerous surveys have shown that the majority of married women would not remarry their current husbands if they had to do it all over again[28].

Is this because women are bitches? Is it because women are stupid? Neither is the case. It's because women are dynamic, constantly changing how they feel. If she loves you now, it's unlikely she'll love you five, ten, or fifteen years from now. If she's sexually attracted to you now, she may not be in three years or even in three months. In many cases this isn't even your fault. It's just how women are.

---

[25] National Center for Health Statistics, American Law and Economics Review, Divorce Source Research Center (Atlanta, Georgia), and various other sources.

[26] http://www.sciencedaily.com/releases/2010/06/100608135114.htm

[27] http://www.nbcnews.com/id/42364656/ns/health-childrens_health/t/us-moms-have-kids-multiple-dads-study-says

[28] http://www.prnewswire.com/news-releases/womans-dayaol-poll-reveals-majority-of-married-women-would-reconsider-their-spouses-36-would-not-marry-their-husbands-if-they-could-re-do-their-i-do--another-20-not-sure-53289747.html

The Alpha 2.0 accepts and fully acknowledges women's fickle, ever-changing nature. He does not ignore it or fight it, which is what betas and Alpha 1.0s spend their lives doing. As a result, the Alpha 2.0 never enters into any long-term arrangements with any women in his personal life with the expectation it will last forever.

Following the beta male or Alpha Male 1.0 path of doing things like:

- Marrying a woman without a prenuptial agreement
- Co-signing a loan with a woman
- Co-signing a mortgage or lease with a woman
- Co-owning a business with a woman in your personal or romantic life

...are all titanic mistakes that will cause severe damage to your life down the road. That dynamic woman you're entering into an arrangement with will likely feel very differently about that arrangement later, and you will pay the price.

That does not mean you can't love a woman, be with a woman, live with a woman, have children with a woman, or make commitments to a woman. You can. You just need to keep the long-term, legal, contractual aspects out of the equation (more details on this in Chapter 14).

Never expect a woman to feel the same way she does now, about anything, many years into the future.

Difference 2: Women perceive blocks of data simultaneously; men perceive one thing at a time.

Women perceive the world very differently than us guys. Whenever a woman takes in information, her conscious mind processes many things all at the same time.

Men are the opposite. Even highly intelligent, perceptive men process one...thing...at...a...time. Our senses detect one item, our conscious mind processes it, then we move onto the next item. Our subconscious mind processes everything like a woman's does, but that's not relevant to this discussion.

Here's a real-world example. When you meet an attractive woman for the first time at a social setting, what do you actually see and process during the first three to five seconds? You probably see and process her boobs and her hair, perhaps her eyes too. Later, you take in much more, but within the first few seconds that's about it.

What does she see in the first few seconds? She sees and fully processes your eyes, your eyebrows, your hair, your nose, your nose hairs, the pigmentation and color of your skin, your facial hair, your five o'clock shadow, your lips, your teeth, your chin, your double chin, your eye contact, the hair on the back of your neck, and the little bits of chest hair sticking out of your collar. Within another few seconds she's processed your hands, the way you move your hands, your dirty fingernails, your watch, and your body posture. While doing this, she is also seeing and processing most of what you're wearing: your shirt, your belt, your pants, your shoes, your socks, your necklace, and any rings on your fingers.

Yes, she really does all of this within just a few seconds. Women are amazing this way. Their brains are built for perception in a way men's are not[29].

This all equates to a very different life experience between you and the women you work with, spend time with, date, or have relationships with. You need to acknowledge this reality or you'll be very confused at women's behaviors.

There are advantages and disadvantages to both the wide perception of a woman and the tunnel vision of a man.

The advantage women have is that women are more perceptive than men. They can very quickly detect detailed information that it takes us guys a longer time to uncover. I think I'm a pretty perceptive guy, but even to this day I'm surprised at how fast I see women pick up on little nuances in their environments; nuances I usually don't "see" unless a woman points them out to me.

Women can also multitask better than men, and are much more conscious and sensitive than men are, one of the many reasons they tend to be more nurturing as parents and friends than a man. Remember I said "tend to," as there are always exceptions to the rule.

The disadvantage women have is that because their conscious minds are constantly being bombarded with information, they can get a little crazy. Everyone knows that women are more emotional and irrational than men (on average), and this is the primary reason. Women are far more prone to emotional outbursts and irrational behavior than men because they perceive so much more of the world at the same time. Women also tend to be far less focused than men, so even if they are able to multitask better, they usually aren't going to stick with whatever they're working on as long as a man can. Again, I'm making generalizations here and this is not always true.

---

[29] http://www.lifescript.com/well-being/articles/f/female_perception_vs_male_perception.aspx

Men are the opposite. Because of their tunnel vision, they tend to act a little more "simple" than women, almost to the point of looking dumb. This is what she's talking about when a married woman complains about how "dumb" her husband is being. She sees everything all at once, and is losing patience for her husband who can only process one thing at a time.

The advantage men have, and it's a massive one that you need to exploit, is that men are far more focused than women. It's been said (though not loudly in this current cultural climate) that if you want to get a job done, give it to man. This is not a chauvinistic statement, because many *women* say this. (For example, surveys show that most women in the workplace prefer to have a male boss, and by a very wide margin[30].) It's a very real observation based on very real biology. Because of our relative tunnel vision, it is much easier for us guys to focus on a task and stick with it until it gets done. We are not going to be distracted nearly as much as a woman might.

So next time you see a woman act a little insane, just remember the flow of data pouring into her mind is far greater than yours is.

Difference 3: Men desire comfort, women desire a range of positive and negative emotions.

This is a big one that directly affects your interpersonal relationships with women.

Men, at least most men, desire positive emotions, namely comfort. As we discussed previously, a man's desire for comfort and happiness is confounded by his own OBW, SP, and the Six Societal Values. Yet a man's desire for positive emotions remains despite these strong Prison-enacted barriers. Once a guy is home from work with a beer in his hand, sitting on his couch, watching the game on TV, he's happy. Moreover, he could (likely) sit there for hours and hours on end, and be just as happy hours later as he was when he first sat down.

Women are very different. Women do not desire consistent comfort or happiness like us guys, even if they say they do. Rather, women desire to experience *a range of emotions*. This means they want to feel happy sometimes, but other times they want to feel angry, or sad, or jealous, or afraid. That's right; they *want* to feel these things. Most women will never admit this, and frankly most women are not self-aware enough to realize they have these desires, but they still do.

---

[30] http://www.businessweek.com/articles/2014-10-16/women-dislike-having-female-bosses-more-than-men-do

A woman who feels happy will eventually do things to make herself feel something else. Feeling happy all the time is "boring" to a woman, and if there's anything a woman can't stand, it's boredom.

Men's tolerance for boredom and sameness is colossal compared to a woman's. Many men can work at a boring job, go home, eat dinner, go to sleep, and do that for 30 years, and be totally fine. He's bored as hell, but that's fine with him. Sadly, billions of beta males all over the world live lives just like this.

A woman living that same life would go insane. Within a very short period of time, a woman in that circumstance would switch jobs, or move to another city, or divorce her husband, or cheat, or end a long-term friendship with one of her girlfriends, or go to night school, or have kids, or make some other radical life change. She cannot be bored. She must avoid sameness at all costs.

The key distinction here is that women will change their conditions even if their life is perfect. If a woman happens to actually achieve a life where she is literally happy all the time, i.e. she has the perfect job, the perfect kids, the perfect marriage, and she's physically fit, for a while she'll bask in that happiness. However, slowly, over time, she will start to feel uncomfortable. She'll start to feel like something is wrong. She will actually start to feel uneasy or guilty. Eventually, she will do something in her life to cause herself unhappiness. It may not even be something she does consciously, but she'll still do it. She's a woman. She doesn't want consistent happiness; she wants a range of different emotions. If she feels happy for a while, she'll want to feel angry after that. Then happy again. Then sad. Then happy again. Then afraid. Difference is what she's after, not consistent happiness or comfort like us "simple" men.

Ever have a woman you were in a relationship with suddenly start throwing drama at you, completely out of the blue, when everything was going great? Did you ever have a woman suddenly leave you when everything was going great? Of course you have! We all have!

Why did she do this? Because she doesn't want everything going great forever; she only wants it going great for a while. After that, she wants things in your relationship to go badly, at least a little. Yes, she really wants this! Then after some rocky times, she wants the relationship to be great again. As always, this is not because women are evil or crazy; it's just how they are.

You've probably heard the old statement that men speak an average of 2,000 words per day while women speak an average of 7,000 words per day. Women process information by talking. What better way to experience a range of emotions in a given day than by talking a lot?

Since (most) men don't have a desire for emotional range, they don't need to say as much. If a guy is comfortable, he's usually pretty quiet. If a woman is comfortable, what is she doing? That's right, she's talking.

If a woman is happy, never expect her to stay that way.

Difference 4: Women desire sex as much or more so than men, but have more self-imposed rules about when sex is "appropriate" for them.

There is massive SP that says women don't like sex, and men are the horny ones. It's grossly untrue. Women's minds and bodies are designed for far more sexual pleasure than a man's. Here's just a few scientific examples:

- During scientific experiments, women respond sexually to images of men-on-women sex, women-on-women sex, animals having sex, attractive women walking down a beach, and attractive men walking down a beach. In the same experiments, men only respond sexually when women were present[31].
- Science has confirmed that when women have high sex drives, they are more likely to be strongly attracted to both sexes. This is untrue of high sex drive men.
- Women can orgasm in multiple ways. Men just have one.
- Women can orgasm multiple times. There is no actual limit to the number. Most men can orgasm a maximum of two or three times during a passionate evening, and those are the lucky ones, since most guys are "one-and-done."

The strange paradox is that even though women are more sexual than men, because of thousands of years of SP telling women to not be sexual, over the ages women have learned to cloak their sexual desire, even from themselves. As a result, women suffer all kinds of emotional and psychological problems surrounding sex that we men never have to worry about. It's a very sad situation and frankly, I feel very sorry for women because of this.

If women want sex as much or more than men, why is it so hard for most men to have sex with them sometimes? It's because of an odd result of the sexual "cloaking" women have been forced to assume. The

[31] *Sex At Dawn* by Christopher Ryan and Cacilda Jethá

symptom of this "disease" is the development of false, self-imposed sexual rules a woman creates in her mind. She then adheres to these rules whether she wants to or not. A few of these rules make perfect sense, like "Don't go home with a man you just met." However, most of the rules are completely irrational and make little sense in the real world with sky-high divorce rates, where women can and do earn their own money, and where men wear condoms.

There are scores of these rules that women have created for themselves, far more than I could list here. Here are a few examples of women's irrational sexual rules that you may have already encountered in your dating life:

- I don't have sex on the first date (or second date, or third date).
- I don't kiss on the first date.
- I don't have sex with a man until he makes me his girlfriend.
- I don't have sex with a man until he buys me several nice dinners.
- I can have sex with a young, poor, very good-looking man without any dates or dinners. This is okay, because we're not dating.
- If I meet a really great guy who I really like and see a future with, I must force him to wait for sex. The converse of this rule also applies: If I meet a man who has zero long-term potential, I can have sex with him very quickly.
- A man I'm having sex with can't have sex with other women even if our relationship is casual.
- If a man makes me pregnant, he must marry me, even if I know he would make a terrible husband and father.
- A man I'm having sex with casually must eventually make me his girlfriend, even if I really enjoy the casual, no-attachment sex.
- I can cheat on my husband, as long as I don't actually love the man I'm cheating with.
- Making out with a guy doesn't count as cheating.

- Sex with that guy doesn't "count" if I regret it later.
- Blowjobs do not count as sex.
- I'm still a virgin after having anal sex.

I could list many more female sex rules, and likely you could too. Notice very few, if any, of these rules actually make any sense. Doesn't matter. To the women who have these rules, these are as iron-clad to her behavior as the law of gravity. Because of anti-sex, anti-woman SP, women have all kinds of rules like these rolling around in their minds regarding when sex is appropriate and when it is not.

It's very important to point out that a woman will follow her irrational sexual rules *even if she doesn't want to*. I can tell you for a fact that I have been on many dates with women who wanted very badly to have sex with me, but because they had a rule like "only sluts have sex on the second date!" installed by SP into their brains, they couldn't bring themselves to do it. They would kiss me passionately, get very wet, adamantly resist having sex with me despite my best efforts, then run back home by themselves and quickly masturbate, then tell me all about it over texts.

Sound insane? To a man, yes. To a woman, no; it makes perfect sense. Her irrational sexual rules take precedence, not logic or reality.

While we men certainly have our own sexual programming to wrestle with (as we discussed last chapter), we usually don't have any rules restricting us from having sex. If we want to have sex with someone, we have sex, or at least try to. The downside to this is that a man with little or no sex rules often comes up against a woman who has tons of them herself.

The number of irrational sex rules a woman has increases with age. A 20 year-old single woman is going to have far fewer sexual rules than a 40 year-old single woman. This is one of the core reasons why I usually don't even try to approach women over the age of 33 for sex unless I already know them personally. In my experience, the age of 33 seems to be when most women in the Western world really ramp-up their own irrational sex rules. I've discussed this topic extensively at my dating and relationships blog.[32]

This means that even though women hit their "sexual peak" at some point in their mid-thirties, they also have a huge amount of rules forbidding them to have sex at around that same time. Therefore despite

---

[32] http://www.blackdragonblog.com/

the fact a thirty-something or forty-something woman may have a higher sex drive than a woman in her mid-twenties, the older woman is going to have far more rules and regulations installed in her brain about when she is, or is not, allowed to have sex with you. She will be harder to have sex with the first time than the younger woman will be, even though the older woman has a higher sex drive.

Crazy, isn't it?

Difference 5: Women have more OBW than men.

We've already discussed the dangers of Obsolete Biological Wiring and how it will sabotage your happiness as a man and an Alpha. Women have even more OBW than men. Women's bodies and brains are wired for some extreme OBW that men never need to worry about. This is mostly tied to ovulation and pregnancy.

Ovulation

I probably don't need to tell you about a woman's once-a-month bitchy time. Any man who's had a girlfriend or wife longer than several months knows all about that.

Women also have a time of the month when they're ovulating. This is yet another form of OBW that exerts powerful control over a woman, including very intelligent, self-aware women. Research has shown[33] that during ovulation, women:

- Are more likely to cheat.
- Are more likely to masturbate and/or watch porn.
- Are more likely to wear perfume and jewelry.
- Have brighter, more attractive skin.
- Dress more sexually and in ways that reveal more skin.
- Are more attracted to men bearing Alpha traits (bigger muscles, deeper voices, more symmetrical and chiseled faces, etc.)
- Speak in higher-pitched voices (so as to appear more feminine and to attract more men).
- Sway their hips more when they walk.

[33] *Sex At Dawn* by Christopher Ryan and Cacilda Jethá

Women aren't doing these things consciously. It's not like a woman wakes up in the morning and says "Ah ha! I'm ovulating! Today I'm going to dress sexy and speak in a higher voice so I can get laid!" Instead, it's all automatic and subconscious, all driven by OBW, whether she knows it or not.

This is why a woman can be very horny one week and be sexually cold just two weeks later. As men, we're static. We're horny all the time. It's confusing to see women be sexual sometimes and prudish others, but that's how they are.

Pregnancy

Perhaps the greatest biological human urge, other than those base urges of survival, is the female's urge to crank out babies. Yes, men also desire to procreate, but men are usually more concerned about the act of sex itself than actual procreation. If we have tons of sex and don't get anyone pregnant, that's fine with us (it's usually preferable!). However with women, they want to consistently have sex *and* procreate.

The OBW that drives a woman to have a baby is ultra-powerful. There is no greater biological urge in her life (other than survival). This is why you see so many women having babies out of wedlock, or when they aren't financially or emotionally ready, or when they really don't want to disrupt their lives or careers with babies, or with men they know would make terrible fathers. A woman's OBW doesn't care. Throughout her life, a woman's OBW is screaming at her to have a baby, even if she mentally doesn't want any!

The fact that society now welcomes, and even encourages, single motherhood and teen motherhood drives this already powerful OBW into the stratosphere, boosted by new false SP. The rate of children born without fathers is soaring. More than half of all American births to women under the age of 30 are to single mothers[34]. 34% of teenage girls will have a baby by the time they reach age 20[35]. Amazing!

Never before in Western history have so many women had their lives destroyed or disrupted by having babies when they shouldn't be having them, all because of irresistible OBW and SP that is further encouraged by society.

Difference 6: Women demand behaviors that will turn them off.

---

[34] http://www.nytimes.com/2012/02/18/us/for-women-under-30-most-births-occur-outside-marriage.html

[35] http://www.capefearteen.org/cfthc.php?section=statistics

Perhaps the most bizarre difference between men and women is that women will actually demand behaviors from men during the courting process that will actually turn them (the women) off to the men doing them. It's the craziest thing in the world, and this oddball trait of women has been confusing the hell out of men for centuries.

For example, when a woman starts dating a man, she will expect him to be nice, sweet, compliant, obedient, affectionate, buy her gifts, treat her to free drinks and dinners, and various other beta male behaviors. The problem is, for the vast majority of women, it is these very same traits which will turn her off sexually. What will turn her on is a man who is confident, outcome independent, doesn't give a shit, acts somewhat aloof (bordering on asshole) and doesn't buy her anything. Yet she will never say to a potential suitor, "Please refuse to buy me anything and treat me like you aren't attracted to me. That will make me more likely to have sex with you."

Instead, she will demand that a man who is behaving in more Alpha ways behave more like a beta, which will actually reduce her sexual attraction for him. It's the damnest thing, and again, most women don't do this consciously. This bizarre behavior is yet another result of anti-sex SP that's been drilled into women's heads for thousands of years.

The Alpha 2.0 is aware of this tendency in women. When a woman demands ass-kissing beta behaviors from him during the courting process, he ignores her requests and proceeds with the Alpha behaviors. These are effective in getting her to have sex with him more quickly, even though they are almost always the opposite of what she's expecting or demanding from men who court her. If she still doesn't have sex with him, no problem. He smiles, wishes her well, and has sex with someone else.

In the next chapter we'll talk about exactly how to do that.

Chapter 14 –
Integrating Love, Sex, and Marriage into the Alpha 2.0 Lifestyle

Let me live deep while I live; let me know the rich juices of red meat and stinging wine on my palate, the hot embrace of white arms, the mad exultation of battle when the blue blades flame and crimson, and I am content. Let teachers and philosophers brood over questions of reality and illusion. I know this: if life is illusion, then I am no less an illusion, and being thus, the illusion is real to me. I live, I burn with life, I love, I slay, and am content.

Conan the Barbarian
Robert E. Howard's *Queen of the Black Coast*

September, 2007.

I sat across from her at her dining room table, eating the beautifully prepared meal she had made me with exquisite care. Even at age 41, which was five years older than me at the time, she was still very beautiful, similar to a young Susan Sarandon, with a body to match. She was intelligent and perceptive too, and we talked for a very long time before having sex, something I don't often do with women. I usually have long conversations with women after sex, not before.

She turned the conversation to marriage, as she often did. Like most unmarried women her age, she was in provider-hunting mode, seeking a man to marry her and take care of her (and to follow her orders, just like any other societally programmed woman). As she went on about her Disney fairytale desires, annotated with strong indications that I could be "just such a man," I interrupted her.

"If we got married," I said, "Do you realize it would damage a large part of what we now have?"

She cocked her head to one side. Having been raised Catholic like I had, my statement directly conflicted with her religious SP.

"How do you mean?" she asked.

"Let me ask you a question," I said, putting down my fork, "Why am I here?"

She was a very modest woman, so she simply shrugged.

"I'll tell you," I continued, "I'm here because I want to be here. With you. That's the only reason I'm here. Literally. If I didn't want to be here, I'd be somewhere else. Right?"

"Right," she said, still not understanding where I was going with this.

"But," I continued, holding up a finger, "Let's say we were married. You've been married before just like I have, so you know exactly what it's like. If we were married, I would come home to you because I had to. You'd be my wife and you'd be living in my house. I'd have to come home to you. I really wouldn't have a choice. Unless I wanted to get a full-on divorce that is, but barring that, I would be spending time because I had to, not necessarily because I wanted to."

I saw her eyes defocus and I could see she was getting it. Indeed she had been married before, and as badly as some divorced people want to get re-married, they never quite forget how crappy traditional monogamous marriage usually is.

"Someone married to someone else, or even just living with someone else," I said, "That person must be with that person even if they don't like that person. Even if that person bothers them. But because they're married, they more or less have to be there. But with you and me, none of that is the case. You know, deep in your heart, mind, and soul that the only reason I'm here with you right now is because I want to be here with you. I have literally no other reason for being here. If I was your husband, that aspect would be gone. I'd be here because I had to be. And you would never know for sure if it was because I actually wanted to be here or not."

She sat back and stared into space for a few minutes. I could tell her wheels were turning. In her entire life, no one had ever explained marriage to her like that. This was because the elites who rule The Prison want people to get married. It makes them easier to control, govern, tax, sell things to, categorize, and manipulate. Therefore, basic realities like the one I relayed to her go unheard of by most of the population.

Several days later we were together again and she had a huge smile on her face as she gave me a big hug.

"You know," she said, "I thought about what you said. And you're right. When I was married to my ex-husband, I was only there because I had to be, and I hated it. The same for him too. He wasn't there for me. He was there for the marriage. Now that you're here with me, I know you want to be here, and, I don't know, that really makes me happy. I never had that when I was married. And now I don't think I ever want to give that up."

Societally-Programmed Relationships

You to not create relationships because they are want you want, or because they are what will make you long-term happy. Unless you're completely liberated from SP and OBW, you (likely) create relationships based on your false societal conditioning.

Let's take a look how normal, SP-based relationships work from the male perspective. Normal men go through life seeking a woman, either for love, sex, or both. They do this in either a needy way (betas) or a touchy, suspicious way (Alpha 1.0s). Eventually, and often in spite of everything they do wrong, they find a woman. They then proceed to operate on autopilot based on their SP.

Beta males usually follow a pattern that looks like this:

1. Go long periods with no sex.
2. Meet girl.
3. Kiss girl's ass.
4. Eventually have sex with girl.
5. Very soon give the girl the "I-think-we-should-stop-seeing-other-people" speech.
6. Beg girl to become his "girlfriend."
7. Get into monogamous relationship with girl.
8. Experience brief and wonderful honeymoon period.
9. Start experiencing drama with girl.
10. Get dumped by girl.
11. Get depressed, sad, angry, or bitter.
12. Wait a few weeks or months.
13. Go back to step two and repeat entire cycle.

After farting around with this ridiculous cycle for years and years, the beta eventually gets married. Then he adopts a new cycle:

1. Get engaged. Feel great.
2. Have a wedding, completely the way the girl wants it.
3. Happy honeymoon phase for anywhere from three to 36 months. Feel "the happiest he's ever been."
4. Start getting (and giving) regular drama from wife.
5. Start getting resistance from wife when he wants to have sex.
6. Have less sex than before. Become accustomed to reduced sex.
7. Suffer from reduced testosterone and a feeling of helplessness.
8. Have a baby. Feel great again (for a while).
9. Work with wife to raise baby. Increased stress.
10. Possibly have another baby. Further increased stress on the relationship as he argues with wife on best ways to raise kids.
11. Wife divorces him.
12. Get financially raped in the divorce. Lose some or all custody of his children. Forced at gunpoint by the government to pay communal property, child support, and possibly alimony regardless of whose fault the divorce was.
13. Go back to dating, and repeat above dating cycle, seeking a new wife to repeat the above marriage cycle all over again.

Of course if the guy is "lucky" he'll never get divorced. Instead he'll stay married, and either he'll cheat on his wife, or his wife will cheat on him, or they'll get gradually bitterer as time goes on until they're both too old to do anything about it.

Yes, there are always odd exceptions to the rule, but with the vast majority of men out there, the above two cycles (or something that looks very close) are the system they follow. Which, of course, is the exact system The Prison promotes via SP and the Six Societal Values.

We can't neglect the Alpha 1.0s. They follow a slightly different cycle:

1. Date and have sex with lots of women. Be a player and love it.

2. Eventually begin to question their lifestyle, and say to themselves things like "Is this all there is?" or "I need to grow up now" or "My life feels like I'm missing something."
3. Find a woman they think is Not Like The Rest™ and get "serious" with her.
4. Cut off all other women.
5. Brief happy honeymoon period. Feel great.
6. Start getting very horny for other women.
7. Cheat on her.
8. Get caught.
9. Drama, fighting, anger.
10. Bad breakup or divorce.
11. Go back to dating lots of women and feel "great to be single again."
12. Go back to step two and repeat entire cycle.

You can see that both of these cycles are utterly incompatible with the Alpha 2.0 lifestyle, as well as the goal of long-term consistent happiness. Moreover, these cycles will severely hamper your ability to pursue your Mission, if not destroy it completely.

The Alpha 2.0 follows a very different system. He cannot allow himself to blindly follow SP or OBW when it comes to women, nor does he have the option of getting needy, possessive, or dramatic with women, even when dealing with a woman he loves. As we discussed in Chapter 12, he lacks the false sexual SP installed into most people via The Prison. As we discussed in Chapter 13, he also recognizes women's ever-changing dynamic nature and never enters into any long-term legal commitments with women in his personal life (except for those impossible to avoid, like child support if he wants to have children).

Most importantly, an Alpha 2.0 does not "pedestal" any woman by making her the most important thing in his life, even if he is living with that woman, married to that woman, and is the father of her children. That doesn't mean an Alpha 2.0 can't love a woman; of course he can, but no woman is ever the most important thing his life.

Instead, women, or even that one special woman, are simply another very important item on the small list of Seven Life Areas that are important to him. His woman life is important, and should be, but it's never the most important thing. You must view your woman life as one of several important pieces to your life, not the only piece, and not even the most important piece. Yes, even if you're in love or married.

The only possible exception to this if the Alpha 2.0 has a carefully crafted Mission that focuses on his woman life. This is a little dangerous, since it tends to violate many of the rules we discussed back in the chapter regarding Mission formation, namely that your Mission cannot rely on one person or small group of people. Yet I will submit that it is possible to do.

The Categories of Relationships

As an Alpha 2.0, you must experience the woman side of your life in a way that brings you happiness without compromising your present or future happiness, life, or Mission. One of the easiest ways to manage this is to view different types of relationships on a scale of categories.

Any woman in your sex life or romantic life will fall into one of nine relationship categories, shown below.

Author's Note: I am about to give you some more acronyms. I realize I've already given you a few in this book to chew on. I try my best not to over-use acronyms but sometimes it's unavoidable. In order to not drive you too crazy, in subsequent chapters I will usually spell out the entire relationship type instead of using its acronym introduced in this chapter. I will continue to use the core acronyms like SP (Societal Programming), OBW (Obsolete Biological Wiring), 6SV (The Six Societal Values) and SLA (The Seven Life Areas), though I will occasionally spell those out from time to time as well. There is also a glossary at the back of the book if you ever need to refer to it.

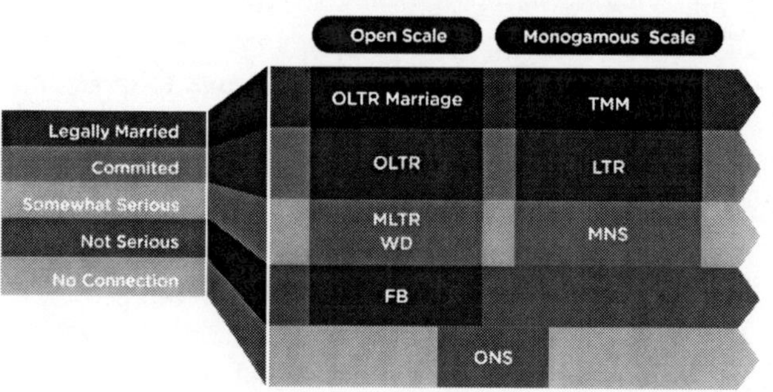

Some relationships are monogamous relationships, others are nonmonogamous ones, usually called "open" relationships or "poly" relationships. I shall describe each, starting from the bottom of the chart and going up.

ONS – One Night Stand

The least serious form of "relationship" isn't really a relationship it all. It's an ONS, or one night stand. This is a woman you have sex with once, perhaps twice, then never see ever again, or at least never again in a sexual context.

I personally don't do ONSs. I don't see the point. I only have sex with women I'm very attracted to, so if I have sex with a woman, I want to have sex with her over and over again, theoretically forever. Regardless, lots of Alphas enjoy ONSs, and if you're one of them, that's fine.

Now we're going to tackle the monogamous relationships scale. These are the types of relationships people in The Prison engage in and the types OBW and SP push people towards.

MNS – Monogamous, Not Serious

A MNS is when you start having sex with a woman and she gives you a little speech about how you are not allowed to start liking her and she is not your girlfriend and how she does not have time for a relationship and this "thing" you and her have is just "hanging out and having sex" and not serious. Oh, and by the way, she says, you aren't allowed to have sex with any other women except her.

MNS relationships are almost universally initiated by females. I have never heard of a man initiating one. When it comes to a MNS, women initiate, and men agree to them. Stupidly.

It should go without saying (I hope!) that the MNS is the single worst type of relationship there is. It's all downside, no upside. Men who are foolish enough, stupid enough, or desperate enough to agree to a MNS when a woman demands one are cutting their own throats.

As a man you should never, ever agree to a MNS for any reason whatsoever.

LTR – Long-Term Relationship

This is the relationship type most people are familiar with, the Long-term Relationship or LTR. "Long" in the long-term relationship is actually theoretical, since the vast majority of LTRs actually don't last past about two years or so.

An LTR is the standard boyfriend/girlfriend relationship most people in The Prison quickly leap into once they start having sex with someone. The promise of monogamy of both partners is either clearly stated or implied, but it's expected regardless. Sometimes LTRs live together, sometimes not. Sometimes two people in an LTR are truly in love, sometimes not, but regardless it's still considered much more serious than just "dating" or "hooking up."

Like all monogamous relationships, LTRs are prone to the usual problems of drama, rules, limitations, compromises, scarcity mentality, and bad breakups. They are relationships based on the Six Societal Values (6SV), not happiness.

TMM – Traditional Monogamous Marriage

The most serious form of monogamous relationship is the TMM, or traditional monogamous marriage. A TMM is when two people get married, do not sign a prenuptial agreement, expect the marriage to last the rest of their lives, and expect no cheating ever by either partner.

Approximately 87% of all traditional monogamous marriages in the Western world created after 1990 fail, thereby resulting in one or more of the following[36]:

- Divorce
- One or both partners cheating
- A bad marriage that never ends

---

[36] *The 87% failure rate (that's failure rate, not divorce rate) of traditional monogamous marriage is a composite percentage of several different statistics, pulled from these and other sources:*
http://www.huffingtonpost.com/robert-hughes/is-the-us-divorce-rate-go_b_4908201.html
http://www.dailymail.co.uk/news/article-1377940/Half-parents-split-16-births-outside-marriage-hit-highest-level-200-years.html
http://www.census.gov/hhes/socdemo/marriage/data/acs/index.html
http://www.census.gov/hhes/socdemo/marriage/data/sipp/index.html
http://www.huffingtonpost.com/2013/06/12/gray-divorce_n_3429703.html
http://magazine.foxnews.com/love/cheating-statistics-do-men-cheat-more-women
http://www.washingtonpost.com/opinions/five-myths-about-cheating/2012/02/08/gIQANGdaBR_story.html
http://magazine.foxnews.com/love/are-you-semi-happy-marriage
http://www.care2.com/greenliving/are-only-17-of-marriages-happy.html

If you get into a TMM, you can look forward to 87% odds of one of those three things happening to you eventually. Despite the fact that TMM no longer works in the modern Western world, most people still eventually attempt it. Such is the power of SP and the 6SV.

Fortunately, the Alpha Male 2.0 has many other options, none of which will harm his current or future long-term happiness. We'll switch now and discuss the nonmonogamous relationship types. Again, we'll start at the least serious and move our way up to the most serious.

FB – Fuck Buddy or Friend with Benefits

An FB is a woman you don't have romantic feelings for at all, but whom you enjoy having sex with. There is no romance or dating. You just meet up and have sex. Maybe you both watch a little TV afterwards or something like that, but that's about it. No dates, no cuddling after sex, no spending the night, none of that. There is no expectation of commitment or exclusivity. A person can even have several FBs at once (I often do).

That doesn't mean you treat your FBs like trash. The "F" in "FB" stands for *friend*. She's your friend, perhaps even your close friend. That means you treat her with kindness and respect, just like you would one of your buddies. Just because you're not romantically serious with her doesn't mean you don't treat her nicely. Plus, treating your FBs like crap invites drama, which will damage your happiness. We don't want that!

FBs are easy, enjoyable, satisfying relationships.

WD – Woman you're Dating

One notch up from FB is WD. A WD is a woman you're dating and having sex with and you do like beyond just a friend. However, you're really not sure where she fits yet. You're not 100% positive if you want to pursue something more serious with her or not.

Unlike an FB, with a WD you are actually doing things like going out on romantic dates and cuddling after sex. However, you're probably not doing super serious stuff like going on vacation together or having her spend the night.

This is how most women enter a man's woman life, whether he prefers monogamous or nonmonogamous relationships. Even pro-monogamy men can briefly date a few women before reaching a decision on just one WD to turn into an LTR (emphasis on the word "briefly").

MLTR – Multiple Long-Term Relationship

An MLTR is a woman you're dating and having sex with on a regular basis, with whom you have clear, strong, romantic feelings for. She spends the night with you and even goes on special events or trips with you. You cuddle after sex and have no problem discussing your feelings with her. You can even be in love with an MLTR.

Just like with LTR, the word "long" in a multiple long-term relationship is not necessarily accurate. Some MLTRs last a few months, others can last many years.

The "M" in "MLTR" means multiple. This means you are not monogamous to, or emotionally exclusive with, an MLTR. You can date and have feelings for her, and you can also date, and have sex with, and have feelings for other women too. You can have several MLTRs at the same time. I often do. The term "polyamory" means you have more than one concurrent MLTR. You're serious, and you care for her, perhaps even love her, but you can care for and have sex with other women as well.

MLTRs are wonderful. I usually have at least one or two MLTRs in my life at all times, as well as a smattering of FBs.

Unlike with FB, an MLTR is actually a scale within itself. You can have one MLTR who is *somewhat* serious and also be dating another MLTR who is *very* serious. They're both MLTRs, but there's a definite hierarchy where you like (or love) some more than others.

OLTR – Open Long-Term Relationship

The OLTR is the nonmonogamous version of an LTR. Unlike with an FB or MLTR, with an OLTR you've actually made some real commitments. You are emotionally exclusive to her and her alone. This means you love her, and are committed to only her. However, you are still allowed to have sex with other women provided those women are FBs and nothing more. Your OLTR is essentially your girlfriend, in a very serious though nonmonogamous relationship.

Because of the committed nature of the OLTR, there are some ground rules you will both have to follow regarding sex outside the relationship. These rules are completely up to you and her, and every OLTR is different. That's one of the great things about the OLTR; they're completely customizable to the wants and needs of both of you. We'll be further discussing the topic of relationship rules in Chapter 18.

Unlike the other forms of nonmonogamous relationships, an OLTR is something a woman must show, through her actions, that she qualifies for it. The rule of thumb is that you should not make any woman your OLTR until she's been a low-drama MLTR for at least six months (though 12 months is better). Awarding "girlfriend" status too quickly to any woman, even a high quality one, often results in drama and other problems down the road.

To review (and to make it easier to remember), just remember the following list:

- You can have as many FBs as you like.
- You can have as many MLTRs as you like.
- You can only have *one* OLTR.
- You can have an OLTR and some FBs on the side.
- You can *not* have an OLTR and some MLTRs on the side. Otherwise the woman you're calling your "OLTR" is really just your favorite MLTR.

OLTR Marriage

This is when you legally marry your OLTR. However, one could also consider an OLTR couple living together but unmarried an OLTR "marriage." Remember that marriage is purely a SP construct, so it's never required, even if you love a woman and want to live and have children with her. The Alpha 2.0 avoids *legal* marriage if at all possible, but if he really does want to get legally married, the OLTR marriage is an option for him.

The OLTR marriage differs from TMM in the following three ways:

1. It's an open marriage, where you are allowed to have sex with other women (ONSs and/or FBs only!) under whatever ground rules you and her agree to.
2. There is an *enforceable* prenuptial agreement signed long before the wedding takes place. Note the word *enforceable.* This means you live in a country, state, or province where prenuptial agreements are actually enforced by the government if challenged in court. Many parts in the Western world, such as California, England, Australia, and others, offer prenuptial agreements but do not truly enforce them. In these areas, OLTR marriages are effectively impossible, and you must simply refrain from ever getting a legal marriage (or move somewhere else).

3. There are no co-owned debts or assets between you and her. That means only one of you is on the mortgage or lease. It also means all the cars, investments, and bank accounts have your name on them or her name on them, not both your names. It also means there are no co-signed loans between the two of you. Everything in your financial life is either hers or yours, not both of yours. Functionally, your house will be "both of yours" of course. But legally, it will only be in one of your names. If you want to financially support your wife, this is perfectly fine. Give her all the money you want as often as you like; just don't have any joint accounts, debts, or assets with her.

The OLTR marriage is the only responsible way for an Alpha 2.0 to be married to a woman in an era where 50% to 68% of marriages end in divorce, in which case men are usually the ones financially penalized. This is in addition to the fact that as much as 77% of people in long-term marriages eventually cheat anyway, and in most marriages one partner (usually the female) eventually starts resisting sex.

The Problem with TMM

This brings us to the two problems with traditional monogamous marriage (TMM) for the Alpha Male, 1.0 or 2.0.

The first problem is when your wife starts refusing to have sex with you once the honeymoon period wears off (which, as we discussed in the last chapter, is something she is biologically wired to do). As a man and a highly sexual creature, this is a very serious problem. You can't have sex with her, because she won't let you. Because the marriage is monogamous, you can't have sex with anyone else, because you promised you wouldn't, and doing so behind her back risks you getting caught.

You are now at her mercy. Cheat, and risk the entire marriage collapsing in a very bad way, or tolerate significantly reduced or even zero sex, which for an Alpha Male is not possible or feasible.

The second problem is an even bigger one. When you get divorced, and the odds are overwhelming that you will, since as a you were never designed for long-term monogamy, she is now legally entitled to half of all your money and possessions, including things like your house, car, and retirement savings. Even if you have no assets, in many cases she is still entitled to a percentage of your income, often for many years. If you don't pay this to her, you will go to jail, and many men have gone to jail specifically for this reason.

Under a TMM structure, your wife will know all of this. She will know that she can manipulate you by refusing sex and/or by threatening divorce. TMM gives a woman awesome power over your life, your finances, your body, and your future. This is one of the many reasons women crave marriage so much.

Under an OLTR marriage, a woman's twin weapons of divorce and withholding sex vanish instantly. If after the honeymoon period she decides she doesn't want to have sex with you, no problem. It's an open marriage, so you can go get your sexual needs met by someone else whenever you like. If your wife ever decides to divorce you, no problem. She signed a prenuptial agreement in an area that enforces them, and her name isn't on any of your assets, so the divorce doesn't disrupt your financial life in any way. Divorce is never fun of course, and you'd still be upset, but it no longer becomes this terrible, life-destroying event it is to betas and Alpha 1.0s living in The Prison.

The Dating / Relationship Cycle for the Alpha 2.0

Now that we've covered the dating / relationship cycle of the beta male and the Alpha 1.0, as well as the different types of relationships, let's take a look at the cycle that Alpha 2.0s follow in their woman lives. It looks quite different from their beta and Alpha 1.0 brothers.

1. Have sex with many women.
2. Categorize some women as FBs, others as MLTRs.
3. Dump any FBs or MLTRs who give him drama or demands. Continue to have sex with and date other FBs and MLTRs who make him happy.
4. Maintain happy, low-drama, years-long relationships with multiple FBs and MLTRs.
5. Possibly fall in love with one special MLTR and promote her to OLTR or OLTR marriage.
6. Continue having sex with FBs on the side, replacing any FBs who drop off.

That's it. This is the model I have been following for many years now. The advantages to a man are massive:

- I never have to deal with cheating, because all my relationships are sexually open, which means cheating is impossible by definition.

- I never have any bad breakups. All my breakups are amicable, and 94% of the women who break up with me return to me later anyway.
- I never go without sex, ever. I have sex at least three times a week, every week, unless I choose not to (which is rare).
- I can satisfy my male need for sexual variety at all times, even while being in love with one special woman.
- I can have very strong romantic feelings, even fall in love, with a particularly special woman if I chose and if the feelings take me. Romantic love, even intense love, is allowed under MLTR and OLTR relationship models. It's actually required for the OLTR.
- I can experience everything I could normally experience with a traditional girlfriend or wife.
- I don't have to "babysit" any of my women like most normal men do. My women can go out and do whatever they like when they're not with me. It's great for me, since I don't have to concern myself with them. It's great for them, because they can be independent women while still being in a relationship with a fun, successful, motivated, low-drama man they care about.
- I am 100% free to do whatever I want with my life, including pursue my Mission, with no interference from a woman who "won't let me do that."

It is the best of both worlds!

I know what you're thinking. "But I want to settle down and have kids someday and be with that one special woman!" No problem, that's what the OLTR marriage is all about. When an Alpha 2.0 is ready to do this, he follows this model:

1. Commit to his OLTR and move in with her. Preferably not get legally married, but if he does want marriage...
2. Write up a prenuptial agreement with his OLTR and have her sign it. The sexually open aspect of the marriage is clearly spelled out in the prenuptial agreement, so she knows exactly what she's getting into.

3. Write up a parenting plan with his OLTR and has her sign it.

4. File all legal documents in accordance with his country, state, or province, making them official and legally enforceable.

5. Marries his OLTR. All debts, assets, and bank accounts are still kept separate, though he may still financially support her if he chooses.

6. Continues to discreetly have sex with ONSs and/or FBs on the side in accordance with what his new OLTR wife has already agreed to. Brings new FBs into his life as needed.

7. Has children with his wife, and raises them just as a "normal" married couple would.

If there's a divorce, which is very possible, since women are dynamic creatures and may end up changing their minds down the road, then the following occurs:

1. Divorce occurs in accordance with the prenuptial agreement. He loses no assets and no money. The divorce takes 30 days or so and then it's done.

2. There is no custody battle, since all the details have already been spelled out in the parenting plan she already signed. He does pay child support, since there's no getting around that, but he pays his ex-OLTR nothing else, and he continues to see his kids and maintain at least 50% custody.

3. Throughout the entire process he's still having sex with his FBs on the side. Never throughout the entire divorce process does he go without sex unless he wants to.

4. After they part ways, he starts dating MLTRs again just like he was before the marriage.

5. His finances are undamaged; his sex life is undamaged; his relationship with his children still intact, and he continues on with his Mission.

I don't want to paint too rosy a picture here. Of course it's possible that the wife could try to contest the pre-nup or the parenting plan in court, but it's very unlikely unless the Alpha Male 2.0 is extremely wealthy. It's even more unlikely that the court will override those documents, unless you were doing something horrible like physically abusing your children.

OLTR marriages really do end that quickly and easily the vast majority of the time. I know one married couple who were moved out and divorced within 30 days, no fighting, no custody battle, no drama; because they had a prenup in place and were never monogamous. To this day, almost 10 years later, they still get along great. Another Alpha 2.0 I know actually has his ex-OLTR wife set him up with women to date. Those are just two examples. How often do you see things like this in the TMM world?

Structuring an OLTR marriage correctly makes the entire divorce experience a polar opposite to those getting divorced under a TMM framework.

Now you should have a very good idea for where the woman, or women, in your life fit within your Alpha 2.0 framework. In the next few chapters, we're going to discuss exactly how to bring all of these women into your life, and how to keep them there.

Chapter 15 –

How to Become Internally Attractive to Women

I may have faults, but being wrong ain't one of them.

Jimmy Hoffa

Summer, 2010.

She was one of the most beautiful women I had ever dated in my life, one of those "perfect tens." She sat in the passenger seat in my car as we sped down the freeway to my house. As usual with younger women, she had to have the car radio on, blasting terrible top 40 music. The particular song we were listening to was "There Goes My Baby" by Usher. She was dancing in her seat, or trying to, her jet black hair whipping back and forth.

"Oh my god," she said, "I love Usher so much! I want him to have sex with me while he's singing. But he has to be wearing that white suit."

"Singing? While he has sex with you?" I asked.

"Oh yeah," she said, really getting into the music and his voice.

I pictured Usher in my mind. He didn't seem like a particularly good looking guy to me, but as a guy myself it's often hard for me to tell.

"You think Usher is hot?" I asked, a little confused.

"No," she said.

"No? You just said you wanted to have sex with him."

"Oh yes! While he's singing! He's so sexy!"

"He's not hot, but he's sexy," I said. I had heard this exact sentiment about Usher and a few other male celebrities before. My own daughter once made a similar observation about him.

"Well…yeah," she said, like it was an obvious concept and I was a doofus for not understanding it, "He's not hot at all. He's kinda plain. But oh my god, he is sooooooo sexy!"

Being Internally Attractive to Women

This shows something very valuable about women most men tend to miss. That is, what makes you attractive to women is not necessarily your looks. Yes, looks are important; so much so that I've devoted the entire next chapter to your external physical appearance. Poor looks can indeed “break” you in terms of meeting, dating, and sleeping with women. However if you have good looks but lack confidence, outcome independence, and skill with women, your looks won’t get you far. I have been working with men in the dating arena for many years, and to this day I am still surprised at the number of very good looking men out there who have trouble getting women to have sex with them.

Conversely, much of the success I’ve had with women in the past was when I was:

- Over 50 pounds overweight, with man boobs and a big double chin.
- Clearly thinning hair.
- Extremely pale skin.

Yet despite all of this I still was able to quickly and easily sleep with many beautiful women, many of whom were 20 years younger than me, spending a grand total of zero to twenty dollars to do so. This was because my confidence and outcome independence were always operating at very high levels, and this made me internally attractive to women. I’m very happy to say that these days I’m no longer that overweight and I’ve addressed my thinning hair (though I’m still pretty damn white.) The point is this: A smooth, confident, relaxed guy who doesn’t give a shit is just as attractive to women as big boobs on a woman is to men.

This is a critical point. A lot of guys out there focus on techniques and routines in order to score with women. Some technique is good and valuable. However, many of these guys have fantastic technique, and can quote you chapter and verse regarding pickup lines, routines, games, and other gimmicks to attract women, yet these same men are neither confident nor outcome independent, thus their results with women are lacking.

When I first got back into the dating game many years ago after my divorce, I was the exact opposite. My dating “technique” was terrible. I mean terrible. I was very beta in my technical approach to women. Regardless, because my confidence and outcome independence were decently strong, I was sexually successful, to a degree at least, despite my horrible technique. Confidence and outcome independence are about 80% of the equation. Technique is the other 20%.

Internal Attractiveness

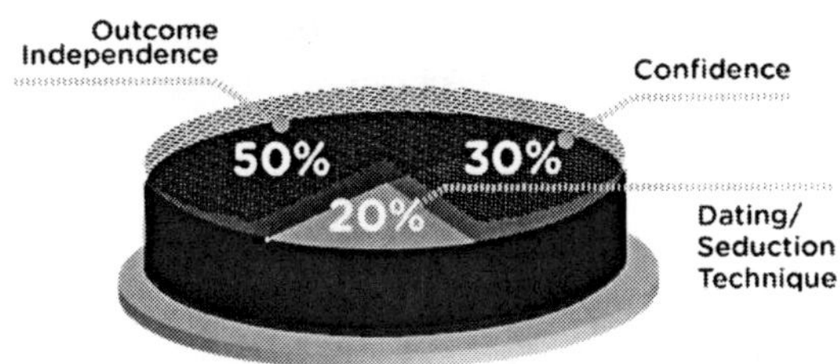

Thus, in order to be attractive to women, you must address the *inner* issues (confidence, outcome independence, emotional control, etc.) as well as the *outer* issues (fashion, grooming, fitness, etc.). Both areas are critical. Over-focusing on one of them while downplaying the other is a mistake.

In this chapter, we're going to discuss the inner qualities that make the Alpha Male attractive to women even if his appearance is subpar. In the next chapter we'll address physical appearance.

The two key areas to inner attractiveness are confidence and outcome independence, or OI. A third key area is emotional control. However, once you get confidence and OI down, emotional control comes almost naturally. I have found that men who lack emotional control tend to lack confidence, outcome independence, or both.

Let's tackle confidence first.

Confidence

When I say "confidence," I'm really talking about self-confidence. This is the full trust and belief in your power, strengths, and reliability. It's the knowledge that you've got things under control, and can handle any aspect of the situation you're in. Confidence means you can sit across from a woman who is an "LA ten" or a billionaire CEO and be totally relaxed, unafraid, and at ease.

You might be thinking of a certain type of quality that I'll call "situational confidence." This means you are confident in some areas but not others. For example, if you're really good at math but naturally poor in language skills, when you go in for a big math test, you'll be confident, but when you have to take an advanced English test, you'll be anything but.

I'm not talking about that type of confidence. I'm talking about an overall sense of confidence that hangs over everything you do in life. This sense of confidence never vanishes from you, even if you are doing something brand new. It's part of who you are.

You've probably seen this before. You've met truly confident people. They're confident no matter what they do. Even if they're in a situation where they have little or no experience, they're still self-assured. Perhaps not as confident as they usually are, but the air of confidence and steadiness still permeates through their actions, tone of voice, vibe, and body language. If I'm out on a first date with a gorgeous woman, or sitting in a business meeting, or giving a speech in front of a large crowd, I'm a confident guy. I've done all of these things many times before and have gleaned positive results from these situations. If you forced me to do a speech in front of 5000 people on a topic I knew absolutely nothing about, I would still be confident. I would not be as confident as giving a speech on dating or business, that's certainly true, but I would still be reasonably confident in any new situation as well, because I'm a confident guy overall.

Having this kind of confidence instantly makes you attractive, both to women on a sexual level and to other men on a friendship level. As soon as you meet a genuinely confident man, you know it instantly, and it's a nice thing to be around.

Confidence is demonstrated by actions like speaking strongly and deeply, slow movements, solid eye contact, a relaxed, kicked-back demeanor, laughter, a big smile, and a strong but relaxed posture. Confidence is not about acting cool or tough. Confidence is being relaxed, at ease, in control, and in charge.

The Sources of Confidence

Confidence comes from three sources:

- Past successes
- "Faking it 'till you make it"
- Positive reinforcement from others

It's easy for me to be confident on a first date with a beautiful woman because I've had sex with many beautiful women over the years by going out on many first dates. I have many past successes built up in my subconscious mind that instantly make me confident in these circumstances.

You're probably thinking, "That's great for you, but what if you haven't had successes in a particular area, like dating?"

The good news is that confidence from success in one area can overflow into confidence into new areas. For example, many years ago when I started going out on first dates, I was still very confident on those dates even though my level of dating skill was quite low. Why? Because I had many other past successes in other areas of my life, especially business, that made me a more generally confident person. My past success in the business world gave me a certain level of confidence when going out on first dates, even though dating was a relatively new thing for me.

It doesn't always work like this of course. I'm just saying it can and often does. Any time you feel less confident in a particular area, all you need to do is remind yourself strongly about a past success you had in a completely different area. Feel the feelings of achieving those successes, and you'll suddenly feel a little more confident in your new area. This is exactly what I did and it worked very well.

Sometimes, reflecting on past successes won't be enough. Or you may be a younger guy with no real major successes in life to reflect upon. That's okay. I started out as a young guy with no successes also. I left home at age 18 with no education, no money, little job skills, and a complete lack of people skills. Within a few years I was making serious money, and by age 27 I was making a six-figure income. We all start somewhere. The idea is to not stay there.

This is where "fake it 'till you make it" comes in. These days that phrase has become a little cliché, but it's still a viable way of achieving results. Assuming the actions and thoughts of a confident role model, and acting the part, will indeed help make you a more confident man.

The best way to do this is to observe a very confident guy you know personally and model your behaviors like him. How does he speak? How does he stand? Walk? Shake hands? Joke around? Later in this chapter I'll give you a specific list of confident body language behaviors.

If you don't know anyone personally who fits the bill, use Hollywood as your guide. Study any James Bond movie, any old Arnold Schwarzenegger action movie, or study men in movies like Humphrey Bogart, Marlon Brando, Steve McQueen, Jack Nicholson, George Clooney, Patrick Stewart, Morgan Freeman, Ed Harris, Sean Connery, Jason Statham, Mark Walberg, or Ryan Gosling. There are many examples of confident men in movies and on television, far too many to list here. Pick one or two of your favorites and model them.

Practice being like these men. Walk around your house, in front of the mirror and in front of friends, emulating how these men move, walk, and talk. Do it over and over again.

Years ago, when I felt myself drifting and needed to feel confident for a new client, business meeting, or speech, I would channel Peirce Bronson or Roger Moore, both of whom were James Bond. You can't get more confident than those guys! When I would go out on a first date and feel my confidence slipping a little, I would model guys like Arnold Schwarzenegger or James Woods.

I'll be honest. At first it felt a little silly. However, over time it started to work better and better. Today, this is all automatic for me. I have become that confident, and I don't need to pretend any more, but I promise you there was a time in my life where I did have to pretend in certain areas; at least a little.

The third source of confidence is positive reinforcement from others. This one may not be an option for you, but if it is, you certainly should take advantage of it. Getting regular positive reinforcement from a circle of friends and/or family members can indeed boost your confidence, soon to the point where you won't even need the reinforcement any more.

We've all read news stories of young, hyper-confident celebrities doing outrageous, arrogant, ridiculous things, thinking they can get away with anything (and sometimes being right). Most of that confidence is because these people are surrounded by a team of sycophants who are constantly telling them they're amazing and can do anything. The same was true of kings and emperors in ancient times.

Having other people boost you up in a positive way really does improve your confidence. You don't want to go overboard with it of course, but you should certainly use this method if you lack confidence.

Outcome Independence

Outcome independence is a fancy way of saying that you don't give a shit. OI means that the specific outcome of any singular, particular situation is irrelevant to you. For example, when you're on a first date with a very attractive woman, you literally don't care how things end up.

- If she rips off her clothes right there at the bar and leaps on you, great.

- If she calls you an asshole, throws a drink in your face, and storms out, great.
- If she ends up being cool and fun, great.
- If she ends up being a bitch, great.
- If you end up having sex with her really quickly right after the date, great.
- If the date ends up nowhere, great.

No matter what happens, you don't give a shit.

When I go out on a first date, I have extreme levels of OI. This is because I'm always dating at least three women at a time, so if this date goes nowhere, no problem, I'm still having sex tonight with a fantastic woman. Moreover, when I go out on first dates, I always make sure to schedule many first dates with many "prospects." That way if this first date fizzles, I quite literally don't care. I have another four or five first dates with attractive women already on the schedule.

With all that in place, do you think I give a shit if the first date doesn't work out? Nope. That's OI.

Compare this to the typical beta male. When he goes on a first date, it's usually because he's not having sex with anybody, and is looking for someone new. That's problem number one. Problem number two is that this first date is the only first date he has on his entire calendar. He has no other prospects.

Therefore, when he's sitting across from her, he needs the date to succeed. Badly. He doesn't want to "screw it up." He wants it too much. He's the exact opposite of OI.

Women pick up on this quickly. Even if he has some level of confidence, his outcome dependence will ooze through him, and she'll smell his neediness and desperation; and it will immediately turn her off.

On the other hand, when a woman goes out on a date with a relaxed, confident guy who doesn't give a shit, suddenly she's attracted to him, *and she doesn't even know why.* The old saying "women chase what runs away" is very true.

Outcome independence is the single most attractive non-physical trait you can have. It's the closest thing men have to a love potion. The more attractive a woman is, the more this is true, since attractive women are more than accustomed to men fawning all over them. Even confident guys tend to be outcome dependent around very beautiful women. When you come along and don't give as shit, she will be instantly attracted.

The side benefit of OI is that it helps you on other areas in your Seven Live Areas (SLA) as well. In business, negotiations, friendships, and family, having OI will assist you greatly. It has vast applications far beyond those of dating women.

Once you get into relationships with women, OI gives you a ridiculous amount of power. It's been said over and over again yet people still don't get it: in a relationship, the one who cares the least is the one who is happiest and has the most control. Would you like it to be her or you?

If your knee-jerk answer was "both," then you have some more SP that needs cleaning out. A true 50/50 relationship is impossible in the real world. Eventually, one of the two people come out on top, even if it's only 60/40.

There are many ingredients to the Alpha Male 2.0, and they're all important, but if you forced me at gunpoint to pick the most important one, it would be outcome independence.

By the way, the only difference between an Alpha 1.0 and an Alpha 2.0 is OI. The breakdown of the three male types looks like this:

Beta Male – Neither confident nor outcome independent.

Alpha Male 1.0 – Confident, but not outcome independent.

Alpha Male 2.0 – Confident and outcome independent.

The downfall of the beta is that he is not confident in himself and is always wedded to the outcome. The downfall of the Alpha 1.0 is that he is strong and confident in himself, but if people don't behave exactly the way he thinks they should, he loses his cool and gets upset, or at least very uncomfortable. This is why long-term *consistent* happiness for the Alpha 1.0 is impossible. His well-being is permanently attached to the outcome of what other people do.

The Alpha 2.0 doesn't have any of these limitations. Not only is he confident in himself, but he also doesn't give a shit. If a woman he's dating turns out to be a bitch, no problem, he just smiles and has sex with someone else. If he fails to get that new client, no problem, he just smiles and calls on some more prospects. He's structured his life and his outlook to be happy no matter what happens or what other people do.

Outcome Independent with Everything?

This raises a question. How can the Alpha Male 2.0 be outcome independent if he wants certain things? Doesn't that make him outcome dependent? Isn't he outcome dependent if he wants to achieve his goals or Mission? If he's out on a date with a beautiful woman, certainly he wants to have sex with her, doesn't he? Doesn't that make him outcome dependent?

The answer is no. Is this a contradiction? No, and I'll explain why. Remember above that I said that outcome independence is not giving a shit about a singular, particular event. It does not mean being completely indifferent regarding the big picture.

For example, the Alpha Male 2.0 does care about hitting his long-term goals, absolutely. At the same time, he knows that he does not need any one particular person, any one particular client or customer, any one particular business, or any one particular woman to achieve those goals. So if any one of these people or things fails him, he doesn't care. He knows (with his confidence!) that he will eventually hit his goals regardless.

When he goes out to have sex with a new woman, of course he wants to have sex. However, he doesn't care which attractive women he has sex with. He might have preferences of course, but he knows he'll have sex with at least one of them, and all of them are attractive to him, so any particular one is irrelevant to him. If one doesn't work out, he knows he'll soon be having sex with someone else. That's why he's outcome independent on any one particular date.

Desiring results from the big picture is not outcome independence. Desiring specific outcomes in particular, singular circumstances is.

The Sources of Outcome Independence

Outcome independence comes from two sources:

- Redundancy
- "Faking it 'till you make it"

Redundancy is a core concept of the Alpha Male 2.0, and you will never be able to live the Alpha 2.0 lifestyle without a full understanding and practice of it. We're going to cover redundancy in more detail in Chapter 20, but for now, I will briefly cover how it's used in your woman life.

As you already know by now, I'm always dating at least three women at a time. This way, if one woman starts throwing me drama, or "falls out of love" with me, or moves away, or whatever, it's no problem. My sex life continues on its merry way. This also means that no woman can ever exert control over me by threatening to break up with me or stop having sex with me. She knows there are other women who will immediately take up the slack. It's a very nice place to be.

Compare this to men in monogamous marriages. If she's a bitch or throws drama at him, he has to either put up with it or go through the life-catastrophe of a divorce. Sure, he could "command" her to stop doing it like an Alpha 1.0, but that only works short-term, not long-term. If she refuses sex and he can't convince her to provide it, he goes without sex whether he wants to or not. His only other option is cheating on her, making him a liar, and forcing him to act like a thief in the night, living a secret, double life that he hopes she won't discover. Not very Alpha. If she threatens to leave him, he cowers and obeys.

This is all because he has only one source of sex, romantic love and feminine energy. If that man had two, three, or four sources of these things, he would never (or at least very rarely) experience these problems.

When you apply the powerful concept of redundancy to all of your SLA you will suddenly become a very OI guy. It's impossible not to be.

However, like with confidence, perhaps you're not quite there yet. Perhaps you haven't built up a truly redundancy-based Alpha 2.0 lifestyle. This is where you're going to have to "fake it 'till you make it" just like I described above.

Finding men in your life who are truly outcome independent might be difficult, since the world has many more confident men than OI men. Fear not, for once again Hollywood can help us out. Watching and studying stand-up comics like Robin Williams, George Carlin, and Steven Colbert will really give you a crash course on what OI looks like. Wild actors like Jim Carrey, Kevin Kline, and James Woods also demonstrate huge amounts of OI in their performances.

If you really need an immediate example of what extreme outcome independence looks like, watch some of these guys:

- James Purefoy in the HBO series *Rome*
- Robert Downy Jr. in the *Iron Man* and *Avengers* movies
- Guy Pearce in the movie *Lockout*
- Idris Elba in the movie *Prometheus*

All of those performances are fantastic examples of what OI looks like.

Emotional Control

Emotional control is many things, but here are the three biggest examples from your woman life:

1. The ability to keep your cool when someone, especially a woman, pisses you off.
2. The ability to control yourself physically when you get extremely turned on.
3. The ability to keep yourself under control when you really, really like or love a woman, and want to start telling her how beautiful or amazing she is, or want to make promises to her you probably won't be able to keep.

All of these applications are important and valuable. Fail to do item one, and you'll enter the world of the Alpha Male 1.0, experiencing regular anger, frustration, and upset throughout your life. Fail to do item two, and you're going to be the victim of unwanted pregnancies and STDs, as well as a host of other problems. Fail to do item three, and you'll enter the world of the beta male, being taken advantage of by women and being a slave to their ever-changing desires. If freedom and long-term happiness are what you want, emotional control is absolutely critical in so many different areas of life.

To this day I am still amazed at the sheer number of otherwise intelligent, strong, capable men who simply can't (or chose not to) keep their emotions in check. These guys are constantly getting into trouble with women, having conflict in their interpersonal relationships, having trouble at work, getting banned from online forums or blogs, and blowing otherwise easy opportunities for women, money, friendship, and other life advantages. All because they simply refuse (or don't know how) to pause for just ten seconds and calm down before they take action. It's such a simple, tiny thing, yet millions of men all over the world, who theoretically should know better, refuse to do it.

An entire book could be written on the topic of emotional control and how important it is to happiness and success in life. Here, I'm simply going to say that you cannot live the free, perpetually happy lifestyle of the Alpha 2.0 if you're flying off the handle all the time. If you insist on this kind of behavior, Alpha 1.0 status is the best you can hope for.

The good news is that emotional control is a natural outgrowth of confidence and OI. Once you have a strong degree of confidence and OI in your life, especially OI, you will suddenly find it's very easy to keep your cool when you someone pisses you off or when a woman really turns you on.

I am not saying that emotions are bad. Positive emotions are what life is all about. The entire concept of this book, the entire point of an Alpha 2.0 existence, is to feel happiness as often and as consistently as possible. Happiness is an emotion, and I'm all for it. Yet I'm talking about *positive* emotions, not all emotions. Flying into a rage because someone says something you don't like isn't a positive emotion, and it doesn't matter if you were really happy the day before you were angry. Completely screwing up your chances with a woman because you were acting too horny will also result in negative emotions for you.

Emotional control is not about suppressing emotions. It's about creating a framework for experiencing more positive emotions while avoiding the negative ones. Make sure you get that, because every time I talk about emotional control, someone always wants to say that either I'm "against emotions" or that somehow feeling bad is a good thing because feeling bad is "human" or something. I addressed this already back in Chapter 2. Feeling like crap might be human, but so is feeling really good. So stick with the good, chuck the bad. To me, that's human. It's also smart.

Body Language

Confidence and OI is carried from your inner world to your outer world primarily by body language. This includes your voice. What follows is a list of the many ways confidence and OI is demonstrated. Make sure you are consciously aware of all of them, and soon, they'll become automatic for you.

- Walk straight and tall. Imagine a string attached to the top of your head, pulling you upward like a puppet.
- When you walk, swaying your arms is great, but don't sway your torso back and forth. If you're not sure what I'm talking about, find a wall of mirrors and practice walking in front of them. Stand straight, sway your arms but not your torso, and you'll see what a huge difference this makes.
- Make sure your head is up, your shoulders are back, and your chest is out.

- When sitting, especially on a date, lean back and relax. Don't slouch, don't lean forward like you're interested, and don't sit up ramrod straight like you've spent ten years in the marines. Lean back. Chill. Relax.
- If you're in a business meeting you do want to sit straighter, but you still want to have a relaxed, I-don't-give-a-shit demeanor about you.
- Control your movements. Think slow and controlled. Strong, classy, confident guys don't have quick, wild movements; their movements are slow, deliberate, and powerful. (There are exceptions to this though; there are plenty of high-energy, spastic Alpha 2.0s out there.)
- Don't be afraid to use your personal space. When you move, feel free to make big movements. Feel "big."
- Always keep good eye contact.
- Always have a relaxed look on your face. Smile a lot. Alphas smile!
- Laugh. A lot. Life is really funny.
- Speak as slowly and as deeply as possible. I have a good voice; it's one of my natural strengths. However even after years of professional speaking experience I still have a habit of occasionally talking too fast. Do your best to slow things down. Slow and deep. If you have a quiet, or high-pitched, or nasally voice, I would strongly recommend you spend $200 and get in a few sessions with a professional speech coach. It helps tremendously.
- Don't try to act tough. Don't try to act cool. That's what Alpha 1.0s do, along with a few miscalibrated betas. There's no point, because as I said above, a truly confident man who doesn't give a shit what people think and would never try to act cool or tough in a million years. Acting cool or tough means you care. That's not OI. An Alpha 2.0 doesn't give a shit. This gives him "permission" to be relaxed and happy.

Your Mission Makes You Attractive

All the other advice given in this book, specifically about having a strong Mission, automatically makes you more attractive to women (and to men in friendship and business contexts).

A man with a strong Mission he's devoted to instantly carries with him an air of command, control, and masculinity that women love. Recall the story I told back in Chapter 9 about the woman who said "I want a man with a twinkle in his eye, but I don't want to be that twinkle." That's exactly what I'm talking about. Men with Missions are far, far more attractive to women than men without them.

Interesting Skills Make You Attractive

Lastly, interesting skills will also make you attractive to women. When I say an "interesting" skill I'm talking about anything appealing you know how to do that's not too "introvertish." For example, skills like being a good dancer, knowing how to cook, being a professional speaker, knowing how to ski, or being skilled at martial arts would all be considered attractive, or at least interesting, by most women. More introverted skills like being really good at computers or knowing how to write well would not be. These skills are valuable, and I have many of those more introverted skills myself, but they likely aren't going to make you more attractive to females.

If you don't have at least one "interesting" skill, go learn one, even if that means you need take some dance classes or something else outside of your comfort zone. Not only will it make you more attractive to women, it will increase your overall confidence as well.

Chapter 16 –

How to Become Externally Attractive to Women

You make your day. You make your life. So much of it is all perception, and this is the form that I built for myself.

Brad Pitt

November, 1989.

It was the weekend and I was in my bedroom. I had taken a shower but I hadn't really done anything else. My hair, which as a senior in high school was huge and thick like a 1980s rock star, was a wild animal on my head.

I got hungry and opened my door to the bedroom, but then stopped. I heard a commotion downstairs, and remembered that my sister, who was a freshman at my same high school, had a bunch of her little freshman girlfriends over.

Dammit. I was in my underwear and nothing else. I groaned as I pulled back into my room, picked my jeans off the floor, shook them off, and put them on. I rummaged around a big pile of dirty clothes, found a ragged black T-shirt, and threw that on too.

Then I shambled downstairs to the kitchen to shove a bagel in my mouth.

At the bottom of the stairs in the living room, my sister and about seven other girls were sitting around and chatting. When I walked through, my sister said, "Hi Caleb!"

I grunted a response and kept moving, my mind on food.

However, being the teenage boy I was, I did do a quick scan over the girls. None of them impressed me, until my eyes rested on one; the only one with blonde hair. I had, and still have, a huge thing for blonde women. The girl looked at me for a minute and held my gaze. She was very cute. I glanced at the other girls and then went into the kitchen.

The kitchen and the living room were all one room, so I could still see the girls and the backs of their heads as I rummaged around looking for something to eat. Every time I looked at the girls, they were all looking at my sister as she held court...except the blonde girl. She was always looking at me. Every time our eyes met she quickly looked away, but every time I looked, I caught her gazing at me.

Being a teenage dumbass, and still very inexperienced in the ways of the female (I was still a virgin at the time), I didn't put two and two together, nor did I take advantage of the situation.

The next day, my sister and I were taking about her little gathering and I mentioned the blonde girl.

"Ohhhhh yeah," she said, "That was Lana. Oh my god, she would not stop talking about you when you went back upstairs."

"Huh?" I said.

"Oh yeah. She had all kinds of questions about you and wanted to know everything about you. She thought you were hot."

"How could she have thought that?" I asked, honestly surprised, "I looked like shit. I had just rolled out of bed."

"No, she thought you were hot. She likes rock star guys and she thinks Richard Marx has the coolest hairstyle in the world, and she loved that you made your hair look just like his. She just thought you were so hot. She wouldn't shut up about you."

"I didn't do shit to my hair," I said, "That's just how it looks when I don't do anything with it."

"Well, you're in luck, because that's exactly what she likes."

Long story short, Lana and I ended up dating briefly and she was a lot of fun.

(Not that much happened though. Not only were both of us under age 18 but it was not yet my time to lose my virginity. Sadly, that would have to come a few years later in my early 20s.)

Your Physical Appearance

Looks matter. In terms of being attractive to women, physical appearance is an important factor whether we want to admit it or not. At the same time, it's not the be-all and end-all a lot of men make it out to be. Throughout the ages men have made a big fuss about how they look in order to attract women, when in fact, as I already made clear in the last chapter, women will be just as attracted to your non-physical attributes as they are to your physical ones.

Men have a tough time with that concept, because as men we are purely visual. If she's hot, we want to sleep with her. It's that simple for us. Of course other factors may come into play, but it really starts with physicality with us, no matter how smart or evolved you think you are as a man. The physical attractiveness of your lover/girlfriend/wife is a critical component of how you feel about her. It's a core part of our OBW.

The more physically attractive you are, the higher your odds of success with women become. Yes, ugly guys can get women. Chubby guys can also get women. I was quite chubby a few years ago and still did fine in terms of meeting and dating women without having to spend any money on them. However, the uglier or chubbier you are,

- The more women you'll have to meet and hit up.
- The more effort it will take.
- The more rejections you're going to get.
- The more overall time it will take to go from zero to sex.

The reality is that the better you look, or at least the "less-bad" you look, the easier everything else with women will be. The less a woman has to "get past" your negative physical appearance, the more your internal attractive attributes will work for you. Therefore it's a worthwhile investment of time (and sometimes money) to optimize your personal appearance.

Contrary to what you might think, improving your physical appearance is probably the easiest technique we're going to cover in this book. Looking a little better physically is much easier than creating a Mission, building outcome independence, setting non-SP goals, or getting good with time management.

Physical appearance is really just a checklist of items. Do these things, and you'll look better to women. Fail to do them, and your looks will be something you'll have to overcome when trying to have sex with a woman or find a female partner. Ideally, you should look the best you can possibly look, especially right before a situation where you know you'll be spending time with a woman you want to have sex with (like a first date, or when going out to meet women).

One of your overall goals as an Alpha Male 2.0 is to look the best you possibly can within the constraints of your age and genetics.

The Checklist

Your appearance falls into three categories: Your body, your grooming, and your fashion. Here is the checklist of items in all three areas you need to address.

Part One: Your Body

Skin

- ✓ Avoid skin that is too white or pale. Keep a decent tan; either a real tan or a fake one. If you have very pale skin like I do, address it as best you can. I use self-tanning lotions and similar to look as "least-white" as I can, but there are many other methods.
- ✓ Address any acne you may have. Visit a dermatologist if necessary.
- ✓ If you're over the age of 35 or so, maintain a daily skin regimen to keep your face looking tight and healthy. Wrinkles actually look good on men (they're masculine) but you don't want too many too soon. Plus, women can tell when a man has unhealthy-looking skin. Your skin regimen should include moisturizer, exfoliant, face wash or astringent, and sunblock protection. You may think that moisturizing doesn't sound like a very masculine thing to do. You're right. However the Alpha 2.0 seeks long-term happiness, so looking great when you're 31 and looking like crap when you're 57 won't make you very happy. The Prison is filled with unhappy old guys who used to be gorgeous, and you don't want to be one of them. Not if you want to be and stay happy.

Baldness / Thinning Hair

- ✓ If you are bald, have a big bald spot, or have very thin hair, you have two options. The first is to shave your entire head. This looks way better, both to men and women. At least try it. Force yourself to keep that look for one month. If absolutely hate it, you can always go back. Don't forget to tan if you have pale skin! Think of all the time and money you'll save when you never have to wash or style your hair ever again!
- ✓ The next option is to spend some money and get either a nonsurgical hair restoration system or hair restoration surgery. Both of these procedures do work (I opted for the nonsurgical option and I'm very pleased with it) and both have their pros and cons. Research, weigh the options, save the money, and get it done. Do not just "put up" with thinning hair. Clearly thinning hair makes you look much older and heavier than you actually are, and looks very unhealthy.

Teeth

- ✓ Having problem-free teeth is huge. To most women (at least those in the US), having bad teeth is an instant deal breaker. If you have very yellow teeth, dark spots, clearly crooked teeth, a snaggletooth, or whatever, address it, even if it costs you some money. This may even more important than addressing thinning hair.

Height

- ✓ If you are under 5'10" or so, that's a negative you're going to have to do your best to alleviate and overcome, unless you live in a part of the world where men under 5'10" are the norm. Guys like Al Pacino and Joe Pesci overcome this challenge by having larger-than-life Alpha 1.0 personalities. That's one way to do it. Another method is getting shoe lifts or height-adding shoes or boots. Nothing wrong with that at all. I would not add more than one to three inches to your height, however. If you do that you'll later have some explaining to do.
- ✓ On the flip side, extremely tall men (as in men well over 6'2") are often going to be perceived as overly intimidating. If you're this tall, it will actually help you with women to be a little nicer and less dominant. Remember I said a little.

Weight

- ✓ It goes without saying that the chubbier you are, the more you're going to have to overcome that negative to attract women. This is something I know a little about. Of all the Seven Life Areas, fitness has always has been my weakest area by far. I've been overweight off and on throughout my adult life, so this has always been a challenge for me. That being said, I recently lost 40 pounds, so I do have enough credibility to say this: if you're fat, address it. Get it under control. Do whatever you need to do. Just get it done. I know it's hard for some of us. Believe me, I know. I'm not saying you have to be ripped with 6% percent body fat. I'm also not saying you can't be an Alpha 2.0 if you're chubby. You can. I am saying the more chub you have, the worse it will be for you and your woman life. You'll have to work harder and put in far more numbers than men of your equivalent height and age who are less chubby than you. Not to mention the myriad of health risks you're incurring which are sure to destroy your long-term happiness.
- ✓ I'm not sure I even need to tell you this, but I'm just saying it to be clear: resistance training like weight lifting, thereby getting big muscles, does help in attracting women. You will attract more women more easily if you're more muscular. Moreover, lifting weights increases testosterone and gives many other health benefits

critical to an Alpha 2.0 lifestyle. Having larger muscles also increases your confidence, and many scientific studies have proven this to be the case. I lift weights regularly and will be doing so for the rest of my life. You should do the same. I consider regular resistance training to be one of the non-negotiable minimums of the Alpha 2.0 lifestyle.

Part Two: Grooming

- ✓ Any facial hair you have should be part of a predefined look, not something that just happens because you're lazy or want to look "natural." If you want to be clean shaven, always shave cleanly. If you want facial scruff, pay attention to it and manage it. Don't let it run wild. More often than not, women do like facial hair on men, but if you've got wild, curly hair coming out of your sideburns or the side of your neck, this is not good.
- ✓ Be aware of your own body odor. Some guys really have no odor at all (I am one of these lucky men). Other men can paralyze a horse with their BO as soon as they start to sweat even just a little. Be aware of this and use cologne, body wash, lemon juice, vinegar, or whatever you need to offset this if needed. A significant change in diet may also be in order.
- ✓ If you do use cologne, don't overdo it. Lots of men wear way too much. One tiny, distant spray under each armpit is all most men need (unless you're one of those horse-killers).
- ✓ Shave the back of your neck once a week.
- ✓ If you're over age 35 or so, address nose hairs and ear hair once every two to three weeks.
- ✓ If you have very big or very scruffy eyebrows, trim them. Comb them upwards and then trim anything that goes above the natural upper line of your eyebrow with a small pair of scissors.
- ✓ Get a cool hairstyle. Think edgy. If you have no idea what's cool, a few Google searches or a quick scan through a current men's magazine like GQ will tell you. Pick a style you like, rip out the page, show this to your stylist, and make it happen. It's worth it to go to an actual salon (as opposed to the $14 haircut place) and get a professional stylist's advice. You only need to do this once. Once you've got the style down you can always go back to the cheap place and duplicate it.

- ✓ If you're a blue collar worker, clean your fingernails, daily if necessary.
- ✓ Shave off any hair that grows on the front of your neck (if any), and any chest hair that pokes through your collar.
- ✓ If you're a hairy bastard, shave off any hair that grows on your back, shoulders, and upper arms (if any) at least once a month. There are long-handled electric razors you can order online just for this purpose. If you're particularly hairy, there are some surprisingly inexpensive laser and dermabrasion options available that you should definitely look into.
- ✓ If you have lots of very bushy chest hair, buy the adjustable clippers that hair stylists use, set it to a one or a two, and shave your chest hair down about once every two to four weeks. You will be amazed at how much better you look. I don't have a lot of chest hair, but when I did this myself as an experiment years ago, I was sold. Note I said shave your chest hair down, not off. Surveys show, and my experience shows, that the majority of women actually like a little chest hair. Moreover, shaving chest hair completely off looks bad, feels weird to a woman touching it, is itchy as hell, and the effect only lasts a few days until it looks weird again. Unless you have the body of a ripped professional bodybuilder, shave down, not off.
- ✓ Everything I just said about chest hair applies equally to, if you have it, excessive pubic hair, excessive armpit hair, and/or unusually hairy arms. Shave it down, but not off. As an aside, I have had more than one woman tell me stories about men they've slept with who had shaved off all of their pubic hair. In every case, the woman considered it was a turn-off. As always, shave down, not off.

Part Three: Fashion

I'm no fashion expert, believe me. Outside of wearing suits and ties, which is an area I know pretty well, I personally know very little about fashion, men's or otherwise. So if you're looking for detailed fashion advice, you'll have to look elsewhere. Here, I'm just going to remind you that fashion is an important part of your appearance that you need to pay attention to, and give you a very general overview.

What I can tell you, and what I practice, is that all of your clothing must adhere to modern, current styles. Way too many men dress like they used to dress when they were in high school, even if that was a decade ago or more. I was guilty of this for many years.

Your pants and shirts, the shoes you wear, the jackets you wear, the style of your collar and sleeves, everything must be in modern cuts, fits, and styles. Women are very sensitive to when a man dresses in a current, cool way vs. when a man dresses in outdated styles.

Color is also extremely important. Women's eyes and brains perceive color far better than we do[37]. There are certain colors that look great on you and ones that look terrible on you, based on your skin tone, eye color, and hair color. You must know what these colors are, so you can wear more of your "good" ones and avoid your "bad" ones.

My favorite color, by far, is black. I wore pretty much nothing but black, white, and grey from puberty all the way to about age 30. Finally, at the urging of some of my co-workers, I spent about $150 and went to an image consultant to improve my appearance for my public speaking. They made it clear to me that because of my pale skin, dark hair, and blue eyes, wearing black and white made me look terrible. I was furious. I didn't want to believe it. Black and white looked good on Antonio Banderas in *Desperado*, so why the hell wouldn't it look good on me?

They told me to instead focus on colors like blue, purple, and red, and to avoid colors like green, yellow, and orange. As a final insult, they said I should never wear black or white unless it was below my waist. Thankfully, they said I could still wear gray shirts and suits as long as they weren't too dark.

Though I was upset and reluctant, I took their advice on faith and changed the colors of my clothing. To my shock, they were right. Just like in some clichéd TV show, when I started wearing colors that complimented me, I actually had women I didn't know giving me compliments. This had never happened to me before.

If you'd rather not spend money on an image consultant, then at least take a feminine woman you trust under age 30 and have her take you clothes shopping. Even better, take more than one. While there, have her put different solid-color shirts up to your face and get her opinions about what colors she thinks work for you. This is one of the very few times I will ever recommend you take a woman's advice about anything dating related. You don't necessarily need to pay attention to what clothes she says to buy; instead focus on what *colors* she says look good on you. Thus armed, you can dramatically improve your wardrobe.

---

[37] http://www.asu.edu/news/research/womencolors_090104.htm

Chapter 17 –

How to Get to Sex Whenever You Want

If I don't have a woman for three days, I get terrible headaches.

John F. Kennedy

January, 2009.

It was a day I knew I had finally crossed over into a new world. In fewer than twelve days, I had:

- Been on four first dates.
- Been on two second dates.
- Had sex with a new woman, a gorgeous 25 year-old, a marathon runner and very fit.
- Had sex with another new woman, a 24 year-old blonde college student.
- Had sex with a third new woman, a spunky 19 year-old.
- Got to almost-sex with an attractive corporate VP in her mid-forties.

After looking back at that activity, I was shocked to realize that I had accomplished more in my woman life in twelve days than it took most men I knew several years to accomplish, if ever. Even more significantly, accomplishing this was easy. It was not the long, hard slog of trial and error that it had been the year or two prior when I was figuring out all this "woman stuff."

In the span of about 18 months, I had achieved a level with women that I could only dream of in my wildest fantasies during most of my adult life, both as a married man in his thirties and a young single guy in his early twenties. I had truly stepped into a new world.

Abundant Sex

Today I live the Alpha 2.0 lifestyle, where I can bring new attractive women into my sex life literally whenever I want, very quickly. Over the last eight years I have fulfilled pretty much every sexual fantasy I've ever had in my life. From cheerleaders to minor celebrities to threesomes to "perfect tens" to mother/daughter couples to all kinds of other crazy stuff. You name the typical male sexual fantasy and I've probably done it, all quickly and easily, without spending any money on prostitutes or expensive dates.

The average face time with a new woman from meet-to-sex for me these days is around two and a half to three hours, usually spread out over two dates. My average total money spent to get to this sex is around $14. Over one third of the time, its zero dollars.

This usually means I will meet a woman via online dating sites, or in person during the day ("daygame"), or through my social circle, then have a very quick first date that runs for about an hour, then meet her for a very quick second "date," usually at my house, and have sex within another hour or so.

I have repeated this exact system scores of times with a very high rate of success. It works with women of all types, ages (with one caveat I'll describe in a minute), races, personalities, income levels, and intelligence levels. A few years ago I even published ebooks laying out the exact system I use to do this, located at blackdragonsystem.com

As we discussed in detail back in Chapter 1, the Alpha 2.0 lives an abundant sex life. This means he can and does have sex often, with whomever he wants, and with women who are very attractive (at least to him).

A man who does not know how to bring new women into his sex life quickly is not an Alpha 2.0, and never can be, unless for some reason he has an extremely low sex drive. Even then that's probably not a great idea, since sometimes a very low sex drive for a man under the age of 60 is often indicative of other health and/or psychological problems.

Back in Chapter 1 we discussed the sexual baseline necessary for an Alpha lifestyle. To review, the baseline is:

1. The ability to have sex with at least two new women within four weeks of losing your current source of sex, be that a girlfriend, wife, friend with benefits, or whatever.
2. Having sex at least twice a week, regardless of whether or not you currently have a girlfriend or wife.

3. You consider these women at least "cute." Only having sex with ugly or average-looking women isn't going to satisfy you in the long run.

Baseline number two, the ability to have sex at least twice a week, every week, is usually a *relationship* baseline, and as such we will be discussing that in a later chapter. Baselines one and three are *dating* baselines. We'll cover those here.

Sexual Success

The single most important hallmark of being sexually successful is the ability to quickly have sex with new attractive women whenever you want. The reason for so much depression, angst, fear, neediness, and anger with beta males is because they lack this ability. Once their girlfriend dumps them, or their wife divorces them, or their friend with benefits moves on, they're suddenly in a situation where they simply can't have sex, since they cannot quickly replace the woman who left with a new quality one quickly.

This fear of lack of sex drives betas into all kinds of ridiculous and destructive fear-based behaviors, things they would never do if they had the ability to bring new women into their sex lives whenever they wanted. Once you reach the point where you know, not think, but *know* that you can go out and have sex with a new attractive woman whenever you want to or need to, this alone brings a sense of confidence and power most beta males will never experience. If you break up with a woman, no problem. You'll be having sex with another one just as smart and good-looking relatively quickly. If the woman you're with gets bitchy or demanding, you have no fear, since you know that you can have sex with another attractive woman no matter what happens.

I'm usually dating around three women, but even if all three women broke up with me on the same day, my sexual sustenance would still not experience a major disruption. Within a week or two I'd have two or three new women in my sex life. Of course I might be a little sad that someone I cared for broke up with me, but I'm talking here about the sexual aspects, not the emotional ones. We'll cover the emotional aspects in the next chapter.

This knowledge brings me an immense sense of happiness, peace, and internal security.

This is why one of our three Alpha Male 2.0 sexual baselines is to get to the point where you can meet and have sex with at least two new women within four weeks at the latest. A true Alpha 2.0 lifestyle is not possible if you lack this skill. As I mentioned above, it took me about 18 months of intense focus to get to the point where I could snap my fingers and bring a new woman (or women!) into my sex life whenever I wanted. It was 18 months well invested. Now, and for the rest of my life, I will never go without sex, for any reason, unless I chose to (though I'm not sure why I would do that).

Why Two Women?

Why do I say you must have sex with two women and not one? Because when you're horny and needy and end up having sex with just one woman, it invites neediness, scarcity mentality, and often, monogamy. These things make the freedom and happiness-based lifestyle of the Alpha 2.0 impossible.

If you're in the hunt for new sex or new companionship, only having sex with one woman will subconsciously cause you to start clinging to her as your "only" source of sex and feminine energy. Therefore it is critical that you can bring in at least two new women within four weeks, not just one. This does not mean you need to be some kind of super-player who is having sex with several different women all the time. Two women are more than enough for a lot of men.

Sexual Parameters

There are a few provisos to the three sexual baselines, since not all sex is the same.

Even the most pathetic guy out there can whip out $200 and have sex with an STD-ridden prostitute. Almost any guy can get lucky with a very ugly or overweight woman or a drugged-out meth addict.

On the other side of the coin, almost any guy can beg his monogamous girlfriend or wife for sex and eventually get it. Almost any guy can take a woman out on four, five, six or more expensive dinner dates spread out over several weeks and then finally, maybe, get inside her pants, assuming she doesn't get bored with him before then and dump him for the next sucker.

These examples are all sex, but none of these examples are Alpha. Therefore, when we talk about bringing new women into our sex lives fast, we need to set some specific parameters around this.

1. Spending significant money to get the sex doesn't count. If sex with a woman requires that you take her out to dinner several times at $80-$100 a pop, not only is that not quick, but the financial expense of doing so is going to damage both your lifestyle, happiness, and self-esteem (unless you are an extremely wealthy multimillionaire). Therefore, spending a significant amount of money to get sex does not count towards our baseline of having sex with at least two new women within four weeks. This means the following types of women would not apply towards the Alpha 2.0 sexual baseline:

- Women who demand several dinner dates (or similar) before sex.
- Women who have a "three date rule" or "five date rule" or similar restriction regarding when they have sex with a new man.
- Women who promise to have sex with you only if you fly them to Vegas, Europe, or other similar gold digger bribe.
- Women with whom you have an "arrangement" with, such as those you would find on a sugar daddy dating site.
- Prostitutes.

I'm not saying you can't have sex with the above types of women. I'm saying that if you do, they don't "count" towards the Alpha 2.0 sexual baseline. I have no moral or ethical objection if you want to have sex with hookers, sugar babies, gold diggers, or dominant "ladies" who demand multiple dinner dates before sex. If having sex with any of those types of women truly makes you happy, then go for it. That's your business. When I become a very old man, I may even sample some of those above options myself; but even then they still won't "count" towards the Alpha 2.0 sexual baseline.

The reason is because if you know the only way to fulfill your sexual needs is to spend several hundred dollars of your hard-earned money every time you want to have sex with someone new, you will never experience the outcome independence, sense of abundance, peace, and internal security that a true Alpha Male 2.0 does.

Again, if you're a wealthy multimillionaire with money to burn, then you may be the one exception to this rule, but for the remainder of this discussion, I'm going to assume you're not in that category.

I don't have to spend hundreds of dollars to have sex with new women. If you do, your thoughts on this won't be as peaceful or abundant as mine are. I will be happier longer-term than you will be. It's that simple.

Again, I'm talking about spending hundreds of dollars, not spending money in general. A little expense is perfectly fine. Taking a woman out to a bar on a first or second date and buying her a drink or two is perfectly acceptable and I do that all the time.

2. Ugly women don't count. I've known a lot of men who eventually become accustomed to having sex with ugly or average-looking women. If you're having sex with unattractive women because you think you can't get better, obviously that's an area of needed improvement in your life.

Like with hookers, I have no philosophical objection to this. The Alpha 2.0 is about happiness, and if having sex with clearly unattractive women truly makes you happy, on the surface it's fine.

The problem occurs when these guys finally have sex with a really pretty girl. Then they often fall hard and fast, and soon they're in a monogamous, beta male relationship in which the new pretty girl owns their balls. All the usual drama and problems then ensue.

I'm not saying every woman you have sex with must be a 19 year-old supermodel. The third sexual baseline states that any new women at least "cute." Not "average," but cute. You know what cute means. Cute means better than average. Ugly, average, or "homely" women don't count.

My own rule in this area, and part of my Code, is that every woman I sleep with must be an "eight," to me, on the one-to-ten attractiveness scale. This is subjective of course; a woman who ranks as an eight for me may rank as a six for you, and a woman who ranks as a ten for you may rank as a seven for me. It doesn't matter. If she's not an eight to me, I pass. I don't ever want a new woman who is significantly better-looking than the rest to cause me to lose my outcome independence.

Routinely sleeping with women you consider less than "cute" will eventually damage your self-esteem, destroy your outcome independence, reduce your confidence, and create a false scarcity mentality when you think about women.

3. Lying to get sex doesn't count. If you have to lie to women to get sex, you're likely in for a very high-drama lifestyle, which is clearly outside of Alpha 2.0 standards. Resolve today to be 100% honest with all women you sleep with if you are not already.

One critical point about that: being 100% honest means you don't state any untruths. It does not mean you blatantly spill the beans about absolutely everything you're doing. Being 100% honest does not mean you tell a woman on a first date, "Hey, by the way, I had sex last week with a woman seven years younger than you, and it was fantastic! I just wanted to let you know." That's not being honest, that's being stupid. Do you think women tell us all their sexual dirty laundry on a first date? Or second? Or third? Of course not, and neither should you.

Being honest does mean that if a woman asks you if you had sex with another woman last night, and you did, you don't say no. You instead say yes or you refuse to answer the question. Either way, you aren't lying. We'll discuss this further in the next chapter.

4. The sexual conditions must be conducive to your lifestyle. Your personal lifestyle and preferences may not be conducive for certain conditions that other men may have no problem with.

For example, some men pick up women at bars and clubs late into the evening, as in well past 2am. For younger men, or more extroverted men, or men without strong careers, that's great. It's compatible with their lifestyle, and it's what they like to do. However, as a man in his forties who runs three small businesses, has two children, dates at least three women at a time, travels often, and is an introvert at heart, I learned very quickly that staying up late into the evening in order to bring new women into my sex life was not a very smart thing for me to do. After trying it a few times, I was tired, stressed, got very little sleep, had to wake up early the next morning to get to work, and had the entire next day shot because I was so sleepy. This negatively affected my productivity, my results in all my SLA, and my happiness.

Therefore, I resolved to not stay up past 11pm at night in order to meet or have sex with new women. For many years now I have successfully stuck to that rule with very little exceptions.

This is just an example. You need to examine your own life and ensure that your sexual activities don't degrade your performance in your other key SLA. Establish any parameters around this aspect of your woman life you think are necessary, and then stick to them.

Core Dating Concepts

So far in this book you have:

- Become aware of your own limiting sexual SP.
- Learned how women are not like you when it comes to sex and relationship desires, and how foolish it is to expect women to act like men.
- Determined exactly where new women fall into your life.

- Learned the importance of being inwardly attractive to women via confidence, outcome independence, emotional control, your Mission, and unique skills.
- Learned how to boost your physical appearance to maximum levels.
- Learned the need to develop the skill of having sex with two new women within four weeks, any time you need to, without having to lie, spend a lot of money, settle for women you don't think are pretty, or damage your key SLA.

Now we can finally talk about exactly how to bring these women into our lives. It's very important you do this within the framework of the concepts we discussed in previous chapters. Too many enthusiastic guys leap into trying to pick up women without considering any of the items above (with the possible exception of external appearance), and these men always, and I mean always, end up either:

1. Spinning their wheels, working very hard for little results, and getting discouraged.

Or

2. Settling for a monogamous girlfriend or wife who owns their balls and orders them around like a little drill sergeant.

Make damn sure that as you read though the techniques and principles in subsequent chapters, you keep these within the context of the critical concepts we've already discussed.

Game Styles

There are four ways to meet, "pick up," date, and have sex with new women. Each of these methods, or game styles, have their own sets of pros and cons. All game styles work, but some styles work better for some men than others.

Club Game

Otherwise known as night game or bar game, club game is the art of picking up women during the evening at bars, dance clubs, parties or similar venues and events.

Pros:

- Lots of very attractive women all in one place, making concentrated pickup easy.
- Many women are there specifically looking for sex.
- Many of them have been drinking, making sexual activity easier.
- Clubs, bars, and/or parties are enjoyable for more social or extroverted men.

Cons:

- Women are often "on guard" against guys picking them up in these kinds of venues.
- Requires staying up very late into the evening, even on weekdays when you may have to go to work the next morning.
- Loud music is very annoying and a barrier to communication.
- Lots of possible cock-blocking from other men and women's female friends.
- Women are usually in groups, requiring you isolate them.
- Can only be done during the evening.

Daygame

Otherwise known as street game, daygame is the art of picking up women during the daytime in "traditional" venues. This could be on the street, at a bookstore, mall, coffee shop, grocery store, or similar.

Pros:

- Women can often be found alone, making things easier.
- Women are more relaxed and less guarded during the day.
- Wide range of women available who could never be found at a club or on an online dating site.
- Can more easily be integrated into your schedule, since there are more hours in the day than at night.

Cons:

- Often extremely time consuming meeting women, establishing comfort, getting phone numbers that go nowhere, and dealing with flakes.
- Often harder to find attractive women, requiring more time to look around (though experienced daygamers know the "hot spots" in their city).
- Harder to get to sex quickly because of poor daytime logistics.
- Women are often in a hurry or on a tight schedule.
- Can only be done during the daytime.

Online Game

This is getting good at setting up first dates with women via online dating sites or social media sites.

Pros:

- Can contact massive amounts of women very quickly.
- Can be done literally at any time, 24 hours a day, and seven days a week.
- Very time management friendly; even dates can be scheduled whenever is convenient for you.
- Older men have easy access to younger women they normally would not have in real life.

Cons:

- Low response rates, requiring a ridiculously large amount of online "openers."
- Attractive women often harder to find, requiring culling through many less attractive women.
- Many women online are husband-hunting, and will thus expect a traditional 1950's first "date" where dinner is served and money is spent.
- Lots of flakes; many women will terminate the online conversation without warning and seemingly for no reason.

Social Circle Game

This is where you game women you already know, or at least know somewhat, through other friends, family, or co-workers. For it to work you need an outgoing personality and a reasonably wide social circle where you know lots of people.

Pros:

- Ridiculously easy if you do it right.
- No uncomfortable, cold "pickup" required; the women already know you.
- Very inexpensive, often requiring zero "dates" and zero expense.
- Other fun (nonsexual) actives are often involved.

Cons:

- Many women who know you have already placed you in "friend zone" making sex very difficult.
- Once you run out of women you know, you're out of luck. So you need to be constantly re-filling the social circle "funnel."
- Not viable for more introverted men.
- Not consistently reliable like the other three games styles. Social circle game is not systematic or predictable like club game, daygame, or online dating.

Just about every method you can possibly think of to meet or date new women will fall, at least in some way, into one of the above four game styles. You must choose one of these and completely focus on it. That's the fastest way to get good.

Be very sure to choose a game style that most accurately reflects your personality and lifestyle. This is important, because many men out there attempt to get good at game styles they aren't suited for.

As I mentioned above, I'm terrible at any type of night game or club game. I also hate doing it. Therefore, pursuing night game would be a huge mistake for me regardless of any advantages I see to that type of game. However, with online dating, I'm one of the best in the world. I've published several ebooks on exactly how to get from the dating site to sex very fast and with minimum money spent. (Go to blackdragonsystem.com if you're interested in those.) I'm also pretty good at social circle game under certain conditions, and have had some success with daygame, but online game has always been my focus.

Focus is the key. Shot-gunning this stuff and trying to get good at radically different game styles at the same time is never a pathway to fast success. Pick just one game style and get very, very good at it. Keep working at this until you get to the point where you know you can snap your fingers and bring at least two women into your sex life within four weeks or less, any time you want. Then, and only then, play your hand at the other types of game (if you still want to).

Putting in the Numbers

Dating is a numbers game. Once you choose a game style focus, your entire system must revolve around putting large numbers of women in the "funnel." No matter how suave, good-looking, or skilled with women you are, you will never master the skill of dating if you don't maintain a strong focus on putting in lots of numbers of new "prospects."

With club game and daygame, this means lots of women you walk up and talk to. With online dating, this means lots of women you send messages to. With social circle game, this means meeting lots of new people in your normal day-to-day life and bringing them into your circle, often and consistently.

By "lots" I don't mean ten or twenty, or even fifty; I mean hundreds and hundreds over a concentrated period of time. Yes, that's what this will require. There is no getting around this. Get comfortable with this reality, or at least accept it.

Here's an example of how the funnel process works with my favorite type of game, online dating. Don't get hung up on the exact numbers I use in the diagram; it's just an example to give you an idea of how this works.

Numbers Funnel Example

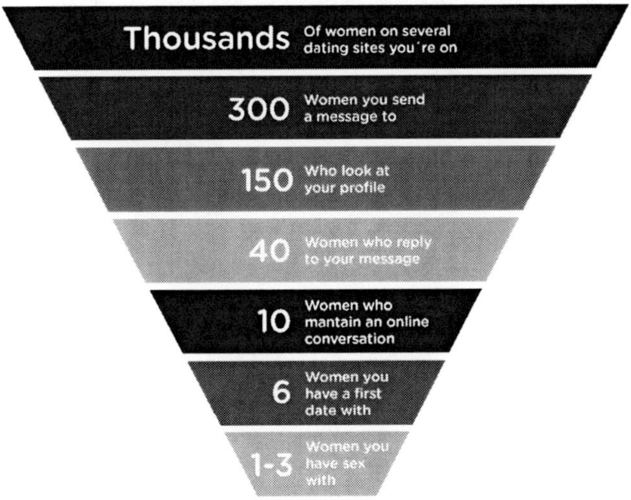

Thousands Of women on several dating sites you're on

300 Women you send a message to

150 Who look at your profile

40 Women who reply to your message

10 Women who mantain an online conversation

6 Women you have a first date with

1-3 Women you have sex with

This very clearly illustrates how the process works in real life. I've seen men complain that online dating "doesn't work" because "I sent messages to 11 women and didn't get one date!" Well of course you didn't. Just like you can't walk into a club, approach four different girls, have all four of them blow you off, then walk out of the club in a huff saying "club game doesn't work."

Putting in the numbers is an absolute requirement of any man who wants his woman life under control. Too many men seek an "easier" way to get consistent fast sex from attractive women by not putting in the numbers. It doesn't exist.

You must plan in advance to put in the numbers, and put in the time and energy necessary to reach those numbers. Refusal to do so will mean constant frustration in your woman life.

Key Seduction Techniques

It would not make any sense to list pages and pages of specific dating techniques here, since techniques vary according to the four different game styles. For example, there are some things you want to do during night game you would never do during daygame. Moreover, since I follow my own advice about specializing in one style, I am not an expert in all four styles, so I couldn't advise you on all of them anyway.

That being said, there are some overall techniques that do cover all types of game and dating. I and others have used these techniques to get effect, and you need to become proficient at all of them.

1. Sexual Frame

You must always exude a calm, confident, slightly sexual bearing. This vibe should pour through everything you do. The way you sit, stand, move, talk, the way you dress, your eye contact, your tone of voice, your facial expressions, the things you say, and the things you don't say.

Remember that this is a *calm* sexual frame. You do not want to be a hyper, horny guy. You don't want to be telling her she's pretty every five minutes nor staring at her boobs and drooling. That's a hypersexual demeanor, not a calm one.

Picture guys like James Bond, Johnny Depp, and Don Draper. Think sexual, not horny; confident, not needy; outcome independent, not desperate.

2. Confident, Outcome Independent Sexual Escalation

Sexual escalation is the series of physical actions you take with a woman to initiate sex. You need to have the confidence and outcome independence to kiss a woman, or touch her jewelry, or caress her leg, without asking for her permission. You must strongly initiate. You must move the physical process of sex from one step to the next; touching (or "kino"), kissing, removing clothing, and sex. Every step of the way, you're gently pushing her forward.

If she resists or says no, of course you stop. The point is if she does resist and you stop, it doesn't bother you, scare you, or make you upset. The possibility of a negative reaction doesn't stop you from trying, like it does with beta males. You confidently move the sexual process forward, and if she doesn't like it, no problem, you'll dump her and go have sex with someone else.

This all goes back to confidence, outcome independence, and emotional control as we discussed back in Chapter 15.

3. Kino

Kino means touching a woman, sexually or otherwise. At various times during a date (or "meet"), you should be touching her. Touch her hands, back, shoulders, and hair. Play with her jewelry. Eventually you should be touching her arms and legs. Physical touch is extremely powerful, and touching a woman gently, sensually, and confidently is a strong way to ramp up attraction and set the sexual frame of the interaction. By the way, you do all of this before kissing her or doing anything sexual. Usually I am kinoing a woman within about 20-30 minutes of the first date, just as we're talking, well before any kissing or anything sexual.

Most men wait for a long time with no touching at all, then suddenly and awkwardly try to kiss a woman at the end of the date. This is often a very awkward experience for man and woman both, and demonstrates very little confidence on your part. It's also harder to turn that kind of sequence into fast sex. You might get a kiss, but you won't get anything else.

4. Avoid Date-Behaviors - Women's Three Buttons

Every woman has three large buttons installed on her forehead. One button says "No," another says "Sex," and the third says "Make Him Wait."

If you show up to a date burping, farting, and bitching about your ex-girlfriend, you're pressing hard on the "No" button. You're not going to have sex with her. That much is obvious to most men.

There's the "Sex" button which, when pressed, will cause a woman to have sex with you very quickly. Most men understand that one too, more or less.

However, most men are completely unaware of the "Make Him Wait" button. That's the button which, when pressed, causes her to think, "This is a good, responsible, nice guy who can take care of me. I don't want to screw this up by having sex with him too fast. Then he might leave me or not respect me! So we need to have many dinner dates, walks in the park, movie dates, and other activities. After a bunch of that stuff, if I'm not bored with him by then, and if he makes a bunch of commitments to me, then I'll have sex with him. Maybe."

While you clearly don't want to press a woman's No button, it's the Make Him Wait button that really causes problems for most men. Men who press this button spend a large portion of their woman life meeting women with little or no results, going out on many expensive and time consuming dates, wasting massive amounts of time and money with little or no sex.

Don't get me wrong, you *can* get sex by doing this. It's how beta males do it. Yet the process is slow, tedious, draining, disappointing, and expensive. It also violates our baseline of a four-week timeframe to have sex with two new women.

The way you press down on a woman's Make Him Wait button is by engaging in traditional date-behaviors before you have sex with her. There are many of these, but I'll give you a few common examples:

- Buying her dinner, especially at a nice restaurant.
- Buying her lunch.
- Buying her more than a drink or two.
- Buying her gifts, including things like flowers.
- Taking her somewhere she's specifically asked to go.
- Giving her compliments, particularly about her appearance.
- Avoiding kino (because "it wouldn't be appropriate").
- Avoiding any conversation about sex or related topics (because "I don't want to creep her out").
- Long dates, i.e. many hours into the evening.
- Getting upset or uncomfortable when she brings up the topic of any of her ex-lovers.
- Asking her nicely if it would be okay to kiss her (or have sex with her, or similar).
- Waiting until the very end of the date to give her a kiss.
- Bragging about your income.
- Talking about your great job or career.
- Expressing a desire to get married or have a "serious relationship" with someone.
- Getting too needy with her too fast, such as talking about a serious relationship or marriage with her on the first or second date (yes, men actually do this!).
- Texting her daily.
- "Event" dates, like going to a play, rock-climbing, or other things far beyond just getting a drink at a bar.

These date-behaviors will instantly place her mindset into a 1950's dating frame, and she will set her expectations accordingly. You're the dashing man who wants to be her husband or boyfriend, and she's the classy lady. Classy ladies don't have sex on the first, second, or even third date. Oh no. Classy ladies get wined and dined by classy men, only having sex after many dates and many promises have been made.

Instead of pressing on the Make Him Wait button with your date-behaviors, you want to press down on her Sex button by purposely avoiding date-behaviors and establishing a strong, relaxed sexual frame instead. That's the quintessential difference between the beta male and the Alpha Male when it comes to dating.

For contrast, here's a simple list of what my first dates look like, the same ones that end up in sex the vast majority of the time, usually within three hours total face time from meet to sex. Compare this to the above date-behaviors list.

- Location of date is where I choose, not her.
- Meet at a cool bar or a mall. Never a restaurant.
- Don't buy her any food.
- Buy her one drink, and myself a drink, max, and that's it. One-third of my dates cost zero dollars. The average amount of the rest is around $14.
- Limit the first date to 60 minutes or less and then get the hell out of there. Meet up again for the second "date" at my place a few days later and get to sex within 30-90 minutes.
- Heavy kino throughout the date. By the end of the 60 minute first date, I've usually touched her hands, arms, shoulders, hair and thighs, in all in a very relaxed, confident, outcome independent manner.
- Lots of casual and fun sexual innuendo, eventually becoming sexually explicit conversation. Women love talking about sex, more so than men.
- Lots of laughter.
- Relaxed, casual, outcome independent body language, tone of voice, and frame.
- No kissing at the end of the first date, with lots of kino and sex talk instead. Kissing ramps up "buyer's remorse" between dates one and two, whereas not kissing leaves her curious, even eager, for more.

You can see how I'm specifically avoiding date-behaviors that press on a woman's Make Him Wait button, while pressing down hard on her Sex button. You can also see how my sexual frame is being established and maintained.

5. Avoid Women Over Age 33 (With Two Exceptions)

At my dating and relationships blog for men, blackdragonblog.com, I've spoken about the differences in women's age groups and how this directly relates to your sexual success. Here, I'm going to give you the bottom line to all of this. It's this one simple rule:

If you want fast sex, avoid dating any women over the age of 33 unless you already know them well.

Once a woman has reached about age 33, she's had three full decades of Prison existence during which all kinds of false sexual SP has been drilled into her head. Moreover, she now believes (accurately or not) that she's running out of time. She believes (accurately or not) that any non-serious sexual stuff with a man is wasting her limited time available to have children and/or find a husband.

Back when she was 19 or 26, having sex with a man fast was no problem; even fun. Now, because of these two forces, it's something she will absolutely not do. She's "a lady now." Because of her extreme SP, sex is now only allowed under a restrictive arrangement called a "relationship." Getting to sex very fast with women over the age of 33 is extremely difficult.

There are two exceptions to this. One is if you're a very good-looking and young (or young-looking) man who clearly has zero provider potential. If you're that guy, getting to fast sex with over-33 women should be no problem as long as your confidence and sexual frame is strong. However, if you're over the age of about 30 or you aren't really good-looking, you're out of luck if you want sex from these women quickly. Stick with women under age 33, or resign yourself to the reality that getting to sex with women over 33 will usually require several dates and a decent amount of money spent. In many cases it will also require promises made that violate Alpha 2.0 standards.

The second exception is if the woman already knows you reasonably well. I think women in their thirties and forties are very attractive, so I have had very fast sex with many women over the age of 33, but these were all women I already knew who were already comfortable with me well prior to sex. In other words, they were all social circle game.

If an over-33 woman already knows you reasonably well, then go ahead and give it shot if you want to have sex with her, following all the techniques and frames outlined in this book.

This means that if you are working on women you don't already know and desire fast sex via club game, daygame, or online dating, you need to avoid women over the age of 33. Your efforts are better spent focusing on women of age 18 to 32, and/or perhaps women over 33 you already know.

Further Techniques

If you're interested in more dating details beyond this chapter, you should read my Alpha Male 2.0 blog at blackdragonblog.com and my ebooks at blackdragonsystem.com where I cover many more proven strategies, principles, and techniques related to the woman side of your life.

Now we're going to switch gears and discuss women in Alpha Male 2.0 relationships.

Chapter 18 –

Serious Relationships, Alpha 2.0 Style

Don't you hate it when you're in bed with three women? And the least attractive one says "Save it for me!" Man, that's a drag.

Jim Carrey

November, 2012.

"So," she said, choosing her words carefully, "What if I brought over my girlfriends to your house every week, and you could fuck them? Then could I move in with you?"

We were in bed, relaxing after sex. She was in her mid-twenties, and we had been together in an open relationship for almost four years. She had accepted the open aspect of the relationship long ago, but her offers for further commitment were growing ever more creative.

"Well," I said, thinking about it, "Your girlfriends are pretty hot..."

It was true. She was hot herself, a petite Asian girl with big eyes and full Angelina Jolie lips. Using her looks she regularly had sex with very attractive women in her age group whom she met from Facebook. I had shown her exactly how to do it.

"But," I continued, "I suggested that before and you said you didn't want me having sex with your girls, remember? Not since I had sex with Laura last year."

"Well yeah," she said, "But one of my co-workers has an open relationship with her boyfriend, and she was telling me that they had sex with people they knew, instead of what we do, you having sex with women I don't know. Maybe we could change that around. You could fuck all of my friends like you did with Laura and Beth last year."

"You mean instead of me fucking women you don't know?"

"Yeah."

"And then you move in with me?"

"Yeah."

"I don't know," I said, "Sounds complicated. What if I want to fuck your friends when you're not around? Like at work or something?"

"That's fine!" she said, her eyes getting wider, sensing my possible consideration of her offer.

"And you realize that if you gave me any drama you'd have to move out."

"Of course," she said. She knew me well.

"Well, I'll think about it," I said, "At a minimum you need to prove to me you won't be jealous if I start having sex with your friends again. That will take at least six months."

"I know," she said smiling, "That's fine."

I smiled, turned over on my back, pushing the back of my head into my big pillow. I thought about what it would have been like if the married, monogamous, beta male, ten-years-younger version of me had taken a time machine forward ten years to witness this conversation.

I would have loved to have seen the look on his face.

Relationships Based on Freedom and Happiness, Not Societal Programming

Back in Chapter 14 we discussed the nine different types of sexual/romantic relationships and where they fit into our lives as Alpha 2.0s. We also talked about the examples of how betas and Alpha 1.0s incorrectly integrate women into their lives in ways that cause drama, conflict, and lack of freedom. In this chapter we're going to talk about exactly how to create and maintain sexual and/or romantic relationships with women in a way conducive to the consistent happiness, freedom, and abundance of the Alpha 2.0 lifestyle.

Living that lifestyle, I am usually dating between two to four women at a time. I try to keep it at around three, since more than that starts encumbering my Mission and my other important SLA. Per the terminology in Chapter 14, some of these women are Friends with Benefits (FBs), women I like as friends and have sex with, but that's really about it. Other women are Multiple Long-Term Relationships (MLTRs), women I have romantic feelings for and actually "date." There have even been times I have been in love with an MLTR, bringing her to Open Long-Term Relationship (OLTR) status or close to it.

Since I never lie to women, every woman I date knows there are other women in my sexual life, yet they keep dating me anyway. Most women have been in my life for many years. Other women date me for a while, leave me to pursue monogamy elsewhere, then become bored or get cheated on, and then return to me.

It's a pretty good deal. I can have deep romantic relationships with a woman (or women!) I care about deeply, but I can still have sex with whomever I want. I can sleep with intelligent women I have a deep connection with, and I can also sleep with hot dumb bimbos. All of it is wonderful and all of it integrates into my lifestyle seamlessly.

Unlike monogamous people in The Prison, relationship drama is almost nonexistent in my life. Almost never do I have any woman raise her voice at me, complain, demand I do or not do certain things, or argue with me. If any of that happens, I temporarily remove her from my life and go have sex with someone else. Once she calms down (and she will calm down, since as we discussed in Chapter 13 women are dynamic, ever-changing creatures who don't stay mad forever) she comes back into my consistently happy life.

I usually get asked several questions about this:

What about STDs? I use condoms on all women unless they are long-term, very trusted partners. I also get tested for every STD under the sun every three to four months whether I think I need to or not.

What about unwanted pregnancies? I have had a lot of sex in my life and I've slept with huge numbers of women, and I have never gotten a woman pregnant on accident. Condoms, responsibility, and self-control do work. I am under the opinion that there is no such thing as truly "accidental" pregnancies; there are only pregnancies when people are being irresponsible, stupid, or drunk, as well as people who really did want to get pregnant (or impregnate) but are lying about the whole "accident" thing.

What about marriage and/or living with a woman? There is no need to ever get legally married, but if you really want to get married, have an OLTR marriage (which we talked about in Chapter 14).

What about having kids? We'll talk about having kids in Chapters 23 and 24, but there are millions of Alpha Males all over the Western world who have discreet open marriages with their wives or OLTRs, often while raising kids. I have known, worked with, and communicated with hundreds of them.

Before we get to any of these big topics, we need to first start with the core of how romantic relationships function within an Alpha 2.0 framework.

Alpha 2.0 Relationships

As an Alpha Male 2.0, with the goal of long-term consistent happiness, and with the additional requirements of freedom and abundance, traditional societal relationship structures derived from SP are not going to work for you. These models exist to serve The Prison and its elites, not to make you happy. The standard relationship model involves monogamy, rules, drama, the eventual withdrawal of sex once a woman gets sexually bored, cheating (on the part of the man or the woman), then a bad breakup where one person leaves while the other wants the relationship to continue. On top of all of that, you often have legal entanglements such as divorce, custody battles, alimony, financial and credit chaos, and even criminal charges.

All of this garbage leads to hurt feelings and resentment, often lasting decades.

For fearful, submissive, or low-sex-drive beta males, that system works fine. It doesn't make them happy, but it does give them the false semblance of security that they desire.

For domineering, higher-drama Alpha 1.0s, that system is also acceptable to a degree, in that it allows the Alpha 1.0 to control "his" woman, at least for a while, and causes all kinds of conflict, which many (though not all) Alpha 1.0s secretly derive validation from.

However, for the Alpha 2.0, none of this is going to work. Not being allowed to have sex with whomever he wants, often having to obey rules he doesn't want to obey, often fighting with the woman in his life and thereby damaging his happiness, and on and on, the standard relationship model encouraged by SP and OBW of The Prison can, in no way, work for an Alpha 2.0 life.

A new model is needed.

Alpha 2.0 Core Relationship Requirements

A romantic relationship is based on caring, passion, mutual respect, compatibility, and trust. All of these things are important. For the Alpha 2.0, the quality and desirability of a romantic relationship with a woman requires three additional factors; aspects that usually get left out in SP-based relationships:

1. Extremely low number of rules she places on you.
2. Extremely low frequency of drama.
3. High priority placed on sex.

For a relationship to be conducive to your long-term happiness, it must have infrequent drama, frequent sex, and a small number of rules you're required to follow. If any of those three items become untrue, your long-term happiness will be jeopardized at best and impossible at worst.

Beta males ignore all three of these factors. They commonly get into relationships or marriages where once the initial "honeymoon period" is over, women throw all kinds of drama at them, enforce all kinds of rules over their behavior, and slowly begin to resist sex as the relationship ages.

Alpha 1.0s are usually pretty good at maintaining frequency of sex and resisting a woman's rules. However, because of their controlling tendencies, they almost always end up with relationships or marriages with regular drama. They set all kinds of rules and boundaries for their women. Naturally, their women eventually violate those boundaries, and the Alpha 1.0s get upset. When a woman throws drama at an Alpha 1.0, he'll throw it right back, and then you've got a war on your hands.

The Alpha 2.0 closely adheres to all three factors. He has relationships with women where they have sex often, whenever he wants (within reason of course). Drama is minimal or zero. The women in his life don't enforce any rules over his behavior, to the point where he can even have sex with other women whenever he needs to.

If at any point any woman he's with violates one of these three factors, by resisting sex, throwing drama at him, or issuing orders, rules, or demands, he instantly removes her from his life, temporarily or permanently depending on the severity of the violation, without any argument or fighting, and has sex with someone else.

What about Love?

The first thing someone might say reading those three things would be "What about things like love and connection and commitment?" Love is extremely important, of course! Love is one of the greatest emotions a human being can feel, and since the Alpha 2.0 craves happiness, romantic love is always a welcome addition to his life. I have been in love a few times over the course of my life and every time was wonderful beyond words. Alpha 2.0s love just as much, if not more, than any other type of man.

The difference is with how the romantic love is integrated into his life.

First of all, sex comes first, love comes second. Many people, especially over-33 women, have an SP-driven Disney fantasy agenda that assumes love or connection come first, and then sex comes second. That may sound nice, but this is actually the opposite from how men are biologically designed.

First you have lots and lots of sex with a woman within a purely sexual or semi-romantic context. After months of doing this, then and only then do you move into more a loving and committed relationship, assuming she qualifies for such a thing in your life. We've already discussed back in Chapter 14 how most men leap into monogamous, committed relationships very fast, often after only having sex with a woman two or three times. We've also talked about how some women will demand things like romance, romantic dates, and sexual exclusivity way too early in the dating interaction, even before sex has occurred!

Both of these types of people are making a colossal mistake. They are creating relationship structures that are literally designed to create drama and unhappiness down the road. For the happiness-seeking Alpha 2.0, spending time with a woman and having lots of sex with her, for many months, comes first. Love and commitment come second.

The second aspect of love and commitment is that it's only available for certain types of women in your life. Love should never be given to women who are FBs, and rarely is it for women in MLTR status unless she's a very high-end MLTR. Therefore, love is reserved only for high-end MLTRs or OLTRs.

It's similar with commitments. *No* commitments are made to FBs or MLTRs. While dating these women you are free to do whatever you want with your life. *Some* commitments, though not many, are made to an OLTR and a few more are made in an OLTR marriage, but the commitments are few as compared to standard SP-designed relationships. Of course, monogamous relationships like Long-Term Relationships (LTRs) and Traditional Monogamous Marriage (TMM) are jam-packed with all kinds of extreme commitments and rules, but as I just explained, these relationship types are fundamentally incompatible with an Alpha 2.0 lifestyle and should be avoided.

The point is that love, commitment, living together, having children, even being married (under the structure of an OLTR marriage only) are all perfectly acceptable under an Alpha 2.0 framework even though the usual relationship parameters (like monogamy) are absent. Don't think for one minute that being an Alpha Male 2.0 requires you to never be in love or committed to a special woman. Quite the opposite is true.

The issue of commitment leads right into the first of our three relationship requirements.

Extremely Low Number of Rules

Perhaps the greatest difference between Alpha 2.0 relationships and normal relationships required by The Prison is the virtual absence of rules both partners place upon each other.

Normally when two people start to date and have sex, each of them figuratively hand their "list of rules" to the other. They (figuratively) each say to each other, "Okay, now that we're having sex, here is the list of rules you must obey in order to be with me. If you don't obey these, I'm going to be upset with you, my fragile feelings and ego will be hurt, and we're going to have drama. If you really violate these rules, I'm going to leave you."

The list of rules people give to their lovers is often vast and extreme.

Women will often give men rules like:

- "Don't ever be late for dinner."
- "Don't ever leave your socks on the floor."
- "Pay for our dates."
- "Don't look at other women when we're together."
- "Never wear that shirt again."
- "Stop watching porn."
- "Don't ever disagree with me in front of our friends."
- ...and a thousand other rules in between.

Men, particularly Alpha 1.0s who love to give women rules, will often give women rules like:

- "Don't ever text any other man."
- "Take those photos off your Facebook page."
- "Have dinner ready at 6:00pm every night."
- "Always keep your pussy shaved."
- "Always stand by me when we go out. Never leave my side."
- ...and a thousand other rules in between.

Both men *and* women will give each other the "standard" rules of SP and OBW-based Prison relationships, such as:

- "Don't ever have sex with anyone else but me."
- "Don't ever flirt with anyone else but me."
- "Don't say anyone of the opposite sex is attractive when I'm around."
- "Always tell me where you are."
- ...and a thousand other rules in between.

There's a fundamental problem with all this crap: *human beings are designed to break relationship rules.* If you set a rule in your relationship, even a small one, there is damn near a 100% chance that at some point in the future, assuming the relationship lasts long enough, that person is going to break that rule.

Remember, women are dynamic, ever-changing creatures. Any rule she agrees to now she's going to break later. It's how women are hard-wired.

What happens when she breaks one of your many relationship rules? You'll get upset and have to go "correct" her. How will she react to this? Will she bow and say "Oh, yes master, of course you are right and I'm sorry," then immediately correct herself? Of course not. She'll fight back at least to some degree. Then, say hello to call kinds of drama and arguments.

If the rule she violated is a bigger one, you're probably also going to feel fear or anger, possibly a sense of violation, and have hurt feelings. The entire relationship may even be threatened. It's the same in reverse if *you* violate one of *her* rules.

None of this can work within an Alpha 2.0 framework, for obvious reasons.

The problem gets even deeper than that. Let's say you live in a magical Disney fantasyland where the woman in your life never breaks any of your relationship rules. How you are going to know for sure? You're going to have to constantly monitor her behavior. You're going to have to watch her like a hawk 24/7. You're going to have to pull time and effort away from your Mission, goals and other SLA in order to babysit her to ensure she doesn't break any of your rules.

You may think I'm exaggerating, but I know plenty of men who live lives like this with their wives or girlfriends and I'm sure you do too. Perhaps you're one of them! You cannot be long-term happy, and you cannot be outcome independent, if a portion of your life is spent monitoring the activities of "your" woman (or women).

The answer to all of this is the following:

- Never agree to any relationship with any woman, no matter how wonderful she is, who insists on installing multiple relationship rules into your life. Quickly move on from any woman who insists you follow her rules.

- On the other side of the coin, don't give rules to any woman you're in a relationship with, even a moderately serious one, other than the fundamental human-to-human basics like "don't steal my stuff" and "don't murder me."

- When the woman (or women) in your life isn't around, let her do whatever she wants. Ignore her behavior when she's not with you, and use that time away from her to focus on your Mission, key SLA, or other women.

Of course a small number of rules may be necessary for more serious relationships. You can picture it as an ascending scale:

- FBs and MLTRs may have virtually no rules.

- An OTLR will have a *few*.

- A live-in OLTR will have a *few* more.

- If you have children with her, perhaps you'll add a *few* more.

The key parts in those sentences is the word *few*. You should always be thinking "minimum number of rules," both rules from her to you, and rules from you to her. More than a few rules either way is unacceptable.

Let's say you're in an OLTR with a woman who's been in your life for quite a while. What are some acceptable rules? If you're in an OLTR with a woman you don't live with and have no children with, you might agree to these rules:

1. Always wear a condom when having sex with another woman.

2. Don't spend the night or go on any romantic dates with another woman.

3. Don't plaster pictures of you and other women on your Facebook page.

These three rules are probably fine, though you might be able to get away with not agreeing to the third one.

What if you're living with her but have no kids? This might require one additional rule:

4. Don't ever bring other women to the shared home. Another variation might be to not bring other women to the shared home unless she (your OLTR) is out of town.

I'm not saying that rule is required; I'm saying it would be something acceptable to agree to. The key point is this: notice that we're now in a very serious, live-in relationship, and you're only agreeing to four rules. Just four! Compare that to the typical non-live-in, SP-based, monogamous relationship that probably has scores of rules.

Less rules means more freedom and less things to argue about; a win/win for the Alpha 2.0.

Extremely Low Frequency of Drama

The next factor that distinguishes an Alpha 2.0 relationship is the absence, or near absence, of relationship drama. Per my blog at blackdragonblog.com, the term "drama" has a very specific definition when I use it, which is:

Any harsh negative actions directed from a woman to a man where the man is the target of said negativity. Screaming, nagging, complaining, arguing, demands, crying, threats, ultimatums, the "silent treatment," refusing sex because of non-medical reasons, all of these things are drama, and there are many others. Drama is not "anything negative." Specifically, it must be harsh (sweetly lying would not be considered drama) and focused at the man (angrily complaining about her boss at work would not be considered drama).

There is also guy-drama, which is a certain type of drama favored by Alpha 1.0s, but is also common with beta males. The definition of guy-drama is:

A particular form of drama directed from a man to a woman. Unlike drama, which is feminine and takes many forms, guy-drama takes the form of a lecture issued in order to correct behavior. "Setting her straight," "straightening her out," "laying down the law," commands to "respect" him, or issuing "rules" are all forms of guy-drama. Guy-drama is extremely ineffective at managing a relationship and only creates more drama or at best simply delays (instead of preventing) future drama.

Both types of drama are either completely absent from an Alpha 2.0 relationship, or they occur very rarely, as in less than a handful of times per year. As I type these words I am dating four different women right now, and I have to think very hard about the last time any of these women argued with me, snipped at me, or complained about anything. Most other men I know who have typical wives or monogamous girlfriends experience this stuff on a weekly, if not daily basis.

Rule number one in low-drama relationships is to limit the number of rules you place on a woman, and limit the number of rules she places on you. We've covered that already.

Rule number two in low-drama relationships is to not give women any drama yourself. At all times you must keep an outcome independent frame. Calm down. Relax. Focus on your Mission. Remember the key trait of emotional control we discussed in Chapter 15.

Whenever I see a man giving a woman drama I always think about how he likely has little or no strong, long-term meaning in life (no Mission, no Code, no important goals), and/or how he lacks basic, adult-level emotional control.

Rule number three is to temporarily remove a woman out of your life whenever she starts giving you drama. This is called the "soft next."

Soft and Hard Nexting

Soft nexting is a technique by which you temporary remove a woman from your life with zero drama. This temporary period usually lasts from 48 hours to seven days. During this time you maintain radio silence with her, ignoring her contact, then resume the relationship after the nexting period is over, just like nothing ever happened. The soft next is the greatest and most powerful weapon a man has in his relationship management arsenal. The first time you try it, you will be shocked at how well it works.

I go into detail on when and how to do a soft next in my ebook on how to create and maintain open relationships (located at haveopenrelationships.com), but I will give you a general overview on how to do it here. When woman you're in a relationship with starts raising her voice at you in anger, or starts making demands, or starts crying "at" you, or starts complaining, or starts throwing any other drama at you, you simply smile, turn around, and leave. You don't argue or fight back, since that would be more drama. You just get in your car and drive away. Then you don't communicate with her in any way for two to seven days. When she tries to call you or text, you ignore her. After the two to seven day nexting period is over, you simply meet up with her again like nothing bad ever happened and resume the happy relationship. When the relationship resumes, not only will she not want to keep arguing, but she will be the nicest and sweetest she's ever been with you. Try it and you'll see.

I realize that procedure sounds extremely bizarre if you've never tried it before, but I have soft nexted many women, many times, over many years along with thousands of other men who have used this technique, and all of them have seen it work wonders.

It works because women's single greatest craving from a man is **attention**. Women desire your attention more than sex, more than security, even more than love! When you're screaming at them, arguing with them, or lecturing them on proper behavior, they're still getting attention, so they somewhat "like" the drama.

However, when you turn around and leave, then don't communicate with them for a few days, the withdrawal of attention is extremely painful and powerful. It sends a message far greater than any yelling, screaming, or lecture you could deliver.

Even better, it strongly establishes your outcome independent frame with her. She realizes that:

1. You're not needy.
2. You don't need her.
3. You don't fear her absence.

This does two things. First, it causes her to fear, even if inaccurately, that you may leave her. Second, it boosts her attraction for you because outcome independence is extremely attractive to women. Once again, "women chase what runs away."

In addition to soft nexts, there are also *hard* nexts. A hard next is a permanent removal of a woman from your life. It's when you leave and never talk to her ever again. Thankfully, hard nexts are rare. Of all the women I've ever dated, I've only had to execute two hard nexts in my entire life. The only time a hard next is required is if a woman does something truly horrible, such as physically endanger you or someone close to you, steal from you, use you, or something similar. While hard nexts are rare, the Alpha 2.0 is never afraid to use them if needed.

For more details on nexting and other drama management techniques, refer to the ebook at haveopenrelationships.com.

High Priority Placed On Sex

In most normal relationships, particularly marriages or non-married, monogamous, cohabiting relationships that last beyond three years, there is hard-coded OBW within a woman that causes her to become sexually bored with her male partner. This has been scientifically proven many times[38]. Just about every man who's been married longer than about three years has had the wonderful experience of wanting sex from his wife only to get a bunch of excuses about how she's not in the mood; excuses she never gave him back when the relationship was new and exciting. Hell, back then she probably initiated a lot of the sex herself!

Marriages or long-term relationships are not the only types of relationships that suffer from a lack of sex. Many girlfriend-boyfriend relationships are plagued by girlfriends who want to go spend time with their boyfriend but without sex. Reasons can include things such as because they're in a bad mood, or mad at their boyfriend, or "tired," or whatever.

As we've discussed, Alphas, both 1.0s and 2.0s, tend to be men with healthy, strong sex drives. Many betas have high sex drives as well. Men are horny, and because of our static natures, unlike women many of us don't stop being horny just because a certain point of familiarity in the relationship has been reached, or because we happen to be temporarily upset at our partners, or if we had a bad day. I'm not saying men never get sexually bored in relationships; sometimes they do. However, by and large it is the female who usually gets bored first. Again, the statistics, studies, and likely your own anecdotal experience all verify this.

Men need sex all the time, constantly, regardless of context. Alpha Males even more so! This is a fact of life we, and the women in our lives, cannot deny.

Therefore, a relationship with a woman who refuses sex for non-medical reasons is simply impossible for an Alpha 2.0. If you don't live with her, then ideally every time you spend time with her you have sex. Per our Alpha Male 2.0 sexual baselines, if you live with her, you should be having sex several days a week, every week, unless one of you is out of town or very sick, Moreover, this pattern should continue for decades, not just two or three years.

---

[38] http://www.nytimes.com/2013/05/26/magazine/unexcited-there-may-be-a-pill-for-that.html

Remember above I mentioned *non-medical reasons*. Of course if a woman is physically unable to have sex because of real medical reasons, that's fine. I'm talking about real medical reasons that prevent her from having sex, like when she's vomiting sick or recovering from surgery. Saying she "doesn't like sex while on her period," or "is really tired," or her "knee hurts" are not medical conditions rendering sex impossible. Those are just excuses. Women are masters at inventing real-sounding excuses to get out of sex with their husbands or long-term, live-in boyfriends.

This begs the question: if she resists sex, what does the Alpha 2.0 do?

Let's first talk about what he doesn't do. He doesn't do what the beta male does, which is to whine, complain, and argue, only to eventually surrender and go jerk off to porn.

He also doesn't do what an Alpha 1.0 would do, which is to start some drama by angrily issuing orders about his sexual rules. "This behavior is unacceptable! You will have sex with me whenever I want! Or else! Now get in bed!" Like that won't start a huge argument. Alpha Male 1.0s view the world as if today's modern, Western woman will meekly and obediently respond with "Yes master" type stuff whenever he tries to lay down the law. No, instead she'll get indignant and throw drama right back at him, and now they're arguing. This is why throwing demands around is completely incompatible with our low-drama relationship requirements.

So what does the Alpha 2.0 do? He attempts to have sex, tries one or two more times if she resists, then immediately soft nexts her. Then he does something fun or productive, like work on his Mission or go have sex with another one of his women.

Frankly, often you won't have to go that far, since often as you're walking out the door she will suddenly change her mind and magically want to have sex with you, and without any of the arguments the beta male or Alpha 1.0 has to deal with.

Even if she doesn't change her mind, you're still getting sex that night if you want it; just not from her. Moreover, she'll never forget what you did, so she will be hesitant to restrict sex from you again. As always, soft nexting is extraordinarily effective, and even better, it usually involves zero drama.

The bottom line to all of this is that the women in your life need to accept you as a highly sexual man. Women who can't (or won't) accept this about you cannot be in your life, at least not long-term and not at any status above a Friend with Benefits (FB). The reason most women restrict sex from their male partners, or make men wait for sex during the dating phase, is because *they know men will put up with the lack of sex*. Simply choose to not be one of these men, and most of these problems are solved from the very beginning. Starting from the very first minute of your first date together, a woman will know clearly through your sexual fame that you're not in that category, and won't treat you that way.

Do Women Really Let You Do This?

If you have zero experience with nonmonogamous relationships, much of this is not only going to be outside of your comfort zone, but also hard for you to believe. I have dated huge numbers of women, from age 18 to late 40s, many of whom have been in my life longer than four, five, and six years, and never once have I promised sexual monogamy to any of them, and all of them knew that I was sexual with other women. Millions of men all over the Western world are also doing this. It's far more common than you may think.

However, even these numbers don't include the millions upon millions of more SP-influenced marriages where the man is cheating, the wife knows it, but she stays in the marriage with him anyway. That's not the ideal way to have a nonmonogamous marriage of course, but you can see the point I'm making.

Nonmonogamous people don't exactly advertise they're doing all of this of course. Open relationships and open marriages are a direct violation of lots of SP and the Six Societal Values (6SV), so people tend to keep quiet about this stuff. Yet they're still doing it, and in great numbers.

Another thought you may be having is that the only women who would possibly agree to relationships like this are dumb bimbos. While I have certainly slept with a few bimbos in my day, most of the women I've had in ongoing relationships were and are nowhere near this category. As I mentioned earlier in this book, I have been in relationships like this with women over 30, women over 40, Ivy League educated women, women with Masters degrees, and women who were corporate vice presidents, attorneys, teachers, corporate executives, accountants and more.

In living this way for many years, working with many other people (men and women both) who live this way, writing about living this way, and teaching these techniques over many years, I've come to the following conclusions:

- About 90% of women, of all ages and personality types, will agree to an open relationship within at least an FB framework, provided the man does everything correctly in establishing the relationship, starting with the very first date.
- About 65% of women will agree to a long-term, serious, nonmonogamous relationship or marriage, again provided the man does everything right during the initial and mid-range phases.

The trouble is not that women won't agree to these kinds of relationships. The trouble is that men are clueless about how to create and maintain them, and do everything wrong when attempting a relationship like this.

Most men's haphazard attempt at creating an open relationship is to get monogamous with a woman, "go beta" and treat her like a girlfriend or wife, and then many months or years later try to retroactively transform the existing relationship into a sexually open one. This is extremely difficult to do, though it is possible if the guy knows what he's doing. I wrote an entire ebook on how men can convert their monogamous marriage into an open one, located at www.open-marriage.com, but it still not an easy process. Women have a tough time going "backwards" in a relationship.

Let's discuss exactly how to correctly establish a nonmonogamous, Alpha 2.0 relationship. I describe it in step-by-step detail in my open relationships ebook[39], but I will provide you with a detailed summary here.

The Three Phases of an Open Relationship

You don't create an open relationship by suddenly telling your monogamous girlfriend you want to have sex with other girls. Talk about inviting drama! Nor do you create one by telling a woman on a first date that you want to have an open relationship with her. Both these methods are direct, open assaults upon a woman's SP, OBW, and 6SV. All you're going to get is a bunch of drama, shock, or hurt feelings for your trouble. Instead of a 90% success rate of establishing open relationships like I have, you'll have perhaps a 5% success rate, if that.

In order to get to that 90% success rate, you create an open relationship by slowly, gently, but confidently moving a woman from one open relationship phase to the next. Each phase builds on the prior phase.

---

[39] http://www.haveopenrelationships.com/

The first phase is the **EFA Phase**, which lasts several weeks, starting from the very first in-person interaction with her. EFA means Early Frame Announcement. Per the glossary at the Blackdragon Blog[40], the definition of EFA is:

EFA: Early Frame Announcement. The strongly conveyed but unspoken overall message to a woman non-verbally conveying who you are and why you're there. Your EFA begins on the first second of the first date and continues for at least three months before it can be softened if necessary. Examples: A nervous, talkative guy on a first date is demonstrating the EFA of a beta male. A guy constantly telling a woman she's pretty, buying her dinner and flowers, and getting angry when she talks about other men would be the EFA of a monogamous boyfriend. A guy who acted like he didn't care, confidently talked about sex, and had lots of pretty girls all over his Facebook page would be the EFA of an Alpha Male. A woman will almost always conform her behaviors and expectations to fit the EFA of a man she's interacting with.

We discussed this in the last chapter when we talked about not pressing down on a woman's "Make Him Wait" button by acting like a boyfriend or establishing a 1950s dating frame. Instead, you want to establish the EFA of a confident, sexual, outcome independent Alpha Male.

The second phase is the **Implicit Phase**, which usually lasts between three and five months. During this phase you date a woman as either an FB or MLTR, and you continue to date other women as well. During this phase, you do not talk about your relationship in any way, and you avoid all questions she has about the nature of the relationship. You just spend time with her, have sex with her, be close to her, and enjoy your time together.

During this phase you are implicitly showing her that there might be other women in your life, but you are not stating it verbally. For example, you might leave an earring on your kitchen counter for her to see, and she might see flirty messages on your Facebook page regarding other women. Women are extremely perceptive and will pick up on this stuff fast. It will be implicitly clear to them what kind of guy you are, and what you're doing, without you ever saying one word about it.

Most men don't realize that women have a three month "relationship timer." This means that for about three months on average,

40 http://www.blackdragonblog.com/

if you don't bring up the relationship, monogamy, exclusivity, or anything like that, she won't either. Due to modern-day SP, women in dating situations try very hard to act tough, non-needy, and independent. Most women are pretty good about not getting too needy with a guy too fast. Frankly, it's usually men who get needy first, and too fast.

Therefore, if you just shut your big dumb mouth about "not seeing other people" or similar relationship-speak, you can date her for about three months while having sex with ten other women if you want. As long as you don't verbalize it, it's okay.

After about three to five months on average, finally a woman will start to really pressure you to define the relationship. This is where you enter the third phase, the **Verbalization Point**. Here, you finally verbalize to her exactly what the relationship is and is not. If she's an FB, you nicely tell her that this relationship will never go beyond where it currently is. If she's an MLTR, you hold her close and tell her that you care about her deeply and want to be with her forever, but only if that's true; remember, an Alpha 2.0 does not lie to women! However, you also tell her that you cannot be 100% monogamous to her, ever. That's simply not the man you are. You tell her that you hope she understands, but you make it clear that if that's unacceptable for her, you will sadly let her go.

What usually happens is she will get a little upset or perhaps even cry a little. Then she'll go away to "think about it." After a few days, when you see each other again, the relationship will resume as normal. Only now, it's "officially" open.

I have followed this exact procedure many, many times with many women of all ages and types over many years, and my success rate with this is between 65% and 90%, depending on various factors. If you do this, and do it correctly, it will work for you too.

Essential Relationship Mindsets for the Alpha Male 2.0

I can give you all the techniques in the world on how to make a happy, nonmonogamous relationship work for you, but if you don't have the proper mindsets first, it will be difficult for you to take correct action, or to maintain such action.

There are two mindsets you need to adopt to make Alpha 2.0 relationships work. They are what set the Alpha 2.0 apart from his Prison-bound beta and Alpha 1.0 brothers.

Mindset Difference One: Cream of the Crop Model vs. Screening Model

This is a core difference in how the Alpha Male 2.0 chooses a long-term partner as opposed to how men in The Prison choose.

Most beta males quickly get serious with whichever woman has sex with him. Alpha 1.0s and more confident betas do something a little different, something I call the Screening Model.

The Screening Model is when a person has a mental checklist of all the things a proper mate should have. Every person has a different checklist, but with men it usually includes things like she must be smart, educated, have a good relationship with her family, have not had sex with too many other men, and similar traits based in "quality" and "purity." We've already touched on some of those aspects in previous chapters, and just by reading that list you can see SP and male OBW bleeding though.

Any woman this man meets or dates who does not measure up to his screening efforts either gets dumped, relegated to a one night stand, or at best becomes a very temporary FB. The first woman who comes along who seems to check all the man's "boxes" gets the prize. He gets serious with her, and often moves in with her and/or marries her, only to later suffer all the usual negative consequences of long-term monogamous relationships, since no amount of screening can change a woman's nature, as we discussed back in Chapter 13.

By the way, if this model sounds familiar, it's because this is the model women use, most especially those over age 33. You've probably been on a first date where you can tell the woman was simply going through her SP-based checklist of all the things a proper "gentleman" boyfriend/husband should have. The Screening Model is actually a very feminine model despite the fact so many men enthusiastically adopt it.

Alpha 2.0s follow a very different model for mate selection, a much more effective, enjoyable, and masculine model. It's something I call the Cream of the Crop model. When an Alpha 2.0 is ready to get serious with a woman, or move in with a woman, or get married (OLTR marriage of course!), he goes out and has sex with many, many different women. He's responsible and uses condoms of course. More importantly, he doesn't "screen" anyone. As long as the women are attractive to him and don't give him drama, he takes all comers. Low quality women, moderate quality women, and high quality women, he has sex with them all, and sees all of them regularly or semi-regularly as FBs or MLTRs.

Soon, many women drop off and leave him, seeking monogamy or more submissive men. Others prove to be bitchy or problematic, causing him to soft next them. A special few of these women make it "through the cut," and stay with the Alpha in a very happy and harmonious relationship for a long time. Out of these, one woman will always end up standing out from all the rest. *That* is the woman with whom he gets serious (or moves in with, or marries, or has children with, or whatever).

It's a far more enjoyable process than the Screening Model, as you can plainly see. It's also far less stressful, hurts far fewer women, is far less disappointing, and maintains an Alpha abundance mentality instead of embracing the scarcity mentally that the Screening Model embraces.

Mindset Difference Two: Inconsistent and Long-Lasting vs. Consistent and Short-Lasting

The vast majority of people in The Prison follow a monogamous relationship structure. Even if they eventually cheat, which most human beings eventually do if the relationship or marriage lasts long enough, women, beta males, and Alpha 1.0s at least try to maintain a semblance of monogamous existence.

In most monogamous relationships, particularly in non-married ones, both partners are together consistently for a set amount of time, then they break up or get divorced, and then never have sex again. Sure, sometimes people will hook up with their exes, but usually it's a very brief encounter or two before that person moves on to the next monogamous partner, never to have sex with their ex again.

In other words, monogamy is a consistent but short-lasting model.

In many ways (but not all) the Alpha 2.0 relationship model is the exactly the opposite. Many of the women I have dated in a FB or MLTR open relationship eventually will leave me to pursue monogamy elsewhere. Over time, as these women get bored with betas or fed up with Alpha 1.0s, they will come back to me and resume the relationship as normal. Sometimes it takes them a month or two to do this. Other times it takes as long as three years or more. Regardless, 94% of the time, they come back. I know that number precisely because I carefully track everything I do in my woman life, just like I do in my financial life. This is the only way I can reliably and consistently improve my results.

I've had women leave me, get a monogamous boyfriend, break up with him, and come back to me. I've even have women do things like move far away, or have babies with other men, or even marry other men, have babies, then get divorced, and then come back to me. Alpha 2.0s are very rare in society, and at a very deep level, women know and feel this. That's why they come back.

I've been doing this for many years. There are women who were in their mid-thirties when I first started dating them who are now in their mid-forties, and are still coming back to me. There are women who were 18 years old when I first started dating them, who are now in their mid-twenties, and still coming back to me. I am an oasis for these women, a place to retreat from the clinginess of beta males and the demands of Alpha 1.0s. Since I follow the Cream of the Crop model, I don't "screen" any of these women, so I always accept them back as long as they don't give me drama. I have developed very strong bonds with many women by doing this.

As a result of these bonds and the pattern of behavior these women have established, I plan on having many of these women going away and coming back, for the rest of my life. That's right. Many of these women will still be going and coming back to me over the next several decades.

In other words, the Alpha 2.0 relationship model is inconsistent, but long-lasting. It's the opposite of monogamy.

I can see your immediate objection, so don't worry! You may be concerned that you can't ever have a long-lasting consistent relationship required for a live-in relationship, marriage, or parenthood. That's what OLTR and OLTR marriages are for. Remember I said many women do this. Not all of them are inconsistent. The Cream of the Crop women will indeed stay with you, for many years, consistently, if that's what you want.

Part Five

Your Money

Chapter 19 –

Work That Frees You

Money buys the things love can't.

Gene Simmons

Monday, September 23rd, 1996. It was one of the greatest and most important days of my entire life.

That morning, for the very first time, I walked into my completed office, the office of my very own company, Draxx Computer Solutions. It was a small computer consulting business with one employee: me.

It was my very first day of full-time self-employment. From that day forward, I would never have a job again. I would set my own financial destiny.

Never again would a boss yell at me about how I was late to work or wasn't allowed to have a desk by the window.

Never again would my income be limited by whatever salary was dictated by my job title.

Never again would I have to check with a boss to get permission to take time off, or check in with co-workers to take a 15-minute break.

Never again would I be reliant on a too-low paycheck that never grew noticeably larger regardless of how hard or how well I worked.

Never again would I have to put up with incompetent, dishonest, or lazy coworkers (who were never fired!) who made a mess of my hard work.

Never again would my work or income be subject to the whims of some distant management I had zero control over.

Never again!

A Quick History of My Business Life

At the age of 24, I had finally fulfilled a life-long dream. It was something I had been thinking about, fantasizing about, and planning since I was a freshman in high school, jotting down business notes during class when I was supposed to have been listening to the teacher lecture us about really important, real-world stuff. You know, things like 18th century American literature, Greek gods, and how cilia worked on microorganisms.

I finally had my own business. Not just a part-time business that I worked on in the evenings or on weekends in addition to my job; I had been doing that for several years prior. No, this was a real full-time business, with my own office, checking account, letterhead, and computers; the works.

My first office was not much to look at. It was a 200 square-foot rectangular room on the second story of a house renovated into a tiny commercial building in the northeast side of Portland, Oregon. Across the hall were two other offices, both artists. Below me was a woman's clothing store. The house was ancient and small, and it smelled like an old sock.

I didn't care. To me, that little room, on that first day, was a cathedral more beautiful than the Sistine Chapel. Because it was mine. I was the president and CEO, with complete power over exactly what the business would do and not do. Instead of my job steering me to its destiny, the business would facilitate *my* destiny. My goal was to make a six-figure income as a young man, and now that the corporate shackles of a J-O-B were gone, it was actually possible. The feeling was intoxicating, almost orgasmic.

I entered my office and slowly sat down at my desk, a crappy wooden hand-me-down my dad would have thrown away had I not scooped it up. I looked out the window, looking down at the street with all the people shopping and passing by. I was just one story up, but I felt like a Wall Street CEO in a high rise. I ran my fingers over my brand new computer, the primary tool I would use to achieve my destiny.

What an exciting time that was. I can't help smiling when I think back on it.

The euphoria was short-lived. My first few years in business were rough. I floundered and made all kinds of mistakes. I screwed up my marketing and pissed off prospects. I mismanaged my very limited funds, and ended up wasting thousands of dollars on stupid crap that I should never have spent money on. I got so far behind on my bills at one point I even talked to an attorney about filing bankruptcy. She said I was a "good candidate" for it. I didn't like the sound of that.

After thinking it through, I decided that the concept of taking money from companies and never paying it back was not an honorable thing to do, so I forgot about bankruptcy and forced myself to make it work.

I started focusing hard on sales, referrals, and customer service. Soon, I started making a little money. This motivated me even more. In the midst of all this, I got married and quickly had two children, which dramatically raised my monthly expenses since my wife at the time was a stay-at-home mom.

I busted my ass, working 70 and 80-hour weeks by selling, marketing, consulting, managing, and driving. Slowly the business grew. Soon I had four employees, including one of my brothers.

Finally, after three and a half long, hard years, late one evening at the office I ran a twelve-month profit and loss report showing my personal income. There it was, at the top of the sheet. Personal Income: $102,342. In fewer than four years, I had gone from unable to pay my bills to a six-figure income, all by the age of 27.

I shouted with glee and danced around the office like a goofball. Fortunately my employees had gone home by then. Another life-long goal achieved, that of a six-figure income. It was a ten-year goal I had set way back when I was a just 18 years old, and here it was achieved, an entire year ahead of schedule.

It still wasn't all roses. I was working a horrible schedule. My wife at the time and my kids were complaining I was never home, and they had a point. I remembered the fate of my father, having to work his ass off at a job he hated, and the stress it caused him throughout his life. So I shifted focus from income to lifestyle. I wanted to keep my income at that level, but while working fewer hours. I re-vamped my entire business to make it Alpha Male 2.0 compatible (I describe exactly how in the next chapter).

By age 30 I was done with the conversion, still making the six figures but now working only about 30 hours a week, usually taking Fridays off as well as the entire weekend.

With all of my big financial goals achieved in life, I started to drift. I had no Mission. My motivation left me, my passion for life stagnated. I was still a generally happy guy, but the fire was gone. My income stayed the same until around the early 2000s when I had a very bad year. We had to sell our house, sell our cars, and the four of us had to move into a small apartment.

It sucked, but once again it lit a fire under my ass. By the mid-2000s I was back to six figures again, and back in a nice home. Still, that passion and excitement I felt in my twenties had not quite returned. I was motivated, but it felt like I was running through the motions, my financial life in limbo. I was still making money, but I started to realize my financial life, as well as the rest of my life, was moving down the wrong path.

Then came 2007 and 2008. Two tremendous upheavals in my life arose like tsunamis and changed everything, both within the same twelve-month period.

I got divorced, sending my financial life into a tailspin. I had to place all my business ventures on hold while I dealt with the chaos. Then, just as I was stabilizing the damage, October 2008 arrived, and the entire US economy crashed into the worst recession in almost 90 years. Based on my economic forecasting, I figured the economy would crash in 2012, not 2008. I had guessed wrong, and with the recession hitting four years before I had planned, I was completely unprepared. Being jarred from the divorce also meant I was not at the top of my game even if I had been ready for it.

So in the midst of my divorce proceedings, the big crash of 2008 wiped out 60% of my customer base in my largest business within three months. Things were bad.

Yet again, it was up to me to turn things around.

However, this time something was very different. I had finally embraced myself as the man I knew I was meant to be. My Mission was perfectly clarified. No longer married, I was now completely unencumbered by the overhead of monogamy, rules, limitations, financial expense, and drama that traditional marriage entails. More importantly, in 2006 I had rediscovered my passion. Just like in my early twenties, I had meaning, excitement, and focus once again.

Financially, things were chaotic in late 2008 and in 2009 as I repaired the damage to my businesses (even though my woman life was on fire, in a very good way). Soon I had things turned around. More importantly, for the first time in my life, all the businesses I ran were structured for the Alpha 2.0 lifestyle, rather than being structured based on SP, which is the structure most businesses are based upon, including my own prior to 2002.

Today things are very different. I work every day, seven days a week, but just for a few hours a day. I do it because I love it. I make plenty of money certainly, but the work excites me, motivates me, and is directly attached to my Mission, Code, and non-SP goals. Just like those earlier years in my mid-twenties, today I'm excited to get out of bed and get to work. My favorite day of the year, by far, is January 2nd, the first day of the work year, when it's time to attack the new year with Mission-achieving work after a relaxing break during the holidays.

Learning from so many business lessons of the past, today I work out of my home. I can afford a separate office but there is no point.

While I had employees before, today I have zero employees, and that's the way it's going to stay. I never have to worry about employee problems, nor the myriad of ridiculous laws surrounding the hiring, managing, and firing of employees.

Most of my income is location independent, meaning I can be anywhere in the world to maintain it.

My work is also schedule independent, meaning I can do it whenever the hell I feel like it. Too many business owners have to "report" to an eight-to-five workday just like their employees do. What's the point of that?

I run three small businesses, all three in completely different industries. That way if one industry ever has a downturn, I'll still make enough money to be okay. This was one of the big reasons I survived the crash of 2008. Many of my self-employed buddies crumbled under that recession because they had only one business, one source of income. Since I was diversified, I was able to pull through.

Best of all, its work I love to do. About 80% of the work I do on a regular basis I would probably do for free.

Work That Facilitates the Alpha 2.0 Lifestyle

Back in Chapter 1 we discussed the life requirements of the Alpha 2.0. To review the key points from that chapter that directly relate to business and finance:

1. Two of the four required freedoms of the Alpha 2.0 are Freedom of Action (being able to do whatever you want, whenever you want) and financial freedom (being free from circumstances created by financial lack in your life).
2. The Alpha 2.0 lives an abundant life. He doesn't have to be rich, but he has the ability within his current income to provide the kind of life he really wants. This means he should ideally make an income of at least $75,000 per year (perhaps adjusted a little upwards or downwards based on where he lives) since lower than that amount will likely

cause him unhappiness due to its inability to provide experiences that make him happy.

3. The Alpha 2.0 has the ability to maintain his income on fewer than 40 hours a week on average.
4. The Alpha 2.0 has the ability to recover his income within 6-12 months even if he loses it due to circumstances outside of his control. He has true internal security: the security of his own business abilities.

In the next few chapters we're going to discuss exactly how to accomplish all of the above in the financial side of your life. Your financial life is every bit as important as the woman side of your life and every other slice of your Seven Life Areas. Without money and without meaningful work, a man cannot be an Alpha 2.0.

Your Work

Men are creatures of work. A man without a steady outlet for his need for work, or a regular income that more than adequately pays his bills and supports his lifestyle, is like a ship floating down a river with no motor, sails, or rudder. Between brief moments of relaxation and fun, you'll constantly be crashing into debris, rocks, shoals, shorelines, and other boats. No matter how far you get in other areas of your life, you'll constantly be in damage-control mode, either logistically or mentally.

To be compatible with the Alpha 2.0 lifestyle, your work must match the below three objectives.

1. Your work must have purpose and meaning to you. Ideally, it should be clearly attached to your Mission in some way.
2. You must always have all of your regular monthly bills paid for without relying on any financial assistance (gifts or loans) from others (friends, parents, lovers and government included). The Alpha 2.0 is not a creature dependent on others.
3. You cannot allow your work to consistently dominate your life.

Generally speaking, younger men are going to have a challenge with item two, older men are going to have a challenge with item three, and men of all ages may have to wrestle with item one. We'll discuss all three.

Work With a Purpose

Unless you are completely unemployed or retired, you are at one of four levels when it comes to your job, career, or business. In order, they are:

- Entry-level job (like it or not).
- Job or business you don't like.
- Job or business without purpose that you like.
- Job or business with purpose that you like.

Your goal is to constantly be moving up that ladder until you reach level four.

You must have a job (or own a business that actually makes money) that has a specific purpose or objective in your life. If your Mission has anything whatsoever to do with your financial life, then your work must be 100% married to and congruent with your Mission. Even if your Mission has nothing to do with money, your work must still have meaning and purpose to you and should not detract from your Mission in any way. Working just to pay the bills will never make you long-term happy.

That does not mean you must have a job that you love, or a job that you're planning on sticking with forever. If you're a younger guy, or a man of any age who has recently switched careers, you may be in the phase where you have to work at a crappy stepping-stone job until you can get something better. I certainly went through that phase, as will you if you haven't already.

However, just because you have an entry-level job doesn't mean that job can't have a specific purpose or objective. For example, a good plan could be: "I will work here at Acme Corporation as a paid intern until I get promoted to <whatever> which should happen in the next 12 months or less." Another example would be something like "I will work at Domino's Pizza for seven more months until I finish college. Then I will…."

You get the idea. People stuck at crappy or entry-level jobs for long stretches are always people who lack a specific goal or purpose beyond that job.

A true, complete man never engages in any time-consuming activity without purpose. Never work just to work. Never work just to pay the bills. Every job or business you engage in must have a higher purpose or objective, otherwise you are literally waiting around to get old and die.

If you're past the entry-level phase in your career, the next item you need to tackle is to make sure you are doing something you like. I'm amazed at guys in their thirties, forties, or fifties who complain they are "stuck" in jobs they "hate." That's insane!

I'm about to tell you something you're really not going to like, but I say it with love and with a hope that you'll better your life. Ready? Here it is: **if you're over the age of 30 and are still working at job you hate, something is very wrong with your life.** You need to stop right now and make a specific battle plan to make some drastic changes. Continuing to waste your life like this will not work. Nothing else in your life will bring you long-term happiness as a man unless you address this right now. I know it's hard to do. I know it will take time; perhaps even years. You need to do it anyway. When you have some quiet time, sit down, think it through, make a plan to change, and then DO IT.

One clarification about liking your job: you don't have to like 100% of everything you do. I think that's pretty rare, nor do I think that's an achievable goal for most people, myself included. As I mentioned above, I passionately love about 80% what I do. I'm neutral about another 10% or so. The remainder is 10% I don't like at all and actually irritates me. That 20% is the price I pay for the 80% of work that I love. Moreover, even the 10% irritating work is still strongly wedded to my non-SP goals and my Mission, so even if I don't love it, I still consider it important, which further motivates me to do it. So when I say "like/love what you do", I mean you like/love what you do in general. I don't mean you absolutely must love 100% of every minute of every workday.

That brings us to level three. This means you have a job (or own a business) and you actually do enjoy it. That's great, and you should feel good about that, but your work still must have a greater purpose. I run into men all the time who have jobs they clearly enjoy, but they're aimless, floating around life, with no clear Mission or purpose. Surprise, surprise, these men usually have all kinds of problems in the other areas of their lives.

In your business or career, first you must achieve *survival*, then you must achieve *like*, then you must achieve *purpose*. The Alpha Male 2.0 lives at level four with his work. He likes his job or business, and it has great purpose for him.

Not Being Financially Dependent on Others

If you are able to pay 100% of all your taxes, bills and living expenses every month in order to maintain a reasonable lifestyle for you (and your family if you have one), without ever having to rely on financial help (loans or gifts) from:

- Credit cards
- Loans (including student loans)
- Parents
- Friends
- Family
- Church
- Charity
- A girlfriend or wife
- Government (that includes unemployment, food stamps, welfare, social security, etc., even if it's money you "paid into")

...then, and only then, you may skip this section and continue on to the next section below. If not, and you do rely on anything in the above list to pay your monthly obligations, then it's time for some more tough talk, you need to listen well to what I'm about to tell you.

Since discovering the seduction community / dating industry many years ago, I have been horrified at the number of men out there who are in their twenties and thirties who haven't yet taken care of the fundamental basics of supporting oneself financially. I have run into too many guys, way past the age of 23, who are still dependent on parents, or who are unemployed for long stretches (as in years at a time) often by choice, and even well before the economic troubles of 2008 began. I have met way too many men who have made it well into their thirties and still have never made more than $25,000 a year.

Invariably and perhaps not surprisingly, even if these men are good with women, they still run into all kinds of woman problems, like neediness, cheating, and bad breakups. They often have other major problems in their other Seven Life Areas.

Listen pal, if you are over the age of about 23, and still can't pay all of your monthly bills completely by yourself, you need to MAN UP,

RIGHT NOW. Again, I'm not saying you need to be rich! I'm not saying you need to make six figures or be a millionaire. All I'm saying is you should be able to regularly pay all of your monthly bills by yourself. A real man doesn't need to rely on others to pay his bills, at least not for long stretches.

We all have financial problems occasionally and sometimes some of us need help. I get that. As I talked about above, I've had a few rough patches myself. However, if you've gone past six months or so where you still can't pay your bills, you're doing something very wrong, and the Alpha 2.0 lifestyle will not be available to you until you grow up and get some self-responsibility.

Yes, I know it's hard. Do it anyway. I don't care if you need to drastically cut your expenses. I don't care if you need to get a job you hate for a while. I don't care if you need to move to another city. I don't care if you need to get some roommates. Suck it up and do it. Your number one objective for the moment is to get to the point where you can pay your bills, every month, without anyone's help. Being successful in the long-term with women, and being happy in the long-term is simply going to be impossible until and unless you do this.

I'm serious. Stop screwing around and get to work.

Your Work Cannot Dominate You

Strangely, this is the opposite of the first two objectives. The first two objectives are about getting there. This objective is about not going too far.

You may be the kind of guy who, like me, has a job or business that makes money that you thoroughly enjoy, that motivates you, and that has true purpose in your life. That's fantastic. You're Alpha. You're a dying breed in the Western world today, and I salute you...but you're not done.

I know plenty of men who devoted their lives to their job or business, working 60, 70, 90, even 100 hours a week, only to have their entire financial lives destroyed when their wives had enough and divorced them.

I also know unmarried men who are consumed by their jobs or businesses, and their relationship lives are a complete mess. Either they never, or rarely, have sex with women and spend what little free time they have masturbating and watching porn, or the opposite: women constantly come and go from their lives in disruptive ways, with many rules going in and massive drama going out. Cheating, fighting, arguments, and sometimes even violence are not unusual for these guys. At the office these guys are great, but out of the office, they're a damn mess.

I also know many beta males who are very successful in their business or careers, yet when they go home are constantly bitched at by a jaded, unhappy wife. These men are bosses at work, but slaves at home.

In terms of your SLA, your job/business should indeed be in the top three or four most important things in your life, but if your goal is to be happy in the long-term, to become an Alpha 2.0 your job/business cannot be the most important thing above all others, at least not for a long span of time. It's a recipe for disaster, and I've seen way too many intelligent guys make this dreadful mistake.

I need to qualify what I'm saying. When you're doing something like starting a new business, yes, it will often be necessary to be out of balance while you work long hours for a while to get things up and running. That's fine. I've put in those kinds of hours myself during the initial phases of my own businesses.

However, just like the guy who's been on unemployment for years and years, you should not be working 50+ hours a week for years and years on end. Eventually, you must crank your hours back to 30 or 40 hours a week maximum, so that you can enjoy your other SLA and the wonderment the Alpha 2.0 lifestyle has to offer. If you've been working longer than about 55 hours per week longer than about two or three years, then you might be a tough and motivated guy, but you're not Alpha 2.0. Your work controls you; the Alpha 2.0 controls himself.

My work is extremely important to me. I cherish it and consider it a beloved thing in my life. However, just like with women or even one special woman, it is not more important to me than my life as a whole. My children are just as important as my work. My dating and relationship life with women is just as important. Travelling around the world, another passion of mine, is just as important. My physical health is also just as important. Your focus should be all the SLA as a whole, not just one slice of the pie.

You are bigger than your work!

Plugging Your Work into the Alpha 2.0 Lifestyle

At this point, your business, career, and financial goals should have already been run through all the procedures and techniques we've already covered in prior chapters.

- You've established long-term happiness as your primary goal in life, and thus know your work cannot interfere with that goal. It must enhance it.

- You are aware that you have very powerful SP and OBW that will compel you to pursue work that will satisfy the 6SV of The Prison, but not yourself. If the only reason you're an architect is because your dad was an architect, or if you think making a healthy six-figure income is impossible by working out of your home on just 30 hours a week, you have some strong but false SP in your mind that you need to weed out. If you have a strong desire to have employees even though you know in your heart you don't need them to provide a lifestyle you enjoy, or if you persist in a career that you hate but looks good to your peers, you have some of the Six Societal Values and some OBW to work through.
- You have a well-defined Code, Mission and non-SP goals, and your business or career is perfectly wedded to all three. If you have any goals or situations in your financial life that do not mesh with any of those three items, you need to re-orient yourself, and fast. Again, having a non-financial Mission is perfectly okay. In that case, your work doesn't need to be "wedded" to your Mission, but it cannot interfere or detract from your Mission.
- You use the E3D and/or the Check System for your time management in achieving your business, career, and financial goals.

The techniques in the next few chapters assume you have done all of the above, so don't forget that the business advice in this book is strongly interlinked with the life planning advice given in the book's first section.

Chapter 20 –

Creating an Alpha 2.0 Business

Instead of wondering when your next vacation is, you ought to set up a life you don't need to escape from.

Seth Godin

Summer, 1995.

I was sitting outside on a bench deep within Nike World Headquarters in Beaverton, Oregon. I was sitting by a beautiful man-made lake in the center of the Nike campus, surrounded by pristine new buildings, parks, hills, trees, spotless clean sidewalks, and smiling, young Nike employees.

I was one of those employees, working the technical side of Nike's worldwide sales force. Currently on my one-hour lunch break, I was reading a business magazine featuring an article on Donald Trump. Trump was in the business news as being the Comeback Kid. After being on the brink of personal bankruptcy, he had brought himself back, and was back on top of the heap once again.

I was mildly impressed, though it always bothered me that Trump was born rich, his father handing him $3 million to go buy buildings right after he graduated high school. I wasn't that lucky.

However that wasn't what caught my eye about the article. In it, Trump mentioned that he took off work at 2pm one day to go visit his daughter in school. He just stood up and walked out of his office.

This tiny little detail probably didn't even register with the vast majority of people reading the article, but for me it was the most valuable, important, and motivating point.

At 2pm on a workday, Trump felt like visiting his daughter, so he just left his work and did so. He didn't have to ask any boss permission to do it. He didn't have to pre-schedule it in advance on some shared vacation schedule with other co-workers. He didn't have to negotiate with his fellow co-workers regarding the specific day and time he was allowed to leave his office ("Okay, I'll take this afternoon off, and then I'll cover for you on afternoon of the 15th.") He didn't have to explain to a scowling boss about why he wanted to take the time off. He just got up and left.

It wasn't Trump's billions that impressed me, nor was it his hot wives or private jets. It wasn't the money or the success he had. It was the freedom he had, the freedom to just get up and walk out of his work whenever the hell he felt like it for any reason he wanted. Here I was, checking my watch to make sure I wasn't late reporting back to work at 1pm, or else I would have some explaining to do. There was Trump, doing whatever the hell he liked.

I wanted that kind of freedom. I clenched my fists and my blood boiled, knowing that I didn't have it. Like most corporate employees, I was trapped in The Prison, the eight-to-five universe, reporting to work at certain times, leaving at certain times, and taking breaks at certain times, like a five year-old in kindergarten.

It wasn't just the scheduling limitations. Across all of my jobs in the corporate world it was always the same. My boss was always right and I was always wrong. If I was lucky enough to have a competent boss, *his* boss was a moron, and once again I was directed to work on stupid, wasteful tasks. Then there were the frequent, boring, utterly useless two-hour meetings that required my presence.

Such a waste of life. It was unacceptable.

I looked around again at Nike's beautiful campus. The perfectly trimmed trees swayed gently in the breeze. The sunlight reflected glasslike from the lake. The majestic white and silver buildings shined. The attractive employees moved to and fro. It was all beautiful, and it was still a Prison, all designed to make me forget I was living in bondage.

Nike was, and still is, a good company. That's not the point. The point is I was somewhere I did not belong. I was living a life I was not designed for.

I was destined to be free.

Self-Employment

The Alpha Male 2.0 is self-employed. There is no getting around this. If you have a job where you are required to be somewhere at certain times of the day, or certain days of the week, or else you'll get yelled at, you simply cannot live the Alpha 2.0 lifestyle. Just like being traditionally and monogamously married, having a traditional job directly violates Freedom of Action, a mandatory ingredient of an Alpha 2.0's life. Having a job, even a good job, even a great job, means you are not free. Jobs are for people living in The Prison. You must run your own business.

There are only two exceptions to this rule:

1. If you are in 100% commission sales where you have 100%, complete control over your own schedule (barring the occasional mandatory meeting), this is acceptable.

2. If you have the type of job where 100% of it is done online at your home and all your work can be done literally whenever you want, this also would be acceptable.

The vast majority of people are not going to have jobs like this, so barring those two exceptions, having a job is not compatible with the Alpha 2.0 lifestyle and you must have your own business.

This means that if you currently do not own your own business that pays 100% all of your monthly taxes, bills, and other obligations, then one of your primary goals in life is to get to the point where you have that. The goal of owning a small business should be integrated into your goal list if it's not there already.

If you already have your own business, that's good, but you're not all the way there. Only certain types of businesses are valid for the Alpha 2.0 lifestyle.

Alpha 2.0 Business Criteria

The business owned and operated by the Alpha 2.0 must follow all of the following criteria:

1. The business must have zero employees. There are unusual exceptions to this rule, but they're somewhat rare. For example, having one or two employees you never need to personally see might be acceptable depending on the specific structure of your business. The vast majority of people who own businesses with employees are not free. It's just as bad as having a job with a boss; often it's even worse. Realize that I'm talking about employees here. Utilizing help from contractors, subcontractors, temporary workers, volunteers, consultants, coaches, or advisors are all okay and often necessary.

2. As we discussed in the last chapter, the business must generate enough income after taxes and expenses to pay 100% of all your monthly obligations. I shouldn't even have to say that, but based on a lot of small businesses I've seen out there, it looks like I have to. If you own several small businesses that all combined pay all of your bills, that's acceptable as long as all of your businesses match the other Alpha 2.0 criteria listed here. Also remember the Alpha Male 2.0 income goal of $75,000 per year (or the equivalent in your city).

3. The business must be location independent or very close to it. If you must live in a certain city for your business to operate, it does not qualify as an Alpha 2.0 business. You should be able to make money anywhere you go, anywhere in the world (within reasonable constraints of course, like having paved roads or an internet connection available).

4. The business must have an extremely flexible schedule. That doesn't mean you can never schedule appointments or meetings. It means that if you have to constantly report to a certain company or person at specific times not of your choosing, it's not an Alpha 2.0 business. The Alpha 2.0 can sleep in until 11am if he wants, and he can work or take time off whenever the hell he feels like it, while still making money and without having to check in with anyone.

5. The business cannot be paperwork intensive. Having to carry around or store huge stacks of hard copy paperwork isn't going to cut it in an Alpha 2.0 life.

6. The business should not require more than 40 hours a week of work on average. Ideally it should require only 30 hours a week or less. As discussed last chapter, the only exception to this rule is during the initial start-up period of the business. Yet even then, that period should not exceed three years. If you're working longer than 40-hour weeks for longer than three years, something is wrong.

7. Ideally, the business must be 100% owned by you and no one else. That means no investors and no equity partners. Having investors can be just as bad as having a boss, and having partners is often even worse. I've seen many real-life horror stories of Alphas doing great in business only to have

a sudden catastrophe because of a partner's screw-up, change of heart, divorce, health problem, or other challenge completely outside of the Alpha's control. That being said, there are lots of exceptions to this rule. Sometimes investors or partners may be required on a short or medium term basis, such as real estate investing in a start-up, where you plan on selling your stock or ownership and exiting within a few years. I'm also not saying you should never rely on other people in your business; you can and probably should. My point is that these people don't need to own an equity share in your company. They can have their own separate company and you can pay them as a subcontractor. The bottom line is to be extremely careful when entering into a primary income source that requires you to co-own stock with other people, and always remember that Freedom of Action is just as important as a high income. Lastly, I'm only talking about a *primary income source* here. You can certainly be one of many investors in a company as an investment or side-income instead of a primary income source.

8. Obviously the business must be 100% congruent to your Code, your Mission, and your goals.

Examples of Alpha 2.0 Businesses

I don't want you to get negative or discouraged after reading all the requirements for an Alpha 2.0 business in the last section. Because of your own SP, after reading that section you probably said, "Oh that's bullshit. You can't make money at a business with all of those requirements!"

Well, here you go; a list of some real-world examples of some Alpha 2.0 businesses to get your imagination juices flowing.

- Selling manufactured products that have at least a five to one, preferably a ten to one margin, where orders are processed and drop-shipped directly to the customer without your involvement.
- Doing independent sales and/or marketing for someone else, selling or marketing a product or service you personally do not provide, and taking a fat commission.

- Consulting or coaching, all done online, using services like Skype.
- Selling information products such as books, ebooks, educational audio, courses, or videos. This area alone is huge. It can range from business advice, to travel writing, to teaching people how to install speakers in their cars. It's very likely you have some piece of knowledge within you that a niche market would love to hear all about, and pay for.
- Professional speaking, either being hired by organizations or doing your own seminars, keynotes, or workshops. You'll need to be a little careful with this one, because if you go too crazy it can and will destroy location independence. I know plenty of successful professional speakers who make a lot of money, but spend more than two hundred days per year on the road. These people are not free.
- A small business with 95% of all of its functions outsourced to non-employees. I once met a man who owned a $100+ million dollar electronics company with just four employees. Impossible! How did he do it? Easy. From the ground up, he always outsourced everything. His entire business model was based around it. (He was an exception to the "no employees" rule.)
- Translation or other language services, delivered online.
- Continuity programs, such as newsletters, online magazines, coaching programs, members-only web sites, paid internet forums, training courses, or even hard products. You can really get creative and profitable with this. One web site I know sells a "pasta of the month" program where customers are automatically billed every month and regularly receive some new exotic pasta and sauce. Another guy I know sells a monthly newsletter for, get ready for this, $3500 a year! His newsletter is highly niched in the oil industry.
- Real estate investing. You must be very careful about keeping everything location independent, however. This means using competent property managers to operate your rental properties.

- Selling artistic works, ideally online. Examples would be a graphic artist, fiction writer, voice-over actor, photographer, etc. The challenge is selling art of any kind can be a tough road, and often doesn't pay very much even if you're good. Often a good deal of luck is involved with success. If you wish to pursue this, please do, but once again, always remember the Alpha 2.0 income goal of $75,000 per year or the equivalent. The "starving artist" might be cool, but he's not Alpha 2.0.

- Writing, copywriting, or editing of any kind. If you have decent writing skills, finding gigs on sites like Elance and Odesk make this relatively simple. Years ago Tim Ferriss profiled an American living in Panama who had a twelve year-old daughter making $500 a month writing blog posts for various clients she found on a freelancer site, using mostly Wikipedia as her information source (I'm unable to locate the link, though the video of the father is likely still somewhere on YouTube). So come on, if a friggin' twelve-year old girl can make $500 a month in an Alpha Male 2.0 business...

- Any work that can be 100% performed and delivered online. This covers a huge range of services, from I.T. consulting to research, virtual assistant work, and a thousand other things.

You can get even more creative for some really wild ideas that do work. I know a woman who sells used women's underwear online. She gets all of her girlfriends to give her their used panties, then she sells them online to perverts. Laugh all you want; the last time I spoke with her she was making big bucks and was only working about 15 hours a week. True, she's a woman and thus not Alpha 2.0, but she was certainly following the Alpha 2.0 business structure.

I once worked with a guy who had a full time job with a large phone company but who also had a complete Alpha 2.0 business on the side. His business was selling and installing phone systems for hotels. He did very little of the work himself yet he had no employees, instead using subcontractors for everything. He only worked one day a week on his business; about seven hours every Saturday. He made almost as much money from these seven hours as he did from his 40 hours working his day job.

There are many good books that describe businesses that fit nicely into the Alpha 2.0 lifestyle. Books like *The E-Myth Revisited*, *The 4-Hour Workweek*, *The $100 Startup*, and many others are great places to see exactly how businesses like this are created and maintained. These are all medium to high-income businesses that require very few hours per week to maintain and can usually be done from anywhere in the world without any employees.

Take your interests and your abilities and plug into one or more of the examples above, and start a small business, even if it's just a part-time business you do on the side in addition to your full time job. Work it and grow it, and always make sure to keep heed of the requirements we discussed in the prior session.

If you already own a business, transform it into an Alpha 2.0 compatible business. Yes, this may require some radical action and some serious balls. You still need to do it. I did it myself. Here's how.

How I Transformed My Business from Prison-Based To Alpha 2.0

Back around the year 2000, I had a decent small business humming along nicely. I had an office, four good employees, and I was making good money. The problem was I was working about 70 hours a week, and most of those hours were not hours I enjoyed. Stress was common. Financial screw-ups were the norm and the employees often pissed me off even though they were all good people. My clients were sometimes upset with me, and there was way too much paperwork to deal with.

Like most Prison-based businesses, to the outside world I looked very successful. My friends and family were extremely impressed. Yet I wasn't happy or free.

In 2002, after much research and soul-searching, and taking the advice I received from Brian Tracy and others (that I described back in Chapter 10), I decided to make a radical change. I wanted the business to serve me and my lifestyle, not the other way around.

The first thing I did was to take advice from another one of my mentors, Alan Weiss, and "fired" the bottom 25% of my clients. These were the clients that gave me the most grief, even if they represented a significant income, which they did. I wrote a letter telling them that I was no longer available to provide consulting and that I would be happy to help them find a replacement.

Result: 90% of my client problems instantly vanished.

Next, I announced to my employees that I was downsizing the company and was laying all of them off. However, I would keep them on the payroll until they had all found new jobs. I would even help them find new jobs. All my employees were good, honest people, so I gave all of them glowing letters of recommendation and references if they asked. One by one, they all found new jobs, leaving only one employee left: me.

Result: My 70 hours per week dropped to about 45 hours per week. Later they dropped again to about 30 hours a week.

Next, I moved my family into a house with a big garage, and using the money I saved by not having to pay any employees, I remodeled half of the garage into a home office. I let the lease expire on my current office, sold all of my extra computer equipment, moved out of the office, and set up shop at home.

Result: An almost 50% reduction in the amount of money I had to earn every month to pay my bills. This was in addition to the savings caused by no longer having any employees.

The year after I did this, my personal net income went up by 72% and my work hours went down by about 42%. I remember that year, sitting in my office, thinking, "Why the hell didn't I do this ten years ago?"

The answer was that I had a bunch of Alpha 1.0 SP in my mind about how a "real man" should own a "real business," with employees and a big building with his name on it and a secretary and all that crap. Men who worked out of their homes don't have a "real business." That was for business wannabes.

Oh, how wrong I was. I counted myself lucky that I had figured that out by the time I was 30. Millions of business owners live their entire stressful lives never figuring this out. What a waste.

Once I had a much more, but not completely, Alpha 2.0-compatible business, I set out into the next stage; that of setting up redundant sources of income to truly secure my financial future.

Redundancy

You may have noticed that much of the Alpha 2.0 lifestyle incorporates the concept of redundancy. We covered how this applies to women back in Chapter 15. There are many meanings of this word, but here I'm talking about the definition used in computers and electronics, which is:

The provision of additional or duplicate systems that function in case an operating part or system fails.

As we discussed in prior chapters, one of the problems with traditional dating and marriage (i.e. monogamy) is that if the one woman in your life turns out to be a bitch, or starts refusing sex, or anything like that, you have a very serious life problem. You can try to work it out, but if you can't, then either you put up with it and remain unhappy, or you need to remove her from your life in a very severe way (break ups, moving out, selling the house, getting divorced, screwing up your kids, etc). Both of these violate the long-term happiness requirement of the Alpha 2.0.

Dating multiple women, or at least having an open relationship, mitigates or even eliminates this downside. It's a redundant system.

Your business and financial life should work the same way. Today, I don't own one business. I own three. All three of them are in completely different business sectors and industries.

Why in the world would I mess around with three businesses instead of just having one? Wouldn't having one business be simpler? Perhaps a little, but then I would miss out on all of these benefits:

- If one of my businesses fails, I might be upset, but I'm still okay. I'm still able to pay my bills and carry on with my life. If I had just one business and it failed, my life would be seriously disrupted and my happiness would be destroyed.
- They're all in separate industries, so if one industry suddenly has a downturn or becomes obsolete, again I might be upset, but on the whole I'd still be okay. I do not have to have my entire income and livelihood reliant on just one industry, which is subject to change at any time in this world of constant technological growth, social upheaval, and hyper-change.

Here's a great example. During the 1970s my grandfather made really good money owning a calculator and adding machine sales and repair company. He had three locations and was doing great until the late 1980s. Care to take a guess as to what happened then? The personal computer was invented, and suddenly no one wanted to spend money buying or repairing adding machines or expensive calculators. In less than 18 months his entire businesses was completely wiped out. He then had to rely upon his grown children for his retirement.

- Having 100% of your income reliant upon one single industry is a bad idea in the modern era. Alpha Males back in the 1800s or 1950s could do this since technology and social change didn't evolve as fast as today. You and I don't have that luxury.

- I never get bored. Because I have three completely different businesses, every day my work experience is completely different. It's fun, exciting, and stimulating.
- This is an interesting side benefit to this I didn't anticipate. Because I have three businesses, none of the businesses need to make a huge amount of money. As long as the incomes from all three businesses add up to what I want to make, I'm happy. This is a completely different feeling I had back when I was 100% reliant upon one business to make these huge income numbers I wanted. My current system makes income goal achievement far less stressful.

It is simply amazing to me that everyone talks about diversifying your investments, yet no one ever talks about diversifying your <u>income</u>. Your income is just as important as your investments, if not more so.

When I was a young guy a very sharp businessman once said to me, "You have a spare tire in your car, don't you? Then why don't you have a spare income?" He was more right than I could possibly imagine at the time.

The Alpha Male 2.0 has structured his entire business and financial life to be a redundant system, just the way his dating and relationship life is structured. This way, whenever depressions, recessions, revolutions, technological changes, sociological changes, or any other challenges come along, while all those beta employees and Alpha 1.0 business owners are screaming the sky is falling, the Alpha 2.0 just shrugs and proceeds on his happy merry way.

Chapter 21 –

How to Get to High Income Fast

To become a successful philosopher king, it is better to start as the king than as the philosopher.

Nassim Taleb
Antifragile

February, 2000.

"I just don't understand how you did this," my dad was saying.

We were having one of our regular breakfasts at one of our favorite places, a dirty truck stop that served omelets the size of campfire wood and cinnamon rolls the size of laptops, both of which I devoured with gusto. The cigarette ash served in the food always gave it that special yummy punch.

It was just me, my dad, and a bunch of smelly truck drivers in the place. My dad was looking over my profit and loss statement from the prior year showing my new six-figure income.

"I just don't know how you did it this fast," he continued, shaking his head.

Normally I would have been a smartass and bragged, but this was my dad, and there's something about not being a braggart with your dad that's hard to explain. You probably already know what I'm talking about. So I just shrugged and shoved another hunk of greasy hash browns down my throat.

My dad eventually got to six figures himself, long after I grew up and moved out of the house. It took him about 15 years of self-employment to do it, 30 years of working total. I had done it in 3 years of self-employment, 9 years working total.

I thought about something else my dad once told me, several years prior during the early 1990s. When I was working at a large bank and considering a move to another company, my dad warned me this would be a very bad idea.

"You don't want a resume full of a bunch of jobs you only had for a year or two," he had said, "That will look terrible to employers and no one will want to hire you."

I remember that advice making sense to me at the time, yet my real-life experience was the opposite. I had found that employers didn't give a shit at all how long you worked at a prior job, just as long as you had the experience they were looking for. Very quickly I had discovered that the only real way to increase your income quickly when living the corporate employee life was to force yourself to go out and get a new job every 12-24 months.

Interesting. Here he was again, flabbergasted at not only my income, but how fast it had increased.

Was his advice and confusion wrong? No, it was just 40 years out of date. Back in the 1950s, his advice about resumes would have been accurate. Also back then, any guy saying he was going to make $100,000 a year, even if adjusted downwards for inflation, within three years of starting a business from scratch, would indeed have been laugh-worthy.

Times had changed. The 21st century had arrived, and nothing was the same.

Getting to High Income Fast

Last chapter we discussed the requirements of an Alpha 2.0 business. In this chapter we're going to talk about proven principles and techniques, used by me and millions of small business owners all over the world, on how to get from zero to the money as quickly as possible.

Why is getting to high income important, other than the obvious reason of wanting more money? There are two answers to that question.

Lifestyle

The first answer to that question is that, as we've already discussed, an income of below $75,000 will likely not provide you with optimum happiness. This does not mean that you need to live in a mansion, drive a Ferrari, and wear Armani suits (though if any of those things are real goals of yours, I support you completely). Regardless, most men in the modern era and in the Western world need a few things in their lives to ensure consistent happiness:

- He needs a *decent home* to call his own. I'm talking about a small to medium-sized nice house or a cool apartment, decorated the way he loves. Equally important, he should be able to pay for this easily without having to rely on any roommates, wives, or live-in girlfriends. The Alpha 2.0 cannot live in a crappy home unless he's very young and hasn't earned his $75,000+ annual income yet.

- Unless he lives in the middle of a large metropolitan city, *he has a dependable car.* It doesn't have to be a new car; I drive a car that is eight years old. However it does have to be a good, quality car that runs perfectly and looks nice.
- He *is able to afford nice clothing.* The definition of "nice" is completely up to you, but he has a few outfits that cost some real money and make him look good.
- He has *very little debt.* Ideally, he has zero debt. Even more ideally, his home is completely paid off. Being debt free should be one of your core goals in life. After that, paying off the mortgage to your home as fast as possible should be the next goal if you have not done so already.
- He has *enough money* to travel to the cool places around the world he likes. That doesn't mean he's constantly traveling, but he has the money to take several big trips per year, including international trips, without breaking the bank.
- He has an income high enough and expenses low enough to be able *to save or invest money every month.* Spending all the money you make every month is insane. Even if you plan on never retiring, you're going be unable to work the hours you now work someday, so you must have long-term savings / investments you contribute to on a monthly basis. As I said earlier, being happy now but miserable as an old man is not Alpha 2.0.

All of those things are accessible to the unmarried man who stays out of debt and makes around $75,000 or more in most areas of the world. He's not rich, but he lives well. Money is not a problem for him.

I will be fair here and adjust all of this based on your age. If you're 20 or 25 years old, I don't expect you to have all of the above yet; though I did when I was 25, so if you want it, you can get it if you desire it strongly enough. Set this kind of lifestyle as one of your goals, and get to work.

However, if you're over the age of about 35, certainly over the age of 40, then I do expect you to be living a life like this. You've had plenty of time to get your financial house in order. If it isn't, you're behind schedule and have some serious catching up to do.

Wait! Are those some excuses I hear? All right, let's deal with those.

Yes, I realize that if you've gone through a divorce this might make all these lifestyle parameters a little tougher. You're preaching to the choir, brother. I went through that too, and it did screw up my financial life for a while. I still recovered from it pretty damn quickly, and so can you too if you focus on it.

Yes, I know that if you have lots of kids this is harder.

Yes, I know that the economic conditions lately are not that great.

Yes, yes, yes. I'm sure you and I could sit around the campfire and go on for hours and hours about all the reasons you're in your thirties or older and are still having all the financial troubles of a man twenty years younger than you. Shut up, stop making excuses, take stock of your life, develop a Code, a Mission, set a goal to clean up your financial life, and get to work.

Excuses are never going to make you happy. Never.

Toil Does Not Equal Happiness

The second answer to the question of why getting to high income fast is important regards the old myth, first developed during the late industrial revolution of the 1920s, of "putting your nose to the grindstone."

There is some very outdated SP that states a "real man" busts his ass for 40, 50, 60, 70 hours a week for 30, 40, or 50 years, and then, and only then, after all those decades of back-breaking work, is he "allowed" to reap the financial rewards of his labor. If you have a grandpa who is still alive, or a very elderly father, you may have heard some SP like this come out of his mouth from time to time.

It's horseshit. Busting your ass for decades at a job you don't love will not make you happy, and will destroy any semblance of an Alpha 2.0 existence. Way too many good men out there throughout history, my own father and grandfathers included, followed this path of mass unhappiness for decades, followed by a brief fun time in very old age. It's all SP of a bygone era, and you don't want any part of it.

If you have any SP in your mind about how success, especially financial success, must be hard, or risky, or take a long time, you need to re-orient your brain immediately, using the techniques we discussed in Chapter 3.

Love and respect your father. Love and respect your grandfathers. Just be very careful about taking outdated advice or listening to SP from anyone.

How to Get to High Income Fast

Here I will cover the core techniques that others and I have used that work very well in bolstering income fast. All of them work. All of them require work. None of them are easy, but all of them will dramatically increase your income very quickly.

The following techniques assume that you are self-employed and are running an Alpha 2.0 compatible business (or close to it), with all the requirements we discussed in the last chapter. If your only income at the moment is from a job, or if you own a business that is not an Alpha 2.0 one, you're more than welcome to apply these techniques as best you can, but for the remainder of the chapter I'm going to be assuming an Alpha 2.0 business framework.

Technique 1: Focus On Sales and Marketing

Every business has three elements.

Sales, finances, and operations. You have to sell it, then you have to make the widget or perform the service and get it to the customer, then you have to track the money. All three areas are critical, and all three areas require some of your time as a business owner.

The problem is most people who start a business are more excited about the widget they're selling than they are about actually selling. When the business is new, they get excited about the process of opening a business. They get pumped about things like their new fancy desk, their business cards, and what bookkeeping system to use. They focus on their widget, fall in love with their widget, sleep with their widget every night, and spend all day working with their widget. In the end, their time and mental focus looks like this:

The Typical Business

Perhaps the biggest mistake I see men (and women) make when running their own businesses is that they spend most of their time, effort, money, and focus on non-sales and non-marketing tasks. Sales is scary, and marketing costs a lot of money with no guaranteed results. Working on their widget is exciting and fun.

You've seen the stats that reveal that most new businesses fail within five years, often within two years. This is why. Business owners spend all their time on the areas of the business that cost money rather than make money.

If your goal is to stay in business and make lots of money to improve your lifestyle, your focus in business should look like this:

The Ideal Business

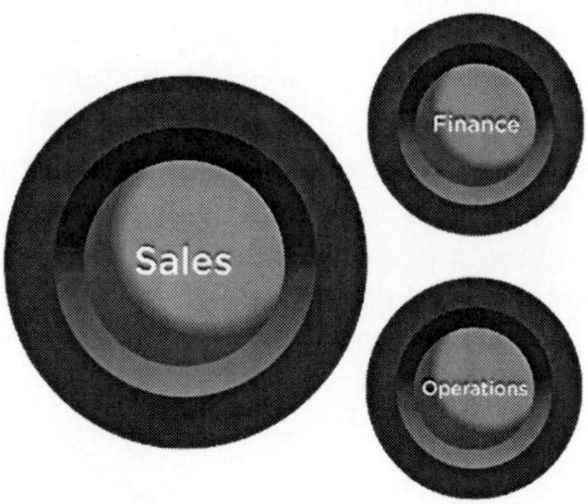

It's perfectly fine to be involved with operations and finance as a business owner, especially during the initial phases of your business. But for every one hour you spend in operations or finance, you should be spending two or three hours in sales or marketing.

This, in my opinion based on the hundreds of companies I've worked with over my business career, is the number one reason for small business failure. Since the owner or managers of a business "don't like sales" or find marketing and promotion somehow sleazy or dishonest, they shy away from the one function of a business that keeps it alive, focusing instead on the "fun" parts of a business like working on their widget.

You must force yourself to spend the majority of the time in your business in the sales and marketing aspects of it. You must overcome the SP you have in your mind about sales being seedy or beneath you, or promotion being deceptive, selfish, or narcissistic. Your business cannot survive without a strong sales and marketing focus. Think of it as a 1-to-3 ratio.

- For every one hour you spend in operations or finance, you should spend three in sales.
- For every one book you read about finance or industry, you should read three books on marketing or sales.
- For every dollar you spend in operations or finance, you should spend three in marketing or sales.

A business can, and often will, survive a major problem or catastrophe in the operations or finance area, but it will never survive a catastrophe in the sales or marketing area. I see it every day. There are numerous businesses in the Fortune 500 that waste a mind-boggling amount of money every year on stupid crap. We're talking hundreds of millions to even billions of dollars a year. Yet every year, these companies stay in business. Why? Because they have strong sales. Try to think of an example of the reverse. Name a business that stays alive year after year with zero help from the government that has excellent operations, flawless finance, but horrible sales.

See my point?

Focus on sales and marketing at all times.

Technique 2: Niche Yourself

Which man makes more: the general practitioner attorney or the attorney who focuses on mergers and acquisitions? The second man of course. Even though both are just as smart, just as educated, and just as capable, the second man might easily be making double what the first man is without working any more hours per week.

Let's take it a step further. Which attorney makes more: the attorney who focuses on mergers and acquisitions or an attorney who focuses on mergers and acquisitions strictly for the food industry? Again, the second attorney probably makes more. He gets clients easier and faster than the first guy, even though he's likely charging much more money for his services.

The more you niche,

- The more money you make.
- The more you can charge for your products or services.
- The easier it is for you to find customers.
- The more likely your customers will be repeat customers.
- The less customer turnover you'll experience.
- The less hard you'll need to work for the equivalent income of the guy who isn't niching himself.

Way back when I started my first business, my small computer consulting practice, I didn't niche at all. I took the business from whomever I could find. Over time, I noticed that in my part of the country, lumber and wood companies were very common and doing very well. Because I followed my own advice and always focused on marketing and sales, I started crafting my marketing materials to position me as the "computer consultant for the lumber industry." Instantly my income went up.

I did this a second time, presenting myself to law firms as the "computer consultant for legal firms." My income shot upwards again.

By the way, that's another secret to this. You can niche yourself in multiple areas and it's perfectly fine. At one point I was the "expert" in the legal, lumber, and construction industries. It was not a lie. I knew the technical side of these industries very well and I was providing a quality service. If I had to do it all over again knowing what I know now, my niching strategy would have been very different, and I would have chosen different industries, but the concept still applies.

Later I started moving into business consulting and professional speaking, and again I niched myself. Instead of speaking about "customer service" or "change" or any of those other things most speakers were talking about, I niched myself as speaking only about business productivity via technology.

Many years later, as I started teaching men about dating and relationships, instead of selling the standard information about "dating" or "picking up women," I was very careful to niche myself. I focused on the niches of online dating, older men dating younger women, and open relationships. Two of those three niches were things virtually no one was talking about at the time, at a least at commercial level. Again it worked, and I made money quickly and easily.

The more you can niche, the better. Ideally, you should micro-niche, meaning finding a niche within a niche. The best example of this was a guy I met once at an annual convention of the National Speakers Association. This guy, whom I'll call Joe, was a very simple guy. Nothing amazing about him at all, but there was something very amazing about his speaking business.

Joe had one speech. Just one. It was only 45 minutes long. He charged $5,000 for this speech, and always had a minimum of 120 booked speeches per year, with almost no marketing whatsoever. Do the math on that one. That's a gross income of $600,000 year, not even working the entire year, and in true Alpha 2.0 style, Joe worked out of his home with no employees.

The rest of us speakers were floored. Everyone who talked to Joe, me included, wanted to know his secret. How could such a simple guy pull off something this incredible?

Joe's answer: "I niche myself."

Joe didn't just niche himself, he micro-niched himself. Instead of doing what most professional speakers do, speaking on some generic topic like "sales," his topic was extremely niched. It was workplace safety. Boring right? Say what you want, but it clearly worked.

He didn't stop niching there. He niched himself a second time by only speaking to electrical companies. So his entire speech, his entire message, and all the supplemental stuff he sold, including stickers, flyers, pamphlets, and all kinds of other materials, was specifically geared towards that single niche: workplace safety in the electrical industry. Now that's niched! That's why simple old Joe was putting all of us to shame, pulling down $600,000 a year without breaking a sweat.

Technique 3: Don't Be Afraid to Charge High Prices

When it comes to setting prices, the age-old advice is to research your competition, find out who's charging low and who's charging high, then price yourself in about the middle.

That's BS, or should I say, SP.

You should instead determine how much money you want, niche yourself, focus on sales and marketing, and charge as much as you like.

At one point I was one of the highest-priced consultants on a per-hour basis in my industry in my entire city, yet my calendar was full of appointments anyway. If I had been charging low or medium rates, I would have been a fool. I provided a very high-quality service, was very easy to work with, was decently niched, and focused on marketing and sales. Charging high prices was no problem at all.

Yes, there are sometimes external factors that prevent you from doing this. Sometimes, based on industry or economic conditions, you may have no choice but to keep your prices low or mid-range. Fortunately, these situations are rare. At one point during an economic recession I indeed had to cut my consulting rates, but it was a temporary situation and soon I raised them back up to where they belonged.

Sometimes you won't be able to raise your prices because it's not feasible for your target market or your industry. Sometimes this is acceptable and sometimes it's not. If you're pursuing an Alpha 2.0 business, you should avoid businesses that are subject to these kinds of pricing limitations. You should have the freedom to set whatever prices you want, based on your own income goals, and nothing else.

The bottom line is that there are many businesses out there that are doing very well, even during poor economic times, while still charging high prices. During the economic troubles of late 2008 through 2010, as horrible as the economy became, I still continued to see mobs of people lined up at Starbucks to buy their five dollar coffees and tiny eight dollar sandwiches.

Charging high prices is a business model that works, and you should always seek to integrate that model into anything you're doing. Of course I'm presupposing that you are:

- Selling a very high quality product or service.
- Treating your customers/clients very well.
- Offering great value for the money you're charging.
- Niching yourself.

You should be doing all these things anyway! Why not charge high for the high value you're providing?

Technique 4: Use All the Other Techniques in This Book

One of the great advantages of being an Alpha Male 2.0 is that many of the techniques and principles overlap into many different slices of your Seven Life Areas. For example, many of the mindsets and techniques of dating and relationships directly apply to business success, and vice versa.

As just one easy example, when you really get outcome independence down, not only will you suddenly find it much easier to attract women into your life and keep them there, you will also find it much easier to do things like get new customers and negotiate favorable business deals.

Almost everything we've talked about in this book can be directly applied to business for fantastic gains even though they may have been originally described in different SLA contexts. This includes:

- Confidence. You'll close sales faster and more often if you're more confident. You'll also be able to close bigger deals and get higher-paying customers.
- Masculinity. Generally speaking, most men and women in business will be more apt to do business with you if you clearly emote masculinity. There are even studies that show bald men exude greater business leadership potential than men with hair[41].

---

[41] http://online.wsj.com/news/articles/SB10000872396390443862604578032541863652264

- Financial freedom. The less pressured you are by your finances, the more picky you can be with the type of work, industry, or customer you choose to engage with.
- Social freedom. The less socially inhibited you are, the more options you'll have in your life for financial gain.
- Abundance. The stronger your abundance mentality is with money, the easier money will flow into your life. It's very hard to noticeably increase your income when you think making money is hard or that rich people are evil.
- The Happiness Change Curve. This is crucial when starting any new business venture or project. Rarely do you get to the big money before some short-term pain first.
- Overcoming SP, OBW, and Six Societal Values. I've already talked about how dangerous it is to base your career around what others want for you instead of what you want.
- Technology. This is how the modern-day Alpha can leverage himself in ways the Alphas of history could not.
- Globalization. You can and should sell to the entire world, not just your current city. Who has more money to give you: your town or the entire planet?
- Increasing liberal attitudes. One of my regular income sources is selling books on how to have sexually open relationships. Do you think I could be making decent and consistent money doing that if it was 1950?
- Your Code. Your odds of consistent, long-term high income go up if your career is aligned to your pre-defined Code.
- Your Mission. This puts greater purpose in your work, motivating you to work harder and better, and helping you persevere through the rough times.
- Your goals. Empirical data has repeatedly shown that people with written goals make more money than people with no written goals[42].
- The E3D System and/or the Check System. Improving your time management, and more specifically your daily focus,

[42] http://cdn5.sidsavara.com/wp-content/uploads/2008/09/researchsummary2.pdf

will help ensure you to get the right business tasks done at the right times.

- Jealousy management. More than once, I have seen otherwise capable men damage their own careers and income potentials because of problems in their personal and business lives directly caused by jealousy.

- Understanding women's differences from men. In selling to, working with, negotiating with, and collaborating with women in a business context, understanding their hidden differences will give you an edge over other men who do not.

- Emotional control. Keeping the positive emotions in and the negative emotions out will keep you focused and motivated in business (though a little temporary anger to help boost a sense of friendly competition might be okay; technically that's not "negative").

- Physical attractiveness. This is probably obvious, but empirical evidence has shown that better-looking people make more money[43]. One of the biggest reasons I lost weight was because I knew I had a very real financial incentive to do so.

- Fashion. As above. The classier you look, the more money you'll likely make.

- Alpha 2.0 relationship parameters (low number of rules, low drama, etc.). Business drama is just as stupid, useless, and destructive as relationship drama, if not more so. You will make more money over your working lifetime if you spend more time focusing on real work instead of wasting time dealing with workplace drama.

All of those above items can and will help you in your business life. It would be useful to re-read this book a second time once you finish it, and keep in mind all the business and financial applications you can apply using many of the concepts above, including the woman ones.

This is why being an Alpha 2.0 is so wonderful! Every new skill improves your life exponentially and in a multifaceted way. Most men

[43] http://online.wsj.com/news/articles/SB10001424052970203687504576655331418204842

learn a skill and apply it to just one of their SLA. As an Alpha 2.0, you can often apply that newfound skill to three or four areas, if not more.

Technique 5: Always Keep Overhead Extremely Low

I purposely saved this one for last. That's how critical it is.

This is one I screwed up twice over my business career. Once was when I first started my business and overspent on startup costs. The second time was when I got married. I allowed my Mission to drift by letting my wife at the time guide many of my financial decisions.

Numerous times I have worked with companies who complained when I handed them an invoice for a few thousand dollars, only to see them the very next week purchase a $10,000 leather couch for the reception area or a $13,000 first class plane ticket to Asia for one of their mid-level employees. I have seen brand-new new businesses purchase desks for every employee that were several thousand dollars each, rent ridiculously expensive offices, or spend hundreds of thousands of dollars on big, complicated, frilly web sites that never made one dollar in actual revenue. I have seen companies pay six-figure salaries to people who sat around and accomplished virtually nothing, and if you've been in the corporate world long enough, you've seen this too.

I've seen Fortune 500 companies do this, but I've also seen small businesses do this. Hey, if you own a company like General Motors that grosses $155 billion a year and you want to waste money on a bunch of stupid crap, then I guess go ahead. However, as an Alpha 2.0 with the goal of long-term consistent happiness, you can't be doing this.

You must be absolutely ruthless, and I mean ruthless, about where you spend your money in your business. I already relayed the story about how I shut down my office, dumped all of my employees (though nicely) and started working out of my home. For many years now, my entire business infrastructure has been a single room in my house, a desk I purchased used 16 years ago, a single laptop, and cheap laser printer on the other side of the house I almost never use because I run a paperless office. That's it! That's my entire company; all three of them. I usually don't even have business cards or letterhead.

I want to be the one spending the money I earn, not my business. The more money I spend in my business, the more money I have to go make, the more hours a week I'll have to work, and the more accounting work I have to do. Screw that.

One of your eternal and over-arching business goals should always be to maintain extremely low business overhead. Even if you ignore my advice about not having employees and have a more conventional, non-Alpha 2.0 business, you should still stick with this goal. Michael Dell, founder of the Dell computer company, has talked about how for the first several years of the business, even after they were making good money and had many employees, he still would not purchase any garbage cans for any employees. Instead he had them line cardboard computer boxes with garbage bags[44].

Sound crazy? It's not crazy; it's damn smart. Today, I do the same thing. The "garbage can" under my desk is the big cardboard box that my paper shredder was shipped in about 14 years ago.

This technique goes hand-in-hand with a sales and marketing focus. If you have a business where you are really focused on sales and marketing and you're keeping expenses really low, you have instantly eliminated 95% of the reasons why people go out of business.

Think about that for a minute.

---

[44] *Direct from Dell* by Michael Dell

Chapter 22 –

Dominating Your Finances to Maximize Your Lifestyle

The purpose of money is to create the environments in which you can experience the things that money cannot buy.

Fredric Lerhman

February, 2007.

It was over. I had made up my mind that my marriage needed to end, or at a minimum, needed a serious break.

I had known for a quite a while that a divorce was likely. I had been purchasing gold coins and throwing them into a safety deposit box. It was my "divorce emergency fund" if I ever needed it. Well, the day had actually arrived, and now I needed it.

Because of the American government's insistence on printing billions of dollars whenever it needs more money, I knew gold had been slowly and steadily rising over the years, which is why I had been buying it. However, I hadn't had the gold very long; most of it was fewer than two years old.

At my computer, I swallowed hard as I pulled up current gold prices. For a separation, and likely divorce of minimal drama, I would need some quick cash to pay a moving company and put a deposit down on an apartment, not to mention paying the expenses of two households for a while. I needed cash, outside of a bank checking account where the wife could access it.

Damn, I really needed my gold to be up in value!

Having purchased most of the gold at around $370 an ounce, I crossed my fingers as I read the data on the screen. Then I leapt out of my chair with a war cry of victory as I saw that gold was now $620 per ounce. A staggering 40% return on my investment! While there were many problems I experienced moving out and getting a divorce, living costs weren't one of them. While many divorced or separated men I knew had their separations force them into financial chaos, debt, and even bankruptcy, the profits from my gold investments ended up financing my entire separation.

Managing Your Money

Making money is one thing. Managing it is something completely different.

In modern society, beta males hand their money over to their wives, who usually spend it with wild abandon on more-expensive-than-necessary cars, homes, vacations, clothing, and the biggest one of all: toys and activities for the kids. While married I was guilty of this myself.

Alpha Male 1.0s tend to be better at handling money, but not much. They often spend money on "big stupid guy stuff" like garage workshops, boats they rarely use, big expensive trucks, and way-too-expensive hobbies.

Assuming they have money to invest, almost all men invest in things The Prison tells them to invest in, like 401Ks and the stock market. Every ten years or so, like clockwork, these same guys freak out as they see double-digit losses in their investment portfolios whenever a recession hits.

On top of that, since the divorce rate for people married after 1990 is over 60% in most American and European cities, and since only 3% of married couples actually include a man with enough balls to get a prenuptial agreement,[45] even very capable and intelligent men get financially raped in divorces with stunning and depressing regularity.

Once, while working at one of my client's offices, a close work friend of mine, a man in his mid-fifties, actually started to cry while describing his recent divorce to me.

"I was planning on retiring in two years," he said with water forming in his eyes, "I had all the money invested and it was in the bag. Now, because of the divorce, I have to work another 16 years."

He was planning on retiring at age 57, but because his wife fell out of love, left him, and took half his money, forcing him to liquidate retirement assets and pay penalties and taxes, he now had to work until he was 73.

You don't want to be that guy.

[45] http://online.wsj.com/news/articles/SB10001424052702303615304579157671554066120

In this chapter we're going to discuss how you manage your finances for maximum freedom, maximum benefit, minimal unpleasant work, and minimum risk from external factors outside of your control. Making a lot of money only to lose it to taxes, debt, divorce, inflation, or recessions is not Alpha 2.0.

Living a Low-Cost Lifestyle

Last chapter, we discussed keeping your business expenses low. Now we're going to expand that concept to the rest of your life.

In Chapter 1, I laid out a list of minimal lifestyle items you should have access to in your life, such as decent place to live, a few decent outfits, the ability to travel occasionally, etc. To live a low-cost lifestyle, you acquire these lifestyle trappings and then stop. That's right. You stop worrying about increasing your lifestyle beyond that point.

Once you are out of debt, have a decent place to live, some decent clothing, a decent car (unless you live in a downtown area where you don't need one), the ability to travel, and a few of the other items we discussed in that chapter, that's all you need. You can stop spending now. All the rest of your money, beyond your monthly living expenses, should go to charity and into long-term investments and savings.

I spent most of my twenties with some SP-based thoughts that I wasn't successful unless I lived in some massive $3 million dollar home or drove a $130,000 Mercedes. Wow, was I wrong! At one point in my marriage I did indeed live in the third most expensive neighborhood in my state, with a huge house worth three-quarters of a million dollars.

Don't get me wrong, I liked the house, but it didn't make me happy. Having a mortgage that big really stressed me out. Even back then, one of my big goals was to pay off my home mortgage and live mortgage-free, but with a mortgage that big, it seemed like something insurmountable.

If you want to get really rich, please do it. That's great! Regardless, I'm telling you right now that as long as you have the minimal lifestyle items described earlier, you do not need a multimillion dollar home, or a six-figure car, or suits that cost thousands of dollars, or a $40,000 Rolex on your wrist, or a private jet. It is likely that these things will not make you significantly happier than living a zero-debt, $75,000-per-year lifestyle.

That being said, if you have looked inward and discovered that your true calling and/or your Mission is to acquire one or more of those extravagant things, then please don't let me stop you. Just remember that your financial life is just one part of your SLA, and if you focus too many hours per week or too much of your life in pursuit of those kinds of massive financial goals, your long-term happiness will likely suffer. The higher and more extravagant your income or financial goals are, the more likely you are to live an unbalanced life. Be very, very careful.

Living a low-cost lifestyle solves all of these problems. Here's specifically how you can do it.

Live in a Low-Cost Area

I know several people who live in tiny apartments in downtown Manhattan or San Francisco. In many cases, their entire home is smaller than my living room. I love these people, but their lifestyle choice makes zero sense to me. These folks pay double, even triple on rent or mortgage payments than I do living in a two story, two car garage, three bedroom house with three bathrooms and two living rooms.

If for some reason you must live in an ultra-expensive area like New York City, London, or Tokyo, in order to achieve your Mission or because you truly love it, then that's fine, especially if it's part-time or temporary. Do your best to live there only as long as you need, and while there, go out of your way to live as simply and cheaply as possible.

If you own an Alpha 2.0 business, your income will be largely or completely location independent. That means you have the freedom to live wherever the hell you want. There are some very cheap places to live out there. If you live just an hour or two outside of moderate-sized city, you can live in a huge house for less than $25,000. If you really want to go crazy, you can move to Thailand or the Philippines and quite literally live like a little king on what would normally be a meager income in the Western world.

I know of a few guys who do things like live in super-cheap Thailand but work with clients in super-expensive New York. SP and The Prison views these guys as strange, perhaps even losers. I consider these men the smartest guys in the universe.

Google "cost of living comparison calculator," possibly adding "international" at the end, and let that be the start of your research. Get the facts and make a battle plan. Take your location independent income from your Alpha 2.0 business and move to a very inexpensive location where your money will be double, triple, or even quadruple the value it would be in some large metropolitan city. If you currently live in a high-priced area, one of your primary goals should be to relocate to a low-cost region unless your Mission absolutely forbids it. The lifestyle gains by doing this are tremendous, not to mention the reduced stress of not living 24/7 in a big, busy city.

Don't Worry About Keeping Up with the Joneses

This may sound strange coming from a guy whose last name is Jones, but busting your ass to keep up with the "Joneses" is a destructive idea for the freedom-loving Alpha.

An outcome independent man doesn't care if his neighbor drives a cooler car than he does, or if his brother has a nicer house than he does, or if his buddy just bought a cool boat, especially they went into debt in order to get these things, which they probably did.

If you're the typical American who grew up in the suburbs like I did, you likely have some powerful SP that compels you to constantly buy more and bigger stuff; a better house, a better car, a better lawn mower, whatever. You need to get to the point where if someone ends up with some shiny new keeping-up-with-the-Joneses item, it doesn't even bother you. Whenever I see one of my buddies end up with an item like that, I shake my head at the stupidity of all the debt they're accruing; unless they actually purchased the item with 100% cash; then I have great respect for their accomplishment but I still don't want to buy the same item.

I have lived most of my life in the suburbs, and let me tell you something: the damn suburbs are an entire culture of keeping up with the Joneses. It's all about how nice your lawn is or how big your boat is compared to the other people on your street. Back when I was married, my wife at the time was very stressed out about how the neighbor's grass looked nicer than ours, how so-and-so had a nicer fence, and how so-and-so's kids rode nicer bikes than ours. By embracing conformity (one of the Six Societal Values), this was a huge concern for her and she spent a lot of time worrying about this kind of thing. She was just one example among millions, and was very typical of people who live in American suburbia. Most of the other people I know that live the suburban lifestyle spend a lot of time stressing out about the exact same things. They aren't happy.

The vast majority of the furniture in my home are crappy hand-me-downs I acquired free from friends and family after my divorce many years ago. Guess what? I don't give a shit. Often I will have guests that are surprised that a man of my income level has such crappy furniture. I still don't give a shit. My goal is a low-cost lifestyle, and I'm very happy having accomplished that goal.

Screw the Joneses! Let them stress out about working 50 or 60-hour weeks for the rest of their lives and going into debt to buy stupid crap. You have a life to live, a Mission to accomplish, and happiness to experience.

Don't Borrow Money – Stay Out of Debt!

In America, the balance of the average credit card with debt is over $15,000. The average consumer has 3.5 credit cards. That's just credit cards; the average student loan debt is over $33,000 [46]. 24% of Americans admit to not being able to pay their bills on time[47], which means the real number is likely above that. Europeans aren't faring any better. People all over the Western world are destroying their financial lives and happiness with debt. I won't even get into the topic of government debt, which is even more catastrophic.

Looking back over my business and financial history, I can tell you for a fact that every major financial or business problem I have ever had in my life was because I had too much debt. Most people, especially most business people, will tell you the same thing. And yes, this includes my divorce and the 2008 economic crash. These events would have been ten times easier had I not had the debt load I was carrying at the time.

You simply cannot achieve and maintain freedom, abundance, or long-term happiness if you choose to go into debt. It's not possible. I realize how alluring debt can be. I realize that it does solve a lot of short-term problems and can be emotionally satisfying in the short run. Believe me, I know. It's like the sirens luring Odysseus to the rocks.

Beating the debt game involves several steps, all of them easy to explain but emotionally tough to do:

1. Resolve today to never, ever, ever borrow money for any reason ever again unless it's to purchase real estate. Yes, that means no car loans. Yes, that also means no student loans. I don't care if the interest is low, or if the payments are deferred, or whatever. Debt is debt. Resolve today, as part of your Code, that you will never buy anything unless you already have the cash saved to do so. If this means you have to put yourself through college by working a job or two, that's what it means. If this means driving around in a piece of shit car for three more years while you save up to get a new one, that's what it means.

Remember that if you're following the advice in these money chapters, you'll be making $75,000 or more at some point soon, so this isn't as bad as it sounds.

---

[46] http://www.nerdwallet.com/blog/credit-card-data/average-credit-card-debt-household/

[47] http://www.mainstreet.com/article/smart-spending/quarter-americans-dont-pay-their-bills-time

2. Set up a $1000 to $2000 cash emergency fund to cover any unusual problems that arise in your life. Just doing this alone will boost your financial confidence. Knowing you've got money ready to go in case the car or roof suddenly needs repairs or an unplanned medical bill pops up really helps. Most importantly, having this cash reserve will help fight the urge to borrow money when you have a sudden emergency.

3. Set a goal to pay off all of your debts, including your home mortgage if you have one. The most Alpha men on the planet are men who have no debt and who live in a completely paid-off house. That's the club you want to join as fast as humanly possible.

The fastest way to get out of debt is to cut back frivolous monthly expenses and dump all that cash on your debts, starting with the one with the smallest balance. When that's paid off, move to the next largest balance, and so on. Most middle-class people can become completely debt free within two to five years just by doing this on their current incomes.

Live a Low-Tax Lifestyle

There is a dark reality of the Western world. The biggest expense of your entire life, bigger than your home, bigger than your education or your car, bigger than your spouse or even your kids, will be taxes. Because of this, as a self-employed Alpha Male 2.0, you need to become an amateur tax expert.

Right after I left high school to go into the business world, I read about 600 books on business, sales, finance, customer service, marketing, and taxes. Why were taxes in there? I had no desire to become an accountant, so why was I spending time learning about taxes? How boring! It was because I knew then what I just told you: taxes are the largest financial expense of your entire life. You need to learn how to legally pay the minimum amount of taxes required by law.

For better or for worse, approximately 95% of tax deductions and loopholes are written for businesses, not individuals. Just by owning a small business you are able to take advantage of all kinds of tax benefits. Add to that all the things you can do with corporate entities and trusts, and you can really save a huge amount of money on taxes, and should do so. Consider tax knowledge one of your core areas to learn.

Just like there are expensive areas in the world and inexpensive ones, there are high-taxed areas and extremely low-taxed areas. You need to live in a low-taxed area. If you don't currently live in one, you need to move to one as soon as you're able.

I did this myself. At one point I lived in Portland, Oregon where I paid all kinds of very high municipal, county, and state income taxes. I simply moved 20 minutes north, right across the river to Vancouver, Washington, where there is no county tax, no state income tax, and no municipal taxes. The one downside is that Washington has a sales tax and Oregon does not. No problem. Whenever I buy stuff, I just drive 10 minutes across the Oregon border and buy it there.

My income instantly went up 13% by making this simple move, and that's not including the lower cost of living I enjoyed. Within the United States there are all kinds of tax havens such as Nevada, Washington State, New Hampshire, Texas, and Florida. All over the world there are extremely low-taxed countries, and in some countries, like Andorra, there are no taxes at all.

You must live in a low-tax area if you want to facilitate a high-income, low-expense, free lifestyle.

Always Keep Separate and Protected Finances

Because of decades of false SP, beta males and Alpha Male 1.0s living in The Prison are expected to destroy their financial lives whenever their wives divorce them, which is inevitable in most cases because that's exactly what women are designed to do as we discussed in Chapter 13. When they get married, and in some areas even if they just move in together, men are expected to instantly combine all of their finances with their wives, and they are not supposed to get prenuptial agreements, since according to SP prenups are "mean," "not romantic," "cold," and "don't work" because they "could be challenged in court."

If we were living in a society with a 5% or 7% divorce rate, that advice would be perfectly fine. However, as we've discussed, we live in a society with an over 60% divorce rate in most American and European cities. Therefore, this advice is insane. I mean that. It's insane. If you ever get legally married to a woman and combine your assets with her and/or don't get a prenup, *you are insane*. Long-term happiness will be impossible for you. You are literally asking for huge problems down the road.

I didn't say you couldn't ever get married, nor did I say you can't ever live with a woman or have kids. Those things are perfectly fine, but if you chose this path you must structure an OLTR marriage rather than a traditional monogamous marriage (TMM). As we discussed back in Chapter 14, an OLTR marriage is a sexually open marriage with an enforceable prenuptial agreement and no combined debts or assets.

An "enforceable" prenuptial agreement means the following:

- You live in a country where prenuptial agreements are actually enforced by the legal system even if challenged by an angry wife. This means if you live in England, Australia, or California for example, you're probably out of luck. If you live in a country or state like that, either move to a different country or refuse to ever get legally married. Do the "unmarriage" described below instead.
- She has signed the prenuptial agreement at least six months prior to the wedding. A year is better. Doing this ensures she can't go back to court someday saying she was "under duress."
- Her signing of the prenup was witnessed by a judge. You can pay a judge a small fee to witness the signing, which means he'll actually explain to her what she's signing, and put his signature next to hers. Doing this ensures she can't go back to court someday saying she "didn't understand what she was signing."
- There are no co-owned assets or debts with her. (That means no joint checking accounts too!)

The "Unmarriage"

Of course you can skip all this complicated prenup stuff by simply refusing to ever get legally married. You can move in with your special lady, even have kids with her if you like, without ever getting legally married. This has been called the "unmarriage."

If you want to get "unmarried," study up on common law marriage and cohabitation laws in your area. Make a phone call to an attorney to get your questions answered if necessary, even if it costs you a little money. Then with the attorney's help, write up a cohabitation agreement and have her sign it in the presence of a notary. Now you can move in with her, even have kids with her, and as long as you do what's necessary to avoid common law marriage, you're completely covered.

If your special lady complains about any of this, remind her that the two of you can do everything legally married people do, such as,

- Have a wedding.
- Get wedding rings.
- Have her legally change her last name to yours (check your local palimony laws on this though).

- Have a fantastic, romantic honeymoon.
- Introduce each other as "husband" and "wife."
- Have children.
- Etc.

There is no law that says a legal marriage is required for any of these things; just false SP.

Structuring an OLTR Marriage or an unmarriage are the only intelligent and responsible options for an Alpha 2.0 regarding a long-term, live-in relationship in the modern era.

Save and Invest

There are a myriad of books, articles, and web sites out there on how to best save and/or invest your money. I'm not going to give you any specific investment advice here, nor am I qualified to give such advice. That being said, I have never lost money in an investment in my entire life, so I can give you a general overview in regards to saving and investing under an Alpha 2.0 framework.

The main thing about saving and investing is that you must actually do it. I know way too many men in their 30s, 40s, even 50s who really have no money invested or saved anywhere. This is ridiculous. You've worked for decades on end and have no money saved? Reckless! Absurd! What happens if you ever get into an accident and can no longer physically perform your work? What if you have a health problem that does the same? You simply must save a percentage of your income throughout your working lifetime. There is no avoiding this.

You don't have to save a lot. You can start with a goal of saving/investing 5% of your income, and slowly work your way up to 10%, eventually getting to 15% or more. If 5% seems like too much right now, then start with 1%. The point is to start. Don't be an idiot and put this off. Don't expect friends, family, or government to be around later in life to help you financially because you didn't bother to save. Governments are technically bankrupt all over the Western world, including and especially Europe and the US.

The best advice I ever heard about investing, advice I really took to heart, is to *never lose money*. Not "make a lot of money." Not "maximize returns." Not "invest in your 401K." No. Your goal is simply to never lose money. When you re-orient your entire savings and investment plan around never losing money, it forces you to invest in things that are very boring and conservative. Investments that are "sexy," like stocks, are almost never investments where you'll never lose money. My late grandfather made several million dollars over several decades investing in...wait for it...municipal bonds. That's right, municipal bonds. Boring, right? Not fun like stocks or strip malls; just stupid old bonds. He was smart. He never lost money.

My secondary goal is to try to get annual returns that are at least 3% above real inflation. That way, I don't need to always be looking for that special investment that will get me a 15% or 25% return. 8% or 9% returns are just fine with me, as long as I never lose money.

I strongly suggest you do the same. There is nothing Alpha about venturing into old age with no money because you were too lazy to save, or because you were too full of SP and invested in sexy stuff and lost money, or got financially raped in a divorce because you didn't get a prenup when you knew you should have.

When to Spend Money

Much of the advice in this chapter may make the Alpha 2.0 sound like a financial tightwad. Well, that's partially true, in that the Alpha 2.0 is very careful and methodical about avoiding SP that will cause him to waste or lose his money. This doesn't mean he doesn't enjoy his money or spend it on pleasurable things.

Here are some ways you should spend and enjoy your money:

- **Nice clothes**. If you love nice clothes, go for it and buy some. Nicer, higher-quality clothing makes you look better, feel better, and increases your confidence. The clothing will also last longer, causing you to buy less clothing and rendering a good investment.

- **Travel**. As we'll be discussing in later chapters, the Alpha 2.0 is a man of the world. He goes wherever he wants, whenever he wants. If you want to fly across the world to new and exciting places, spend the money and do so. That doesn't mean you need to stay at $400-a-night hotels whenever you travel (though you could), but you should have no guilt about spending $1500-$3000 every few months on a big international trip. Some of the greatest joy and richest experiences of my very full life were, and are, due to international travel.

- **Quality items you use daily**. You should always think cheap. However the one big exception to this rule is when you're purchasing something you will be using literally every day. In that case, really spend some money and get the highest quality you can afford. The mattress you sleep on every night shouldn't cost less than $800. The chair you sit on every day in your home office every day should be a very, very good chair, so if you have to spend $300 or $600 or more on that, go for it. That's money well spent. Same goes for things like your laptop, your phone, your shoes, and your electric razor. For daily-use items, spend the extra cash and get the best. You deserve it. Plus again, doing this often ends up being less expensive in the long run because these things will last longer and have fewer problems.

- **Rewards and events.** A great way to stay motivated with your goals is to promise yourself a special event you will treat yourself to if/when you accomplish a big goal, or even a mid-term goal. This can be anything from a classy dinner at a posh restaurant to a weekend retreat at the beach. As long as you don't do it all the time, and as long as you're attaching it to goal achievement, treating yourself with your money occasionally is a very smart thing to do. It ensures the child part of your subconscious mind will keep you working hard so you can get more "prizes."

- **Outsource drudgery**. I never do yard work. I don't edit my videos or podcasts. I never clean my bathrooms. I never wash my car. Either one of my MLTRs are doing these things for me, or I pay someone a small amount of money to do them. As we discussed back in Chapter 6, with today's technology and marketplace, you can cheaply outsource any and all grunt work from your life. With sites like Elance, Freelancer, Odesk, Taskrabbit, Craig's List, and a myriad of others, there is no reason to not make use of low-cost providers to streamline your life (unless you're really cash-strapped). This increases your happiness and gives you more time to focus on your Mission. Taking precious time away from your Mission or your key Seven Life Areas to mow your lawn or scrub your toilets is horrible time management.

- **Donate to charity**. As I mentioned back in Chapter 2, I donate 5% of my income to charity. I personally think this is not enough, so one of my biggest financial goals in life is to double this to 10%. Donating your time or money to responsible, charitable causes you believe in does wonders for your happiness, self-worth, and abundance mentality. If you're not donating either your time or your money (or both) to a charitable cause on a regular basis, you're really missing out on one of the greatest and most fulfilling experiences of life.

- **Cheap thrills.** Regularly spending money on inexpensive but highly enjoyable activities is perfectly okay. I'm a big movie nut, and I go to the movies almost every week. I really enjoy movies and the eight or nine bucks it costs me every week is really no big deal. When the weather is nice, hiking and camping bring me huge amounts of personal pleasure. Once the equipment is purchased, the costs of doing this is often almost zero. I also really like sex obviously, and I get that for free from my FBs and MLTRs whenever I want. There are probably several things you have access to in your life that make you happy but cost very little. In your local area there are likely many enjoyable, low-cost activities like small local concerts, stand-up comedy shows, kart racing, or even bungee jumping. Find them, and do them often!

Part Six

Your World

Chapter 23 –

The Alpha 2.0 Father: When (And When Not) to Have Kids

The heart has its reasons, of which reason is ignorant.

Pascal

February, 2001.

I sat at the dining room table with my two children. My daughter was three, my son nine. While their mom was busy in the kitchen, the three of us were giddily unwrapping our Valentine's Day chocolates.

My son and daughter were each given a small heart-shaped box of chocolates, while I, Big Daddy, had a huge, two-pound, double-layer box. As we all started stuffing our faces, I was reminded about how when I was young, my siblings and I would trade our individual candies after our Halloween hauls. We would trade the candy we didn't like for the candy we did. If you played your cards right and were a good capitalist, you could end up with a pile of candy you liked, rather than a pile of some candy you liked and some you did not.

"Hey!" I said to my kids, remembering this, "We should trade our chocolates. So we can all end up with the kinds we like." After all, some of the chocolates I had I wasn't crazy about, and I was sure it was the case with my kids as well.

"Do you want to trade?" I asked my son.

"Naw," he said, "I like all mine."

"How about you?" I asked my daughter, "Do you want to trade?"

Her big brown eyes went wide as she said, "Okay, Daddy!"

She then proceeded to climb down her chair, walk over to me with her tiny box of chocolates, place her box before me on the table, and with a big smile, pick up my huge box of chocolates, and then walk away.

As I watched her dumbfounded, my son started bursting out laughing, crying out, "You got screwed, Dad!"

Seeing my two pounds of chocolate slowly vanish down the hallway carried by a very happy three-year old with a major score, I got up and went after her. I then had the very awkward conversation of explaining to said three-year old that Daddy didn't mean trade the entire box when he said "trade."

With my son still laughing his ass off in the background, my daughter scowled at me as I gently handed her back her tiny box and retrieved mine. It was quite apparent that despite Daddy's big words, he was clearly ripping her off somehow.

In the future I tried to remember to explain myself better when conveying capitalistic concepts to three year-olds.

Raising Kids as an Alpha 2.0

As you might expect, living the Alpha 2.0 lifestyle, with its many aspects that directly contradict the SP, OBW, and 6SV of The Prison, presents its own unique challenges when it comes to raising kids as opposed to living the societally-approved life paths of the beta male and Alpha Male 1.0. Betas and Alpha 1.0s have their own significant challenges as we've already discussed, so living the life of the Alpha 2.0, even as a father of children, is still a much more desirable path. Yet, we must address the unique needs and situations that arise as an Alpha 2.0 father.

In this chapter we're going to specifically address the parameters of when an Alpha 2.0 should have kids and when he should not. Having children at the wrong time or under the wrong conditions will create chaos and problems for all involved, especially you, regardless of how skilled you are as a father. In the following chapter we'll discuss exactly how to raise happy, successful children while still living the free, masculine, abundant life of the Alpha 2.0.

Rule 1: Delay Having Children for as Long as Possible

This is rule number one for a reason. It's also the rule men have the most trouble accepting or understanding.

You should avoid having any children until you have achieved your big dreams in life. Having kids is a massive commitment that lasts 20 years, and takes a huge amount of time, resources, energy, emotion, and money away from you, your Mission, and yes, your happiness. I'm not saying to never have kids. If you want to have kids, have them. I'm saying put in the years, or decades, required to achieve your big life goals, and *then* have your kids. There is no rush.

If you already have kids, change this rule to "Don't have any more kids" or at a minimum, "Delay having any more kids for as long as possible."

The world is full of great examples of high-achieving Alphas who purposely delayed having kids until they accomplished their big goals in life. Men like Arnold Schwarzenegger and Matthew McConaughey purposely waited until they were 40 years old before they started having kids. David Letterman waited until he was 56. Self-made billionaire and Wall Street legend Jim Rogers waited until he was 62.

One of the dumbest things men do is have kids too soon. I made this mistake myself, having kids at age 25. I should have waited at least another 10-15 years. I made things work, but I delayed and damaged both my Mission and my big life goals by having kids too early. If I could wave a magic wand and could do it all over again, I would have, without question or hesitation, had my same two children, but when I was 40 years old instead of 25.

This brings us to that key age. If you currently have no children, you should set it in stone right now that you will never father any children under any circumstances until you turn 35 at the very soonest. Make it part of your Code. Putting your goals, dreams, and Mission all on hold during the prime time of your twenties and early thirties just to crank out some kids is a terrible idea for a man pursuing an Alpha 2.0 lifestyle (and remember our Mission parameters from Chapter 9 about not designing a Mission that relies on just one or two other people).

Oh yes, I can already hear your SP excuses screaming in protest. "But I don't want to be some old man in my sixties who can't throw a ball when my kids graduate high school!" Then here's a thought: make one of your core goals to be in excellent health as an old man so you *can* throw a ball around when you're sixty. Liam Nesson is in his sixties. Does he look like he would have any trouble whatsoever throwing a ball around with a 20 year-old son? Go watch some 1990s Sean Connery films when he was pushing 70. Does he look like he would have any trouble whatsoever doing this?

Then why won't *you* be able to do this at that age? Really think about that.

Set a goal to be young and vibrant and healthy in your post-60 years. Hell, that should be one of your big goals anyway. It's certainly one of my primary life goals. That way you won't be worrying about this silly "old dad" excuse.

The next excuse I sometimes hear is when men point out to some of the sky-is-falling medical news about how older fathers have slightly higher odds of passing on birth defects to their children. If you dig into the numbers behind these scare-stories, you'll realize this is just hype. The odds of a healthy "non-old" man producing birth defects in his children are often a fraction of one percent[48]. That means that even if they were to "double" or "triple" because you're older, they're often still just a fraction of one percent. Even if you were to father children in your sixties, your odds of giving your children birth defects are minuscule. A recent Cambridge University study concluded that *"paternal aging does not affect the risk of miscarriage and increased paternal age on its own is not an indication for prenatal diagnosis since the absolute risk for genetic anomalies in offspring is low...there is no clear association between adverse health outcome and paternal age but longitudinal studies are needed."*[49]

Still worried? Fine. For around $1000, you can have your sperm frozen and stored at a sperm storage facility. Frozen sperm lasts indefinitely; women have been successfully impregnated by sperm that had been frozen for 25 years. So go get some young sperm frozen, and use that to have children later in life after you've accomplished your big goals. The time and expense to do that will be far, far less than it would to actually crank out some kids before age 35.

Bottom line, wait until you're at least 35 before you even think about having kids. Don't make the mistake I made, and that too many other men make every day.

Rule 2: Don't Have Kids until Your Budget Says You Can

This is another big dumb mistake men make, particularly younger men, but many older men who already have other children fall prey to this too.

Whether or not you're married, you should not have any kids until an accurate budget of your financial situation, including income, taxes, and expenses, clearly shows that you can afford several hundred dollars a month above and beyond your current expenses, for the next 20 years. If you can't afford to spend an extra several hundred dollars a month, every month, for a very long time, then you are not ready to have kids.

Kids are extraordinarily expensive, far more than most people who've never had kids can imagine. Worse, the cost is growing every

---

[48] http://www.cdc.gov/ncbddd/birthdefects/data.html
http://www.babyzone.com/pregnancy/fetal-development/birth-defects-risks_70721

[49] http://books.google.com/books?id=-SlaAQAAQBAJ&pg=PA104#v=onepage&q&f=false

year. A government report released in the summer of 2012 found that a middle-income family with a child born in 2011 will spend $234,900 in child-related expenses from birth to age 17[50]. That's about $14,000 a year for just for one child. If you want more than one, you're looking at a hell of a lot more.

By the way, that figure does not take into account all the taxes you'll have to pay for child-related expenses throughout their lifetimes, pregnancy expenses, or any other expenses required for your children after they leave the home, such as college (not that I'm a big fan of the concept), other post-high school education, bailing them out of financial problems, helping them buy their first home, etc. Believe me; the expenses continue for a very long time after your kids turn 18 and move out!

Moreover, none of this takes into account the fact that if you ever have to pay child support and fail to do so, you will go to prison.

How does all that grab you? Still think you can afford kids right now?

Having a child when you can barely pay your own bills is insane. It will severely damage, if not destroy, any opportunity you have to live an Alpha 2.0 life. Instead, you'll be stuck in a beta male hell while you bust your ass to pay for kids you can't afford.

Although I screwed up and had kids at too early an age, I did not mess up on this second rule. In my early twenties I forced myself to not have any kids until I knew for a fact that I could afford them. I wanted kids before I knew I could afford them. I forced myself to wait anyway. You should do the same.

Rule 3: Avoid Legal Marriage – Remember You Can Have and Raise Children without Being Legally Married!

I mentioned this in prior chapters but it's so important it bears repeating. "I must get legally married in order to have kids" is pure SP. You are more than able to move in with a woman you love, have children with her, raise your children with her, all without ever legally marrying her. Legal marriage is not required to have and raise children.

Just because you want kids does not mean you should suddenly forget that legal marriage is simply another false, anti-man, societal construct created by the rulers of The Prison. Having kids should not automatically expose you to all the legal, financial, and drama deathtraps that modern-day marriage represents.

---

[50] http://www.usda.gov/wps/portal/usda/usdahome?contentid=2012/06/0197.xml

Rule 4: Create and File a Legal Parenting Plan Prior To Any Pregnancy

Once you've determined that you are at the right age and income level to have kids, and you've found that special woman to share them with, you need to write up a legally-binding parenting plan before you get anyone pregnant. A parenting plan is a legal document you and your special lady sign that spell out issues such as parenting, visitation, and custody. It prevents or mitigates any future disputes or custody battles you may have with the mother of your children down the road in case of breakup or divorce. If a breakup ever occurs, you simply refer to the parenting plan, and that's what happens. No argument or legal battle is needed.

Every state, province, and country has their own laws regarding parenting plans, and some states/countries have more legally enforceable parenting plans than others. Research the laws in your area and find out how to acquire the template or form, fill it out, get it signed, and if necessary, get it filed with your local government. Make sure a notary is present when you and her sign it so she can't later say you forged her signature.

Do not get any woman pregnant without a completed, signed, and filed parenting plan in place first.

Rule 5: Get a Legally Enforceable Paternity Test Immediately after Childbirth

You may have already read about the huge percentage of fathers out there who are unknowingly *not* the biological fathers of their children. The percentages I've seen range from 18% of fathers all the way to 29%, depending on the city or country.

The last thing you want to do is waste your life raising or paying child support for a child you thought was yours but wasn't. I've seen way too many men find out years later that their kids weren't their kids, and by then it's legally too late to do anything about it. Even if they get divorced, even if DNA tests prove they are not the father, they're stuck paying child support for those kids for the next 18 years, or they go to prison.

I don't care how much you love your OLTR/LTR/wife. I don't care how much you trust her or think she's "different from all the other women." As soon as the baby comes out of her at the hospital, you need to immediately get a DNA sample and have it locked and transported to a legally approved testing lab to get a DNA paternity test. *Do not sign the birth certificate until you get the test results back that show the baby is indeed your baby.*

If the baby ends up not being your baby, at least now you can make an informed decision on what to do, and more importantly you're not legally liable for the child's 18-year-long expenses. However, you will be liable for these expenses if you wait a few months or years after the birth to get your DNA test. Don't wait! Test that baby as soon as it's born.

Rule 6: The Mother Must Be the Primary Caregiver

This is going to be a tough one. It's going to fly in the face of a huge amount of SP and OBW in your psyche. It's also going to be politically incorrect in our current strong-woman, feminine world that we discussed back in Chapter 6. Regardless, it's one of the most critical concepts you'll learn in this book if you plan on having children someday (or do now).

As I explained way back in Chapter 1 when discussing Freedom of Action, while it is possible for an Alpha 2.0 to have children, it is not possible for an Alpha 2.0 to be the primary caregiver of such children. It is literally impossible to be a free man, to live your life as you choose, to diligently pursue your Mission, to focus on your goals, to have sex with whomever you like, to travel the world and live your life, if you have to be home by 5:30pm every night to change diapers or help kids with their homework.

If you insist on choosing that lifestyle, or more likely, submit to a woman who demands you surrender to that lifestyle, then an Alpha 2.0 life is going to be impossible for you, at least until your children get older. At very best you'll be a domesticated Alpha 1.0.

I'm sorry. I realize you probably didn't want to hear that, and you're probably coming up with all kinds of excuses to invalidate what I just said, but what I just said is accurate. You cannot live an Alpha 2.0 life if you choose to submit to regular caregiving responsibilities to small children. It renders Freedom of Action impossible. Can you still achieve aspects of the Alpha 2.0 lifestyle? Yes. Can you live the actual lifestyle and reap all the benefits of the long-term happiness from such a life? No.

This does not mean you can't be an integral part of your children's lives every day. Having the woman be the primary caregiver does not mean that you're "never there" or "do nothing." It does not mean that your special lady is constantly slaving over a hot stove and dirty diapers while you're out having sex with cheerleaders. Of course you will help out all you like, and you will spend lots of time with your children if you choose. The point is that you have the *option* of doing so or not doing so.

Let me repeat: none of this means you're an absentee father. You can still live with your kids and care for your kids daily and probably should. It simply means that their mother must handle the vast majority of the regular "grunt work" tasks involved with raising young children.

As we briefly covered back in Chapter 1, the Alpha 2.0 father has two options:

- Not living full-time with his children.
- Living full-time with a woman who has agreed to cover 90% of the regular grunt work needed in raising a child.

My situation is option one. My kids live with their mother most of the time, and go to school in her town. They live about 40 minutes away from me, and I have my daughter most weekends, during which time I don't see any women. I also have her much of the summer in addition to most holidays. My son is grown, out of the home, and has been for several years now.

This way, I spend a large amount of time with my daughter and get plenty of dad time, yet I still have a huge amount of time away from my kids to pursue my Mission, get my strong sexual needs fulfilled, enjoy my life, travel, and work very hard. It's the best of both worlds in many ways.

The other way to do this is the method recommended by Kevin O'Leary and many other Alphas, and that is to only have kids with a woman who agrees beforehand that she will be responsible for about 90% of the grunt work required to raise the kids, especially when the children are smaller. I'm not saying their mother spends 90% of the time spent with the kids. You can spend as much time with the kids as her, if not more. I'm only talking about the grunt work.

You know what grunt work means: cooking for them, cleaning after them, helping with homework, driving back and forth to soccer practice, changing diapers, folding clothes, and other oh-so-fun parental drudgery that women sign up for when they decide to have kids (unless they are wealthy and can afford full-time nannies, in which case this entire conversation is irrelevant).

The modern-day SP method of men raising kids involves a 50/50 split of this grunt workload with the mother. It's a system where, when the baby starts crying at 3am in the morning, your wife elbows you and commands, "Your turn! Get up!"

That kind of arrangement is perfectly fine for betas. It might also satisfy all kinds of politically correct SP in people living in The Prison, as well as make for some funny Hollywood moments in TV shows and movies, it's not going to cut it for the Alpha 2.0.

If that arrangement sounds unfair for the mother, remember that I said you only have kids with a woman who agrees with this system *before anyone get pregnant.* This means before anyone get pregnant, you sit down and discuss this in detail with any woman you want to have children with. You can love her, financially take care of her, and give her the children her SP and OBW craves. In return, she understands that she handles most of the grunt work involved in raising the kids, while you work on your Mission and provide financially for the family. She can still work and generate her own income if she likes, via a full or part-time job or business (preferably a stay-at-home Alpha 2.0 business; women can run Alpha 2.0 businesses too!).

If she refuses this arrangement, then you have a decision to make. Either you surrender to a beta or Alpha 1.0 lifestyle for 15-20 years and have a 50/50 arrangement with her, or going to have to look elsewhere for that special woman to bear your children.

I realize this arrangement may sound offensive to certain people with modern-day SP, claiming that it's a throwback to the 1950s. It might be in some ways, but that's not why you're doing this. You're doing this to maintain Freedom of Action, one of the core Alpha Male 2.0 requirements. 1950s or not, if you are responsible for 50%, or even 30% of the regular child-rearing tasks for your kids, especially if your kids are small, Freedom of Action is going to be impossible. Your Mission will suffer, as will much of your happiness. Studies have shown that men actually lose testosterone when they are involved in day-to-day child-rearing tasks for babies or small children[51] so there's science behind what I'm saying.

Bottom line, there is simply no other way to raise kids who live with you full-time while maintaining a strong level of freedom.

It's Not as Hard as You Think

You might be thinking, "I'll never find a woman like this." Wrong.

Remember from Chapter 13 that the strongest OBW a woman has is the desire to have babies. Therefore, despite all the SP in modern society about "strong, independent women," you would be very

[51] http://www.scientificamerican.com/podcast/episode/baby-makes-daddy-lose-testosterone-11-09-13/

surprised to find the sheer number of women, in the Western world, who will agree to this arrangement, especially with an externally and internally attractive, strong, low-drama Alpha 2.0. These men are the most attractive to women in all of society. Over the past several years I have had multiple women offer to take me up on this (and so far I have declined their generous offers). If you follow all the advice in this book, you will also receive such offers from the many women in your life even without asking for them.

Also, remember women's ever-changing dynamic nature. Just because she enthusiastically agrees to this system now does not mean she'll feel the same way about it five or ten years down the road. If she does change her mind, that's okay. She's signed a parenting plan and you've already budgeted for child support, so if there is a breakup or divorce, you're covered. She's also not legally married to you or has signed an enforceable prenuptial agreement, so you're not out of any cash or assets other than child support if she decides to leave you.

I'm not saying she will change her mind. She may not, since women have strong OBW to be mothers and caregivers to children. Regardless, if she does, you're covered, unlike all of those beta and Alpha 1.0 fathers.

Rule 7: Take Full Responsibility as a Father for at Least 18 Years

You must take 100% full logistical responsibility (within the parameters of rule number six we just discussed above), emotional responsibility, and financial responsibility for any and all children you bring into this world until that child is at least 18 years old. Alpha 2.0s do not go around creating babies they can't afford to pawn off onto society and unprepared women to take care of.

This means:

- Paying child support and/or other necessary finances to support the child for their first 18 years of the life, whether or not you are still with the mother, like the mother, or are even in contact with the mother.
- Being there to support the child whenever you are needed (within reason).
- Being a resource to the child, a support system for the child, and a source of guidance, advice, and moral support.
- Spending lots of time, regularly, with the child to nurture growth.

- Always showing through your words and actions that you love the child unconditionally. We'll discuss this in detail in the next chapter.

Fathers who abandon children they chose to bring into the world, either financially or emotionally, are scumbags in my opinion (I am not talking about fathers who were tricked into pregnancies). The world has way too many of these men already. Alpha 2.0s make the world a better place by achieving long-term happiness via pursuing their goals and becoming better men. As we discussed back in Chapter 1, they are not barbarians who trample over other people or make the world a worse place, especially not by bringing children into the world for other people to worry about.

Rule 8: Limit Your Children's Access to the Other Women in Your Life

Living the Alpha 2.0 lifestyle possibly means you will be dating, having sex with, and being in relationships with many different women. This is a good and wonderful thing. However, presenting your small or teenage children a constant merry-go-round of women flying in and out of your life is not a good idea at all. Children require consistency, structure, and stability. You demonstrate the exact opposite of that if you present to them a constant flow of new women all the time.

Despite my pro-open-relationship sexual stances, I am very saddened for children who have parents, be they male or female, who constantly introduce them to a new boyfriend or girlfriend every year or two. Even worse are the people who move the new girlfriend or boyfriend into their homes, often with kids of their own, live with them for two or three years, then kick that person out, only to shortly later move in another new boyfriend/girlfriend and repeat the entire process. I've known small children who have gone through this three or four times by the time they're teenagers.

This is horribly damaging to children on many psychological and emotional levels. I really feel sorry for the kids whose parents do this to them.

I have lived the Alpha 2.0 lifestyle for eight years now, and never once have I ever moved in with a woman. There are several reasons for that, but one of the biggest is because I didn't want my kids seeing me move in with a woman, then move out, then move in with another one. (Now that youngest child is older and getting ready to move out herself, my attitude on this is changing.)

Along those lines, I do not allow the vast majority of women I have sex with to meet, or even go anywhere near my children. A strong part of my Code is that a woman must be in my life consistently for at least eight months or so before I even think about introducing her to my kids in any way. That woman must prove to me, through her actions and not her words, that she is going to be a long-term and consistent presence in my life. If she demonstrates in any way that she will not be like this, I keep her away from my kids, even if she's an otherwise wonderful person I care for very much.

You should do the same. Date and have sex with all the women you want. Have all the friends with benefits, one night stands, and MLTRs (Multiple Long Term Relationship women) you like. At the same time, think very carefully about giving your children access to any of these women until and unless one of them shows you with her actions that she's going to stick around in a low-drama way.

Implement at least a six-month rule. Limit access to your children only to your OLTR (Open Long Term Relationship) or a long-term favorite MLTR who has strong OLTR potential. Mid to low-range MLTRs and FBs should not allowed to spend time with your kids.

Respect your children's need for a stable upbringing. You're the only father they will ever have.

The Decision to Never Have Children

This chapter and the next one assume that you want to have kids someday, assuming you don't already. I've included these two chapters because it's very clear to me that the vast majority of men, including Alpha 2.0s, do indeed want to father children someday.

However, it's very possible you never want to have kids. That's great! I love my children and I don't regret having them. I also completely respect a man's decision to have kids and think it's a noble calling. Regardless, it is still an undeniable fact that one of the best moves you can make as an Alpha 2.0 for your long-term happiness is to simply refuse to ever have kids at all.

As I've talked about at blackdragonblog.com and other places, numerous studies over many decades have clearly shown that adults are happier when they do not have children living with them. This includes men, women, married people, and single people. When an adult has no kids, they're generally happier. As soon as the first baby comes and the work begins, their overall happiness levels drop, at least somewhat. These happiness levels stay reduced for many years until the last kid grows up and leaves the house. Then surprise, surprise, the happiness of the parents shoot back up again.

Having kids is a damn tough job, even for a man with a woman who does 90% of the child-rearing work. The time commitment, financial expense, limits on personal freedom, and emotional tolls are all extreme, even if you have great kids and a great spouse. If you choose to never have kids, my hat is off to you, and achieving and maintaining long-term, consistent happiness will be an easier process for you.

If this is you, you're free to skip the next chapter and move on to Chapter 25. If instead you already have kids or plan on having them someday, let's now talk about how to raise them to become happy and successful adults.

Chapter 24 –

The Alpha 2.0 Father: Raising Children

Beat them all! Do more than survive, my son, as I have survived. Live! Be true to the callings in your heart.

Zaknafein
R.A. Salvatore's *Homeland*

Summer, 1998.

I was on the side of my house moving some boxes, when I noticed a large hole at the bottom of the wooden fence gate. I cocked my head sideways. That hole wasn't there just a few days ago. Immediately I knew that the culprit was either my son or one of his friends.

My son was seven years old at the time. A while back he had come into my life with his mom, and now he was my son. He called me dad and spent no time with his biological father. He was a very extroverted, high-energy boy, and in his younger years he was a handful. I loved him very, very much and still do. His energy brought a vitality to my life I had never known.

I was reasonably convinced this same vitality was the cause of this large hole that had been smashed into my fence gate.

Later that day I sat him down on the couch and had a little father-son chat. It became a wonderful lesson in parenting, kid-logic, and kid-speak.

"Do you know anything about that big hole in the fence on the side of the house?" I asked.

"Nope," he said with a smile.

"Are you sure?" I asked again, this time my voice more grave.

His face darkened. He said nothing, only shrugging his shoulders guiltily.

"I know your mom didn't do it," I said, "I know I didn't do it. Your sister can't even walk yet, so I'm pretty sure she didn't do it. Are you sure you know nothing about it?" I glared him like an angry god from Mt Olympus.

"Well..." he squeaked, "Um. Well. My friends."

"Your friends what?" I said in a low voice.

"Well, my friends. You know, we were playing."

"And?"

"We were playing."

"Yeah, I got that part. Are you saying one of your friends did it?"

"No."

"Okay. Then what?"

"Well, we were playing guns."

"Okay. That's cool but that still doesn't explain anything."

"Well, we were playing guns and we were shooting each other."

"I figured that."

"Well, the fence was closed, and we needed a hole to shoot through."

Ah. I nodded, already knowing the rest of the story.

"And?" I said.

"Well, we didn't have a hole to shoot through."

"Yeah?"

"So...so I kicked it."

"You kicked a hole in my fence," I stated flatly.

"Well," he said shrugging, "We needed a hole to shoot through."

Glowering as I was, I tried not to laugh at the thought of my son kicking a hole in the fence so he could shoot one of his friends with his toy laser gun. It's exactly something I would have done when I was seven.

Parenting

I have two children. As I write these words, my son is 22 and my daughter is 16. My son became my son at age five when I married his mother. My daughter came a year later. I love them both in a way that is hard to describe. I am with them often and think about them even more. Children are indeed one of a man's greatest sources of both joy and frustration. In this chapter we're going to discuss raising children under an Alpha 2.0 framework.

I do not in any way claim to be a parenting expert. I'm simply relating my experiences and techniques in raising two happy, successful children from birth to young adulthood, half of that time under an Alpha 2.0 framework.

While I'm no expert, I have been a successful father. Today my son is sharp, happy, and extremely charismatic. He has never had any trouble with drugs, alcohol, or hanging out with a bad crowd. He's currently in college majoring in political science and international business with a high grade point average. He's a capable guy with a bright future. I couldn't be more proud of him.

My daughter is frighteningly intelligent, extremely perceptive, and sharply sarcastic. Her artistic skills are amazing, and even as a small child she was creating paintings that astonished everyone who saw them, and writing short stories with complicated twist endings. Like my son, she is a very happy and dynamic person with a bright future. She has never been problematic with any of the garbage so many children and teenagers become involved in these days. No drugs, alcohol, depression, pregnancies, or any of that nonsense.

So both my kids are, at least so far, huge success stories. I consider them on my short list of my life's greatest accomplishments. This chapter is about how you can raise children under an Alpha 2.0 framework so that they become independent and happy adults who are as free of SP, OBW, and the Six Societal Values as possible.

Beta Male Fathers

What I'm about to say in these next few sections may be upsetting to you, because it's going to challenge some strong SP in your mind. Regardless, everything I'm about to say has been verified by studies, psychologists, and therapists the world over.

Since most men in the Western world are beta males, most fathers are beta male fathers. Many children today spend their entire childhoods watching their beta fathers argue, cower from, and obey their strong mothers. Little boys and girls watch as their mothers bark orders to their beta fathers and have dads obey like slaves. Since their parents model their lives based on the Six Societal Values (conformity, security, control, drama, validation, and not being alone), little boys and girls watch endlessly as their mothers and beta fathers get into frequent fights (drama), go into debt and suffer financial upset in an effort to live a lifestyle that looks like their neighbors (conformity and validation), and boss each other around, often with much resistance (control).

Because of all this, little boys in these families grow up to be adult beta males, spending the rest of their lives being bullied by women, unable to structure lasting, happy relationships with women, and unable to take life by the balls and confidently stride forward in pursuit of their goals, much less a Mission.

Little girls in these environments grow up to be bitchy, angry drama queens, expecting men to kiss their asses and getting upset with men when that doesn't happen. They go on to often have children too early and outside of a stable relationship (because, no problem, mom will help me take care of my baby!) and end up leaving the vast majority of men they get into relationships with via breakups or divorce.

Alpha 1.0 Fathers

Some kids have Alpha Male 1.0 fathers instead. These fathers are loud, scary, and overbearing. They impose a myriad of all kinds of dictatorial rules and regulations on their children down to the minutest of details. I've seen Alpha 1.0 fathers do things like mandate that electronics will only be used from 5:30pm to 6:30pm in the evening, make their children write reports on daily activities, or determine the very specific shades of blonde or brown hair colors appropriate for their teenage children. Other Alpha 1.0 fathers make their teenage children sign huge multi-page contracts full of "dad legalese" that would make attorneys faint. Divorced Alpha 1.0 fathers impose strict times of when their children are supposed to call them and update them on their activities. Some divorced Alpha 1.0 fathers even force their kids to read to them over the phone nightly.

When the kids disobey, which is exactly what children's OBW forces them to do when too many rules are imposed upon them, Alpha 1.0 dads punish harshly, often screaming, threatening, lecturing, and/or physically assaulting their kids.

Little girls raised with overly domineering Alpha 1.0 fathers grow up to be adult women who fear men and find it almost impossible to ever trust men, causing all kinds of chaos throughout their lives and in their interpersonal relationships with men. This also includes platonic relationships with men at work, in their families, and in their social circles. Often these women become overly submissive to abusive husbands or boyfriends.

Little boys with dads like this grow up with inferiority complexes, thinking they will never be good enough and never measure up to the perfection their Alpha 1.0 fathers always demanded. This makes long-term happiness for these men extremely difficult to find as adults. Of course it goes without saying that many men raised by Alpha 1.0s become Alpha 1.0s themselves, regularly upset that people aren't doing what they command.

Having No Father

All of these scenarios assume that two parents are present during the upbringing of the children. Since over 40% of births in the U.S. are to unmarried mothers[52] and 34% of single mothers have never been married[53], in many cases little boys and girls are raised with no father around, beta or Alpha. Then we have an even worse situation. Fatherlessness in society is a huge problem with massive negative repercussions. Society has only just begun to pay the price for this.

Women raised with no father spend their entire adult lives looking to be endorsed by men, romantically, sexually, platonically, and at work. I'm sure you can imagine the problems and unhappiness this creates for these poor women, and have seen these problems play out in your own life.

Men raised with no father have it even worse. They often become more beta than even men raised by beta fathers, always seeking to be dependent on a strong female, just like they were dependent upon their single mother throughout their upbringing.

Men being raised by beta fathers, Alpha 1.0 fathers, or no father. It's all bad news. Is it any wonder why the Western world is so full of beta males today?

Alpha 2.0 Fathers

Alpha Male 2.0 fathers, like Alpha 1.0 fathers, are strong, confident, and masculine role models for their children. Unlike Alpha 1.0 fathers, they don't impose a lot of rules on their children, just a very short list of a few basic ones. They seek to raise their kids via example, not control. Alpha 2.0 fathers also do not seek to dominate the child's mother, and children seeing any drama between their mom and their Alpha 2.0 father is an extremely rare experience - even if their parents are divorced or no longer together.

When kids violate the small number of rules imposed by an Alpha 2.0 father, the father punishes his kids swiftly, sharply, and fairly, however he never gets angry or emotional about it, he never raises his voice, and he never physically hits them. His entire tone during a punishment is a neutral one; it's simply something that must be done, then it's over, resuming the happy relationship between father and child. Alpha 2.0s never feel angry or "disrespected" because of their children's

[52] http://www.cdc.gov/nchs/fastats/unmarried-childbearing.htm
[53] http://www.singleparentcenter.net/single-parent-statistics.html

failures to adhere to his rules or standards. He knows his children are simply children, sets his expectations accordingly, and loves them regardless, both in thoughts and deeds.

Of course Alpha 2.0s are human beings and are not perfect. Sometimes they can lose their cool with their kids just like everyone else, but these occurrences are rare and unusual rather than being regular, expected events.

I'll never forget the one time I ever raised my voice at my son in anger when he was little. It was when my daughter was a baby, and he (at age six at the time) got upset and hit her. I told him to go to his room, but I said it loudly, in anger. Both him and my wife at the time looked at me with shock, since I had never raised my voice to him like that ever, and to my recollection, never have since.

Yelling, screaming, overbearing rules, and harsh punishments are ether non-existent or extremely rare in your Alpha 2.0 parenting style. The four core concepts of Alpha 2.0 parenting are:

1. Not losing your cool.
2. Few rules, but swift, consistent, and fair punishments for violating those rules.
3. Leading by example, not by control.
4. Demonstrating unconditional love.

We're going to tackle each one of these. If you're a more Alpha 1.0 guy, you're going to have trouble with not losing your cool and not setting too many rules. If you're a more beta guy, you're going to have trouble with issuing punishments. Just about all men are going to have trouble with leading by example and demonstrating unconditional love.

Not Losing Your Cool

Losing your cool in front of your kids is not cool, for you or the kids, and your spouse if you have one. Having your kids see you getting mad, raising your voice, or acting irrationally angry actually damages your credibility as both an authority figure and as a role model. On the other hand, keeping your cool even when your kids are misbehaving, and even while you are punishing them, raises your children's respect for you in ways that no lecture, threats, or punishments ever could. I know that seems counterintuitive, but it really is the case.

My dad was an Alpha 1.0, though fortunately not an extreme one. When I was young, he was a stressed-out guy. He worked very hard at a job he hated for many decades. As a result of this and his troubled upbringing, he had a short temper. Like many Alpha 1.0 fathers, he flew off the handle often, and got upset very quickly at very little things. After observing him do this many times with me and my siblings, I began to view him as almost a child, since the only other people I saw who would get visibly upset at little things were other children. It damaged my respect for him. Of course, since he was a big, loud guy who could and did punish me, I still feared him, but my respect for him as a father and as a role model was lessened.

Garnering *fear* from your children is easy. Garnering *respect* is not. Too many angry, stressed-out, or Alpha 1.0 fathers don't realize that all their efforts to induce respect from their children actually end up damaging that respect, gaining only fear instead.

I'm not saying that instilling a little fear is bad. As their father, your children should fear you, but just a little. The reason women, especially single mothers, have so much trouble and angst around raising children is because kids don't fear their mothers (I'll demonstrate this in a minute). So a little fear is good. However, overdoing the fear at the expense of respect, admiration, and even love is never a good idea.

Not losing your cool with your kids means the following things:

- Not raising your voice to them in anger.
- Not punishing them because you happen to be upset at their behavior.
- Not punishing them because you've had a bad day.
- Not arguing with your spouse in front of your kids.
- Not arguing with any other adults in front of your kids.
- Don't *ever* physically hit your children. As we'll discuss in the next section, there are some extremely effective ways to punish your children that will really make them suffer without you ever having to hit them or get upset with them.

In terms of specific actions you can take to facilitate these things, here are some examples:

- While punishing your kids, always keep a normal tone of voice and neutral expression on your face while doing it.
- Think before you punish. Are you punishing or raising your voice just because you happen to be pissed off, or because the child really deserves it?

- Make a rule with your special lady (hopefully a OLTR and not a traditional wife) that you will not argue with her in front of the kids. Develop a system with her where if either of you are upset at the other, you will either table the argument for another time if the kids are present, or you'll take it outside or to the other side of the house where the kids can't hear the two of you. Now remember, since she's a woman, she's dynamic and ruled by her emotions, so she will happily discard this rule down the road even if she initially agrees to it, so plan on this. You still need to set this system up and work with it as best you can. This may mean that when she starts screaming at you, you'll have to stop her if the kids are present, or lead her into another room or outside. Actually get up and leave yourself, causing her to either follow you or stay but stop screaming and calm down.
- Come up with a specific type of punishment that is painful for the child that doesn't require any raising of voices or physical punishment; this includes spanking. We'll talk about this in the next section.

The Importance of Punishment

Lest you think that reading the above means you have to be a pussy father who never punishes your kids and always parents with a light hand, lets now switch gears and talk about how punishing children, sometimes very harshly, is absolutely necessary and a required component of Alpha 2.0 parenting.

As a parent, you have two primary long-term goals when it comes to raising your children:

- Demonstrate unconditional love for them.
- Teach them the universal law of cause and effect.

If you successfully do both of those things with your kids during their upbringing, you "win." Your kids will grow up to become happy, successful, fulfilled adults who have most or all their SLA functioning well.

If you fail to demonstrate unconditional love, your kids will grow up to be pussies, always seeking validation from others and having all kinds of problems in their relationship and work lives.

If you fail to teach them cause and effect, your kids will grow up to be lazy, frustrated, easily angered, despondent brats. They will sit on their asses expecting the world to do them a favor, and will get very upset whenever the world doesn't do that. Which, of course, it won't. Others will go to the opposite extreme and develop a form of OCD, which is an irrational attempt to regain control over cause and effect.

The way you instill the concept of cause and effect into a growing child is by rewarding the child when he/she does well, and punishing the child when he/she does bad things on purpose.

Most parents in the modern era have no problem with rewarding kids. If anything, most parents over-do that. In this section we're going to talk about the importance of punishments. Specifically, punishments that are harsh, but appropriate and fair.

Female Parenting vs. Male Parenting

This is something you've probably seen many times, or perhaps experienced yourself.

Picture a woman in a grocery store, doing some shopping with her hyper little boy, Johnny. Johnny, being the typical high-energy little boy, is bouncing off the walls and driving mom insane. Like most mothers, mom often screams, threatens, negotiates, and bribes her kids, but rarely punishes her kids.

So first mom starts *screaming* at Johnny. "Johnny! Stop! Stop it right now! Johnny??? I said stop it!" She does this for about five minutes, over and over again, and gets more and more upset. It doesn't work. Johnny doesn't fear his mom, since he knows mom screams a lot but never punishes him. She's all bark and no bite, as Johnny figured out by the time he was about three years old.

As mom gets angrier, she starts to *threaten* Johnny. "Johnny! If you do that one more time, I'm taking your Xbox away as soon as we get home! I am so serious right now!" Since Johnny knows mom rarely follows through with these kinds of threats, he ignores her and keeps right on being hyper.

So then mom enters the next phase. She starts *negotiating* with Johnny. She attempts to logically reason with him as if he was an adult. "Johnny? Are you making good choices right now? Johnny? Remember what we talked about when we go to the grocery store? Are you behaving like we talked about?" Of course, this doesn't accomplish anything either. Johnny is six years old. He could care less about something that happened a few hours ago, much less a conversation from a few weeks ago.

When this fails, assuming mom isn't furious by now and losing her cool, she tries to *bribe* Johnny. "Johnny, if you stay quiet until we're all done shopping, I'll let you pick out a candy bar when we get to the checkout stand." This is the first smart thing mom has done. Sometimes it works, sometimes it doesn't. It really depends on the day, what Johnny ate that day, Johnny's mood, and the alignment of the planets.

Let's say it still doesn't work, and Johnny is still bouncing off the walls. Now mom really loses it. She starts screaming in the grocery store, creating a scene. Maybe she even slaps Johnny in the mouth. I've noticed the only way mothers actually do punish children is by slapping them, usually in the mouth. The problem is they always do it when they (the mothers) are angry with their children, which introduces anger and unfairness into the interaction, just like an Alpha 1.0 would.

Now let's paint a slightly different scenario. Let's say that fortunately for Johnny, he's one of the 60% or so of kids who actually has a live-in dad, who happened to be on the other side of the store when Johnny started acting up

Dad returns to mom and Johnny. He sees Johnny misbehaving and his distraught mother.

"Johnny is not behaving," the exasperated mom says to dad.

Dad turns slowly to Johnny and glares at him with eyes of steel.

Instantly Johnny shuts up. Instantly. Dad never needed to scream, yell, argue, threaten, negotiate, or bribe. Hell, dad didn't even actually need to say anything. One look was all that did it.

Why did this happen? How could dad accomplish in two seconds what mom couldn't in 15 minutes of drama?

It's because Johnny knows that, unlike mom, dad actually punishes. Johnny does not want to be punished.

That's just an example. I'll give you a real-life situation that occurred more than once back when I was married and my kids were small.

Sometimes I'd be in my home office in the evening working diligently on my Mission. While this was going on, my wife at the time would tell the kids "Okay guys, bed time!" Then the kids would proceed to give their mom all kinds of hell. Running around, laughing, ignoring her repeated commands to go to bed, making up excuses to stall for time, they'd pull every trick in the kid playbook. Mom, in typical mom fashion, would scream at them over and over again to no avail. She would yell, threaten, negotiate, bribe, and all that other crap, anything but punish, and as usual it wouldn't work. The kids would not go upstairs to their bedrooms.

Finally, after 10 or 15 minutes of this chaos, she would come into my office, infuriated, and say, "Could you please put these kids to bed?!?"

I would smile and say, "Sure!"

Then I would walk out into the living room, and with a neutral expression on my face, I would say in a very loud, booming, but non-angry voice, "In bed on the count of three or no TV all day tomorrow! ONE!"

Both kids would instantly stop in their tracks with terrified looks.

"TWO!"

Both kids would dash across the living room and bound up the stairs.

"THREE!"

Both kids would dash across the upstairs hallway, run into their rooms, and leap into their beds.

I would look at her and say, "There you go," then go back to my home office and continue my work.

I'm not exaggerating. This is exactly what happened many times. I accomplished in about five seconds what she could not do in 10 or 15 minutes of screaming. The worst that would sometimes happen is that one of the kids would whine and complain, perhaps even cry a little bit as they were going to their rooms, but they would still go.

Ease of parenting isn't the only reason for punishing when it's necessary. The more important reason is the teaching of cause and effect. If you want your kids to grow up to become happy, independent adults, you must instill in them this critical life concept. Specifically I mean this:

When you do good things, good things happen to you.
When you do bad things, bad things happen to you.

One of the huge problems with kids today is that they grow up into young adults not understanding this basic reality. Kids in the modern era are growing up thinking they can enter the adult world with their hands out, while sitting on their asses, and get all of their needs and desires met. This is because of things like:

- Divorce
- Single motherhood
- An epidemic of beta male fathers
- Political correctness in schools

- The every-kid-on-the-team-gets-a-trophy culture

Children in The Prison are constantly rewarded for no reason and are rarely punished when they do bad things on purpose. Oh, they're threatened and yelled at a lot, but not punished.

When you reward a child only when he/she does something good, and when you harshly punish a child when he/she does something bad, suddenly the child realizes, at a core psychological level, that he/she better focus on doing good things and avoiding doing bad, irresponsible, or harmful things. He/she then carries this forward into adulthood, and becomes a great person who helps not only themselves but also the world around them.

The great news is that you don't have to wait until they're adults for this change to take place. My son is very intelligent, and both as an adult and when he was small he always got good grades. However, when he was about eleven years old, he started hanging out with two buddies who were fun guys but complete losers. As a result, his grades went from As to Ds. Back then I was still married to his mother, and his mom was in charge of grades and homework.

As you might expect, his mother did all the usual ineffective feminine stuff of yelling, bribing, negotiating, and threatening, but never punishing, and my son's grades continued to decline.

One day he handed her his report card, and it was filled with Ds. She lost it, and screamed, "That's it! I'm tired of this! If you don't improve your grades, I'm going to put dad in charge of your school work! And I'm going to let him do to you whatever he wants!" (Notice the beta-assumptive language of "I'm going to let him…," but I digress).

My son reacted in terror, "Mom! No! Please! I'll do better! I promise!"

Mom relented, and "gave him another chance." Still no punishments.

Of course, three months later my son brought home yet another terrible report card.

That day, responsibility for my son's grades and schoolwork shifted to me. I made his mother promise me that I would not get any resistance from her whatsoever if/when I had to punish our son, since I knew that watching their children get punished is a very hard thing for women to do, even if they know the punishments are necessary. I always maintained my rule of not arguing in front of the kids. While reluctant, she was fed up with my son's bad grades, so she agreed.

I had a sit-down meeting with my son. I told him that I knew the only reason he was getting bad grades was because he wasn't doing his homework. I was well aware of this phenomenon, since as a child I sometimes received bad grades in school for the same reason. I told him that he had exactly one month to start doing his homework regularly. After 30 days I was going to speak to all of his teachers and get a full report on his missing homework assignments, if any, and get his current grades in all of his classes.

I told him that if any teacher reported any missing assignments, or if he was getting anything lower than a C in any class, I would remove all electronic devices from his room and lock them in the storage garage. That meant no phone, computer, Xbox, iPod, stereo, or TV. All of that stuff would stay locked away until he brought his grades up. As I relayed all this I was calm, relaxed, and not mad. I was simply stating facts. I also told him the choice was his to make. If he wanted to continue to get horrible grades and have no electronics in his life, that was perfectly fine. I left the choice up to him. I was not issuing commands or orders; I was imply informing him of cause and effect.

You can probably realize the horror this instilled in him. Just picture a pre-teen with no electronic devices in his life! He told me he would absolutely, definitely get his grades up, and promised me that when I called his teachers in a month, they would give him a glowing report.

I simply smiled and said, "We'll see."

A month later I called his teachers. While he had improved a little, most of his teachers reported he was missing assignments and he still had a D in two classes.

That evening, my son, daughter, and their mom watched in reverent silence as I disconnected every electronic device from my son's room and moved them, one-by-one into the locked storage garage. When I was done, his bedroom looked like a wasteland.

My son was never a natural reader, so from then on, when he had to go to his room for evening bedtime, he had literally nothing to do, often for hours. It was torture for him.

The result of all this? Within two months his grades went from Ds to As. I happily put all the stuff back in his room, but reminded him that if his grades ever slipped again, "I'll be back!" like the Terminator.

From then on, his grades maintained an A average all the way through high school and into college, where today his GPA is 3.98, and that's with a dual major.

Punishments work.

How to Punish Correctly

You need to follow a specific and consistent system for punishing your kids. Punishments must be:

- Swift
- Harsh
- Age appropriate
- Situation-appropriate
- Not involve any hitting, spanking, or raising your voice in anger

The absolute best way to do this, which worked wonders on both of my kids, is a correctly executed "time out." Time out is an old term these days, and most people either don't do them or do them very wrong. If you do them right, they work wonders. They will turn around problematic kids into wonderful, happy kids; but again, only if you do them right, since they're very easy to do wrong.

Like women, kids crave attention. If you act like a woman and scream and yell at your kids, you're giving them attention, and they like that. They'll keep right on being bad so they can continue to maintain your attention, even if your attention is negative.

The ultimate punishment then, is to completely remove your attention from the child. That's ultimate pain for most kids. They'll hate it. It works for almost the exact same reasons a soft next (that we discussed back in Chapter 18) works on women.

There's one exception to this. Some more introverted kids love being alone and love to do activities by themselves. Removing attention won't work on these kids. They might even like it. I was like this when I was a kid. I loved hiding out in my room all alone and curling up with a good book for hours and hours. My two sisters, on the other hand, were normal kids who constantly craved parental attention. Often my sisters and I would be driving my dad insane with our childish crap. My dad would finally lose his temper and scream, "That's it! All three of you, go to your rooms!"

My sisters would start crying, screaming, and protesting, not wanting to go to their rooms, but I would pump my fist and say "yes!" then happily run to my room, shut my door, and read a book. My dad's traditional SP method of child punishment ("Send them to their room") did not work on me at all.

Therefore, the time out technique you use must be adjusted to work well on *all* types of kids, both introverted and extroverted. My daughter liked being alone when she was little, my son hated it, but correct time outs worked like magic on both of them.

Here's exactly how you do it:

1. Set up single child-sized chair in a room in your home where no one ever hangs out. This means a room like the kitchen or family room would not suffice. You also cannot use the child's bedroom for this. Use a spare room, bathroom, master bedroom, den, or a baby's room when the baby isn't in there.

2. Set the chair up facing the corner of the room. Make sure no objects are within reach of someone sitting on the chair.

3. Get a kitchen timer with big numbers on it and set it by the chair.

4. When child is doing something bad on purpose, give them one warning. Just one. "If you keep doing that you're getting a time out." Don't use the feminine method by giving the child three or ten or twenty warnings. **Just one warning, that's it**. Any more than one warning damages your creditability as an authority figure.

5. As soon as the child violates your one warning, execute the time out. Don't get mad. Don't yell or scream or threaten. Just say, "You get a time out now. Let's go." If they scream or refuse, pick them up and move them yourself. Just make sure not to grab them harshly. The great thing about kids is that they're small and portable.

6. Have the child sit on the chair facing the corner. Make sure no one else is in the room! Time outs will not work if there are any external stimuli in the room like other people, or a TV on, or music playing. It must be empty of people and 100% quiet in this room.

7. Set the timer for one minute for every year of the child's age. So four minutes for a four year-old, eight minutes for an eight year-old, etc. Then place the timer on the floor where the child can see it but not be able to reach it with his/her arms or legs.

8. Tell the child, "As soon as this timer goes off, you can get up out of the chair and join us in the living room again. If you make any sounds with your mouth, hands, or feet, I'm going to come back in here and reset the timer all over again."

9. Then leave. No other discussion, even if the child tries to continue the conversation, which they probably will.

10. Do not re-enter the room during the duration of the time out and make sure no one else does either. Once the timer goes off, the child can get off the chair and join you again.

11. If during the time out period the child makes any noise whatsoever, go back in, say nothing, reset the timer, and leave again. Do this as many times as necessary. It won't be very many times; kids learn very fast, believe me. Note that I said *any sound whatsoever*. So if the kid says they need to go to the bathroom, that "counts" as a sound. Ignore his/her request, reset the timer, and then leave again. Other sounds that "count" would be if the kid kicks the wall or pounds a table. If they do that, reset the timer, and then leave. No discussion. Kids will use every trick in the kid playbook to get your attention during a time out. Be strong, don't fall for it, and stay the course.

12. Once the time out is over and you let the child return, ask the child this question: "Do you know why you got that time out?" Be sure to keep a calm, neutral expression on your face and a relaxed tone of voice. If the child answers your question correctly, just nod and drop the subject, and proceed with your day as if nothing happened. If the child refuses to answer the question or answers incorrectly, then tell the child exactly why he/she received the time out in one sentence, then drop the subject and go on with your day. Do not get into a big conversation about this. If you feel a conversation is warranted, save it for another time, like later that day or the next day. Never "combine" time outs with other forms of punishments or lectures.

That's it! Using that method above, you now have a very effective way to punish your children harshly, but without getting mad and without hitting them. Trust me, once you do this to your kids two or three times, they will think very carefully before crossing you again.

Sitting in a chair facing a wall in a room with no people or television for a prolonged period of time is extremely painful for kids, and they'll do whatever they can to avoid this in the future.

Why Not Spank Or Hit?

You may be wondering why I recommend against any physical punishments for children, including spanking. There are several reasons.

First, I think hitting, slapping, or spanking children is cowardly and weak. It's just way too easy for vastly bigger, stronger adult to smack around a small child when the adult is upset. It shows a complete lack of both emotional control and outcome independence, two key Alpha 2.0 traits.

It's a weak move to hit your kids. It takes a strong person to *not* hit a child when you're really upset with them. It takes a weak person to slap the kid in the mouth or on the butt whenever you get pissed.

It also shows that you know of no other way to properly punish your kids, and it shows that you don't have the balls to punish your kids in a way that removes attention, which is what kids really fear.

Secondly, parents who hit their kids don't realize that hitting is attention. This is why hitting doesn't often work very well. Yeah, kids don't like physical pain, but they do like the attention they're getting while you're hitting them. Whereas kids hate the isolation of the time out and will move heaven and earth to get out of those.

Lastly, hitting your kids is completely illogical and sends all kinds of conflicting signals to your kids. I'm amazed when parents scream at little Johnny, "Don't hit your sister!" and then slap Johnny. What the hell? What the kind of message is that? What kinds of conflicting, irrational, illogical signals are you sending Johnny? What kind of adult will Johnny grow up to be with you sending all of these strongly-conveyed illogical signals to him throughout his childhood? What do you think Johnny will think of you as he grows up?

It really is insane in a very real sense. Do you want your kids to grow up hitting people? Even worse, do you want your kids growing up becoming accustomed to people hitting them? No? Then why are you hitting them?

Leading By Example, Not By Control

Rules are important for children. Unlike adults, children are not fully responsible for their actions, thus they shouldn't be accorded the same level of freedom that adults enjoy. On the other hand, parents imposing too many rules upon children create many unwanted side effects, including but not limited to:

- Causing kids to rebel against their parents in ways they never would have without all the oppressive rules.
- Creating more conflict and drama between parents and children.
- Creating more conflict and drama between father and mother due to disagreements over the imposed rules on the kids.
- Damaging the respect kids have for you as their father, as we discussed earlier.
- Damaging the love your kids have for you.
- Creating kids that turn into adults who are either frightened to take risks or troublemakers who cause all kinds of chaos for themselves and others.
- Causing your kids to grow up and impose all kinds of silly rules on their own lover and children, creating a never-ending cycle of needless conflict and hurt, not to mention divorce and screwed-up children.

The Alpha 2.0 father leads not by controlling his children's lives, but by living by example. My kids benefited greatly from watching me as their father achieve positive things in my life. Having my kids see me do these things enriches them in ways that no rules, regulations, or lectures ever could.

Throughout the years within my Alpha Male 2.0 life, my kids have observed me:

- Working hard at starting and growing my own businesses.
- Taking a strong and exciting passion in my work.
- Being happy, upbeat, and smiling all the time.
- Having happy, drama-free relationships with women.
- Paying attention to what I eat (at least the vast majority of the time), and taking vitamins every day.
- Exercising daily, even on days when I might grumble I'm not feeling like it.

- Lead other men (and some women) in my work life.
- Travelling the world, filling my life with rich and new experiences.
- Always trying new things, new foods, new places, new languages, and new experiences.
- Reading often.

Compare all that to a bunch of rules I could have made for my kids, like "You must run for 30 minutes every morning, or no video games!" or "You must practice the piano for 30 minutes a day, or I'm taking your car keys!" or slapping them across the head if they don't smile at people. These things might sound ridiculous but there are millions of fathers all over the world who impose rules like this, or ones much sillier, with dire punishments for kids if they don't comply.

Instead of being an outcome dependent Alpha 1.0 and spending huge swaths of your life away from your Mission and your happiness by running every aspect of your children's lives, lead by example. Live a disciplined, rich, wonderful, happy and free Alpha 2.0 lifestyle. Make sure your kids see what you do. Talk about your life with your kids. Whenever appropriate, invite your kids to come along in your journey and share it with them. I love traveling with my kids, discussing politics and literature with my kids, seeing the world with my kids, and working with my kids on business or career issues.

Your full and abundant life as an Alpha 2.0 is one of the greatest gifts you can give your children. Don't screw all that up by trying to run their lives like some little-man dictator.

Demonstrating Unconditional Love

Your kids need to clearly know from your words, but more importantly from your actions, that you love them. They must also know that you love them no matter what. That "no matter what" part can be difficult for a lot of us manly-men fathers. Your kids must know, not suspect but know, that you will love them 100%, always, even if…

- They don't take your advice.
- They live a lifestyle you fundamentally disagree with.
- They don't follow in your footsteps.
- They do stupid things.
- They make very bad mistakes.

It's easy for fathers to love their children when they're living their lives exactly the way the fathers want. However, when the father, who is a doctor, suddenly hears his son say he wants to be musician, or when the Asian father has to watch his daughter date a man outside his race, or when the conservative, religious father finds out his son is gay, or when the submissive, beta male, pacifist father watches his son go into the Marines, that's when all this unconditional love stuff gets very difficult for a lot of men.

You don't have to agree with what your kids do. You can even disapprove of your child's choices in life. That's okay. What's not okay is for your kids to get the idea that you love them less. Your words and actions, from the day your children are born until the day you die, should be that you completely and unequivocally love and accept them no matter what they do and no matter what mistakes they make in life.

Like I said, this can be tough. I have trouble with this one myself. I'm not a very lovey-dovey guy and I'm sure I could have told my kids that I loved them more often when they were growing up. Regardless, I did my best to make sure that my overall frame with them was "I want you to be happy. I have strong opinions about how to do that, but you need to follow your own path, and I will love you no matter what you do in life."

Here's the biggest point I can make regarding this: unless you're spiritually enlightened beyond us mere mortals, people often forget that the only unconditional love you will ever experience in life is the love you have for your children. All other types of love you will ever experience are conditional. Love for your friends is conditional. As we know from breakup and divorce rates, romantic love is extremely conditional. Even love for your parents is conditional; I know plenty of people who don't love their parents.

Your love for your kids is different. It's something very special and very rare. It's truly unconditional. Don't mess that up. It's too precious.

Don't Try To Be Perfect

A final word of warning about parenting: don't beat yourself up about it. I'm a good father, and I think I've done a good job in that slice of my Seven Life Areas. Despite that, I've made plenty of mistakes in my parenting over the past two decades. Hey, life is life, and you can't be a perfect father, so don't ever expect to be. Shit happens. You occasionally have bad days. You occasionally forget things. You occasionally make mistakes. As long as you're doing the other 95% right, that's okay.

Like with my example above about the one time I yelled at my son, you need to be such a good dad that when you do screw up (and believe me, you will screw up) it will be such an unusual occurrence that everyone will be surprised. It won't be a regular thing where your kids roll their eyes and think, "Yep, there's dad getting mad and yelling again," or "Yep, there's dad getting his ass kicked by mom again."

It's okay to screw up occasionally as long as you're doing all the big stuff right. Focus on the big stuff, and the rest will be fine.

Chapter 25 –
Getting Out of the Box

When traveling and asked where I lived, and I answered "sunny Phoenix," I'd often get the envious sigh, the gee-I-wish-I-lived-there-instead-of-in-X, then the litany of unpleasant things about their home city. This amuses me because apparently they haven't noticed the highway signs in their own town pointing the way out.

Dan Kennedy

May, 2001.

A good friend of mine I'll call Rick was sitting next to me at the circular table in the hotel ballroom. The party was going strong. It was my parents' thirtieth wedding anniversary, and it was a packed house. Both of our wives and kids were elsewhere, eating and socializing, and Rick and I relaxed while talking about work.

Rick and I had been friends for a long time. We had gone to both middle school and high school together. Rick was a funny, casual, good-looking guy. I still remembered the girls I had talked to in high school who had swooned about my "hot friend" Rick.

He and I had both grown up to become successful businessmen; me a consultant, Rick a dentist. He ran a thriving practice with four employees. He made very good money, more than I was making at the time.

Rick was doing what he usually did: complaining about his work. He went on and on about how much he hated being a dentist. Your customers all hate you and constantly complain and fight you. Your employees all hate you. The paperwork is a nightmare. The insurance companies are almost impossible to deal with. It takes forever to get paid. You have to screw around with banks. The equipment is ridiculously expensive. The continuing education was tedious, expensive, and time consuming. I could see the pain in his eyes as he spoke.

"Why don't you just quit?" I asked.

"Quit?" Rick said, blinking fast, as if snapped out of a trance.

"Yeah. Just quit. There are lots of things you could do to make the same amount of take-home money you're making, things that require much less overhead and bullshit. I could even help you out with a battle plan."

"I can't quit," he said, shaking his head, "I went to school for this for a billion years. It was expensive too. I can't just chuck all of that hard work. I have a whole practice now. I have employees and stuff. My dad did this. My uncle did this. Plus my wife wouldn't let me. There's just no way."

Rick's a great guy and I love him, but every time I see him, he is once again talking about how unhappy he is being a dentist. He knows he could do something else with his life, but he "can't."

He's trapped in The Box.

The Box

At this point in reading this book, you've probably come up with some really fantastic and motivational ideas about how you can change and improve your life. At the same time, it's also likely that you're thinking you "can't do that" because of some major condition in your life.

Maybe you think you "can't do that" because...

- You're married and it would be too difficult to get divorced or change your marriage to a sexually open one.
- You have kids and it would be too difficult to live a life of freedom.
- You have a good-paying job you hate, but feel trapped because of the time and effort you've already put into it.
- You're in college, or some other educational endeavor, and you "can't" stop because of the time and/or money you've already put into it.
- You "can't" make a major change because your family, or certain members of your family whom you feel close to will be disappointed, perhaps even angry.
- You're concerned your friends will ostracize you if you pursue techniques or concepts described in this book.

- Your girlfriend or wife "won't let you."
- You feel you "can't" financially afford to make the change you want.
- Etc.

It is very likely you are trapped in The Box, a concept first introduced by Harry Browne back in the early 1970s[54]. The Box is a significant, self-imposed condition that restricts your freedom or your long-term, consistent happiness. It could be a:

- Marriage
- Relationship
- Job
- Career
- Obligation
- Family situation
- Living situation
- Legal or financial limitation
- Or other similar circumstance

It could be a condition such as the fact that you have kids, or have a lot of debt, or are dependent on someone, or feel obligated to someone. It could be a prior commitment you made to someone that you know is harmful and destructive to your life, and perhaps theirs too. It could be that you hate where you live, but fear moving to a new city.

It could even be something as simple as cultural SP. For example, you may have been raised in an Asian culture and are strongly sensitive to how your family would react if you took charge of your own life.

It could be any self-imposed condition that you feel is holding you back from taking the actions in this book to improve your life, your freedom, or your happiness.

The Prison is imposed on you from external sources, namely the elites who run your society. However, the Box is something you have created for yourself. Consider it your own mini-Prison.

[54] *How I Found Freedom In An Unfree World* by Harry Browne

Logic and Facts Sometimes Don't Work

A long time ago I discovered that I could logically explain something to people, have them truly and honestly agree with me, but then say, "Yeah, but I can't do that because…" and then throw their "Box excuse" at me. For example, when I talk about how long-term monogamy doesn't work, and present all the facts, statistics, and arguments that support that, a lot of men will tell me "Yeah, you're right. A 'forever' monogamous marriage doesn't work. That's just not how human beings work. You're right. But I'll probably end up doing it anyway."

One of the many reasons I completely removed myself from politics many years ago, to the point now where I now don't even vote in national elections, is because I found that people would agree with me that the person they were voting for was very harmful to their own core political beliefs. Conservatives would tell me, "Okay, yeah, George W. Bush is for big government and he's a globalist and he's a fiscal socialist and he's pro-abortion, but I'll still vote for him." Left-wingers would tell me "Okay, yeah, Barack Obama obeys the big banks and big corporations and kills a lot of women and children with his predator drones and spies on our email and stuff, but I'll still vote for him."

As I described back in Chapter 2, the world is full of people doing things they know will make them unhappy. Men and women alike remain in marriages they hate, relationships they hate, jobs they hate, cities or countries they hate, and situations they hate. All because of that damn Box.

Therefore, this book would be incomplete without talking about how to break out of your Box.

Breaking Out Of the Box

Unlike The Prison, The Box is something you have complete control over. You can break out of your Box whenever the hell you want, and you should. Yes, there will be a price for you to pay to do this, and breaking out of the box will be uncomfortable, even painful. We discussed that process back in Chapter 2 when we talked about the Happiness Change Curve. It is indeed a law of the universe that you will experience some temporary unhappiness, perhaps even deep unhappiness, when you change major circumstances in order to make your life better. This is unavoidable in most cases.

The good news is that this unhappiness is temporary. If you focus, you can minimize that unhappy phase and get to the happy stuff very quickly. Several times in my life I have had to break through my own Box:

- I refused to go to college when I was younger, deeply upsetting my highly educated parents who were both very pro-education. At the time, my mother was a teacher and my father had two master's degrees.
- I quit my job and started my own business, leaving a very secure, stable, high-income corporate career. I was switching high guaranteed income with maybe-income.
- I pursued public speaking as a source of income. Surveys have shown that people are more scared of public speaking than even death(!). I wasn't that scared of it, but I was scared when I started out, believe me.
- I had to separate from, and later divorce, a woman I was married to for almost a decade, forever changing my family life.
- After my divorce I had to, very uncomfortably, get back out into the dating world, being a decade out of practice.

Breaking out of The Box is never fun, but it's worth it. The new happiness and freedom that comes as a result is more than worth the temporary and transitory pain you feel as you push through the box and enter into a new and better world.

How to Break Out

Here's exactly how to break out of your Box, if you have one. If you have no Box, that's great. Take the things you've learned in this book and get to work. If you do have a Box that's holding you back from adopting one or more of the lifestyle changes described in this book, here's how you punch through and get yourself out, and on to bigger and better things. That Box is continuing to make you unhappy and less of a man. It's time to chuck the damn thing.

Step 1: Clarify the price you're paying by staying in The Box

While you're busy worrying about all the scary stuff that might happen if you break out of your Box, you're not thinking about all the great stuff you're missing out on right now by staying in The Box. You're also not considering horrible stuff that is happening right now, as you stay in your Box. If you think about it, this makes absolutely no sense.

You may forget that by staying in that boring, painful, but familiar marriage, you are paying a massive price. The same goes for that "safe," soul-killing job you hate, that pretty but bitchy girlfriend you won't break up with, that family member you don't have the balls to stand up to, or that friend who keeps taking advantage of you.

By staying in these situations, you have installed a huge pipeline that directs all kinds of pain and unhappiness right into your being on a constant basis. Even worse, you are forever destroying all the other wonderful options out there that you could be experiencing.

I don't believe in reincarnation, nor do I believe in an afterlife where we retain our identity. That means once you die, you're done, and you're never coming back here ever again.

This life is your only shot. If you live through this life without ever having experienced something, you will never get another chance. You will have lost your one and only opportunity.

Therefore, by choosing to remain in your current circumstances, you are paying the greatest, most horrible price you could possibly pay. You think you'll "only" pay a price if you get out of The Box, when in fact you're paying an even worse price by staying within it. The pain you're now experiencing will be forever, while the pain of getting out of The Box will only be temporary.

Sit down and write out a specific list of "prices" that you are paying right now by choosing to stay in your Box. Be very specific, very honest, and don't hold back. Don't leave anything out; put down every negative item. What pain, suffering, unhappiness, or boredom are you now experiencing because you refuse to make a change? What things are you missing out on that would make you happy?

Step 2: Imagine living your life without The Box

What kinds of things would you do if you were completely out of your Box? What would you have? Who would you be? What would you experience? How would you live? How happy would that make you? How else would that make you feel? How different, in a positive way, would it be from your current conditions?

I can very honestly tell you that my life today is a fantasy world of joy compared to the boring, stressful, monogamous, financially strapped, Prison-based life I used to be living just a few years ago. It's night and day. The level of happiness I feel on most Monday mornings is better than what most men in The Prison feel on Christmas. I'm not kidding. It's that good.

Write down exactly how wonderful your life would be if there were no Box. If you were free. Write down everything you would do, have, be, and feel. You might be surprised how large and exciting a list you'll be able to come up with. It takes just three minutes. Grab the nearest pen and paper and go for it.

Step 3: Ask yourself, "What's the worst thing that could happen if I leave The Box?"

Ask yourself that question and get very real for a minute. What is the absolute worst possible thing that would happen to you if you made this change? Write down your answer and examine it rationally.

Don't go crazy into dark fantasies about crap that would never actually happen, but do get specific about the worst that could happen in real life, within reasonable probability.

Let's say you're thinking about divorcing your bitchy, non-sexual wife. The worst thing that could happen could be, "I would have to go through a very terrible divorce, only see my kids on weekends, have to pay my ex-wife $1300 a month in child support and alimony, and my parents would be very upset with me." You would not say something like, "I would never see my kids again!" because that's simply not going to happen (since laws protect you against this kind of thing).

You see my point. Make it the worst thing that really could happen, but don't go into dramatic la-la land.

Let's say you're thinking about quitting your safe but horrible job and starting an Alpha 2.0 business. You could say, "The worst that could happen is that I would not be able to pay my bills for a while, I'd have to file bankruptcy, and move in with my parents for a while." You would not say, "I might end up homeless and die in the gutter!"

Specifically define exactly what would happen in the absolute, but realistic, worst case scenario.

Step 4: Ask yourself the magical question, "Could I handle that?"

Looking at your worst-case scenario, ask yourself, "Could I handle that?" Give yourself an honest, rational answer. The vast majority of people who go through this exercise are quite surprised to discover two things:

1. The worst-case scenario isn't nearly as bad as you thought it would be.

2. You would be able to handle it. You wouldn't like it, but you could handle it. As a matter of fact, you've probably already handled worst things in your past, and you still turned out fine.

Step 5: Specifically define the price to get out of The Box, then develop a battle plan to pay that price and get it over with as fast as possible.

That's what this book is all about. Define your Code and your Mission, set some goals, make some plans, and use the time management techniques we discussed in Chapter 11. Then pay that Box-breaking price and go through that pain as fast as humanly possible. Then you can get to the good stuff, all while avoiding SP, OBW, and the 6SV. Always keep in mind how bad your Box is (or was), the new life you're going to live, and how you'll be able to handle even the worst-case scenario, which is unlikely to happen anyway.

Make a list of tasks that you'll have to complete to get out of your Box. Sort them by priority and sequence, just like we talked about back in Chapter 11. Then get to work!

Also, now that you know your worst-case scenario, you can include aspects of your plan to prevent this from happening. Within a personal strategic plan, preventing disaster is every bit as important as accomplishing goals. You should do both.

Chapter 26 –
Maintaining Maximum Physical Energy

He who breaks a thing to find out what it is has left the path of wisdom.

Gandalf
J.R.R Tolkien's *The Lord of the Rings*

October, 1983.

I stood in line with all the other 11 year-old boys, outside on the playground. I shivered in the frigid Pacific Northwest air, only wearing my gym shorts and t-shirt.

One by one, each boy's name was called by my angry, overweight, cigarette-smoking physical education teacher. Once she barked a boy's name and blew her whistle, he had to run up to the pull-up bar and do as many pull-ups as he could in front of everybody. When he was done, the teacher would notate it into her logbook, and then call up the next boy.

The girls had already gone first. Instead of having to do pull-up reps, they just had to pull up to the bar one time, then hold themselves there for as long as they could. The teacher would then note their times in seconds. The girls were now all relaxed, sitting in the grass and chatting, watching the boys do their pull-ups.

I was not looking forward to this. I was much more interested in doing things like reading than doing anything like playing sports, and my body showed it. I wasn't fat, but I was soft, and my upper body strength was pathetic.

Closer and closer I moved towards the front of the line as more boys ran up to do their pull-ups. I would watch as one boy did twelve, another did fourteen, another did seven, and another did nine.

Finally, the boy in front of me was called, placing me in front of the line. He ran to the pull-up bar and cranked out eight pull-ups like it was no big deal. Then he dropped and ran over to his buddies.

"Caleb!" the teacher cried, "Go!"

I ran up to the pull-up bar, leaped up, and grabbed it. Its metal was ice cold and unforgiving. I pulled as hard as I could. Slowly, ever so slowly, my body lifted upwards towards the bar. My chin still nowhere near the bar, my teeth clenched and my tiny arms burned like battery acid.

"C'mon, Caleb!" the irritated teacher screamed, "Go! C'mon!"

I groaned loudly, pulling as hard as I could, squeezing my eyes against the strain. My body raised another inch. I pulled harder. I could hear my teacher scream at me again but I didn't make out the words in the midst of my pain-soaked focus. My chin was about three inches from the bar, but my body wasn't moving.

"Alright, alright," she said, "Forget it! Drop!"

My arms released the bar and I dropped to the mud, which was sweet relief. The pain vanished and reality returned. I stumbled away from the pull-up bar, muddy and red-faced, feeling the eyes of my entire class on me. Most boys in the class could do many pull-ups. I couldn't even do one.

Angry and embarrassed, I trudged past all the boys and girls sitting and watching, carefully avoiding their eyes.

Someday, I thought, I'm going to be strong.

What about Health and Fitness?

Health and fitness is a huge topic, and a relevant topic to the Alpha Male lifestyle. Regardless, I have purposely avoided that topic in this book for several reasons.

1. I have no credentials whatsoever in this area, therefore it would be dishonest of me to relay advice to you in this realm.

2. As we discussed back in Chapter 7, you will have one or two areas of your SLA where you will be weak. The physical side of my life has always been my weakest area, by far. Although I am very healthy and look decent now, I have been moderately overweight at various points in my life. Again, this does not exactly qualify me to give fitness advice.

3. There is already an excessive abundance of health and fitness information for men out there, almost to a ridiculous degree. If you want to lose weight, improve health, or

increase muscle mass, you're a quick Google search away from more information on those topics than you could possibly assimilate in ten lifetimes. That's just the web; Amazon and your local bookstore are jam-packed full of books on men's fitness. Even if I were to give fitness advice, which I will not, absolutely nothing I would say would be anything new.

However! Just because I'm not discussing this topic doesn't mean it isn't critical to an Alpha lifestyle. You need to be as healthy and physically fit as reasonably possible based on your age and genetics. In addition, as we discussed in Chapter 16, you need to maintain a high level of good looks throughout your entire life, as much as your genetics allow. A skinny, scrawny, wimpy guy, or a guy who's so fat he wheezes like a farm animal as he walks up the stairs, or a guy who's so ugly he scares women off, all of these men are going to have a very tough time living the Alpha 2.0 life. Health, fitness, and personal appearance are a priority to the modern Alpha, no question.

Physical Energy

The one area of your physical life I am going to touch on is the topic of physical energy. As you may suspect, having the rich, full, and often crowded life of the Alpha 2.0 is going to require you to have plenty of energy every day to get all of your to-do tasks done, to stay motivated, to have plenty of sex (and do it well), and to feel great. If you lack the energy to do these things, the odds are good that you won't do them, or won't do them when they need to get done.

Even when I was clearly overweight I have always been a high-energy guy. Don't think it's any coincidence that I've been able to accomplish what I have in my life. More importantly, my physical energy was a choice. It was something I nurtured and maintained on purpose. Frankly, one of the big reasons I started to lose weight was because the weight was starting to sap my energy and slow me down. This was unacceptable to me and my Mission, my goals, my happiness, and my lifestyle.

I'll say it again just to be clear, I am not a fitness expert, not even close. Yet what I can do here is run down a list of things others and I do on a regular basis, that I know work, to keep my physical energy levels at optimal levels.

Does this mean I never have days were I feel lazy or unmotivated? Of course not; I'm human, and those days do happen. That being said, they're pretty damn rare. The vast majority of the time I maintain a high level of energy from the moment I wake up in the morning to the moment my head hits the pillow in the evening. Below are the steps I take to accomplish this. *Important disclaimer!* I am not a doctor. I am in no way qualified to render medical advice, and no advice in this book should be considered as such. Please check with a health professional before attempting anything in this chapter if you at all unsure of the advice.

Exercise Hard At Least Once Every 48 Hours

Never let a 48 hour period pass by where you have not exercised, hard, for at least 20-30 minutes. If you want to exercise more often than that, then fine. I exercise seven days a week, but I consider once every 48 hours a non-negotiable minimum for an Alpha 2.0. I don't care if it's lifting weights or swimming or running or whatever. Do whatever you want, but exercise! Not only are there numerous health benefits, but your brain will have more oxygen which means you will be more creative, motivated, and in a better mood. It will also help with your sleep.

Moreover, you need to exercise hard. If you aren't sweating and panting, you're not exercising hard enough. Spend $40 and get a heart rate monitor and set it so that it beeps at you if you ever go below 70% of your maximum heart rate. This is determined by deducting your age from 220, then taking 70% of that figure. This will ensure you really are accomplishing something when doing your cardio exercise. If you can do sprints or interval training, that's even better, but not required. Just exercise!

Make Eight Hours of Sleep a Priority

Way too many people in The Prison are not getting enough sleep. Then they wonder why they don't have energy and are often depressed, unmotivated, or easily angered. Well, duh.

If you're not getting at least seven, preferably eight hours of sleep every night, there's only one reason: you're not making it a priority in your life. In today's busy world, you must actually make getting a proper amount of sleep a priority and a conscious choice in your life. Do whatever you need to do to make sure you get to bed early enough so that you get in your eight hours.

I have alarms set in my smartphone that go off at certain hours. These remind me to get ready for bed and to actually go to bed. Use any technique that you think would work for you.

I admit that there are people out there who are able to function on fewer than eight hours. That's fine, but we're not talking about what you can do, we're talking about what's optimal. If you are one of those oddballs who feel perfectly refreshed and high-energy every day after only getting six or seven hours of sleep, then make seven hours your minimum daily sleep goal. I personally would never go below seven though, at least on a regular basis.

Sleep deprivation leads to decreased testosterone, increased insulin, increased stress hormones, weight gain, increased heart disease, and increased rates of death (by any cause). Defending your lack of sleep is very dangerous business.

Lift Weights (or Engage in Other Resistance Training)

Nothing increases your day-to-day confidence, self-esteem, personal sense of masculinity, and energy levels like having rock-hard muscles. Even if you're a chubbier guy, having some solid, well-trained muscles under the chub is still worth it.

I'm not saying you need to look like Conan the Barbarian or Dwayne Johnson. You don't unless that's specifically one of your goals. I am saying that you need to be lifting weights (or using similar resistance training) on a regular basis, even if it's a lighter, high-rep workout. Even when I'm not trying to gain any muscle mass, and even when I'm very busy with my other SLA, I always force myself to do a full-body resistance session at least once every four to six days. This keeps my body strong and tough. It also boosts my confidence. There are always other benefits too, not to mention when a women says "Oooo!" when they touch your biceps.

Take Lots of Vitamins

I take a huge handful of various vitamins every day with my breakfast. In addition, every time I eat throughout the day I pop a big Vitamin C pill and a big Omega-3 pill.

Men tend to be very bad at taking necessary vitamins, and you should not be one of them. I'm not going to sit here and list out all the exact vitamins I take. I'm not qualified to give that kind of advice, and your body may differ from mine. You must take the time to do the research and take whatever vitamins you need for maximum energy, health, anti-aging, disease prevention, and longevity. Be sure to base your vitamins based on your age, body type, fitness goals, and medical history. I have read many books on health and vitamins and I've learned a lot. You should do the same.

There is one vitamin that is particularly important to a man and his energy levels, and that's vitamin D. Many people don't get enough sunlight and/or live a sedentary lifestyle, both of which sap vitamin D from your system. Vitamin D also helps improve testosterone levels which are crucial. Get a blood test to determine your vitamin D levels, and if you're low, start taking vitamin D daily. Consult a doctor on specifics.

I have pale skin and live in a part of the world where unimpeded sunlight isn't very common. A few years back I took a blood test that indicated my vitamin D levels were extremely low. I started taking 4,000 IU of vitamin D daily, and within a few weeks I was shocked at how much it improved my mood and daily focus. My testosterone levels also improved. I can't recommend vitamin D enough.

Have Sex at Least Two Days a Week

It's one of the three Alpha Male 2.0 sexual baselines we discussed earlier. Have sex twice a week, minimum.

Way back when I first started on my road into the Alpha 2.0 lifestyle, my goal was to have sex three times a week, every week, without having to promise any woman monogamy. It took me a while, but I eventually hit that goal. These days I have sex at least three days a week, and it's often with multiple women.

The "multiple women" part is optional, and maybe you don't need it three days a week, but sex two days a week is mandatory. Having sex this often will not only help you feel great, but it will keep sex from being a distraction in your life. Men who are distracted by sexual desires or neediness tend to be men who aren't getting enough sex. How many cheating married men have you met whose wife was super hot *and* was having sex with him most days of the week? How many single guys do you know who are addicted to porn while having sex with real-life women many days a week?

See my point?

By the way, I need to state a few things for the record. When I say "sex":

- Masturbation does not count.
- Watching porn does not count.
- Sex with blow-up dolls does not count.

- Sexting, phone sex, cyber sex, and/or video-chat sex with your long distance girlfriend or wife does not count.
- Flirting, even things like ass-slapping, does not count.

When I say "have sex," I mean you're having actual sexual intercourse with a real-life, warm woman in your arms. No excuses on this one. I don't care if you're monogamous or have been married for twenty years. As a man, you need to be having sex at least two days a week with someone. Take the advice you've learned in this book and make it happen.

Don't Sleep in Too Late, Even If you're a "Night Person"

If you're a "morning person," the kind of guy who loves to get up at 5am or 6am even if you don't have to, then you don't need to worry about this advice. However if you're a "night person" like me and you are self-employed where you don't need to report to a job every morning, you need to be very aware of an insidious condition I call Creeping Sleep-In.

It works like this. You finally start your own business and now don't have to report to a job, which is great. For a while, you still get up at 7am, just like you did when you had a job. You just keep doing it out of habit, and because your business is new and exciting.

Over time you start to think, "Hey…I can wake up whenever the hell I want. Screw this 7am stuff." Then you start sleeping in until 8am. So far, no problem.

Over time, 8am becomes 8:30am. 8:30am becomes 9am. 9am becomes 9:30am and so on. You start staying up late into the evening, not going to sleep until 2 or 3am. Soon, you're sleeping in until 11am, noon, or even later.

You might be thinking, "Hey, what's the problem? Isn't feeling the need to get up at 7am a bunch of SP? I'm an Alpha 2.0. Society shouldn't tell me when I'm supposed to get up every morning."

You're absolutely right, but we're not talking about SP here. We're talking about physical energy. If you're sleeping in until noon every day, you will feel sleepy, tired, and shiftless throughout the day. You'll start feeling like crap. Your motivation and energy levels will take a hit.

I'm no doctor, so I don't know why this happens, but I've seen this happen with a lot of guys, including myself at one point. Sleeping way into the mid-morning or early afternoon will damage your energy and motivation levels even if you get eight hours of sleep. Don't do it.

Just like any Alpha 2.0, I can wake up literally whenever the hell I want, every morning, seven days a week. Regardless, I set an alarm and I'm up by 8:30am most mornings. I won't ever let Creeping Sleep-In affect my life, productivity, or energy levels.

Drink a Lot of Water

This should go without saying, because I think most people these days understand the necessity for a high amount of daily water consumption.

Water is the only liquid I drink. I never drink juice, milk, coffee, or alcohol (with the possible exception of a few sips on wine on the occasional first date). Just buckets and buckets of micron-filtered, reverse-osmosis water, every day. I have a water dispenser not only in my kitchen, but I have two more water dispensers located right at my desk in my office so I can always refill my water without having to get up and damage my productive flow. I always keep two big bottles of filtered water in my car so I always have it on the go.

I once heard a saying I never forgot: "You're not tired, you're thirsty." If you're not drinking several glasses of water a day, you're making a big mistake, and your energy levels will suffer.

Avoid Drugs, Especially Marijuana

Here's the deal on drugs. I'm a libertarian. Politically speaking, I think all drugs should be legal across the board at the federal level, and individual states and municipalities can make legal or illegal whatever drugs they like. I have no problem whatsoever on a moral level with you doing all the drugs you want. I have dated many women who did drugs either regularly or occasionally, and have many good friends who do the same. I have no problem with it whatsoever philosophically.

Again though, we're not talking about SP, politics, morals, or philosophies right now. We're talking about what's optimal for your overall health and energy levels, and what's optimal is to stay the hell away from drugs.

I have never done any drugs in my entire life. Just once I took a drag on a weed pipe with two girls I was dating. It tasted like shit and made me cough. That is the extent of my personal drug experience.

Weed (marijuana) is especially bad. Why? Because nothing will sap your energy levels and motivation like smoking weed. More than once in my life, I have seen reasonably intelligent, motivated, dynamic, high-energy people become lazier and less motivated because of their love of smoking weed. They often gain weight too. Of course it doesn't always happen, and I do know people who smoke weed occasionally who are just fine, but I've seen it happen enough to indicate there's definitely some causation there.

As an Alpha 2.0, you should allow all the people in your life to do all the drugs they want (except your kids), but *you* shouldn't do any. You have bigger and better things to do, and drugs will more than likely pull you away from your Mission and your goals.

Avoid Alcohol

Everything I have just said about drugs also goes for alcohol. I have never been drunk in my entire life. I have never consumed hard alcohol in my entire life. There are times I will occasionally sip from a glass of wine, but rarely will I drink the entire glass.

Getting drunk all the time, or even getting buzzed on a regular basis, will damage your energy levels and overall level of motivation. Having a beer or two is fine. If you want to get shitfaced occasionally, like at a special event or when celebrating something, that's also fine. However, artificially altering your mood via alcohol should not be a regular occurrence in your life if your Mission and energy levels are important to you.

Constantly Remind Yourself of Your Goals to Stay Motivated

You should have the biggest and most exciting goals that you set back in Chapter 10 plastered up on your walls, your bathroom mirror, your monitor, and perhaps even on the dashboard of your car. Set up a system in your life where you are constantly reminding yourself of your big, exciting goals. Gold medal winners in the Olympics do this. It works. It will keep you pumped, keep you going, help you through the bad days, and make you feel remorseful when you start screwing around and wasting time, which is good!

Avoid Crappy Carbs

I'm not going to discuss whether carbs are good or bad for you. I have no expertise in this area. I'm strictly talking about energy levels here.

At one point during my weight loss adventure, I was eating nothing but meat, vegetables, and dairy products. Salads were the mainstay of my diet. At one point, I became frustrated at the prep time it took to chop all the lettuce, onions, peppers, and other vegetables needed to prepare my food. Even the pre-chopped bags of vegetables you can buy at the grocery store were still too big for me and required extra chopping.

Ever the time management optimizer, I decided that if I switched from salads to pre-made meals I could cook in the oven or microwave, I could drop my weekly food prep time to near zero. If I kept the calories the same, I would continue to lose weight. It sounded like a win-win to me!

So I chucked the veggies and bought a pile of pre-made meals at the grocery store. From a time management standpoint, I was right. My food prep time dropped to almost nothing, which was great. From a mathematical calories-in, calories-burned standpoint, I was also right. I made sure my total daily caloric intake was exactly the same as before, so I continued to lose weight. The food was also very tasty, which was nice.

However, from an energy levels standpoint, I had made a grievous error. Most pre-made grocery store meals, even the organic and "healthy" ones, include all kinds of high glycemic carbs like pasta, noodles, rice, potatoes, and bread. This was stuff I was barely eating earlier. Within about four days of switching my diet, I was noticeably more lethargic throughout the day and was actually getting a little sleepy in the afternoons. Worse, I became less motivated and focused at work. At first, I had no idea why this was happening. Within about a week or two I finally put it together; my new intake of crappy carbs was sapping my energy levels and making me tired and unfocused, particularly in the afternoons.

So with a heavy heart, I chucked the carb-meals, reluctantly went back to salads (this time focusing on pre-made salads whenever I could to save on food prep time), and my normal high energy levels returned within a few days.

I still chop vegetables sometimes and I still dislike doing it, but the increased energy from these foods is well worth it.

Regardless if carbs are good or bad, needed or not, and regardless of your overall daily caloric intake, complex or starchy carbs like pastas, rice, potatoes, and breads *will* noticeably drain your energy levels. Stay away from foods like this. If you really need carbs, stick with lower glycemic carbs like fruits, veggies, nuts, and beans.

Date Younger Women (Even If You Date Older Women Too)

I have always heard from older men that dating younger women makes you feel young. I always considered that to be bullshit. However, now that I have been doing that myself for the last several years, I can report to you that it is absolutely true. I am often in FB or MLTR relationships with women who are much younger than me. Think that's immature, inappropriate, or gross? Then you'd better check your SP, because you still have some. I also date women my own age, and even older, but there's often some younger women in there somewhere.

There's no better youth potion than dating younger women. I don't think it's any coincidence these sprightly old guys who date much younger women like Silvio Berlusconi and Hugh Hefner look, feel, and act like men decades younger. It's been scientifically proven that dating younger women boosts testosterone in men[55]. It will increase your energy levels, make you feel younger, and will motivate you to stay young and healthy yourself.

I'm not saying you must date younger women, although I am strongly recommending it. If you really want to stick with older women, that's fine as long as long as they're youthful, happy, trim, and reasonably fit.

I'm also not saying you need to get into super serious relationships with much younger women. Keep them at the FB level if you like. Regardless, I highly recommend younger women for higher energy levels as a man.

Keep Your Weight under Control

This should be obvious. I've had to wrestle with my own weight at several points in my life so I know this can be hard if you were cursed with poor genetics in this area.

It's okay if you have a little chub on you. It's not okay if you are fat. If you're fat, you need to put everything else in your life on hold and get that handled right now. The health risks are enormous. Testosterone takes a massive hit. Consistent levels of high energy are impossible. If you're fat, get it taken care of. Even if it takes a few years, do it.

I walk my talk here. At the time of this writing I've lost almost 50 pounds over the past two years. It wasn't easy, because I really love food, but you can do it if you make it a priority and persevere. Moreover, my understanding is that strictly removing sugar and complex carbohydrates from your diet will remove the cravings for these things completely, though I personally haven't accomplished that one yet.

This also means that if you are currently not fat, you need to keep watching your weight as you age. Every ten years you're going to "naturally" gain some weight, so you need to always be on guard against this for the rest of your life.

---

[55] *Sex At Dawn* by Christopher Ryan and Cacilda Jethá

Closely Monitor Your Testosterone Levels, Especially Once You Hit Age 35 and Beyond

Speaking of the rest of your life, the greatest physical source of energy and motivation as a man is the level of testosterone in your system. Testosterone keeps you strong, young, motivated, full of energy, and sexually potent. Testosterone is a core ingredient of masculinity. Since masculinity is a core aspect of the Alpha Male, and since, as we've discussed in prior chapters, femininity and consistent happiness are two incompatible conditions, low testosterone is unacceptable if you want to live an Alpha lifestyle.

Once you hit age 35 or so, you will start losing testosterone as a part of the aging process. Worse, most doctors won't do anything about it. Many men end up going to the doctor and complaining about lack of energy, motivation, or reduced sexual function. The doctor will check their testosterone, see that it's low, and say, "Well hey, your testosterone is just fine *for a man your age*." He'll proceed to tell you that it's "okay" your cock doesn't get quite as hard as it once did or that you don't have the energy you once had.

Unacceptable!

This is absolutely unacceptable if you want to live a full, healthy, happy life as a man into your older years. One of my over-arching lifetime goals is to keep my testosterone levels to the equivalent of a young adult, even if I'm in my forties, fifties, seventies, or nineties. You don't need to be as extreme as that, but you should still make healthy testosterone levels a consistent goal in your life.

Getting a blood test to check your testosterone levels is inexpensive and easy. Do it, and make sure that it shows you have the testosterone levels of a healthy 25-30 year-old man or close to it. If you do, great. Keep doing what you're doing. If you don't, you need to start on some kind of testosterone-boosting program, many of which don't involve any drugs or a doctor's assistance. Often just a change in diet and exercise can do it.

Once again, I'm not a fitness expert, so I can't give you specifics on how to do this; there are a myriad of resources out there you can draw upon. Many of the above items (such as vitamins, lifting weights, getting enough sleep, and dating younger women) will boost your testosterone levels already. Get your testosterone to young, healthy levels as best you can through lifestyle changes. If that doesn't work, look into getting testosterone replacement therapy (TRT) through your doctor.

Chapter 27 –
Exploring the World

No man has found himself in a position similar to mine. The dominions of kings are limited either by mountains or rivers, or a change of manners, or an alteration of language. My kingdom is bounded only by the world, for I am not an Italian, or a Frenchman, or a Hindu, or an American, or a Spaniard—I am a cosmopolite. No country can say it saw my birth. God alone knows what country will see me die. I adopt all customs, speak all languages. You may, therefore, comprehend, that being of no country, asking no protection from any government, acknowledging no man as my brother, not one of the scruples that arrest the powerful, or the obstacles which paralyze the weak, paralyzes or arrests me.

The Count of Monte Cristo

April, 2006.

After many years of fantasizing about it, reading about it, dreaming about it, and learning about it, I was finally there.

I leaned out of the Star Ferry, an old but sturdy green boat, as the sun bore down upon me and the sea air whistled through my hair. I could not keep the big dumb smile off my face and the excitement from my eyes as I looked up from the harbor to see some of the tallest skyscrapers in the world tower over me. More sleek, high-tech, and modern than anything New York, Chicago, or London had to offer.

It was Hong Kong, the freest country in the world, a historic success story about what free men can do. A barren rock with no resources of any kind just a few decades earlier, it was now the number one economy on the planet, with a business climate that rivaled New York, technology that rivaled Japan, and good food that rivaled anywhere.

This was my Mecca, and this was my pilgrimage, my first visit to the greatest city on Earth. Sailing across the harbor on that perfect sunny day, looking up at the majesty of what man can accomplish, it was *Star Wars*, *Blade Runner*, *The Fountainhead*, my birthday, Christmas morning, and going to church all at once. So many years of wanting to be in a place like this, growing up in a small suburb of a quaint and unimportant city. This place was one of the few fulcrums of the world of man, and here I finally was, quite literally a dream come true.

I clung to the side of the ship, leaning far out over the water, surveying the shorelines of both sides of the Kowloon peninsula and Hong Kong island, drinking it all in, I did my best to imprint the experience into my memory forever. I didn't want the moment to end. I wanted to feel like this forever. For the first time in my life I was in a place that felt 100% right, 100% compatible with the universe around me. It was at that moment, thousands of miles from my homeland, I made the decision to live my life congruent to the man I was, no matter what price I had to pay. It was at that moment I knew my life would never be the same.

The Entire Planet Earth Belongs to You

It is impossible to live a full life, and to acquire all the necessary ingredients for such a life, by relying on just the city or country you happened to have been born in. Over the horizon, in lands far from yours, in cultures much different or perhaps quite similar to yours, lies fulfillment, excitement, richness, perspective, spirituality, love, and life, the kind of which you can literally never experience in your own tiny corner of the world.

You need to go see it and experience it, because it's already yours.

I'm going to describe something that may sound a little odd, especially considering my hard-nosed, rational outlook on the world. Yet I don't mean what I'm about to say in a literal or rational sense. This is one of the few times I'm going to be extremely subjective and even a little fantastical.

When I look at the world, at the majesties and experiences it offers, I take an almost godlike view. I view the entire planet Earth as something that belongs to me. All its majesties, vastness, and experiences are all things that were designed for me, and me alone, to experience.

When I stand in front of the huge nine-feet high glass wall in my usual room at the Wynn Hotel on the Las Vegas strip, and I see the lights of the hotels and casinos flash in the dusk, and I see vast desert beyond, the distant mountains beyond that, haloed by flashes of blue lighting, that vista is mine, all of it. No one else can experience the majesty I am experiencing "for me" by seeing it. Therefore, it was created for me.

When I'm swimming in the lagoons of the Bahamas, and huge schools of brightly-colored fish, straight out of *Finding Nemo*, swarm around me with curiosity as I peer all the way to the bottom of the lagoon in the crystal clear water; that entire ocean, all of its majesty and waves and wildlife, were created for me. Just for me.

When I'm sitting on a comfy outdoor couch on the roof of the historic House of Roosevelt, formerly the 1800s headquarters of Jardine Matheson, the company James Clavell wrote about in all of his novels, drinking a (virgin) bloody mary, staring out over the water at the Pudong district of downtown Shanghai, jam-packed with all the largest and highest-tech skyscrapers of the world; all of that steel, glass, history, technology, and majesty was made for me; for me to experience and become a better man.

The entire world is yours. Seize it.

However before you do, you'll need to clean out some cultural SP first.

Your Country Sucks

That's right. Your country, the one you were born in and now live in, sucks. I don't care which country it is. It sucks.

Did I just upset you? Good. I've just demonstrated some extraordinarily powerful cultural SP buried deep within your mind.

All your life you have been told that your country is the best. Or you've been told your country is the:

- Nicest
- Fairest
- Strongest
- Most peaceful
- Most honorable
- Most moral
- Most hardworking
- Most caring
- Most progressive
- Or most something

As a result, you have very powerful, and very false, SP in your mind telling you that your country is somehow special and that all other countries are inferior, at least in some ways.

It's bullshit. I don't care which country you were born in or live in, I can point out several major problems with it. There are 196 countries in the world, and every single one of them has huge, and I mean huge, problems, downsides, and disadvantages to living there.

Yes, of course some countries are better than others. I would far rather live in the United States, Switzerland, or Japan than I would live in North Korea, Iran, or Zimbabwe. However, that doesn't mean there aren't huge problems for a financially and sexually free Alpha Male 2.0 living in the United States, Switzerland, or Japan, just to name three random countries out of the 196 on this planet.

For you to think that your country is somehow special or different or better than all the other countries in the world is not only false and juvenile, it also keeps you from great happiness by experiencing other countries and cultures.

You Don't Owe Your Country Anything

The next chunk of cultural SP you have in your brain is the false belief that says you somehow "owe" your country something. Men have fought, suffered, died, had their families suffer or die, and have even killed themselves because of the false cultural SP that says you somehow owe something to the country you happened to have been born into.

The reality is that you only owe your country two things. The first is the legal minimum of taxes you need to pay while you live there. The second is to follow your country's laws while you live there.

That's it.

Provided you've paid your legal requirement of taxes while you have lived in your country and followed its laws, *you don't owe your country anything else.*

That's hard truth. To think you somehow owe your country your life, freedom, family, fealty, or eternal servitude is simply insane. Whatever benefits your country has given you, you paid for those benefits, via taxes. As long as you've paid your taxes, you're "square" with your country. You don't owe them anything else other than to obey their laws, which you're probably already doing.

We briefly discussed the concept of Natural Law back in Chapter 4. This states that you own you, and no one else owns you. That includes your country. Your country doesn't own you. You own you. Start acting like it.

Once you realize that your country sucks and you don't owe your country anything, it suddenly opens up the majesty and richness of the entire world to you. Just like the Count of Monte Cristo, you suddenly stop becoming a citizen of the country you happened to have been born into, and instead become a citizen of the world; a true sovereign man.

I was born, and have lived, in the United States. I love the United States and think it's a pretty cool place. I'm sure I will always have an emotional attachment to it and fondness for it. At the same time, I know that there are massive problems with the United States, culturally (some of which we covered in Chapter 6), and with its government, wars, social problems, financial system, and economy. This means that there is great happiness and freedom in other countries that is mine for the taking as an Alpha 2.0.

If you live outside the United States, this is also true about your country. Even if you hate the United States, remember that I can easily point out all kinds of truly screwed-up things about your country too.

You must venture out of your home country and experience the world. You can do this by either moving to another country or traveling internationally often.

International Travel

Traveling internationally and experiencing other countries and cultures in a very immersive way isn't necessarily a requirement for the Alpha 2.0, but it's strongly recommended for several reasons.

1. It makes you happy. Happiness is the primary goal of the Alpha 2.0.
2. It increases your level of freedom. The less reliant and "stuck" you feel to your home country, the more freedom you will experience, both externally and mentally.
3. It increases your outcome independence in many ways, some of which are very subtle. For example, if my government threatens to do something conservative like cut Social Security benefits, or something left-liberal like socialize healthcare, everyone freaks out. I don't. I know both in my conscious and subconscious that I'm not "wedded" to anything my country does. If my country does

something really stupid or horrible, no problem. I'll just move somewhere else. Everyone else feels "stuck" here, so of course they get very angry at all kinds of silly political moves the government makes.

4. It opens your life to enriching experiences that are not possible to experience within your own country. There are people who live in downtown New York City who have lived 50, 60, even 70 years and have literally never been more than eight blocks from where they were born. What a frightening thought! Just imagine all the wonderful, enriching, powerful, and beneficial experiences they will never have.

If you wish to pursue the Alpha 2.0 path in life, I strongly urge you to set a goal to travel internationally at least once a year. Work up to the point where you are doing that two or three times a year, or even more if you want to.

When you travel, make sure you really spend some real time wherever you're going. I'm not talking about spending three days there and then coming home. I'm talking about trips that last at least a week, preferably longer. Ideally, you should be spending a month or more at a time in faraway lands when you travel. Having the location independent income of the Alpha 2.0 makes this no problem.

I don't care which countries you visit. That's up to you. Just get out there! It's possible you already have a travel lifestyle and if that's you, my hat's off to you. It's also possible you've never left your home country even though you're over 30 or 40 years old. In that case, get out there! You have a lot of catching up to do.

But Traveling Is Expensive!

Okay, time to deal with the excuses.

First, remember that your goal should be to make at least $75,000 per year in income while keeping your debt, taxes, and monthly expenses low. If you're doing this, covering the costs of traveling internationally once or twice a year will be no problem.

Second, people vastly overestimate the cost of traveling internationally. The most expensive part of international travel is the plane ticket. However, if you hunt hard enough, you can find a plane ticket that will take you damn near anywhere in the world for less than $1200, sometimes as low as $500. If you travel as often as I recommend, very quickly you'll be racking up so many frequent flyer miles that many of your plane tickets will be free. For his 21st birthday, I flew my son and myself from Seattle to the Bahamas for free, all because of frequent flyer miles. This is a common occurrence for me.

Once you get the plane ticket handled, everything else is quite inexpensive. Web sites like hostels.com and airbnb.com offer rooms and apartments for ridiculously low prices. When I go to Asia I often spend less than $40US per night on my hotel accommodations, and these are fully private rooms with internet access located in major city cores like Shanghai and Tokyo.

Food is also cheap if you get creative and plan ahead. I once spent a week in Tokyo, one of the most expensive cities in the world, and spent less than $17US per day on food, eating the *o-nigiri* (big balls of rice with tasty meats inside) available at convenience stores. In many cities in China, including the expensive ones like Hong Kong, you can purchase huge amounts of the best-tasting, high-protein food you've ever eaten from street vendors for the US equivalent of fewer than 80 cents.

Of course if you want to spend more money and treat yourself on your international trips, don't let me stop you. I sometimes do that myself. The point is to not use cost as an excuse to not visit the world.

Live Abroad

The ultimate expression of what I'm talking about here is to actually move out of your country and live somewhere else, even if just for a year or two before returning. I have not yet done this myself but I plan to, and I have many friends who have done this and are extremely happy with their decision. I have yet to meet a person who lived abroad and regretted doing it.

I would consider living abroad as another important, but optional goal you should have. At some point in the next few years, when my kids get a little older, at a bare minimum I will be spending 50% of the year living abroad and the rest of the time at home in America.

Date Women from Other Cultures

One of the most unexpected pleasures I've had from living a nonmonogamous Alpha Male 2.0 lifestyle has been from dating women from other cultures. I'm not saying you need to do this, but I've certainly enjoyed it.

I'm an American white man. While the majority of women I've dated have been white American women, I've also had sex with, or had

FB or MLTR relationships with women from countries such as Russia, Poland, France, China, the Bahamas, Korea, the Philippines, the Dominican Republic, Mexico, Cambodia, Japan, Sweden, and Estonia. This has really given me an education on other cultures, let me tell you!

As a nonmonogamous Alpha 2.0, it doesn't make any sense to restrict your love life or your sex life to just women from your own race or culture. How boring!

Hey, I'll be honest. My favorite type of women are blonde Barbies, and probably always will be, but I would still be missing out on a lot of great enriching experiences if I limited myself to just these kinds of women.

If you have only dated women of your own culture and race, I strongly urge you to break out of your mold a little. If you've ever been even a little curious about what it would be like to date an Asian woman, or Latina woman, or European woman, or whatever, don't limit yourself! The same goes for you if you have a fetish for only a certain type of race outside of yours, such as white guys who *only* date Asian women. Again, try not to limit yourself like this.

Remember that Alpha 2.0s live an abundant life! Live it!

Afterword

The world's mine oyster, which I with sword shall open.

Shakespeare

As I implied earlier in this book, there are times I wish I could take a time machine and go back in time to that wide-eyed kid I was when I was twelve years old, dreaming about the life I wanted to have "someday" when I would be an "adult." I would love to sit him down and tell him that all the amazing fantasies he has for his life would actually come true. There would even be things he was going to experience beyond his wildest dreams. Owning his own business, making a six-figure income without having to work long hours, traveling the world, having meaningful work that excites and motives him, being in love, having sex with many beautiful women, raising two wonderful children, being able to do whatever he wants, whenever he wants, without having to check in with anyone. It would seriously blow that kid's mind.

He probably wouldn't believe me. I've been living this life for many years now and there are times I don't even believe it.

Is it easy to achieve a life like this? Of course not; I've had to work pretty hard at certain points. The good news is that most of the hard work was actually pretty fun, so "hard work" doesn't accurately describe it if your connotation is negative.

Even if the work involved to get here was all negative, I would still have done it, without hesitation. The Alpha 2.0 lifestyle is truly the greatest in the world. Only the Alpha Male 2.0 can live a life of consistent happiness.

Women can't. They crave a range of positive and negative emotions, not constant happiness.

Beta males won't. They want happiness but don't have the courage to go out and seize it.

Alpha male 1.0s won't. They choose control over others instead of consistent happiness.

That leaves us: the Alpha Male 2.0s.

If you're not yet one of us, I encourage you to join us. You won't regret it.

If you don't want to become one of us, but want to integrate aspects of what I've talked about in this book into your own beta or Alpha 1.0 life, that's okay too. I'm glad to be of help.

If you're a man who wants to instead break out of your beta or Alpha 1.0 mold and live a life of freedom, masculinity, confidence, abundance, and consistent happiness, you are the man I wrote this book for.

Greatness is there, right in front of you.

Take it. It's yours.

What will they say right before they put you six feet under? Will you say "I wish I could have, I wish I would have, I wish I should have," or will you say, "I did it all. Thank you and good night."

Gene Simmons

Further Information

If you would like more information on how to design an Alpha Male 2.0 lifestyle, I have a very inexpensive monthly program that includes individualized coaching, private podcasts, a newsletter, and other benefits. The purpose of this program is to improve your income and skills with women.

If you would like to get more information on this program, plus get four free ebooks, go to:

www.sovereignmaninnercircle.com

If you would like to get a hold of some ebooks that give more detailed specifics on Alpha Male 2.0 dating and relationships, go here:

www.blackdragonsystem.com

I also have three blogs where I post articles regularly. The Alpha Male 2.0 dating and relationships blog is located at blackdragonblog.com. My business and time management blog is at sublimeyourtime.com. My personal blog, where I talk about miscellaneous guy topics is at calebjonesblog.com.

It is my hope that this book is the beginning of your Alpha Male 2.0 journey, not the end. Please avail yourself of the above resources. You have a very exciting life ahead of you.

Caleb Jones
November, 2014

Glossary of Terms and Acronyms

Acronym Quick Reference

SP: Societal Programming.
OBW: Obsolete Biological Wiring
6SV: The Six Societal Values
SLA: The Seven Life Areas

E3D: Every Three Days time management system
FB: Friend With Benefits
LTR: Long-Term (monogamous) Relationship
MLTR: Multiple Long-Term Relationship(s)
MNS: Monogamous, but Not Serious
OI: Outcome Independence
OLTR: Open Long-Term Relationship
TMM: Traditional Monogamous Marriage

Glossary

Alpha Male 1.0: A strong, confident, successful man who desires to control others.
Alpha Male 2.0: A strong, confident, successful man who desires long-term consistent happiness.
Beta Male: The typical, needy, submissive "nice guy."
Check System: A simple time management system.
Code: Your personal code of conduct. A (hopefully short) list of standards you will always adhere to no matter what.
E3D: A comprehensive time management system.
Financial Freedom: Being free from circumstances and unhappiness created by financial lack

Freedom of Action: The condition of being able to live your life any way you choose, free from any unreasonable limitations from work, government, family, or lifestyle.

Hard Next: A permanent removal of a woman from your relationship life.

Improvement Work: Work that potentially or definitely will improve your income and/or lifestyle not today, but down the road.

Kino: Sensual touching.

Mission: The single, overriding purpose and direction of your life, or at least for the next 20 years

Money Baseline: The three financial minimums of the Alpha Male 2.0: income of $75,000 per year (or the equivalent), working less than 40 hours average per week, and having the ability to recover that income within 6-12 months if it's ever lost.

Obsolete Biological Wiring (OBW): Strong but outdated biological urges that were needed 50,000 years ago but now only serve to make you less happy.

OLTR Marriage: An open or semi-open marriage with an enforceable prenuptial agreement and completely separate finances between the two partners.

Outcome Independence: The state of uncaring in regards to the outcome of a particular, singular situation currently before you.

Seven Life Areas (SLA): The seven ways in which you can spend your time: financial, family, social, woman, spiritual, physical, and recreational.

Sexual Baseline: The sexual minimums of the Alpha Male 2.0: the ability to have sex with at least two new women within four weeks of losing your current source of sex, and always having sex at least twice a week with women you consider at least "cute."

Sexual Freedom: The option of having mutually consensual sex whenever you want with whomever you like without having to get permission from anyone.

Six Societal Values: The six values society deems as more important than personal happiness. They are: conformity, security (perceived or real), control over others, emotional validation ("drama"), social validation, and not being alone.

Social Freedom: The ability to take action without regard to negative reaction from society.

Societal Programming (SP): Any thoughts you have as a result of society's extreme and constant efforts to install falsehoods within you to further the agenda of the elites.

Soft Next: A short, temporary removal of a woman from your relationship life.

Standard Work: Regular work you must perform in order to pay your bills and maintain your lifestyle.

Unmarriage: Moving in with a woman in a relationship that looks exactly like a marriage (cohabitation, raising kids, a wedding, wedding rings, etc) only without actually getting legally married on paper.

Useless Work: "Busy work" that makes you feel productive but actually accomplishes nothing of value.

Acknowledgements

A man is the sum of those he has experienced throughout his life. This book, nor the wonderful life I now live, would not have been possible without the invaluable assistance of the following people. Not all of you below will agree with everything said in this book, but all of you have given me gifts I can never hope to repay, though I may try (and fail).

Dad, for being the father so many men wish they had. I stand in your shadow, and always will.

Mom, for teaching me what long-term consistent happiness means and looks like. You are the model the world should follow.

My son Josh. At age five you already had abilities it took me 30 years to develop. You are a greater man than me. Watching you grow and conquer is my single greatest pride.

My daughter Indie. You are only the best qualities of your mother and I. Every girl who knows you wants to be like you. Your brother and you are the two children I always fantasized having.

My buddies over the many years who I will always consider brothers. Mike M., Kevin M., Andrew W., David C., Rob R., Rob P., Frank H., Jon C., Eric L., Garret F., Derrick K., and Dirk M.

My personal mentors. Thank you for believing in that scruffy, smartass kid when no one else did. Alan L., Ted T., Doug W., Dan K., Ken C., Shawna S., David R., Sarah V., and Bill C.

My mentors from afar. Most of you I've met or communicated with, some if you I haven't, some of you are no longer here, but to all of you I owe a great debt. Alan Weiss, Brian Tracy, Dan Kennedy, Jay Abraham, Tony Robbins, Dennis McEachern, Harry Browne, Robert Ringer, Rocky Covington, Larry Winget, Dan Burrus, Ray Kurzweil,

Tim Ferriss, Phil Knight, Gene Simmons, Jim Rogers, Arnold Schwarzenegger, Sylvester Stallone, James Clavell, and Isaac Azimov.

The Great Eight. There have been many, but only the eight of you stand out from the rest. If all women in the world were like you, paradise would be a reality.

- Sweet Pea - If only I had your wisdom and humanity.
- Napintas - Everyone loves you, as they should. Your gift will last forever.
- Miss Hawkins - You made me a man. Twice.
- Chaos Queen - You bring more energy to those around you than a nuclear power plant. Never change.
- Punk Rock - Crazy is why you work.
- Sadie - Poise, elegance, class, femininity; you don't even have to try.
- Bomb Bomb - You taught me what no other woman could; to say yes.
- Ghost Rider - *In perpetuum et unum diem.*

Everyone who's ever informed me, helped me, hated me, debated with me, or supported me on any manosphere blog or forum. All of you helped me improve as a man, hone my ideas, and call me out on my shit when needed. There are too many of you to list, but the standouts are Player Supreme, Tubarao, JWS, Money Matteo, Kwagmire, Dennis, GreenTea, Lovergirl, 60 Years of Challenge, Silvertree, and at least a hundred other guys. Thank you all.

All the editors and beta testers for this book. You made this book into something readable and accessible. I can't thank you enough. Scott M., Colin, Mike Thompson, Samim Salim, Vadim Fedorovsky, and about 35 more of you.

Every person who has hired me as a consultant over the past 22 years (has it really been that long?). I would not be here without you.

Every woman I've ever tried to have sex with who said no. You made me improve as a man probably more than anyone else did or could.

Everyone who's ever purchased a Blackdragon product or service. This book would never have happened if it wasn't for you.

All readers of the Blackdragon Blog, the place where these concepts first took shape.

Anyone else I've forgotten to mention. There are a ton of you, but my memory banks are limited. Thank you all.

About The Author

Caleb Jones has two careers. His first is as a time management and business consultant, author, and speaker. His second is as a dating and relationship expert for men.

At age 18 he was working for the seventh-largest software company in the world, the youngest person in a company of 400 employees. At age 19 he purchased his first piece of real estate and became a part-time real estate investor. At age at age 24, Caleb started his own IT consulting firm and reached the top 5% of his industry's earning level within three years. He has since worked with over 300 companies of all sizes including the Fortune 500, all over the United States, Europe and Asia. Caleb's business articles have appeared in national publications such as National Public Accountant, Medical Economics Magazine, and many others. Caleb has spoken to numerous audiences on the topics of time management, productivity, technology, business success, dating, and relationships.

Caleb lives in the beautiful Pacific Northwest USA, loves the outdoors, and travels frequently. He has two children.

Lightning Source UK Ltd.
Milton Keynes UK
UKOW03f2007240517
301939UK00001B/219/P

9 780986 22202